AF483359

MY TESTIMONY

An Autobiography

DEVIN PALADINO

Table of Contents

Introduction

On November 7th, 2013, we were beginning our first basketball game of my 7th-grade year against our rival Eisenhower middle school. All of my friends and family were going to be there. I couldn't wait for school to be over because of how excited I was. After the school day was finally over, I went down to the locker room to get changed and get ready to play. There was going to be a shoot around upstairs before the game, and I wanted to make sure I was ready for tonight's game. So, after I finished getting ready, I hurried upstairs to get in some shots. Slowly, the crowds started getting bigger and bigger, and the more people I saw the more nervous I began to feel. I was scared I was going to embarrass myself and not play well, which was something I did not want to do. I looked in the crowd for my father and sister, but they hadn't showed up yet. I figured they were just running late and would be showing up in a short amount of time. I was not a starter on the team anyways, so it wasn't like they were going to miss me playing. But overall, this was a very big game for us to prove we were a legit team. It was an even bigger game for us because we were playing against our rivals. I loved playing on my team because me and all my teammates had grown up with each other since we were little kids in the city of Rockford, Illinois. We were always playing basketball with each other before and after school, getting into intense games and running into class all sweaty in our green and khaki pants uniforms. Sometimes we would even play basketball at lunch time if we were allowed to. It was even more intense once we got to the lunch table and started talking trash to one another. But this game was bigger than a pickup, this was a chance for us to prove what we could do as a team.

At the beginning of the game, we traded buckets back and forth, watching each team score over and over again. Then, after a timeout, I was finally called into the game and got my chance to play. I instantly looked into the crowd and that's when I saw my dad, older sister, a couple of my friends, and my grandparents in the stands. I was proud to finally get to play in front of them after not making the basketball team last year. All the hard work I put in ended up paying off in tonight's game as I scored multiple times and we won our game. That was the first time in a very long time that I had felt some sort of accomplishment and proud of myself.

Later on, that night, my dad took me and my sister out to eat at this burrito joint to get some food. Even though we were there for my basketball victory, things outside of the court were very rough for us. Our stepmom had just left us and took my two little sisters with her. My father was very depressed and angry. He had tried to do a lot of crazy things to get her to come back to him, like faking a heart attack and going to the hospital trying to get my stepmom to come and see him. Then, when she would come back for a little bit over the summer so my dad could spend more time with my two little sisters, he stabbed himself and tried to frame it on my stepmom so he could gain custody of them. While we were eating at the burrito joint that night, my dad kept telling us that he wasn't going to be around forever. I figured he was just giving us a life lesson, but he kept saying this over and over again on many different occasions. He continued by telling me and my sister that we needed to grow up and always have each other's back in life. We needed to make sure that we always took school seriously and didn't do drugs or get involved with the wrong crowd. It was so weird because the way he was talking wasn't making any sense. I did not know if he was just in one of his parenting modes or if he was going somewhere. Me and my older sister did not have our mother at the time, she was completely out of the picture. The last time we had heard from her was 6 years ago. She had left our life, and this always made us upset because we never understood why. But we also were never allowed to talk about it because my dad would get mad and hit us. While we heard him lecture and talk to us that night during dinner, things would take a turn for the worst and we did not even realize it.

After dinner, we drove home in complete silence. Once we got inside the house, my dad told us he had to leave early in the morning to drive to Wisconsin for work and that me and my sister had to go to our friend's house to catch a ride for school. Another thing that was very awkward was how my dad rented a car when we had a car that worked perfectly fine. He worked at Golden Corral as well so I was not sure as to why he would be going all the way to Wisconsin if he was a buffett worker. I never questioned him though because I would get beat if I did. Even my sisters, and my former stepmom were never allowed to question him because we would all get beat. I was never more afraid of a man in my entire life than I was of my father because of the way he would beat us. So many times, I had been thrown across the room, slammed on the ground, punched, kicked, choked, and even been threatened to be killed. But this was normal to me because I had been going through this since I was 2 years old. I just had to forgive, act like nothing happened, and go about my day. My dad also told me that my uncle was coming by the house to pick up a yellow folder that was full of important documents for him and that me and my sister needed to be home to open up the door for him. Me and my older sister were always home alone, so we were used to this as well. One time when I was 11 and my sister was 13, we were left at home for a little over a week because my dad took my stepmom and the 2 little girls they had together to Disney World. When he went upstairs to sleep, I went down to the basement to tell my sister what was going on and then I headed upstairs to bed because it was late, and I was very tired from my basketball game.

The next day, I was taking a test in my science class, and about 10 minutes in, the 7th grade principal came into the room. This principal was known for giving out referrals, lunch and after school detentions, and tardies. I was just hoping he did not look my way or call me out. But of course, he called for my name and he told me I had to leave the class. Instantly, my heart started racing and my adrenaline was pumping on high. I thought I was in trouble, but I could not figure out what I was in trouble for. I was on time all week and didn't get into any altercations with any of my teachers or other students that could have caused me to be called down to his office. I followed him downstairs and into his office, as he told me to take a seat. That's when he told me I was not in trouble and I was instantly relieved. But out of nowhere my stomach dropped again and I went right back to being nervous when he asked to see my phone. He searched my whole phone as thoroughly as possible. I was now starting to think that someone may have told on me but described the wrong person or accused me of something I didn't do. I asked him why he was going through my phone and he just told me I wasn't in any trouble. I had sat in his office for an hour and a half and during that hour and a half I was totally confused. I even had to eat lunch inside of his office and couldn't grab my own tray, I didn't get to see any of my friends. I was totally lost as to what was going on that day. After 2 hours inside the principal's office, he finally told me to get up and follow him. I followed behind my 7th grade assistant principal and we walked down a hallway into a room I had never been into before. As soon as I got inside, I saw a huge group of people. There were 4 police officers, 3 assistant principals, the head principal of the entire school and my older sister. I was so confused about what my sister was doing here when she was in high school. But I felt a sense of relief when I saw her. They told me to take a seat and I sat down next to my sister. My sister told me "Devin, our dad didn't go to work, he went to our stepmom's house and stabbed her," and we both instantly started crying. It was crazy how I could feel any sympathy for my father after the way he had beat us and treated us like we were slaves. I felt even more sick to my stomach when I found out that my stepmom had been stabbed by him and that she was on the verge of dying. I did not want my stepmom to die and I was scared. On the day of November 8th, 2013, my life was changed forever.

Living With My Aunt And Uncle

After my sister and I stopped crying, they told us what was going to happen next. The police told us that they didn't know where my dad was and that he was on the run. For our safety, the police told us we couldn't be at school anymore in case he tried to come and get us. Shortly after, we were taken out of school to the police station. This was my first ever time being inside of a police car and I was just a scared little 13-year-old boy. Once we got to the police station, we followed one of the officers upstairs while we sat and waited on a bench. I kept asking my older sister what was going to happen, but even she didn't know. We just ended up waiting for a few hours and then our grandparents on my dad's side of the family showed up. After another 30 minutes of waiting, my grandparents came back into the room and told us we were going home with them. Finally, we were able to leave this boring police station.

Once we got into the car, I started asking my grandparents what was going to happen. They told us we were going back to our house to grab all our clothes and belongings that were still there. I felt better knowing I was still going to be able to keep all my stuff and it wasn't going to just be thrown away. Once we got over to my house, my sister unlocked the door with her key, and we started packing all our stuff up and putting it in the back of my grandparents car. But because there was only one car, we could only fit so much stuff inside at once. We would end up having to wait later on until my aunt and uncle got off of work. In the meantime, we drove back to our grandma and grandpa's house and waited. I thought we were going to be unpacking our things and living with them, but they told us we would be going to live with our aunt and uncle. To take our mind off things, my grandpa played cards with us while we waited for my aunt and uncle to get off work and come pick us up. I was very happy when I found out I would be living with them because that meant I would get to see my cousin a lot more. Me and my cousin were like best friends, he was just 5 months older and a grade ahead of me. But we liked a lot of the same things, and we always played Xbox with each other. The only difference was I loved to play basketball and he liked football and cross country. He also loved spending time and hanging out with his friends a lot more than hanging out with me, which started to hurt as we got older. In a way he was like a bully to me, he used to kick me out of his Xbox parties, barely talk to me at family get-togethers, and started shutting me out in a way. But I was hoping that would all change now that we were going to be living with each other. After 2 hours, my aunt finally came to pick us up. My sister and I went outside and unloaded the things from my grandma and grandpa's car while my aunt and grandparents stayed inside the house and talked. Once we finished unloading and loading the car up, we went back inside, and we had to stay downstairs a little bit longer and wait because the adults were still talking.

When my grandparents and aunt finished talking, we followed my aunt out to her car and she asked us if we wanted to go and get some ice cream. I figured she was trying to cheer us up with this. I said yes right away because I loved ice cream and I was also very hungry. After we finished eating ice cream and got back to my aunt and uncle's house, we waited for my cousin to get home off the bus to surprise him. My aunt had a little tracking device where she could see where he was through his iPhone. We saw how close he was and when he was coming up to the door and me and my sister hid. As soon as he came through the door we jumped up to surprise him. We still didn’t know if we were for sure living with my aunt and uncle because they hadn’t told us anything yet, so we told him we were just visiting. But all three of us sat down at the table and told him what had happened with our dad. He was blown away by that and felt sorry for us. He quickly asked where we were going to be living and we told him that we didn't know yet. Once we finished talking, I went into my cousin's room to play Xbox with him while my sister and my aunt stayed in the living room. I asked my cousin about going to Peak and working out with him and his dad because I had always wanted a gym membership. All my friends would always be at the YMCA or Peak playing basketball and I was always left out just to play basketball outside around the neighborhood. This always sucked because in Illinois you could only play basketball outside for so long until it got freezing cold to where your hands would be frostbitten. This was another reason why I wanted a gym membership, but my dad told me no. After about an hour of playing Xbox with my cousin my uncle came home and sat me and my sister down to talk with us. They told us that we would be living with them for now on and they were going to get things set up for us and not to worry about things and that everything would be ok.

After a week of living with my aunt and uncle, me and my sister were each able to get our own rooms. Both of us also got memberships to go to the gym as well. I was asking to go to the gym every day because of how much fun I had playing basketball with the other kids. My dream was to be a professional basketball player as well one day and I thought playing basketball all the time would help me get there. Me and my sister also got brand new phones because the phones we had were taken for evidence for the police because my dad left a voicemail for me and my sister on it. At first, I wasn't sure how to set up my voicemail box but when I listened to it, I knew it was my dad. He was crying on the phone and telling me to behave and be good for my aunt and uncle. After a few seconds of listening to it I stopped because it was too hard. However, there were a lot of downfalls that came to follow after we moved into my aunt and uncle's house due to my dad's actions. We were eventually placed in the foster care system because my aunt and uncle didn't adopt us yet. We were both placed into this foster care agency called Lutheran Social Services of Illinois. This was where we would have to meet with a caseworker and other people once a week. It seemed like every day all these people came and kept asking us all different types of questions. I felt like I was back in daycare or elementary school when I would be taken into an office and have to talk to a man a lot because my dad and mom were going through a custody battle. Every week my dad would sit down with me and my sister and tell us what to say to the people when they came to ask us questions. Whenever we went over to our mom's house, which was once a week, she would flip out when she saw the bruises that my dad left on me and my sister after we told her that he hit us. She always called DCFS and told them what happened to us. But when we went back to our dad's house, he told us to say something completely different and if we didn't, we would get beat up again. He also told us to say bad things about our mom and bribed us with going to Disney World and said all that would be taken away if we didn't tell the people that our mom hit us. I figured because we lied about our mom that caused her to not want to be in our lives anymore.

After a week, my dad was still on the loose, and we were not allowed to be at the house by ourselves. We had to go everywhere my aunt and uncle went. We were also not allowed to go back to school yet and this sucked because I missed all of my friends and wanted to be on the basketball team. It also sucked because now that I was living with my aunt and uncle, I wasn't going to go to Lincoln anymore and my sister wasn't going to be able to go to East either. But it was something that we were going to have to get used to because we'd moved now. I was also wondering where my dad was and what had happened to him. Nobody heard from him or seen him in a little over a week now. But one day, while me and my sister were in a car with my uncle, he got a text message that was sent from my dad. It was also sent to all my aunts and uncles. We all immediately tried to reach out to him and talk to him, but the text messages wouldn't deliver anymore. My dad said he was suicidal and was sorry for what he had done and wished the best for all of us. Later on, the police were able to track where that message came from and they went to the place right away. But it turns out that my dad threw his phone away and some guy found it in the trash and hit send. While my dad was on the loose, me, my sister and my entire dad's side of the family, went through some of the most embarrassing times of our lives. His name was all over the news and everyday people were messaging me on Facebook. Even at the gym or when I went out in public and people knew me, they would ask. But what made things even worse, was the radio station and website announced that he had two kids in the Rockford Public Schools system. It was like me and my sister were now the center of attention. It was just very overwhelming and so embarrassing to be only 13 years old and in 7th grade having all of this going on.

This wasn't the first time my dad had done something abusive. When I was 2 years old and my sister was 4, we first entered foster care because my dad used to break into my mother's apartment and beat her. He beat her so bad one time that he broke her hip, and we were taken away for a while. I don't remember seeing my dad hit my mother a lot because I was too young, but I remember him beating my stepmom. He was very physically abusive to her. At night time, I would wake up to my stepmom screaming or him yelling and hearing her cry from being hit. I remember opening up my door and seeing what was going on and watching him beat her. On one particular occasion she went out to a club with some friends and he got mad at her and took her face and threw it against the bathroom mirror, shattering it and leaving a huge crack. While she was pregnant, he took a dictionary and threw it at her face, leaving her with a black eye. He once threw a vase at my stepmom, hitting her right in the face and causing her to bleed everywhere. After my aunt's wedding, me along with my 3 sisters, my dad and stepmom, witnessed them getting into a fight while he was driving on the highway. He choked my stepmom until she started to pass out. When he finally let go of her, she climbed to the back of the van. He started driving full speed while she begged him to stop and my older sister started crying as well. I saw this from 7 years old till I was 13. My dad beat my mom and stepmom like they were nothing.

My dad was also very physically abusive to me, and my 3 sisters. The first time I ever saw my dad abuse my sister was when we were 7 and he took a baseball bat and hit her right in the hip. The first time I saw him abuse my little sisters was when I was 12 and they were month old babies. They wouldn't stop crying so my dad squeezed them and kept shoving a pacifier down their throats thinking it would stop them from crying but only made them scream more. As my sisters got older, the worse the beatings became. My dad would always get angry with my older sister because she was chubby and he would call her a "fat pig, fat bitch" and mean names like that and do very cruel things to her. If he caught her eating too much, he would take some food and smash it in her face or shove it down her throat while calling her a fat bitch. He always bullied her and put her on Weight Watcher foods while we all ate normal food in front of her. My dad was always calling my older sister lazy and beat her if he caught her being lazy. My older sister had a friend come over and my sister didn't walk her out, so as soon as her friend left, he walked downstairs and beat her and all I heard was screaming and yelling. I hated hearing my sister's and stepmom get beat. My little sisters who were only 7 and 4 at the time got beat if they played too loud, woke my dad up from his nap or were defiant in any way. I would watch him pick my little sisters up and throw them across the room like they were nothing. It was like we all had to be perfect living with my dad, or we got beat, and as for me I got it the worst.

My dad was the hardest on me because I was the only boy. Like my sisters I was beaten for everything I didn't do right in his eyes. If I did not understand or do my homework correctly, I got beat. If he asked me to grab something and I did not do it right or grab the correct thing, I got beat. If I ever changed the tone of voice to him or talked wrong and gave attitude, I got beat. If I did not cheer for the right sports team, I got beat. If I asked too many questions or talked too much, I got beat. If I was too loud while he was taking a nap or one of my friends knocked on the door and woke him up during his nap, I got beat for it. Even if I had hurt myself or got hurt playing outside, I was beat for it. It seemed like I was beat for any and everything you could possibly think of. I was abused and severely beaten to the point where some days I was unable to walk or even talk. At 10 years old I slammed the door while my dad was home and he came into my room and grabbed me by my feet and slammed me down on my face, broke my chin and gave me a concussion. I was unable to talk for weeks and wasn't allowed to go outside because of the bruises. I was 11 years old playing baseball with my friends and hit the ball as far as I could and yelled "homerun" out of excitement and my sister told me to come inside because I woke our dad up. I refused to. Then I moved to the alley way with my friends and continued to play and as I bent down to pick up the ball, I was knocked down. My dad had come outside and punched me to the ground and kicked me before carrying me inside while I screamed for my friends help. I was thrown across the room several times like a ragdoll and punched in my face repeatedly until I almost passed out. I was then kicked in my face and blood ran down and covered my entire face. I was thrown upstairs and told to wash it off, but I could not move. I was then locked in my room and my dad had taken the key to work with him. I pissed on myself that night because physically I could not move. So many nights I was beat. So many days my dad threatened to kill us all.

I was almost killed by my father in one incident. My stepmom had gone to the store and he never liked it when she was upset. When she was upset everything was ruined because all he cared about was making her happy. So as soon as she left, he yelled for me and my sister to come upstairs and I went downstairs and told her and all she did was ignore me. When I told him she was not coming, she got up and slapped me as hard as he could, and I fell. As he walked down the stairs the screams began. I could feel the vibrations of him beating my sister. My blood was rushing, my heart was racing, I was like a frozen deer in headlights. As I ran upstairs and hid in the closet, I heard him stomp all the way back upstairs. As he slammed open the door, he punched me in my face and grabbed me, stomping on my face and body over and over again. When I got up, he threw me up against my desk and punched me in my face some more. I blacked out and when I came to I ran full speed to get out of that room. I don't even know how I did it with how much blood was all over my body and how many marks were all over me, but I ran for my life. He tried to trip me as he ran downstairs but missed. My mind was racing, but I was blacked out at the moment and running as fast as I could into the kitchen. My father followed behind me as I entered the kitchen and I grabbed a knife to defend myself, crying and shaking with blood all over my face and body. I yelled "get back!" My father was in the marines for many years so that was a very dumb move. He twisted my wrist back and the knife fell from my hand and he slammed my face on the kitchen tile. He then grabbed the knife and pointed it to my face saying, "how about I fucking kill you?" I don't know how but I got up with the strength God blessed me with and ran full speed for the front door. It was locked, so I unlocked the top lock and the bottom lock. My father came and grabbed me with all his strength and all his might pulling me back, but I managed to jump outside. As soon as I was outside, I screamed at the top of my lungs "HELP! HELP!" My father did not move another muscle or grab me; he ran inside and shut the door. I ran limping to the neighbor's yard and knocked on the door and screamed for help. They finally opened the door and were shocked at the sight in front of them. My dad came running full speed with his shoes on, but the neighbors would not let him in, and they called the police. I later lied that night so my father would not go to jail.

When I was 10 years old, I finally decided to run away. The night before, my dad came home from work and was sleeping on the couch upstairs. I was playing a game called Rock Band in the basement and was playing the drums too loud. Out of nowhere, I heard loud stomps on the stairs coming down. My dad ran down the steps and once he got to the bottom, he threw me to the floor. He took both drumsticks and hit me with them over and over again until my mouth was bloody, and he cut me on my arm, deep causing blood to be all over the floor. He kicked me in my face and told me to clean it up. I ran because I was playing the video game and accidently dropped the controller, breaking a button. My dad always played video games and anytime we broke anything we got beat. My mouth and body were already damaged from being beat the night before, so I decided to run. I had no shoes on, only my pajamas. My stepmom was yelling at me to go to my room for breaking the controller but I ran right past her and out the door.

I ran as fast as I could and did not stop for anything. I ran like someone was trying to come and kill me. I was so terrified that I didn't notice that I didn't even have shoes on my feet. I was going to run to my grandparents' house and ask them to save me and show them the bruises on my body. While I was running to my grandparents' house, some kids came up to me and asked what was wrong. I told them what happened and then, out of nowhere, all I saw was a black car driving full speed towards me. It was my dad. I guess my stepmom told him I ran away. As soon as he got out of the car, he started chasing me and I ran for my life and so did the other kids. I ran through neighborhoods and made lots of turns and cuts and I could hear my dad right behind me. I ran into this open yard and a couple was outside having a barbeque. They saw me and I immediately screamed for them to help me. They got up instantly and ran to me and they saw my dad and the man told my dad to stop. I couldn't breathe and I was crying, and my dad told the man that I was his son and I acted up at home and he was coming to take me back home. The man then got out of my dad's way and I ripped my body from the lady's arms and ran full speed some more. I just kept running and running. Eventually my dad stopped chasing me and went back to his car. After another 20 minutes of running, I looked down at my feet and saw how bloody they were from the rough ground. My adrenaline was so high that I couldn't even feel any pain in my feet. I was down the street and seconds away from my grandparents' house, when I saw the same black car drive at full speed at me as if it were about to hit me. I immediately ran into someone's yard. It was my dad and he started chasing me again. I came to a fence and I tried jumping it and I felt my dad grabbing my shirt and my leg, but I used all my strength to get over it. When I finally made it over, I felt the metal needle from the fence scrape my leg leaving it all bloody and I had reopened the cut on my arm from falling. I laid on the ground as he watched from the other side of the fence and stood there waiting. I got up with bloody feet, a bloody leg, and a bloody arm and kept running. He stopped chasing me and got back in his car and drove off. After another 2 hours of walking, I was covered in dried up blood and on a busy intersection in Rockford when a lady got out of her car and ran towards me asking what had happened. Then I saw a red car drive up right next to me and another lady ran out of her car to me. It was my stepmom crying and begging me to come home. My stepmom told the lady that I ran away from home and the lady let me go. I didn't want to go home because I was terrified, but the lady told me to go with her. I went in the car with my stepmom and thank God I did not get beat that night. It was probably because I was taken to a hospital after all the cuts and bruises.

When I would open up and tell my aunt and uncle these stories it seems like they almost didn't believe me and my sister because of how well my dad hid the abuse. Nobody ever suspected anything. It was very sad because my stepmom had gone over to my grandparents' house one day crying and begging them to help us. Then, the next Thanksgiving, it seemed as if the rest of my family didn't want anything to do with us and didn't speak to us, as if we were the problem. I missed my stepmom and wondered if she was okay. I didn't hear anything from her besides, she had been stabbed 5 times and was in critical condition. But I knew deep down inside that my stepmom would be ok because she was the bravest woman I had ever known. She would step in sometimes while my dad was beating me or my sisters and protect us. I was very sorry that she had to go through all of this abuse from him. We didn't go to school for a week until we got settled in and had transportation to and from school. I missed playing basketball for my school and I missed all of my teammates. That's when later on in the week after my dad went missing and everyone was looking for him, they finally found him. I felt such a sense of relief that I didn't have to worry about him attacking us in the middle of the night or having to keep going everywhere with my aunt and uncle. When they found my dad, he was caught washing his feet in a bathroom inside of the Gurnee Mills Mall. It turned out he had been sleeping in the bushes outside of the mall. They tracked him down from his credit card purchases and saw that he was spending money there every day. What made things even scarier was he was going shopping, eating, going to see movies, and walking around the mall like he hadn't committed any crime. Then, when they searched his rental car, they found a multitude of knives in the back of his car. Finally, my dad was getting what he deserved and that was being arrested. I no longer had to be afraid of someone beating me for everything I didn't do right. I no longer had to watch my sister get beat or hear her scream. All of the abuse from him was over with and I felt free.

When my dad was finally arrested, my sister and I were allowed to go back to school and be at home by ourselves. But things would take a sharp turn because we did not last very long at my aunts and uncle's house. We did not like living with them because we never got to see any of our friends, and we were too much for them to handle. We got into a lot of arguments, especially me and my aunt. Once, I walked out of their house and said I was walking to Rockford. She grabbed me by my arm and shoved me; I shoved her back and kept walking. My uncle called me that night cussing me out on the phone and threatening to hit me and I told my caseworker what happened. Apparently, my sister and I were ruining their marriage and causing trouble. Things were just hard for us, especially after what had happened and moving to a different city where we didn't get to see our friends anymore. That's when they eventually had enough of us. The last straw for them was when my sister posted how we were not happy and wanted to live somewhere else. When I was 13 and my sister was 15, we were kicked out of my aunt and uncle's house and sent to live in separate foster homes. For the first time ever, me and my older sister were being split up.

Living With The Cat Lady

It was June of 2014 when we were separated. I felt alone. I had always lived with my older sister and had someone to talk to but now I felt like I had nobody. I was very scared and nervous. When my caseworker was taking me to this new home, I cried the entire time. I told my caseworker I was scared and didn't want to live there. She told me this was the only choice I had and only home that was available for me. I asked her if I was going to be put in chains for being bad because my grandpa told me they abuse bad children in foster homes. He told me about a little boy who was put in chains down in the basement of a foster home and had to sleep in a cage. I did not know if he was joking or being serious, but I was terrified. I didn't want to be put in a cage like I was a dog or a cat because I was a human. When I told my caseworker this she started laughing and said no and I would be removed if she even laid a finger on me. I didn't think it was funny because I was so full of fear.

Once we arrived at the house it was a very nice subdivision, right behind Jefferson High School. This meant that I would no longer be going to Lincoln my 8th grade year with the rest of my friends I grew up with and who were attending East High School. I had to go to school at R.E.S.A. (Rockford Environmental Science Academy) Middle School. All of the houses in this subdivision were beautiful, especially her house. There was a very nice flower bed planted in front of the entire yard, nice clean and cut grass and a newly finished driveway. Once me and my caseworker got inside, I met this lady, and her name was Linda Moore. Linda Moore was going to be my new foster parent and she had 2 other boys as well. I met a little 10-year-old named Alex and another boy who was the same age as me, named Austin. She told me to meet 4 of her other kids but they were not kids, they were her cats. There were cats everywhere and I instantly got scared from the cage story. When she told me to go outside and play with the other boys while she talked to my caseworker, I asked the boys if when they got in trouble were they put in cages and they both started laughing. They said this lady was very nice and wouldn't hit me. I stayed outside with them and we walked to the local park and back. I got to know both of them a little. Both of these kids had come from abusive foster homes before this. I told them about my story and situation as well so we both were able to relate.

After some talking, we left the park because our foster parent Linda called Austin on his phone to tell us to come back. We headed back and when I got inside, I had some paperwork to sign. I had to sign that I agreed to this placement even though I didn't, and I had to get my physical to be sure I was healthy and able to stay with this lady. After some more talking, my caseworker eventually left. I was nervous when she left but I was sure I would be okay. After my caseworker left, my foster parent Linda sat down with me and the two other foster kids and we talked about the rules of being here. I had to go to church every Wednesday and Sunday. That was not an option and I had to go to the City First Church. Another rule was no hitting of any kind or I was gone. She had a very low tolerance for this especially since we had all grown up abused. Then we always had to let her know when and where we were going, and if we ever hung out with anyone; she had to meet the people. I thought this lady was very strict right away and I was ready to leave. I told her I did not like all of her rules, and she told me we could call my caseworker to come back and get me but I would have no place to go and would be put into a residential facility. This made me angry and sad, so I just listened and said ok.

After we finished talking, I was shown to my room and it was here I would have to share a bunk bed with Alex the 10-year-old boy. This was a straight slap in the face from having my own room with a nice flat screen tv and my Xbox set up. You could see the anger on my face as soon as I saw this. I took the top bunk. Alex started telling me what drawers were his and which ones were mine. After I got settled in, it was Wednesday, so Linda said we all had to go to church including myself. Every Wednesday, City Church first had a youth group and I had to attend. On the way to this church, I kept thinking about how far we lived from the YMCA and how far we lived from everything. This sucked because I missed going to the gym and seeing my friends. After a 25-minute drive, we finally got to church, and I was told to stay with the 2 boys, and they would show me where to go. It was Fuse Night meaning they were having a huge event at the church for the youth, so it was not a typical Wednesday service. I remembered these events because a girl I went to Lincoln with handed out invitations to me and I went one time with my sister. While we were walking, Andrew told me that the foster parent Linda thinks I'm going to run away so he had to pay extra close attention. I did not respond because I was sad, and I didn't want to be there. I had no words to respond with because of how fast everything had gone by. I was just separated from my older sister, taken to a new home for the first time ever, met three new people and four cats. Now I'm at a huge church event where there are people everywhere; it was too much. Once I got inside, everyone was very welcoming and nice, but I stayed quiet and said nothing. I didn't even say my name to anyone, and let my foster brothers introduce me. I just walked off to an area where nobody was and cried by myself. I had never felt so alone in my entire life.

After sitting by myself and crying for over an hour, the event was just about over. Then one of the workers saw me, who was a staff member at the church and immediately attended to me. I hurried to wipe the tears from my eyes so he wouldn't see me crying. He saw me though, he asked me right away what was wrong, and I said nothing. I did not want to let anyone in. I did not want to talk to anybody; I just wanted to push everyone away. The man told me he wasn't sure what I was going through but as long as you have God with you, you can get through anything. At first, I thought this sucker was just telling me that because he works in a church. Then I started thinking about how to get God involved in my life. I always heard of him but didn't know much about him or how he worked. My dad's side of the family were not very religious, so we didn't grow up hearing about God a lot. We only went to church on random occasions and when we did go, we didn't talk about him once we left the church and got inside the car. When my 2 foster brothers found me, they told me it was time to go, so I walked with them to the car. When I got inside, Linda asked us how it went. I didn't have much to say to her. I was just ready to go back to the house and get this day over with. Once we got back to the house, I went straight to my room and into my bunk bed and Linda called me to her room later that night. She sat me down and told me everything was going to be okay and she understood why I was upset and angry. Then in the middle of us talking one of her favorite cats, Boomer, came up to me. I was scared of cats because the only cats I knew were the street cats that hiss at you if you come close. I just sat there, and this cat would not leave me alone and it kept rubbing up on me like we were at the club and purring. Linda started laughing like it was funny, but I did not like it at all. She told me her favorite cat never does that to anyone and that was a sign from God that it was all going to be okay. I thought this lady was out of her mind and crazy. Last time I checked God was not a cat. After she said that, I told her I didn't know much about God and what the man said to me at church and she told me I had come to the right place to find out.

This lady had a routine every day. Usually, we were not allowed to sleep past a certain time because that was against her rules and she said we had stuff that we had to do. I watched the other two boys get ready each morning: they ate breakfast, they both took two different pills. One was for a vitamin and one for medication. At the time, I did not know what type of pills those were and had never seen that before, so I asked them what that was. She said those were their meds and every kid that came into her house was usually on meds. My stomach dropped right when she said that because in my head I thought I knew this lady was crazy because she's trying to dope us up so she can rape us or put us in those cat cages. She said I would eventually end up on some medication. I was ready to call my caseworker and tell her what was going on, but I had no phone. I didn't trust her after this, I thought she was up to something. Once we finished our morning routine and I finished eating, we went in the car and did errands with her. None of us were allowed to be at the house alone. While we were driving, I asked her about a membership to the YMCA and she said no. I told her we get a free membership paid for by DCFS, but she wasn't having it because she didn't want to drive 25 minutes there and back for one kid. We all had to be involved in this membership. Back at the house, she told me I would be involved in summer camp at R.E.S.A Middle School, my new school and I was really upset. I couldn't enjoy my summer. I had to be in summer school, couldn't get a YMCA membership and see my friends, and now I had to go to church every Sunday and Wednesday. I was just pissed off.

When I started my first day of summer camp, I instantly hated it. I don't know any kid who wants to be in school during the summertime. It was like babysitting; it was one of the worst summers I've ever had. When we first got there, we had to go inside our classroom and stay with the same group of kids every day. We would play a variety of different games and all I wanted to do was play basketball. When I did get to play basketball, it was boring because it was mostly girls, and when the boys would play half of them could not even dribble the ball. But I guess summer camp ended up working well because that's when I met the varsity head coach of the basketball team Coach Jackson. Coach Jackson was the varsity head coach of the football team as well and he asked me to play football right when he saw me, but I was not into football. I loved basketball. He asked me my name and what school I came from. I saw him a few times while I was playing in the gym with the other kids and he would watch me play. One of the days, he asked for my foster parent's phone number and told her he wanted to get to know me better. Then he came over to the house one day and picked me up for church. Once church was over, he walked me over to the basketball court and showed me some basketball drills to do and helped me work on my jump shot. Coach Jackson was a great male role model to me.

After we got to know each other more, he took me over to his house and would show me basketball games and the different techniques they would use in the game. I didn't really have much of a basketball IQ and he helped me understand how the game was played more. I heard him tell me a story about a basketball player who would get up every day at 5am just to work on his game. This inspired me and pretty soon I was doing the same thing. I started getting up at 5am and dribbling a basketball for a week straight. I would work on the different types of crossovers, in and out, between the legs, behind the back, every dribble you can imagine. He always said if you can dribble a basketball you can get anywhere you want to on the court. After a straight week of doing this, the other two foster kids wanted to do the same thing, and pretty soon there were three foster kids outside dribbling basketballs at 5am waking up the entire subdivision. After about two weeks we had to stop because we got complaints, so our foster parent Linda changed the rule to waking up at 7am instead of 5am. We all loved basketball so much that we convinced her to buy a basketball hoop for the driveway. The only time I came inside was to eat lunch, dinner and grab a water bottle. I was just all about the game of basketball. Linda made us get in the summer reading program and we had to read at least one book over the summer, and that summer I read about Magic Johnson and how he dribbled a basketball with him everywhere he went, even to work. This inspired me to dribble outside every day in that driveway. It was like Coach Jackson changed me completely and pretty soon I was not scared anymore. Linda was on board with the entire idea. I would show her the basketball equipment that I wanted and as long as I behaved and did everything she asked and my chores, she would get them for me. Pretty soon I was dribbling a basketball with weighted hand gloves and dribbling under a dribble stick to make sure I kept the ball lower at my waist.

Once the school year started for 8th grade I did not like this new school at all. I had a hard time fitting in because here I am this church good boy, and all of these kids were just bad. This was the first school I had gone to where I knew of 8th graders smoking weed, having sex, drinking and were into fighting other people. These kids all grew up so fast and I could not fit in. I did not want to fit in because this wasn't cool to me, it was very lame. When I did try to make friends, a lot of the kids that I went to school with had already grown up together since they were little. This made it harder to make friends because they already had their groups. It didn't help either with Coach Jackson being the security guard and telling me who to hang out with and who not to hang out with. It felt like every day was the longest day of my life. I just sat by myself or with kids I never talked to during lunch time waiting for the school day to be over. I was just waiting to play basketball for this school and that's it. That's all I thought about and all I wanted to do. Meanwhile, I would still go to church groups every Wednesday and Sunday and dribble my basketball in the morning before and after school daily. One day while I was outside dribbling during the night, I saw that my 8th grade English teacher Mrs. White drove past. She lived in the same subdivision that I did, and she would always tell Coach Jackson she saw me out there dribbling. I was still outside every day for hours.

Once the basketball season rolled around, I didn't have a good season because every Wednesday I had to skip the games to go to church. This led me getting into it with my foster parent Linda a lot, which altered our relationship. It even made Coach Jackson angry because I was easily one of our best players. It got to the point where I started disobeying her and being rude and disrespectful to her. I got tired of going to school at R.E.S.A as well because our team sucked, and we kept losing. I hated losing. I was a huge sore loser and after we lost one of our games to Kennedy Middle School. I cried because I was so upset. Coach Jackson talked about how good winning felt and I wanted to win but we kept losing and I hated that feeling like I sucked. I would be angry at my teammates because none of them took practice seriously or would play good during the games. I ended up acting out in school because I would be so angry and started talking back to my teachers and getting into it with a couple students. I got myself suspended and even arrested, all of this because I hated losing basketball games and was angry at my foster parent. I thought that if I started acting out in school that I would eventually get to leave this stupid school and be sent to another foster home.

I ended up getting arrested for the first time at the age of 14 because I was getting bullied by a few kids on the bus. There was a joke going around the school about me missing basketball games every Wednesday because I was a church boy. One day, these kids on the bus kept laughing about it and making fun of me and then one of the boys said, "it's because he's in foster care and his mommy and daddy don't love him." I ended up lashing out. When I got off of the bus, I confronted the kid and he slapped me in my face and I lost it. I ended up throwing him to the ground and punching him over and over then kicking him in his head and the bus driver saw me. Once the incident was over, I walked home and told my foster parent about what happened, and she immediately called the school and got things figured out. When I went back to school on Monday, I was arrested because the incident happened on school grounds. They put me in the back of a police car and took me to the juvenile detention center. I felt so ashamed of myself because I was a good kid and did not do stupid stuff like this. I just had so much anger built up and it got me here. After about an hour of being down at the police station, Linda picked me up and I was surprised I did not get in trouble with her. She told me that this was my lesson and to not do it again.

Eventually, me and things with Linda got worse and I left her house. I was tired of this school and not having any friends. I was tired of losing all of the time and not being able to play on Wednesdays and missing half of the season because of this. I was tired of living under her roof and abiding by these insane rules. Every time she got angry, she threatened to turn in her two-week notice and have me removed from her home. I always felt I had to be perfect. I never got to go to the movies or football games to see my old friends from school. She had me on medication and this made me even more angry because she put me on the pill and lied to the doctor when we got there. It got too cold to dribble the basketball outside because snow was on the ground and I never got to practice my game anymore. I never got to go to the YMCA and play basketball with my friends. I felt like I was a cat inside the cage, but the cage was this house. It got worse when Andrew left because he was tired of living here and then there was nobody to talk to anymore. I felt like I had no childhood and nobody but myself. She crossed the line with me a few times when we both had gotten into an argument and I walked out of her house and sat at the park for 30 minutes. Her rule was to always let her know where I was going, and I didn't and when I went back, she had locked the door so I could not get in and turned the code off to the garage so it wouldn't work either. I stayed outside for almost two hours in the freezing cold until she was finally ready to open the door. Another time I was at a basketball tournament and was talking to one of my friends from my old school and I took too long and she walked out and told me to find my own ride home and I ended up having to wait all night until someone could take me home.

Finally, three days before Christmas, I was removed from her house. After 6 months, it was finally over. I felt sad about it but then I didn't. It just hurt how she always called me her boy and said we were family but turned her back on me and never let me grow or do anything. When she called my caseworker to come and get me, I grabbed all my belongings. I hugged my foster brother Alex goodbye and thanked him for everything. She told me I was not allowed to take any of the things she bought me, and this led to one last argument. She considered the allowance we got from DCFS her money because she gave it to us, and this made me angry too. When I went to grab the PlayStation, I had bought myself with that allowance she wouldn't allow me to take it. The last encounter we had was me taking the PlayStation and smashing it on the ground. After I did this, I left for good.

After Leaving Linda's House

Once I got inside the car with my caseworker, I was told that there was nowhere for me to go at the moment. We ended up heading back to her office and waiting for a few hours. My caseworker told me I would have to go into respite, meaning stay at someone's house until they found me a new home. We got in touch with my grandparents on my dad side and asked them if I could stay there for the time being. At the time me and my grandparents were somewhat close. Every time I went over there, they just dropped me off at the YMCA for a few hours so they wouldn't have to deal with me. My grandpa loved to play cards, talk about the Green Bay Packers, Chicago White Sox, and the family, so that's all we usually talked about and did. Once I left my aunt and uncle's house things were awkward with everyone on my dad's side of the family. I had four aunts and three uncles; they all had kids and extra room in their house, and they all said no to taking me in. My grandparents had three empty bedrooms in their house, and they said no to me as well. It killed me going to "family" get togethers and I was in foster care with all this family in my face and to know nobody wanted to take me in. I felt like it was because I was half black and they hated my mother.

My father was in the marines and met my mother in Africa while he was stationed in Chad. My mother was an African American woman and a Muslim, and my grandparents hated it. Once my dad went to jail, he would tell us that they disowned him for an amount of time for marrying our mother and that was part of the reason he was so angry with us. He got letters from my grandparents telling him that my mother had AIDS and not to marry her. They hated my mother even more after they said she caused him to get kicked out of the marines. When, in reality, he got himself kicked out because he couldn't keep his temper in order and abused my mother. Then, his life went downhill and he lost all benefits and everything he worked hard for. As I started getting older, I paid attention to all the remarks they made about Trayvon Martin, Mike Brown, and Eric Gardner and incidents that happened and how everyone in that family was all for the police killing innocent black people. I started paying attention to how my grandparents, aunts, and uncles had little to no black friends. I started paying attention to how everyone in this family was against Barack Obama being president and saying every bad thing you could about him. But the big clue for me was when every family get- together, they made jokes about African Americans and their culture saying very ignorant things. The older I got the more I realized these people were not my family and they were borderline racist.

Once I got to my grandparents' house, I stayed at their house for about a week. I overheard my grandma telling my caseworker that they didn't want me any longer than that. I went to the YMCA every day and played cards with my grandpa as usual. But I decided to stop acting like everything was okay and just to not talk about them not taking me in and him choking me and I decided to ask. When I asked him about why he choked me he said it was because I didn't listen to him when he asked me to grab his iPad. This made me angry, so when someone doesn't listen to you, you just choke your 13-year-old grandson and throw him into the fireplace? Then when I asked my grandpa about why none of them wanted to take me in, he said that me and my sister had our chance with our aunt and uncle but failed there, and that me and my older sister had too many problems. I wanted to cry after he said this. Did you expect two 13 and 15 year olds, who have been physically and verbally beat for almost their entire life, never had their mother around and lost their stepmom who was like a mother figure and is fighting for her life, haven't seen their two little sisters, whose dad just went to prison for stabbing that only mother figure we had, and have been getting all this attention from every kid in school and feeling embarrassed every day, to not have problems? As me and my grandpa were talking my stepmom was in the hospital fighting for her life because of their son's actions and they cut her out of every photo for no reason. What about when she used to run over to their house and cry and ask for help because their son was beating us, and they did nothing? That's when I realized I was done with this family.

While I was staying temporarily at my grandparents' house, I went to visit with a potential foster family. This family lived out in Winnebago, Illinois and I was taken to the Rockford Ice Hogs game with them. While I was out with them on a cold December night, I felt uncomfortable the entire time. I never met any of these people, and here I was completely alone with them. I was on guard the entire time and just ready to leave. I used my phone to text one of my friends telling him my situation and that I needed a place to live. I had known him since I was seven years old. I used to go over to his grandma's house all the time and hang out with him and his family. He had an older sister that was my sister's age so all four of us always hung out. They lived with their grandma and she treated us like we were her own grandkids. They were the first people we ever opened up to about us getting abused at home. We would come over to their house every day and stay the night lots of nights. When my dad was not being abusive, he would take me, my sister, and my friend and his older sister to Wisconsin Dells with us or out to eat. Their mom and grandma had been through abuse before and that's when things changed. Whenever we were at their house or playing with them, we had to stop everything and anything we were doing to go home and check in at a certain time every day. No matter where we were, we had to be home at that time, and they found that strange. Another sign they caught onto was we would be at their house for sometimes a week straight then they would not hear from us for days or weeks and we would come back with bruises all over us. They paid attention to the signs and things we would say, and they knew we did not fall all the time to get these bruises. Finally, after they kept asking us where these bruises were from, we opened up and told them everything about the abuse we were going through and what was going on. These people changed our lives and saved us in a way where I can never thank them enough.

The day my stepmom left for good, my dad beat me and then started beating her up in the kitchen. I ran out of the house full speed to my friend's grandma's house and told them everything that was happening. They immediately called the police and told me to stay inside the house. My friends went over to the house with a screwdriver in her hand to grab my sister and bring her over as well. When my sister got back, she told us that our stepmom lied again and didn't say anything to the police but left with her two daughters. My sister said our dad cut himself on his arm to make it look like our stepmom stabbed him so he could get custody of them. After twenty minutes, my dad came walking down the alley full speed and angry. But my friend's mom grabbed her screwdriver and his grandma walked right behind her out the door and as brave as they were, they both stood up to him. They told him we were not leaving the house and we were staying the night until things calmed down. If it weren't for these people, we would have gotten very badly that night. It was crazy that they were there for us more than our own family.

When my caseworker picked me up the next morning from my grandparent's house we went back to her office and she was telling me how I was most likely going to be placed in a shelter because there was nowhere else for me to go. I started panicking and my adrenaline started rushing. I was scared of going to a shelter and I did not want to go. I was begging for my friend to answer his phone to see if I could come and live with him, his mom, and his older sister. I waited at my caseworker's office all day and then he finally answered. I had his mom talk on the phone with my caseworker and thankfully, I did not have to be placed in a shelter. She had to get a background check, and the home had to be looked at by my caseworker that night. Once her background check passed, we planned to head over to her house but first I had to get a physical done. Each foster home I went to an updated physical had to be done and I did not have a regular doctor, so it was always uncomfortable when a new doctor I had never met before was touching my penis for an exam. But I managed to get through it each time. Once we finished the physical, we headed over to my friend's apartment. She lived on the south side of Rockford in the Kishwaukee and Broadway area which was filled with lots of crime. My friend also went to R.E.S.A and played basketball for this school so it was nice I would still be able to play on the basketball team. I talked to Coach Jackson and told him my situation and he came to an agreement with me to still allow me to play as long as I corrected my behavior in school. I was happy to be in a new home and thankful to be living with my friend.

Living With My Friend's Mom

Once I got to my friend's apartment that night, my caseworker met with my friend's mom and talked for about thirty minutes. I heard her bring up getting paid for a foster kid living with them and this hurt my feelings. I was told the money they got from me would be used to pay the cable bill, so I guess I was a free cable provider walking around during this time. I thought this was out of genuine kindness, but I guess I had the wrong idea. When my caseworker left, I was told I would be sleeping on a blowup mattress in the living room because there were only two bedrooms in this place. Soon my friend's mom and I did not get along too well because she became a very rude, mean, and nasty person who said a lot of smartass comments. She did a lot of drugs and had been arrested for stealing on multiple occasions. She had even stolen from her own mother. She also smoked cigarettes a lot which was another thing I was not a fan of. She went through at least a pack a day and I hated the smell. After we got my air mattress set up and got a spare dresser to put my clothes in, we went out to eat. Afterwards, my friend and I started playing PlayStation 3 on his game system and hanging out. But his mom was always overprotective with her kids because I was beating him in a basketball game and joking with him saying he sucks, and she told me if I say something like that again I won't be living with her any longer. Within the first day of living there, I was already threatened with a two weeks' notice.

After a week of living there I got sick of sleeping on a blow-up mattress in the living room. It was very hard to sleep during the night because my friend's sister would have a boyfriend during the night and they were very loud. My friend's mom also walked around a lot late at night to grab a soda from the fridge and light a cigarette at the dining room table. I always looked forward to her leaving and going to work early in the morning so I could have a good sleep. I would wake up early in the morning to a loud scream or moaning noise over and over again coming from my friend's older sisters' bedroom. I would jump up, scared and nervous because I thought someone was being attacked somewhere. We already lived on the far south side of Rockford in a bad area where there was daily a police presence and the last thing that I wanted was to get hurt because I slept in the living room right where people could see me. With this in mind, I got up and walked to my friend's sister's bedroom to see where this screaming was coming from. I knocked on the door loud and asked if she was okay. Then about five minutes later she came walking out with her boyfriend. I instantly knew what was going on and I was pissed because I heard these same sounds for several mornings and realized I was woken up to sex. It was very disgusting and nasty.

While I was going to school at R.E.S.A, I got called into the principal's office a few times because my clothes all smelled like smoke and I was accused of smoking. I explained that I moved to a new foster home and my foster parent smoked and that I never touched any of it. This school had a big problem with kids my age smoking and drinking. When I finally was able to be back on the basketball team and see my teammates, I apologized to the team and coach for my behavior and explained that I could attend all games now because I left my old foster home. My friend who I was living with was a grade younger than me and played basketball for this school as well, so it was nice to know I had a ride every day. We started the 8th grade playoffs the next night and played the team Marshall Middle School and this was a "win or you're done for the year" situation. While I was living with my friend, I was able to go to the YMCA a lot and would stay there for hours practicing, so I was very happy and confident to play. I stopped being angry at my teammates and we had all become closer and it helped out a lot while playing. When we took the floor that night, we played them at West Middle School where this event was held every year. It was a very close back and forth game, but we beat Marshall Middle School. It was one of the best feelings I felt in a very long time. I was so happy to know that our season was not over, and we were going to be able to keep playing. Things would however take a drastic turn for the worse the next morning.

When I woke up that morning, I was feeling very happy after that win the night before. As usual I woke up to my friend's mom drinking her soda and smoking in the dining room. I got dressed and got ready for school like normal, but I wanted to play the PlayStation because I woke up so early and had plenty of time before I had to leave. I grabbed my headphones so that I could listen to music while I played. That's when I heard her yell "don't touch my son's game!" Surprised, I told her he said it was okay if I play it while he is not around. Then she just kept yelling at me to put it down, and added that I have a smart mouth. I told her no and to go ask her son and watch what he says. I put my headphones on as she was talking and sat in my chair and continued to play ignoring her direction. Then out of nowhere I felt a hand come from behind me and rip my headphones off snapping it in half. These were not ordinary headphones ;these were Beats and cost $200 and I knew I was not going to be able to replace them. I was in total shock and got up from the chair and asked her why she did that. She then started cussing me out and that's when I got up and grabbed my coat and went to put on my boots and leave to go wait at the bus stop. When I put my boots on, I went to grab my coat but she grabbed me by my arm. She told me I was not leaving, and I yanked my arm from her arm and then she grabbed me by my neck and threw my head up against the wall. She slammed my head up against the wall. I pushed her to get her off of me, while my friend was yelling at us both to stop. That's when she said, "you're going to jail for pushing me." I told her, "you put your hands on me first, bitch!" I walked out of her house. I never called an adult a bitch at such a young age, but I did not care because I was so angry at the time. When I walked outside, I heard her talking to the police and telling them she had a foster kid who put his hands on her. I got scared and took off running.

It was a very cold January morning, and I was freezing. My

friend's mom yanked my coat off, so all I had was my middle school sweatshirt on to cover me. I had no hat, no gloves, and no coat. I was going to walk to my friend's grandma's house because that's the only place I knew where I could go. The only problem was she lived over five miles away and I was freezing cold and had only walked a mile so far. But I was scared of getting arrested again and I just kept walking and walking and walking. As I got closer to my friend's grandma's house, I could no longer feel my face, my hands, or my feet. I was completely frost bitten and freezing cold. When I finally arrived, she saw how freezing I was and got me a coat and some hot chocolate. I sat down and told her everything that happened, and she listened to me talk. But shortly after I started talking, I saw a police officer pull up.

I freaked out and realized I had been set up by my friend's grandma. When the officer came inside, he sat down and talked to me about what happened at the house and I told him that the lady broke my headphones and slammed my head up against the wall and showed him the cut and bump I had on my head. Then he went over and talked to my friend's grandma about what happened. After he talked with her outside for about ten minutes, he came back inside and told me to walk outside with him. I got up and walked outside with him and he told me that there were four stories against my one story. I told him only two people saw what happened, but he said the other stories matched and I was going to be arrested. I was beyond pissed and when he told me to put my hands behind my back, I ripped my arm away from his arm and the officer grabbed me and I pushed him off of me. He then grabbed me again and tackled me to the ground, turned me over to where I was face first in the freezing snow and had his knee on my back telling me to stop resisting. I wish I had hung out with the wrong crowd at R.E.S.A because I would have gotten a gun and shot that officer that day. I got up crying because of how angry I was and was placed in the back of his car. He tried talking to me and I did not say a word to him. I was in shock. I was being arrested for doing nothing at all but pushing someone to get off of me after they had slammed my head against a wall. I was the victim, and I was the one who ran away from the situation but that didn't matter to him. I was just a foster kid.

I was ashamed of myself that I had been arrested two times at just 14 years old.

On My Way To Aunt Martha's

When I was taken down to the Juvenile Detention Center again for the second time at just 14 years old, I had to sit inside while being chained up to a bench. I waited for about two hours and I didn't say a word. I was filled with hatred and anger. It's crazy how the night before I was so happy that we had won a basketball playoff game and here I was mad with a cut on my face sitting inside of a detention center. I was tired of being bullied at school and tired of not having anyone. At 14 years old, I realized that the only person I had in this world was myself. I didn't ever want to be in another family, and I didn't want to have any more friends. Because of this incident, I stopped trusting people. I didn't even trust the Bible anymore or the pastor. I was just a very bitter person at this time.

After almost three hours of sitting in handcuffs, my caseworker came inside and took one look at me and shook her head. I promised her the last time I was arrested I would never get arrested again and I felt like I had failed her. I was surprised she was here because I thought I was going to be locked up that day, but my friend's mom did not press charges. When I left, I got inside the car with my caseworker and told her what happened. She told me she knew what really happened and apologized to me. I took a look in the mirror to look at my face and I was so angry because this officer had left a huge cut on my face. I asked her where we were going, and she told me she was taking me to Subway to get some food and then I had to wait inside her office until they found somewhere for me to go. I told her I had a basketball game the next day and I had to be there because it was the playoffs and she said we'll see.

Afterwards, we headed back to her office and I had to sit again and wait. I felt like I was at her office every week and this was my hang out spot. I knew almost every caseworker in this Lutheran Social Services building and it was fun when I would sit inside here. I would walk to everyone's office and look for toys, candy, or food that they had and then go to the next one. I used all of them for toys and food, but I didn't like any of these people anyways, so I didn't feel bad. But after the three offices I went to that day, I got upset after everyone kept asking me what happened to my face and I just went and sat back with my caseworker. I started bothering her and asking her where I was going and who would be taking me to my basketball game tomorrow. I was just being very annoying. That's when she broke the truth to me and told me I was most likely not going to be able to play tomorrow because I was going to be sent to a shelter. Immediately, I started crying. I didn't want to go to a shelter. I was scared, and I didn't want to let Coach Jackson down again or my teammates. My caseworker tried cheering me up, but I didn't care what she had to say. I was so angry and sad. That's when the only caseworker I did like came by. He was a nice guy who I talked basketball with, and he told me he would take me down to the YMCA to shoot some hoops to take my mind off of things. I stopped crying and eventually went with him after some convincing.

I saw some of my friends at the YMCA because it was now 6pm and a lot of kids came here after school. They all asked me what happened to my face and I told them what happened, and I said I was going to be put in a shelter home and I asked all of them if I could live with them. A lot of kids my age could not comprehend what foster care was and didn't know what a shelter home or respite home was and basically had no idea what I was talking about. They all thought I was crazy because of how young I was to be going through all of this stuff. I didn't blame them because most of them had parents and a home and I had none of that. It was just something I learned to get used to. Finally, the caseworker I came to the gym with said it was time to go. I got in his car and we left to go back to the office. I didn't care for all of the basketball talk he had to say because I was sad; I wouldn't be able to play tomorrow. When I got back inside the office, I saw my caseworker and her manager, and we had to sit in a room and talk. They told me I was going to be placed in a shelter home called Aunt Martha's Youth Center and I broke down crying again. I asked them if there were any other options and they said no. They knew I was a runner and they told me if I ran away from this office or there I would go to jail. I wanted to call my coach, but they told me no and to sit and wait. This was one of the worst days of my life so far and I was just filled with so much hate and anger. I felt like I had let my coach and team down after promising not to. I was just very angry, depressed, and I hated the world. I started to doubt God and question if he was real or not because if he was why was I going through all of this? When my caseworker and her supervisor were ready, we left at 8pm that night and drove a little over an hour to Aurora, Illinois. The closer we got, the lonelier and the angrier I beacame. I was in for a new experience I had never been through before.

Aunt Martha's Youth Center

In January of 2014 at 14 years old, I arrived at Aunt Martha's Youth Center in Aurora, Illinois. It was better known as a homeless shelter for DCFS wards with no homes or placements to go to. I arrived filled with sadness, anger and hate for people during this time and was ready to leave as soon as I arrived. This was a Victorian mansion that was made into a home for the youth with no place to go. This was a shared boys and girls home just for temporary stay. There was staff working 24 hours a day. It was the biggest house I had ever seen in my entire life. It was a huge blue house with three floors. I remember staring at the ceiling because I had never seen the ceiling inside of a house so big in my life with the long brown wooden stair wells. There were seven bedrooms on the second floor, a huge basement with a flat screen tv and three computers. I guess this was my new home for now.

After I was given a tour of the building, I also had the rules explained to me. I was told about how you could only call people on your list and phone calls could only last 30 minutes. I understood that a lady would cook for us every day and if we did not eat then we would go to bed hungry. This was the first place I had been to where knives were not allowed. I never saw kids use a spoon to smear their peanut butter and jelly before. I was taken to my room where I would be staying. I saw how every room had bunk beds and was on my way to meeting my new bunk bed partner. When I first walked in the room, I saw nothing but WWE action figures everywhere and heard a kid making noises as he hit his action figures with one another. My roommate was a 15-year-old kid named Jake. Jake was a very nice, quiet, shy kid with a stuttering problem. I was so happy he was my roommate because I was the youngest kid there at the time and was scared of all the other bigger kids. The first thing he asked me when I got in the room was, "Do you like wrestling?" I said "yea" dully and the rest of the night we played with the wrestling figurines until we were told to turn the lights off at 10pm. At least my first night was not so bad after all.

The next day I was taken to the school where I would be enrolled at but did not go to school for a week after that. Washington Middle School was my new 8th grade school. At the house I started to get to know the other kids more and learned more about the rules. I had learned the house was split into two sides: a boy's side and a girl's side. I learned the hard way that there was no cable on the upstairs tv only in the basement, and the basement was only open certain hours of the day. Also, computer time was in the basement and we could only get on the computers on the weekends. We were not allowed to have phones, so that always made it worse. On top of that, all the movies this place had were all scratched up. I would watch the same movie repeatedly. I was just so bored all the time. I missed my friends back home and missed going to the YMCA.

I got along with almost every kid there even though a lot of kids tried to bully me all the time by telling me what to do and by trying to intimidate me. One kid in particular was a 16-year-old kid named Kyle. Within the first week of being there, he would say that if I did not do everything, he said he would slap me or punch me. He tried to intimidate me every time he got the chance too. I never feared him though and that's what pissed him off all the time. One day, we were doing our daily chores and as I was sweeping, Kyle got mad that I swept close to his feet. He took the broom from my hand and spit on it and I got mad and yelled at him. Then he got in my face and I pushed him. As staff came through and broke us up, he told me how he would slap me, but I never feared him. Later that night, the staff came to my room and told me I did a good job standing up for myself. They explained that Kyle always tries to pick on people. I finally had something to feel proud of myself for.

I became happier once I learned we could get passes with rec and go play basketball at the Vonn Center. I felt like I was back home again getting to play at the basketball courts against other kids my age and grown men. I was always so competitive when I played. I finally got to get Kyle back as well by beating him on the court. I always had so many people tell me how good I was for a 14-year-old kid. Basketball continued to be my escape from reality. Just a game of basketball could cheer me up for the entire day. That's how much I loved it. I felt like a little kid at Disney World every time I saw a court full of people. I always loved to dribble a basketball. That was my favorite thing to do. At my old foster home, I spent hours doing dribbling drills in the driveway. In fact, I used to be out so late that my 8th grade teacher Mrs. White would see me as she drove home four houses down. She used to tell Coach Jackson about how long I would be outside dribbling. I always had dreams about becoming a pro athlete one day and believed I would make it happen if I practiced every day. I used to annoy the staff so much because all I wanted to do was play basketball every single day. Of course, we never got to go every day because every kid had to agree on where we would go, but we go at least once a week. I always used to tell Jake to vote to go play at the Vonn Center and he always voted for me. But his vote never counted because all he did was play with his WWE action figures there.

I had seen drugs for the first time in my life while I was at Aunt Martha's Shelter Home. They had a policy where if you smoked you could go outside on the porch and smoke for 15 minutes then had to come back inside. I decided to go out there one day because I was tired of being inside. I remember seeing these two kids have green leaves. They tore their cigarettes open and put this green leaf inside, then licked it back together. I remember asking, "what the heck is that?" and they both laughed at me. They never told me what it was, and I went back inside because a staff member yelled at me and told me to come back in. I went back upstairs and into my friend's room named Jordan and Cairo. Jordan was a 17-year-old, 6-foot 4 giant from Oswego, Illinois. I always asked him why he doesn't play basketball because he could go to the NBA. But he was more of a nerd and into comic books and shows on Cartoon Network. I always wondered how someone with that height liked cartoons and superheroes more than sports. Cairo was 16 years old and from Aurora, Illinois. Cairo was into skateboarding and rock and roll music. He always liked to wear these black gloves and put paint on his face. I never understood that and I thought it was only for white people to be gothic and like skateboarding. But when I went into the room and asked them what it was that those kids were smoking outside, they both started laughing. I thought I was seeing things at first. Then they explained to me that it was weed, and they were rolling it up in a blunt. Then we looked outside from their room and saw another staff member doing it with them. I could not believe this small little green leafy thing was so popular.

Once I was enrolled in school and started making more friends, everything became smoother. I did catch myself hanging out with the wrong crowd at school though. I started trying to fit in and be cool with other kids there. I met someone by the name of Kade, and he did not have the best influence on me. He was 14 years old like me and always talking about all the women he had sex with. I could not wrap my head around how a 14-year-old boy was having sex like this even with grown women. He wasn't lying either because he had videos on his phone. I was a really quiet student in the classroom who didn't cause any disruptions. I did love gym class and getting to play basketball again. I was very competitive not only in basketball but in every game gym played. It was something about winning that always sparked me because I was always losing in life. Even if it was a scooter game, I just wanted to win. I told some kids that I occasionally go to the Vonn Center and asked to hang out sometime and play ball, but we could never keep in touch because I did not have a phone. It was cool because when we did go, I saw some of the kids from school playing so I usually joined in and played.

A month and a half had gone by and still no homes were available for me, it got nerve wracking because I still did not know where I was going to end up. When it was my turn to get on Facebook I would check if any of my friends from back home messaged me. They never did. That always hurts the most to be checking your inbox and seeing it empty. I never got any phone calls either, even when I did reach out to people from back home. I could not understand why because right before I left, we were laughing and joking at lunch. I guess you see who your real friends really are when you're alone and feeling down. Not even my caseworker really talked to me and I felt so alone and abandoned. This started to frustrate me and cause me to act out more. I stopped listening to the staff and I stopped wanting to do anything. I did not understand why I could not be like the rest of my friends at 14 years old. Why do I have to be in this stupid shelter? I got into an argument with one of the staff ladies at nighttime when It was lights out and I was told to go back to my room. I refused to go back in the room, and she put her hands in front of me and I pushed it down. One of the older boys saw what happened and he pushed me all the way to my room and yelled at me for putting my hands on a woman. I did not even care, I just wanted to leave this place. That night I thought about running away and never coming back. I wanted to just be normal and have a mother and a father who loved me. I remembered how I had four aunts and three uncles and none of them wanted me. My own sister refused to talk to me. It was like everyone betrayed me. The next day at school I was asked to move to a different seat, but I did not want to change seats. I refused to move, and I ended up cussing the teacher out and calling him many names. In fact, I was almost arrested because of the words I was saying to him. The police came into the room and escorted me out. I had to sit inside the officer's room until people from the shelter came to pick me up. I was filled with anger about everything. I was on a downward path and did not care.

While I was on suspension I was not allowed to just sit around and watch tv. I had to be punished for my actions. Especially when Mr. Jones was working; he was the strictest staff there. I had to sit in my room all day until the night staff came or I had to just write and do work. Even if I did want to do my work I couldn't because everything was on a stupid bendy pencil. Do you know how hard it is to write with a bendy pencil? I refused to do any of that. They ended up taking the tv remotes away so I could not watch tv anymore and I was not allowed to go down to the basement. Everything was taken away at this point, yet I still did not care. To piss them off even more I took plastic cups and filled them up with water, and I walked up to the very top of the stairs. I threw both the cups over the banister and water got everywhere, even on a staff. I ran to the bathroom and hid not knowing that not everyone was at school that day. Mr. Jones kept yelling, "Devin, get out here and clean this mess up!" Eventually, when I decided to come out of the bathroom, I refused to clean it up. Then out of nowhere came Mr. D the big boss of the whole house and he was mad. After I cleaned up my mess, I was given a lecture with Mr. B and with my caseworker on the phone. I was warned that I could be sent to a stricter place if I did not change my behavior. I decided to change it because I did not want that to happen. I felt like a fool giving these people what they wanted. What about me and what I wanted? Did that matter at all or is it just what you think is best for me and what you want? Later that night, I was talking to Jake and asking him, "if I jumped out this window do you think I would make it down okay?" I told him I was ready to run away, so I climbed halfway out the window on a cold snowy February night. I was three stories up from the ground not knowing if I slipped, would instantly fall and die? Here I am trying to be a fourteen-year-old spider-man! I was trying to walk on the thin ledge to another kid's room and talk to them to help me run away. The ledge was not big enough for me to do it, so I smartly came back through the window. I was talking to Jake that night and he was telling me to stay and things would be better. Here I am complaining about being there a month and a half and this kid has been here for over three months. I told him "when we get out of here one day, you will be a WWE legend and I'll be an NBA player and we both will live in mansions!" I'll never forget the excitement on his face when I said that. We later played wrestling the rest of the night and I got to be John Cena and he was Ray Mysterio. I couldn't believe how this kid had managed to cheer me up after feeling down for weeks. I guess it's just the little things that count at times.

While I was still suspended from school, I had to see the counselor once a week at the house and apologize to the teacher. I was fixing my behavior and decided to start doing well and stop being bad. Once I was finally off punishment after about two weeks, we were all going to go out and do an activity. Of course, I voted for the Vonn Center but everyone else wanted to go to a haunted house. I hated haunted houses, but they still made me go. There were eight kids and it had to be a 4 to 1 staff ratio, meaning for every four kids there had to be one staff member. There were only two staff members working that night. As we came to the haunted house I decided to finally go in and I was terrified. It was in a creepy basement and the whole time I had my hands over my ears and slowly walked through. All these weird creepy masks, face paintings, loud noises and people running up to me trying to scare me as if it were funny and I was trying to enjoy this. All the other kids were laughing at me, but I did not care. At least I was man enough to do it and I did it. Once that was over later on that week, we went to another outing at the Chicago Wolves game. At the time a lot of kids started dating at the shelter home which was gross to me. There were five kids who came including myself. The game was very empty, and it was hockey so not many of the kids enjoyed it. Once the game was over and it was time to leave, we went looking for the other two kids. Of course, it was a boy and a girl, and they just so happened to be dating and disappeared. We spent 45 minutes walking around that whole stadium looking for them and where they went. We still could not find them. We searched everywhere and even told the security at the game and had them announce it over the intercom. Still no sign of them anywhere in the stadium. We were finally asked to leave and waited in the car even longer. They still did not come and finally after almost two hours they came walking up to the car. Of course, they got in trouble, but they didn't even care at all. We all knew what they were doing and what they were up to the whole time.

It was now the month of March. Two months and still no word of anyone taking me in. I stopped caring after a while and just learned to enjoy what I had for the time being. I refused to let someone make me angry or get upset about this. I did not want to go back to my old ways of misbehaving and getting my outings taken away, especially since I had just earned them back after being punished for weeks. Things however began to escalate for the kids who lost their privileges to leave the shelter. I had witnessed my first fight inside of the shelter between Kyle and another boy. These two hadn't liked each other for a while now and during the night they went at it. I woke up from shouting in the hallway and heard some cuss words being said to one another. I was thinking Kyle was just trying to bully someone like he always is trying to do. Then as I came to peek my head out to see what was going on, boom, punches were being thrown left and right. All you heard was the staff ladies screaming and the other girls screaming. Silently, in my head, I was hoping Kyle got his ass whooped for always trying to bully me. So many punches were being thrown so fast that I could not even keep track just one after another after another. The way these two were fighting, you would have thought it was Tyson vs Holyfield part three! Then, out of nowhere, they both ended up slamming and crashing into my room and the fight continued into my room. Everyone was trying to break it up, but they just kept going at it over again with punches and kicks. Then, finally one of the boys grabbed a fire extinguisher and hit the other boy with it. We were all told to go downstairs because the police came in and tased one of the boys. After about an hour of staying downstairs, we were allowed to come back upstairs to our rooms. For some reason they arrested the one boy and kicked him out of the shelter and not the other boy, Kyle. I was annoyed that this guy was back in the house again.

After the fight, it seemed as if everyone was in trouble but me and one other person were the only people who got to go on outings. I used this to my advantage, and we went to the Vonn Center all the time and played basketball. I always had fun playing ball, so I never cared. I started going to church on Sundays as well and growing spiritually with God which helped me. I started singing in church which was something I never did. Also, I started sitting through a whole 2-and-a-half-hour church service and then wanting to go back again the next Sunday which I never ever wanted to do before. It was like these people were changing me and I started liking this shelter more and more. I started becoming more disciplined and listening to authority. Every Sunday I went to church. I learned how to pray more and give stuff up to God more. An old saying always came into mind was, "it's all in God's timing and plans." I watched four kids get discharged and still did not wonder or get upset that it was not me, because when it's in God's timing it will happen. The more rec activities we went on and the more talks I had with staff about life, really helped me grow as a young boy. I never would have thought there was so much more to life that I had left being as young as I was.

When we entered the month of April, my caseworker called me and delivered great news to me that they have found me a new home in Rockford! I was so happy they found me a new home and I was going to get to play basketball every day and work out to be a better basketball player. Yet I found it so hard to leave. I had grown a bond with these people. I had learned to trust and open up to these people as if they were my family. I actually felt like these staff and some of these kids were like my new family. It's funny how you never realize what you really have until it's gone. It was unreal that the very next day I would be leaving and going to a new home. One of the hardest people to say goodbye to was Jake. Even though I loved basketball and he loved the WWE, I would never forget all the talks and fun times we had playing with the wrestling men. He really helped me just enjoy the little things in this world. It seems every day we always want more and more as people, yet a couple of $2.00 action figure toys could keep a kid busy and happy for hours on end. This really was something that I had never seen before, especially with a kid my age. As the day came and my caseworker was outside, I thanked all the staff so much for everything and they gave me the number and told me to call if I ever felt down. I had grown a relationship with all these people. I made sure to apologize again for all my childish behaviors and gave them a big hug again. As I went upstairs to say goodbye to Jake, I gave him a few of my shirts and a hoodie because he didn't have any clothes at all. I had never met a kid in my life who did not care about clothes, money, shoes, but was just happy with what he had. Right before I left, he had told me to wait. Right then and there he handed me one of his favorite action figures. As we both walked down the stairs and I said one last goodbye we were told to exchange phone numbers but we both did not have phones at the time. I never would have thought as I walked out the door with a final goodbye, this would be the last time I ever spoke to not only some of the staff but to Jake as well.

When I left Aunt Martha's Youth Center, I was taken to another foster home back in Rockford, Illinois. I did not realize how much damage was done after I had left this shelter home. I did not want any love or affection; it was very different from being in a structure for three months, to going into a normal home. It was like I wanted to leave but then I did not. I was tired of living under these foster parents' roofs where if you don't do everything, then they threaten to kick you out. I had already been through five different foster homes at the time, and it was the same pattern over and over again. I stopped trusting these homes and slept with one eye open at night. Especially after my own uncle turned his back on me. I've been around him and his wife since birth and their son was like my best friend. All we did was play Xbox together and at family get-togethers us three would be outside playing football. I liked him better than my own dad. I wished I were in my cousin's shoes all the time. Me and my older sister were not angels at all, and we made our mistakes, but I was 13 years old and she was 15. We were just two young, damaged kids at the time just leaving an abusive father. It was so difficult being a 13-year-old boy with so much stress, anger, and sadness. My emotions were all over the place and it did not help how we were not allowed to talk about it. It was like we were living under the slogan "children should be seen but not heard." I refused to live by that because I was given a mouth and a voice for a reason. This new and pathetic foster family did not understand that. You cannot just push everything aside all the time and hold it in as if it will just go away. That's exactly what my father would do when he beat us. We were expected to never talk about the beatings and pretend and laugh with him as if nothing just happened. I was tired of living in the shadows. My grandparents did not like this, and this led to my grandfather choking me and throwing me up against the fireplace when I was thirteen as my sister and cousin watched in horror. My grandma was screaming for him to get off, but I did not understand why because when he was finished, she told me to get out of her house. I did not trust anyone anymore.

I was tired of the same cycle where the family was all nice and friendly at first then changed into these tyrants and rude people. I did not want anything to do with these homes. All I wanted was just a place to sleep, food, and a ride to and from places, other than that, I wanted to be left alone. This was a terrible way of thinking but at the time it felt right. I felt that if I could survive in a shelter home for three months by myself with no support, then I can do it anywhere I go. Eventually things went downhill at this new home I was at. I did my own thing a lot and they wanted me involved in their family which was not what I wanted. How can you blame me after my own family turned on me? It felt awkward always being introduced as a "foster son." I felt like I did not belong in any family. When dinner time came, I stayed downstairs and ate on my own. When they tried to pick me up from school, I never wanted to get in. I just wanted to listen to music and walk with my headphones in as this was always my way of coping. I felt like I had nobody anymore, not even my own blood sister. Especially after my sister never called me in the shelter home and always bullied me as a kid. We had gotten into so many fist fights and fights because she felt she controlled me. On the phone one day she even laughed that I was in a shelter home. I had cut off my relationship with her after that happened because she crossed the line. I guess big sisters don't look out for you after all. Some days I would just listen to music and walk all over the city of Rockford. Some days I would even walk to my old childhood home just to reminisce about what happened. I felt like nobody could understand my pain. Even when I told my friends at school they would laugh or wouldn't know what to say really because we were all just young kids at the time. It felt like I was just existing, I was not even living at the time anymore. I never thought suicide would cross my mind at such an early age. I hid my sadness with anger because I did not want to appear weak or vulnerable. This caused me to lash out on people at school and even teachers. I had gotten suspended again from school for yelling at a teacher. It was like I was making the same mistakes all over again.

Eventually, I ended up getting kicked out of this home because I did not want to be a part of their family. I did not want to listen to their rules or follow their directions. I really just kicked my own self out because I was filled with anger and sadness. I was too afraid to join another family and have them turn their backs on me again like the last ones did. We got into many arguments as well because I was not willing to take medication. That was a big thing that was always forced upon me was taking pills. I always had to go see a psychiatrist at Rosecrants as if I was some psycho. I did not need medication. What I needed was someone I could trust and someone who could show me real love and care. It was like once I entered the system nothing, but medication was bestowed upon me. I felt so embarrassed taking these pills and how they made me feel. After I was removed from the foster home, my caseworker came to take me to her office with my things packed. She was telling me how I couldn't keep going from home to home and that I needed to learn how to trust these people and give them a chance. She also told me that they were running out of places to put me and if I kept this up, I would be sent to a residential facility. Meaning, a lockdown place where every day you are told what to do and live in a jail type of structure. I asked her where I was going next. I was ready to give one of these new foster homes a chance after she said this. But she told me, I was going to be going to another shelter home. I immediately ran away from her office and ran outside. I just kept running and running as fast as I could. I felt like I was 10 years old again running away from my dad. But there was nowhere for me to run being in the middle of downtown Rockford. The police station was right across the street, but I did not care, I just ran. I was tired of these foster homes and shelter homes. I wish I could take care of myself and get my own apartment, but I was only 14 and that was impossible. I hated how I was treated like a piece of trash and just passed along from dumpster to dumpster. I was so sick of these caseworkers not doing their jobs and putting me in these crappy homes, or them telling me there were no foster homes at all to put me in. I knew they were lying to me and they just didn't want to deal with me. I was angry how they all got to go home every day and live how they want to live but when it comes to me it's just like the mentality was "place him anywhere." I wish these people could feel my pain and understand my struggle. Maybe then they would take their jobs more seriously and actually find a home out there for me. I wish I could place them in a foster home, and we trade places maybe when they would see how it feels to play with someone's life and to actually see what it's like being in foster care. Even when I tried opening up about what I went through inside the homes but nobody cared because I was just a child who didn't know anything. While I ran away from my caseworkers office, I ended up hiding behind an alleyway dumpster that day for hours playing with a piece of grass. I was thinking about becoming homeless, and this way I would not have to deal with any of these foster homes. Then during the day, I would just play at the YMCA and take showers there. I had this whole great plan figured out in my head of how I would live. Eventually, something changed in my mind and I walked back inside the office and sat there.

When the receptionist called my caseworker and told her I was upstairs in the lobby waiting, she threatened to have the police called on me if I did that again and I would go to jail. I couldn't even hear anything she said because I was so angry. All I kept thinking about was why me. Why at 14 years old can't I live like a normal kid and be happy? Why is life so hard for me and why do I have to be sent to another homeless shelter? I missed all of my friends from school and missed playing basketball at the YMCA. I wish one of my friends was able to take me in, but nobody was able to. I felt like I was just a lost cause in this life. Once my caseworker stopped talking to me and I locked back in, I had to go back to her office. Then I had to speak with her manager about what happened. She threatened to have the police called on me as well, but I did not care about what she had to say. I was told to sit in the corner where they both could see me and just wait. After hours of waiting and sitting in this corner they told me it was time to go. I didn't know where we were going, I just knew it would be another shelter somewhere in Illinois. When me and my caseworker got in the car, she told me that the shelter I was going to was in southern Illinois, meaning I was going to the country. I passed through southern Illinois before when I took a trip to St. Louis. I remembered seeing nothing but corn fields and prairies. I planned on running away from this shelter, but I knew If I tried to run away, there was nowhere to run. We drove almost two hours. I asked my caseworker the name of this place and where it was. She told me the name was Nachusa Shelter Home, and it was a small village outside of Dixon, Illinois. The more cornfields I saw the more I wanted to jump out of this car. I saw people jump out of cars before when I watched action movies, but I was afraid I would hurt myself. We were going super-fast on a highway with cars and a semi-truck right next to us so

I was sure I would not fare well at all if I jumped and tried to roll. I was pretty much out of luck at this point, and that sting of reality triggered my emotions. I tried to hold back tears, but I just started crying on the way there. My caseworker started telling me that I did this to myself, and to use this as a lesson to behave. This made me cry even more because she was right. It felt like one of the longest car rides in my life. I was so scared again and nervous to go to another shelter home. I was thinking the worst things you could possibly think. I thought I was going to get bullied again and this time beat up by the older kids inside of here. I was just totally intimidated. I asked my caseworker if I could use her phone to apologize to my old foster parents, but she told me it was too late.

Nachusa Shelter Home

It was April of 2015 When I first walked into Nachusa shelter home. I was 14 years old at the time. The campus was outside in the middle of nowhere. There was nothing around there besides cornfields and more cornfields. On the campus were four buildings and an outdoor baseball field. One of the buildings was used as a drug rehab center for kids who were both in DCFS and not in DCFS. I had never seen a rehab center where you live inside of one. The second building was where the kitchen was. This is where we would grab our food every day but had to walk along this outdoor path. The third building was a school and this was where I would finish 8th grade and where I could play basketball inside of the gym. The 4th building was our building. It was a short, one story brick building. As we walked inside, I could sense that this was more of a strict and structured shelter. There was one big office in the middle of the whole shelter with two doors and glass surrounding every side of it. It was like one of those hospital booths with one big office and nothing but glass and two doors. The rest of the place was just a long building with brown doors everywhere. One side was covered by carpet and another side with nothing but tile. Then there was a little room in the back behind the office that was covered by glass and had one door to go in and out of. This room had a couch, two tiny pillows, a small tv with a Wii attached to it, and a bookshelf full of books and boardgames. This was the rec room, I was guessing. Then when I walked to the right side, the carpet side, I was taken to my room and saw a small tv on a cart with a box of movies underneath. This is where I saw two girls watching tv and eating popcorn. One of the girl's arms was covered in lines. I thought she was scratching herself, but it was not scratches, these were self-harm cuts. The other girl was about 11 years old, a small little girl. When I was taken to my room, I was in shock at how much this looked like a jail cell. There was nothing but brick walls and a small little desk in the corner. It had one small little closet, and this was all. I sadly unpacked my things and folded my clothes neatly putting them away. I saw something in my bed, I went down to grab it and it was an action figure from my friend at Aunt Martha's. Right then and there I knew that everything was going to be okay.

The very next day I was given a tour around the building and explained what the rules were. I was not allowed to have a phone, a tv, or anything electronic besides a radio. I was told that a lot of the kids have radios in their rooms as entertainment and I was just getting more annoyed. Next, I was told we can only use the phone to call people on our list and we have a limited number of phone calls. Also, we had to be in our rooms at 10pm every night. We were allowed to watch tv but the tv had no cables, so we just had to pick from the movies in the bucket, if they worked and were not scratched up. With good behavior we could go to Family Video and rent movies and do other things like go hiking, fishing, and get ice cream. All of this stuff was so boring to me and I was just ready to leave. I did not want to be here at all. I asked her about the rules to play the game system and was told that we can play the game, but we have to earn it with good behavior. We were allowed to play outside as long as a staff member was present and watching us. I wanted to play basketball all the time and the other girls did not really care to do much of anything besides watch tv. We always had to agree on everything even with movies, so this became very annoying and frustrating for me. I felt like they were running everything because the older girl would boss the younger girl around so it would be two against one in votes. But sometimes the staff had my back and let me get my way. The eating rules were that whatever the kitchen made was what would be for dinner. If we did not eat, then we would go to bed hungry. Similar rules as if I were back at Aunt Martha's.

When I did go back to school it was not the same. I missed all my friends from Lincoln and R.E.S.A. (Rockford Environmental Science Academy) and had no way of reaching out. This place had no computers and a "no electronic policy." Even if I wanted to disobey this rule, I had no phone or tablet so I couldn't. I would not even get to graduate 8th grade like the rest of my friends. I always wondered if any of them ever thought about me. I wondered what they were saying about me. I always thought if I was back home what I would be doing with them right now. I wanted to play basketball with them or go to Skate Land. It just sucked how all the other kids my age were always able to hang out with one another. My childhood was beyond ruined. I never thought it would be too much to ask just to play basketball with my friends. I wanted to play on an AAU travel basketball team with them so bad but was not allowed to leave the state of Illinois. Most friends could not even give me rides or I could not have sleepovers with them because DCFS had to do background checks on all of their parents. It was like I was the police to them, and I lost some friends because of this. Stuff beyond what I could control as a kid. My new school was just a school where I walked across one building to the other. I had to do everything on a computer. Everything on the computer was blocked off besides the website we were supposed to be on. Believe me, I tried to sneak on to other websites, but I wasn't slick. Every day I did my work on this computer for hours and would get up and leave. It seemed like I was doing the same thing every day. I felt like I was not even learning anything by reading off of a computer screen for hours every day.

I was happy I was able to play against some of the boys from the rehab house. I always impressed them with how I was able to score. Most of those kids sucked anyway so it was not really fun. They all liked baseball for some reason. I do not know if it is because they all grew up in the country or what. I grew up in the city, so I was used to playing basketball all the time. But I just loved sports, so we played some games. Yet these kids still tried to bully me on and off of the court. I don't know if it's because of my age or if it was because I was too small, but it seemed like a lot of older kids were always trying to pick on me for whatever reason. I never let that stuff get to me, but I did take it out on them when we played sports. Every time we played basketball, I played real physical defense on them and they did not like that. Half of them couldn't even dribble so I would easily take the ball from them. When I took the ball from this one 17-year-old boy he was embarrassed and pushed me. I fell straight on my stomach. When I got up, I threw the ball as hard as I could and hit him directly in his face. Right after that everyone came in between us and broke it up. He tried to push people out the way, but I had already been escorted out. I got lucky because I knew I would lose that fight to a 6 foot 3, 17-year-old kid and I was 14 and 5 foot 10. I just wanted to let him know I was not going to back down. I had been backing down from people my whole life. I did not even care if it was a grown man; I was not going to back down.

I was told I could no longer play with the kids from rehab because of this incident, so I would just play basketball by myself and practice. I did not care, I was just happy to be playing a sport that I love. When I was able to convince the two girls in the shelter to play basketball with me, we usually played a game of Horse. The game that I loved to play was WII sports that the shelter had. This game was so fun, and I enjoyed beating them in every sports game we played. It was like I loved winning. I was so competitive even with the little girl. I had always lost in life so winning was just fun for me even if it was on a small little video game. This caused them to not want to play with me anymore, so I usually just played against the computer. I found a new fun sport and that was fishing, UFC, and Boxing. We all behaved well, and we were able to go to Family Video to rent videos. All I would rent is nothing but UFC videos, I'm not sure why that was but I heard something about shadow boxing and wanted to learn from them. Also, I was tired of being bullied so I wanted to destroy anyone that would try to mess with me. My favorite fighter of all time was Mike Tyson and I wanted to be like him. I would watch his fights when I rented them from Family Video and shadow box in my room and practice all the time. I had asked the big boss of the shelter, Andrews, if I could get into boxing and he told me only if I kept good behavior I would be allowed to. I made sure to listen to all of the staff and follow directions so I could get involved in this. But I got in trouble one day because I was fake punching one of the girls while shadow boxing. I did not understand how I got in trouble because I wasn't even hitting anyone, I was just shadow boxing. Of course, the staff told Andrews but I did not get in trouble because I explained but I was told I couldn't get boxing or UFC videos anymore. I guess my behavior was changing and I was a threat to them. I still practiced all the time in my room. When we went fishing, I always loved the excitement of trying to catch my first fish. My parents were never around to take me fishing. I had gone a couple of times with some friends, but I never caught anything. I wanted to catch something for my first time but still was never able to catch one.

Me and Andrews became closer when I started asking him about teaching me how to fish. He was a nice guy and told me we could go when he was working. We also became closer when I started asking him to burn me CD's so I could listen to them on my radio. He loved music and played the guitar but the music I liked and the music he liked were total opposites. But I eventually learned to work with what I had because it was this music or no music. I just learned to like these songs. I also always used to make him laugh because I would bring up all types of different "what if" scenarios to be allowed to have electronics. I had a phone at my caseworker's office and was trying to get it, but I never came up with a good enough excuse. I should have told him it was necessary for my health. When he took me fishing and hiking in the woods, I felt a bond forming between us. I started to trust this man and let my guard down. Also, I was bored of being in the shelter all day, so I learned to get along better. Me and him would go mushroom hunting, I'm not sure if he was tricking me or being serious but he showed me pictures of this mushroom where if you found it you would get paid. Every time we went hiking, I would look everywhere for these things and try to find them. I wanted to get paid so I could buy some more action figures or a Rubix Cube. I was never able to find one though and that always sucked because I really wanted some new games to play. He had taken me to the store and let me pick out one thing that I wanted for good behavior.

My behavior started to shift while I was here though. I was tired of living so isolated like I was in jail or a bad person. I missed my friends and my contact with them, so I started to misbehave on purpose. I would not listen to staff when they told me to get off the WII. When it hit 10pm and I had to go to my room I never listened and kept watching tv until they had to physically unplug it. I refused to listen and was tired of this lifestyle. One day, I had enough and was trying to get myself kicked out after being here for a month. I was told to go to my room and refused to and I was told I would have no tv for a week because of this. Then I grabbed the chair and threw it as hard as I could into the window leaving a big crack in it. Then I took my fruit and threw it at the window to leave a nasty smell and even more of a mess to be cleaned up. The staff lady had called the police on me. The police came later that night and handcuffed me and took me down to the station to get processed. I really did not care at this point. I felt like I was already in jail. Why not actually go? I wanted to go home but the sad reality was I had no home. While being processed and fingerprinted, I was not put in jail that night. I'm not sure why, I guess Andrews did not want to press charges on me. We did have a long talk about what had happened, and I really did not care what he had to say. I just wanted to leave. When I did my week of punishment with no tv I started going outside by myself and looking for where I could run away to. I tried to remember every street we came down each time we went to Family Video. I had secretly got on the computer the day at school and googled "Nachusa to Rockford" and there was no way I was going to be able to physically walk that distance.

Plenty of nights in my room I broke down. I wished that I could be any other fourteen-year-old boy out here having fun with his friends. I was told not to keep in contact with my mother, but I called her anyway. I always asked her to come and get me and she always promised that she would but never did. She had been giving me broken promises since I was a little boy. It was crazy how she convinced me that she would come back and take full custody of us. I was convinced in one of my foster homes I would be moving to Buffalo, New York at the time. My mother had told us she bought furniture and she had a nice apartment and all the fun stuff we would do and how I would have a way better life. I had so much confidence in her and always bragged to my friends about how I was moving and told my caseworker so I would not have to look at her ugly face anymore. I had so much confidence in my mother and thought she would truly come through. I even changed my favorite sports team to all the New York teams because I was so confident that I would be moving in with her. Come to find out when we went to court that everything she had told me was one big lie. I got kicked out of my foster home because she told me on the phone that I did not have to listen to them because she was coming to get me. My mother had no furniture and no place of her own, she lived with one of her cousins in an apartment in Buffalo. It was like I truly trusted everything she had said. After she pulled this stunt, my relationship with her was broken. I was totally alone physically and spiritually. Every time I would ask her why she left when I was only seven years old, she would never answer me. It was very frustrating talking to a woman who asked me the same questions everyday but would not allow me to open up with her. It was always the same basic questions and I gave her the same basic answers. There was no bond anymore. When she would call, I would refuse to talk to her at times. I felt as if I could not trust anyone on this planet. My mother was not an angel either, I was whooped by her a lot as well. There would be times where if I said the wrong thing, she would take her high heels and whack me in the face with it and give me a bloody lip. There would be other times she would hold me down and whack me with a belt as hard as she could until some days, I started bleeding. Some days me and my sister were supposed to visit her every other weekend and we would show up to her apartment and nobody would be home, and we would wait outside for hours. This lady did not have a car either, so she made me, and my sister walk all over the city of Rockford. I hated going to her house because of this. She did not know how to cook either, so we always had microwave dinners and she never really watched us when we were living with her. She left us alone while she stayed in her room. I got whooped one time because I put my microwave dinner in the microwave with a fork and I almost broke it and started laughing because I thought it was funny and got the belt. My mother was a very promiscuous woman as well. She had four kids with three different men and lost custody to all of them. Me and my sister would wake up in the middle of the night to get a drink or use the bathroom and catch her having sex with another man right in the living room. There were always new men that were brought around us all the time. It seemed like she had a new boyfriend every week. I did not understand what was going on at the time because I was still a little boy. When I stayed with her on weekends instead of sitting bored in the apartment, I became friends with a little boy named Jose. Me and Jose would run all over the apartment and play with our action figures. This little boy taught me how to steal from Happy Wok as well. He convinced me that the statue with money in the bottom of it was free money but really it was tips for the restaurants. I got a whooping for these as well.

Later that week, I finally decided to run away from this shelter I was staying at. I was sick of living like this and convinced myself that I deserved better and better was out there for me. I was tired of being alone and I missed my friends. I missed playing basketball and watching tv. I just wanted to leave. I hated everything about this place. As I started putting all my clothes inside of this orange backpack of mine, a staff member knocked on the door and caught me. I told her I was leaving and did not care about anything she had to say. There were two staff working at the time and she yelled "call the police!" and the lady had the police on the phone. She tried to block the door with her hands, and I slapped her arms away and took off running. She then grabbed my backpack and I yanked it away from her. I never thought it would be so hard to get past this old, heavyset white woman. She kept screaming at me to stop but I was in fight or flight mode at this point. I had blacked out and my adrenaline was rushing, and my heart was beating so fast. I ran full speed out the front door and ran as fast as I could towards the Family Video Shop. I saw a McDonald's inside and thought I would go there first. Before I could even make it down the street, I saw an all-black car speed right towards me. I thought I was going to get hit at first, but it was the police. I tried to run into the fields away from them, but he tackled me and put handcuffs behind my back. I never felt that type of pain before in my stomach. I was not able to breathe at the time and could not get up. He pressed his knee on my back while putting the handcuffs on and threw me up against the car. He then told me "if you try to run, I will unleash the dog in the back." I never forgot those words because this was the first time in my life I was threatened to be attacked by a dog.

Later on, I was taken to the hospital with the police officer and we had to wait for hours. I had to get into hospital clothes and get my vitals taken. I had no idea what was going on. I had a cut on my arm, but I did not think it would require this much medical attention. I was so hungry, and I finally was given some food after hours of being there. I was so happy I was able to watch TV on the hospital TV screen as well. Even though I had been chased by the police, slammed on the ground and against a car, threatened to have a dog chase me, and had a cut on my arm, it was still a good day. My caseworker later showed up after that and told me I was not allowed back in that shelter. I smiled so hard and was so happy. I was then nervous if I was going to jail, she told me I was not going there either. I was so happy because I thought she found me a new foster home back home in Rockford, but that was not the case either. I was going to be taken to a hospital because my behavior was "out of control." I instantly broke down, especially after my plan had backfired. I was hoping I would be sent to a new foster home but now I have to go to a stupid hospital. I could not understand what was going on anymore. All I knew was things were about to get a lot stricter and a lot worse for me.

I was told I was being sent to a hospital in Kankakee, Illinois. I had no idea where this was, and I had lived in Illinois my whole life and never heard of this place before. I was so mad at myself and my caseworker. I wanted to cuss her out but then the police officer that slammed me was right there. I also wanted to run away but did not want to get slammed again. My plan had backfired big time. I was told I would have to be taken in an ambulance and sit in a stretcher for four hours. I was confused why I had to go in an ambulance and sit in a stretcher when I was perfectly healthy. I could walk on my own. I did not need a stretcher. I refused to get in one at first then was threatened to be taken to jail if I did not get in it. Eventually, I got on the stretcher and was put in the back of an ambulance. I was so full of anger and rage I wanted to just hurt anyone and everyone. I hated this world with everything in me. Why is it so hard to be like any normal 14-year-old kid? Why does all this stuff have to happen to me? I guess only God knows the answer to these questions. If there even is a God in this world.

As the ambulance began to take off, I had to sit in the back with another man. This man was a nice man, so it helped a lot on this 4-hour ride. We talked about a lot of sports and what football teams we wanted to win. I remember when he asked me what my favorite football team was, and I said the Green Bay Packers. When he asked me why I was a Packers fan when I'm from Illinois, I told him I had to be one. My dad would beat me if I wasn't. I once cheered for the Bears and not the Packers when I was in elementary school because all my friends were Bears fans. I was laying down on the floor and the second that I cheered for the Chicago Bears he got up and kicked me in my face and picked me up and threw me across the room. He then choked me and told me to go to my room. The man was in disbelief. He then asked what happened to my father and I told him he was in prison and the man told me that was good, and I could now cheer for any sports team I want too. I asked him if he had ever done that to his son before and he told me never ever would he lay a finger on his son. He then asked me if I had any siblings and I told him I had four sisters and one older brother. But I did not know who my older brother was, and I did not know who my youngest sister was. When he asked what happened to them, I told him they live with their mom and my older sister lives in a foster home. I was not close with my older sister. She was a bully to me, and I hated that. I hated how every time she would go to the movies with her friends or do fun things with them, she never ever let me go. I hated how she always said so many mean things to me and hit me all the time. When he told me that's not how an older sibling is supposed to act, I was in shock. I thought this stuff was normal because things were always like this. Just like I thought every screwed-up thing in my life was. He told me about his kids and how they behaved, and I was amazed. It seemed like this man's life was perfect and I felt like he was trying to brag in my face for a second. But I put my defense down and listened to what he was saying. I was very amazed at how his life was and I remember calling his life perfect. But he told me his life was not perfect, it was just filled with proper love and respect. This was something I had never had in my life.

When I had to use the bathroom halfway there, I was told we could not stop. Even when I begged to stop so I could use the bathroom they both said it would be against the policy to stop. How the hell am I supposed to pee then? I was told there is a plastic bag for urine that I had to use. I was so embarrassed to use that plastic bag. I had never peed sitting down with my legs straight before. Do you know how hard it is to pee laying down with your legs straight? I could not move my legs because they were strapped in the stretcher. I could not hold it anymore. I wish I did not drink anything at the hospital that day. It was either go or pee on myself. Either way I was going to be embarrassed. I finally told the man to give me the bag. At least the whole bag was big enough to where my piss would not splatter all on myself. I then took the bag and forced my legs to open up a little despite having my legs strapped super tight. I put a blanket over what was going on so nobody would see, and just in case it splattered it would not hit me. The blanket was not big enough for me to look as I did it, so I had to do this off straight memory. I admit I did spill a little on my leg, but I did pretty good after all. The weirdest part was putting the lid on it and handing it to the man. I have never been so weirded out or embarrassed when it came to using the bathroom.

When we finally arrived at the hospital, I was so happy that I was going to be able to stand up after being strapped down for four hours. When we pulled up to the ambulance it was a hospital called Riverside Medical Center. I had no idea where I was going or what I had gotten myself into. When the man parked the ambulance on the curb just for ambulances, they both opened the doors and rolled me out of the ambulance. When I told them to take the straps off and get me out of this stretcher, they told me I had to be wheeled all the way up the unit. This pissed me off even more because I was already laying in a stretcher I didn't need to be in and an ambulance I didn't need to be admitted to a hospital. I was ready to snap but I kept my cool. I was surprised I did not snap but it was probably because there were police officers in the front of the hospital entrance. After getting pushed through the lobby, we then went inside of an elevator to the third floor. When we got to this point, there were so many doors I had to go through. I was confused if this was a jail or a hospital at this point.

Every single door had a key scan to get in and another door with a key scan to get in on every hallway. It was as if I was in a hospital jail. When we finally got to the last door, I was finally let off this stretcher. I could barely walk because of how stiff my legs were. As I walked into the unit, I saw nothing but nurses and staff in hospital gear. This was something I had never experienced before.

Riverside Medical Center

I was approached by a male nurse named Ryan. He told me to sit on the bench and was taking my vitals. I told him I was scared and asked if I was in hospital jail, for some reason he laughed but I was very serious. Ryan told me this was the Bolder Unit, a unit to fix the behavior of kids who are out of control, suicidal, and hostile. He told me this is not a temporary place, the max time of being here is two to three weeks on good behavior. I was very happy about this because I had no idea of how long I would be inside of here. While he was explaining the rules to me, he handed me a little tub with a toothbrush, toothpaste, a hospital uniform shirt, pants, and sox with a stick of deodorant. I had to change into this uniform and place everything in a bag that I had until I was discharged. I was told there is a point system, and that I could wear my clothes if I got a certain number of points and earned more privileges with the more points I earned. This was all earned by attending and participating in groups and the group activities every day. Also, displaying good behavior to my peers and staff while following directions played a major part. I was only allowed to call people on my list and the limit was one phone call for ten minutes a day. Every day I had to get my vitals checked as well. I would be sharing rooms with a roommate and each day we had to go to our rooms during every shift change and be in our rooms at 9pm every night. We were not allowed to leave the unit or go outside, so for however long I would be here I would not be allowed to go outside, wear shoes, or leave this unit. This place was a lot stricter and a lot worse than what I could imagine. At least in jail you get to go outside, here I cannot even step foot outside, I thought to myself. I was ready to leave already. At least every day we got to order what we wanted for food three times a day from the kitchen downstairs. Hospital food was always good to me. Every day was a strict schedule that we had to follow, it seemed like now everything had gotten worse.

The first morning of being there we were all woken up at 7:30am and had to do hygiene and breakfast. If we did not get up in time for this or refused group time, then we would have to stay in our rooms for a long period of time. Every shower had a time limit and we had to be at group by a certain time. I was given an assigned seat at the two octagon shaped tables. While eating my food, I saw all the other kids eating their cool foods and what they liked. I did not get a chance to order because I had come in from the hospital late that day. I was stuck with a mini bowl of raisin bran cereal and milk, while other kids had biscuits and gravy, muffins, and omelets. When I finished eating, I was told to sit in the group area. This area had nothing but chairs in a circle, nine chairs in a circle on a carpet floor. I had to wait for my roommate to finish his hygiene so I could complete mine. Once he finished, I was able to do mine. I walked into a tiny bathroom with a tiny single person shower. The timer had begun for me and this water was freezing cold, from then on, I was always trying to shower first. This was the routine every day while living here. On weekends we had group early in the mornings. On Mondays we would do school and a teacher would come in and teach us. I met everyone there and introduced myself. One staff member usually ran a group. During our group we each individually had to participate by answering a question when called on. If we did not answer, then we would not earn points and would be sent to our rooms. Depending on who ran the groups they would be fun or very boring. Once the group was over, then we would go by what was next on the schedule and that would be another group or vitals. During vitals, we all had to sit in the group area and wait for each nurse to take our vitals one by one as she called us. I learned that not every kid in this unit was a DCFS ward. Some of these kids were sent here by their parents for bad behavior. I would get so angry inside to hear that. I would kill to have two parents who loved me and not be in this DCFS system.

When the morning part of the schedule was finished, and it got closer to noon, we would order lunch for the day on the menus with our bendy pencils. I had experience using bendy pencils from my time at Aunt Martha's and remembered everyone there. When we finished ordering, we did another group until food came. The group sessions were strict as well. I put my arms inside of my sleeves because I was cold and was told I could not do that, or I would be kicked out. We also were not allowed to put our feet up on our chairs, we had to sit straight up with our feet on the ground as well. The old me would have been defiant before but I listened because I wanted to leave as soon as possible. I was not trying to spend longer here than what I needed. During one of our group sessions, a boy refused to answer questions and then when he was told to go to his room; he refused that as well. The nurse had threatened to call code 99 and I had no idea what that was at the time. They told him to go again and he refused, and he threw his chair. That's when a loud alarm went off with a flashing yellow light. Over the intercom all you heard was this loud computer voice going off "code 99 boulder, code 99 boulder!" and it kept going off. Then we saw all the nurses, but our group leader gathered together and then at least 15 more nurses came through the door into our unit. I was terrified at this point myself and I did not even do anything. The boy then started throwing punches at the nurses as they all came in and at this point, it was 20 people vs 1 kid. They eventually jumped on him and got him to the ground, and they carried him onto the bed. Each mattress was under a medal frame with metal clings attached to it. They placed the boy on the bed and strapped him down to each metal cling. Now his hands and his legs were isolated and that is when I saw the nurses come in with a shot. Once they gave the boy a shot you heard nothing but yelling and screaming. I was terrified at this point and was going to make sure I followed everything they said. I was not trying to get a shot or get strapped down. I was not sure what the shot did to you but the way he screamed I was not trying to figure it out. I felt bad for him as he just laid there with his arms and hands strapped, he then started yelling really loud but with the door closed we could not even hear him.

After we ate our lunch, we all had to go back to our rooms for shift change. We were allowed to take a book during this time or take a nap. Every room had a camera inside of it so we could not play games or sneak out to talk to other kids because they would know. When I did talk to my roommate, I usually just asked him if he liked this place and when he was leaving. We talked about what we would do if we were out of here. I never asked him what he was here for because they told us that was confidential. I don't think we were really allowed to make friends because they way everything was scheduled it was like there was no time to talk. Even when we were in our rooms, the staff sat in the hallway and would listen to all of us. I guess they were afraid of all the kids plotting together to take over the unit. I seriously doubt that would happen the way all those nurses stormed through the door. I just felt like I was wasting my life being inside of these places. There was so much more to life than this thing and my imagination kept me from breaking. I just always thought of what I would do once I got out of here. I remember being at Aunt Martha's and saying God won't put you through anything that you can't handle. I should know this better than anyone after staying in a foster home with the most religious person I've ever met in my entire life. Her rules to living with her were we had to go to church every Sunday and Wednesday and be involved in the youth group program. Even when I made the basketball team and had basketball games, I still had to go to the youth group program and miss my basketball games. I hated that, especially missing the chance to play against my old teammates and Lincoln Middle School. Even at dinner we read the Bible and had to have the Bible kids' app on our phones and complete a certain amount of progress to live with her. This lady was a church-aholic. This caused me to get made fun of in 8th grade because I missed my basketball games for church. But I tried to explain if I did not, I would have nowhere else to live but these kids didn't understand. They were all beginning to smoke, have sex and try to be cool. The only person who understood me was 8th grade basketball coach, Coach Jackson. He always had me come over to his house and watch basketball and football games with him and take me to church as well. He would teach me basketball moves and take me to watch his son play basketball in college. I was happy he had taken me under his wing to get away from this crazy lady and all eight of her cats. He helped me gain confidence in myself and always gave me drills to do and I practiced them every day for hours outside in the driveway. I know God is important, but we use Him to help us achieve our goals and motivate us not to block us from it. That is what this lady was doing in my life.

When it was time to start our next group and I met the other night staff and these people were a lot better and fun. I saw the nurse Peter from yesterday and met a gentleman by the name of Jamie. Jamie was a funny guy that always had lots of great funny and cool stories that made the groups so much better. He also was good at chess and other games. He would tell us stories about his old high school days and the crazy things kids did when they were here. He always allowed us to have extra free time as well. When it was time for free time, we ordered what we wanted for dinner and got to play games. I never knew how to play chess, so I asked the people to teach me how to play. I never knew how competitive this game could be. It was cool watching all the kids play chess. There were also Legos and a bucket full of action figures and books we could read. This was not the ideal free time, but it was better than sitting in a group all day. Jamie was the king at chest, no matter how hard all of us tried to beat him it was almost impossible. Even the nurse Peter could not beat him. I never realized how fun board games were until I came here and played against the other kids. Once our rec time was over, we did one last group then were told we had to go to our rooms. Every night they played this calm ocean wave music to help everyone go to sleep. I hated it at first but then I began to like it once I realized I had no control over the music. As my eyes began to close, I just kept thinking about being ready to leave and how anxious I was.

The next two weeks of being here were still the same. Every day it was basically the same schedule. On weekdays we did school for about an hour and we at least got to watch some educational videos on the tv screen. I was so happy we could watch tv. I was tired of looking at groups and paperwork sheets all the time. I began getting closer with the staff and learned who the cool ones were, and who the mean ones were. My favorites were Dough and Jamie. Dan was a comic nerd so all we did was talk about comic books and superheroes. He also liked baseball and the Boston Red Sox, but I was a Chicago White Sox fan. I opened up to both him and Jamie and Jamie started teaching me how to win in chess and I enjoyed it more. I did an experiment with getting a shot, the same shot that they give the bad kids when the alarm goes off. I somehow convinced Peter to give me a shot and he gave me one before bed in my arm. That shot hurt because it felt like the needle poked me right in my muscle and I did not like that at all. After about fifteen minutes of getting the shot my entire arm became numb. It felt like I couldn't even move it. Now I see why all that boy could do was lay there after his shot. I started earning more points and more freedom, so I was happy to be wearing some of my own clothes again. But I did get them taken away at times for talking too much. I was having a bad day and I took my blueberry muffin and threw it at the wall and almost had the code called on me. I had to stay in my room the rest of the day. Other than that, I behaved well all the time.

I did see one more code 99 happen. One of my roommates was tired of being here and was thrown out of group and began walking around the unit refusing to go to his room. The female nurse was warning him and then out of nowhere he slapped her in the face. Immediately, the code went off and at least twenty nurses came through the door. This boy was kicking and punching to the point where they gave him a shot while restraining him on the ground. I think he was given four shots, two shots in each leg and two shots in each arm. I felt bad for the nurse lady because she was slapped in the face hard. She was okay though but had gone home early that day. I had now been here for three weeks and got a phone call from my caseworker. This was the first phone call I had gotten since my time in this hospital. She told me I would not be going back to another foster home. I was going to be sent to a facility fifteen minutes from the west side of Chicago. I had no idea what a facility was at the time and I had never heard of it. But I was happy I was finally going to be leaving this place. I had already been here for over a week of the average stay time. I guess this new facility was a structured living environment where I was going to be doing more groups and more counseling. I could not understand why I had to go to a facility though. I was getting sick of these people always controlling my life and where I would go and live.

After three weeks, it came time for me to leave and a lot of the staff were proud of me. They told me I did a great job in groups and opening up and I was one of the best kids they had come in. I felt like I accomplished something while being here and that was understanding how hurt I was. All the long talks and groups helped me realize a lot about myself as well. They told me that I was always free to call and to continue to stay on the path I was on. I wanted to go to another foster home, but I just took this positivity with me to the facility I was going to be going to. I was super excited that I would be finally getting my freedom back and be able to walk outside again and get fresh air after three months with none. While my caseworker was on her way, I had to realize that I would never see these people again. I was not sad or upset about it, but it sucked how people kept coming in and out of my life. It was like everything was a temporary relationship in my life. I wish these people could come with us. I could get their phone numbers and stay in touch. Even when I would call Aunt Martha's I never heard from staff or kids. they did not really like those types of phone calls. I just started to get used to this type of pattern and tried to prevent myself from getting emotionally attached to people. It felt like every time I started to make friends, I ended up not being able to see them anymore. Or the friends I would make turned fake just like they did back home and never messaged me or ask about me. When my caseworker finally arrived, I said one last goodbye to everyone and finally got the chance to walk through those doors. When I stepped outside, I kissed the ground out of happiness. My caseworker told me I was nasty, but I did not care. After three and a half weeks of no outside or fresh air, I was so happy to be back. I never realized how wonderful the smell of fresh air truly is. It is really a smell you cannot describe. I was just so thankful God pulled me through this place and I was outside. I even missed the feeling of wearing shoes after not wearing shoes for so long. As I got into the car, we put in the G.P.S to head to the next destination, Lutherbrook Child and Adolescent Center. The next journey of my life was about to begin. This was a journey that would completely change my life.

Lutherbrook Child & Adolescent Center

Lutherbrook Child & Adolescent Center was a facility located in Addison, Illinois, a west suburb just 17.4 miles away from the West side of Chicago. Lutherbrook was a place where foster kids were sent to correct bad behavior. For example, foster kids who were kicked out of too many foster homes. Foster kids who had just been released from jail or had been hospitalized for bad behavior and I was considered one of these kids. Lutherbrook was structured to be like a jail type of feel. Kids were required to do groups and counseling once a week. Kids were not allowed to have a phone, leave the grounds or go outside of the unit without staff permission. There were six different units on the campus including a school. Two of the units were for boys ages 13-17. Two other separate units were for younger boys and girls ages 6-11. One of the units was a house called "Lake House" that contained young ladies ages 13-17. Lastly, there was a unit called "Collins Group Home"and this was for young men ages 14-18.

When I first arrived at Lutherbrook Child & Adolescent Center it was June of 2015 and I was 14 years old. My first day arriving I was totally intimidated and nervous but tried to play the tough guy role. My heart and mind were racing, and I was sweating. I was 14 years old moving into a jail facility where I had never been. Upon my arrival I had met with a lady named Melissa Perez who was the outreach worker on the unit of Field. She handled all the kids coming to the unit. I had to sign papers, learn about the rules and structure of the campus and was given a tour around the facility and my unit. There was an outdoor and indoor basketball court with a swing set and baseball field. The campus was very big and spread out. There were 4 other buildings not connected to mine. This campus was about the size of a small college. Walking down to my unit was a long tile hallway with a water fountain and eight white bedroom doors. The lights were very dim, and the tiles were very dirty. There were blue walls painted with each Chicago professional team and eight different bedrooms for each client. I noticed two black dots in each corner of the hallways and in the den and those black dots turned out to be cameras. I was introduced to all nine of the other kids I would be living with along with the staff members. They were all sitting in the den, an area with two long couches and two single couches, a flat screen tv and a long table. It was a very small area for nine people all to be in at once. There were always three staff members in my unit because there was a 4 to 1 ratio, so for every 4 kids there was 1 staff and my unit had 9 kids. I could not believe this was my new life at 14 years old. Everyday being told what to do, no more freedom, no more phone, no more seeing my friends, no more anything. Even at night time there was an overnight staff for each unit, and they sat at each end of the hallway. They would open our doors and point their flashlights at us to see if we were still there because I had found out a lot of kids would run away in the middle of the night.

My first month at this facility I got to know who the cool kids on my unit were and every personality of each kid. I became a different person after the first month and started behaving very badly. Within my first month of being there I saw three fights. One of the fights was over a piece of cracker because someone ate someone else's crackers. This was a regular thing fighting over dumb stuff. It almost felt like I was in a school for boxing because of how many fights would happen, not only in my unit but everywhere around the facility. All of the fights however ended in the police being called so it felt like the police were here every day. Some of the staff would even let the kids fight off camera just so they could hash it out or for enjoyment. I learned a lot about each staff member and which ones were the cool ones and the ones that were strict. A lot of staff members at this job had backgrounds or used to be in gangs so not listening to them would not get you very far. Oftentimes the staff members would try to fight us kids if we did not do everything that they told us to do. I witnessed a lot of kids get beat up by staff off camera or even on camera, get slapped or pushed and some incidents even choked. This facility was a hands-on facility so staff could put their hands on us kids and get away with it. There were so many incidents like this it felt normal so us clients knew better to not mess with one of the staff members who did this. I felt like I was back to living with my dad getting abused again and hit by staff. This put a lot of anger inside of me and made me want to not listen to them even more.

I learned the facilities rules of the basketball court and when we were allowed to go play, the rules of the tv and how we all had to agree on a tv show, or who was allowed to play the PlayStation 4. I learned that every day we had scheduled eating times and we had scheduled times of when to be in our rooms which was 9pm every night. Every time there was a staff change, we had to go to our rooms and wait to be told when to come out and if we did not behave, we would stay in longer. Phone calls were limited to 30 minutes a call and you were only allowed to call people on your list. I had adjusted surprisingly well considering I wasn't happy with all of these rules, but I managed to do it especially when I found out about going on outings and the rec unit. Each month every unit was sent a certain amount of money to take us kids who behaved well and did their chores on fun activities and go on outings such as the movies, arcades, baseball, and basketball games, etc. Also, I learned about the Rec department and met the two gentlemen who ran that department named Kevin and Sean. These guys were paid to take the good kids on fun activities and outings. Also, if they really liked you, you could get a job with them and make some money. Some of the fun outings I went on included going to the Chicago White Sox game, Chicago Sky game, playing at parks, and going downtown Chicago. However, I started to lose my outings by hanging out with the wrong crowd.

I started to get fed up with being inside all the time or not being able to go on outings due to other bad kids' behaviors. That's when I started hanging out with more kids on my unit rather than with staff and trying to fit in. I was tired of living off an allowance of $18 a month and tired of being stuck inside all the time. I was also angry with staff hitting me or making fun of me and this made me want to get back at them. That's when me and two other friends of mine started to run away. We always had plans to make it so we wouldn't get caught. We would watch and pay attention to what overnight staff were the laziest and did the worst checking compared to the best. Then we would take all the clothes from our drawers and stuff them in our laundry bags and put it under the covers to make it look like a body and place a hat over the pillow to make it look like a hat. Next, we would quietly slide up our windows and leave out of them while quietly closing them and we found a meeting point of where to go. A lot of the times when me and my friends would run away, we would go car hopping, meaning we would go through neighborhoods and quietly open the doors to cars that were left unlocked and take things. I just changed from being a scared, quiet person to being a total animal. A lot of times we would come back with pockets full of change or if we got lucky a phone, tablet, watch etc. I didn't want to do this, but I was hungry and the food they were feeding us was jail food. It was so nasty that even the staff that worked there didn't eat it. Instead, they went and bought their own food then would tease us with how good their food was while we had to sit and eat this nasty food and it pissed me off. I learned that I could sit around and complain or get up and go do something about it and I did that. With all the stuff I stole I would just sell it for money, then I would use that money to buy food or a pair of nice clothes so I wouldn't keep getting made fun of by staff. I loved to steal phones at the time and try to sell them or keep them because I didn't have a phone of my own. I had almost gotten arrested for one incident when a food delivery driver was inside the unit delivering food and I saw his window was down. While he was inside, I took his phone from his car and ran back to my unit and went outside, turned the phone off, took the chip out, and buried it outside under the wood chips. I never got caught over this incident, but stealing was normal for me at the time. I even used to go to school and see how kids would set their phones on top of their lockers so I would wait till the end of the day when big crowds were in the hallways and just take their phones while they didn't notice and then turn them off and take the chip out. I made money from doing this because I would sell the phones to other kids. Stealing from cars was normal for me too and became addicting and fun because I never knew what I was going to get from a car. It was like a game we were playing, but little did we know how dangerous it really was or the consequences if we got caught. I completely lost myself and who I was during this time because I was mad that everyone had abandoned me, so I acted up. It didn't help either with all of these other kids in gangs and not caring. I felt like I had no positive role models during this time, especially not from the staff after they kept fighting us and bullying us. While I would go steal from cars, I would see other boys from my unit and other units out on the run. I asked them what they were doing and most of them would be on the run to have sex with girls from the Lake House unit. The way they did it was by calling the girls unit secretly and convincing some of them to go on run and have sex with them. It was so sad to see these young ladies just having no respect for themselves or their bodies. There was a secret alleyway that we went to every time we were on the run and we would meet up there and split up what we made between the three of us. But when the guys started trying to get other girls to come, I would go to the alley area where we met up and see three guys having sex with one girl. I could never comprehend sex out in the open like this being a 15-year-old virgin. It was sad and scary to me to see that because I had three sisters of my own and couldn't imagine seeing one of them do this. What made it even worse was some of these girls or boys had STD'S and they were just passing it to each other like it was nothing. I made sure to stay a virgin and never participated in any type of sexual activity with these girls.

I started getting myself involved in drugs at the age of 14. I was ashamed of myself because I always talked down to the kids at R.E.S.A who did drugs but there I was doing it myself. I was so angry with myself because I promised that I would never drink or smoke in my life. I knew I was better than this but at the time I just stopped caring about my life at this point. I felt like I would never amount to anything and that I was a failure. My grandparents called me this, my sister, my foster parents from before and now staff members did as well. I couldn't see a future at the time while I was inside of a jail facility at 14 years old and thought my life was ruined and over. It made it even harder with these other kids around me who were nothing but bad influences, but I felt like I had no purpose anymore. With my dad being in prison since I was 13 and all the people who talked down on me, I just gave them what they wanted. I felt very alone and depressed with my life not seeing my friends anymore and my family betraying me. I was just a very vulnerable kid at the time trying to fit in and be cool. I thought being something I was not would give me friends because when I was the person who I truly was I could never fit in and was bullied for being lame.

A lot of times while we were on the run, we would be chased by the police because as soon as we left the facility grounds, our names and pictures were given to the police. We would spend all night running from the police or hiding from them and to us that was fun; it gave us a thrill jumping over fences or hiding under cars. We usually were caught by the police after we finished what we wanted to finish. Even being picked up by the police we were never arrested or got into any trouble we would just be brought back to the facility. I would run away so much that almost every police officer in that suburb knew my name that summer. It seemed like they would drop us off just to run away again and again. But the real punishment was when we came back to the unit by certain overnight staff. Some nights we would come in from being on the run and the staff members would punch the shit out of us or slap us. This happened many nights. We would come back and 9 times out of 10 we wouldn't even fight back because we know we would lose. One moment in particular, I remember I was coming back from a run and two male staff members came to us and one of them came into my room and slapped me so hard. He slapped me 3 or 4 times before giving me a lecture and leaving. While he was leaving, I could hear the other boy gasping for air and crying while yelling because that staff member had gone into his room and punched and choked him. Stuff like this was a regular thing. Or we were told to go to the "Opp Room" . This was a room filled with blue padding all over the ground and walls where kids would be placed if they misbehaved or had to be restrained. Often staff members would slam kids in there or put them in a submission and sometimes even 3 or 4 staff would be laying on a kid at a time. The kids that were sent here after a run had to sit in this room for hours, sometimes even days with no shower and couldn't leave but just sit there while staff blocked the door. There were many different forms of punishment in this facility.

One of the things I had to learn to deal with once I came to this facility was bed bugs. I had never seen a bedbug in my life up until this point. I got up in the middle of the night to use the restroom and came back to turn the light on and there were nothing but little red bugs in the cracks of the wood and on my bed sheets. It was completely embarrassing and disgusting. I would go to school and have all of these red bumps on me and lie and say they were mosquitoes when really, they were bed bug bites. These bugs lived in the cracks of the wood in all of the beds, and furniture. It became so bad that every unit inside of Lutherbrook had bedbugs. Nobody ever sat on the wood, and staff started bringing their own chairs from home. I started sleeping on the floor by laying a blanket down, then sleeping on that blanket on the hard tile floor because I did not want to get eaten up by bedbugs. Once the problem started getting so bad, we would have to go and sleep at the school on campus or in the meeting rooms so the exterminators could bomb the entire unit. These exterminators must have bombed the entire unit several times and it never worked because they came back again and again. For two and a half years I slept on a tile floor because I did not want to have red bumps all over my body from the bedbug bites.

Addison Trail High School

Once I found out I would be attending a normal high school called Addison Trail my freshmen year I started behaving a lot better because I had the freedom five days a week to go off campus. Every day I walked to my bus stop and just loved the feeling of not being watched or told what to do every second. Sometimes I would leave extra early just to sit inside a McDonald's and watch how this group of old men would come in once a week and eat breakfast together or just to watch other kids with their friends and families. It was great just to see happy people for once or get a peace of mind because my whole life was so negative all the time. We were not allowed to have phones at the time, but I did get permission to have an iPod so I would just listen to music and walk. That was my favorite moment. Some days I would skip riding the bus on purpose just to walk two and a half miles to school because that made me happy.

I had never been to a school like Addison Trail before. This school was beautiful unlike anything I had ever seen coming from the poor city of Rockford and Chicago. When I did ride the bus, it was amazing seeing a 4 -story building with two baseball fields, two football fields, and inside the building was so beautiful. It had nice clean tile floors, water fountains that were electric with cold water, a common area with couches and a flat screen tv to watch tv, a wall full of former alumni with the colleges these kids went to. This school also had four gyms and a field house like I had never seen in my life. Even the bathrooms were super clean with nice tile floors and electronic sinks with granite counters. The cafeteria had more than 1 line and multiple choices to pick from for lunch. Usually back home there were two lines, and we all were served the same thing but here you could get pizza every day or nachos, tacos, etc. I hated the food so much at Lutherbrook that I would beg kids for their lunches at lunch time or use some of the money that I had stolen out of cars just to get seconds because I was that hungry. This school was in the top 6% nationwide. I remember some of my teachers had gone to big name universities and some of the kids in my class had academic scholarships. I was totally blown away. It was just amazing and breathtaking to me that this was a high school especially coming from what I had come from. The kids made the school even more beautiful. Almost 95% of the kids in that school spoke properly and did not sag their pants. You never heard of fights happening and in the classroom kids paid attention and were not on their phones or cussing out teachers. This school was full of kids who wanted to learn and be successful and even in the hallways or bathrooms kids were not skipping class or hiding because everyone was in class learning. This was hard for me to adjust to at first because everyone could tell I was an outcast. Here I am a kid living in a jail facility with barely any clothes, always asking for kid's lunches and a school full of rich, well-educated kids with two loving parents and a nice home to go to. I didn't even have a phone so many times I would just stare at other kids on their phones. A lot of times I was just alone and didn't really have anyone to talk to until one day I was sitting alone and this young lady who was a sophomore asked me to sit with her along with another young lady along with two other young men. I was the youngest at the table and that's where I started making friends by opening up. Then I found out about basketball tryouts and I found out that I was considered "cool" if I played sports. I always loved sports especially basketball so once kids found out I could play basketball I became cooler.

I became really close with a lot of the teachers in this school. I had never met so many nice teachers in my life. Back home the teachers just teach and that's it, but these teachers wanted to help in every way and be supportive. I was a kid who lived in a jail facility and they all treated me with respect and went out of their way to help me every time. I became really close with my guidance counselor Mrs. Myers and a lot of other teachers and I would sit inside of their office and open up to them about what happened at Lutherbrook and the things I was going through. These teachers would actually listen to me and care for me. Some teachers would buy me groceries or pay for me to get an extra school lunch. For Christmas time, all the teachers chipped in and bought me a bunch of new clothes and shirts. What was even crazier was none of these teachers wanted anything in return from me but to see me happy and do good in school. It was really weird having people care for me and help me because I was so used to being bullied and having nothing. It was very amazing and generous of these people to help a poor kid from Rockford, Illinois.

My bus stop was on a street called Green Oaks. It had a basketball court with a park, and this was the hang out spot for a lot of the kids. I used to stay up late and play basketball against kids from that school just to show I could play and become cool. I would get off the bus at 4pm and be out there until 7-8pm, just playing basketball for hours or sometimes just sitting inside McDonalds because I did not want to come back. I became friends with a lot of these kids from this apartment complex, and they started to have my back more and I became cooler. Unfortunately, I would often get into trouble when I came back from school to Lutherbrook because they knew I was lying about tutoring, so oftentimes the police were called, and they would find me playing basketball at Green Oaks and I had to come back. A lot of kids hated that because I would make the "block hot" meaning this block was a big spot for drug dealing and drugs so a lot of the people had to hide when the police came. I really didn't know anything about drugs or drug dealing until I came here. A lot of times I would leave in the morning to go to school and kids who went to alternative schools or the Lutherbrook school on campus would give me $10 or $20 to get them weed. This is where I started seeing just how big drugs were in this block. Drug deals were often made down in the laundry rooms of this big apartment complex so the police or others couldn't see. A lot of kids smoked weed down there as well. At the time I started smoking weed too and I would get high before school or hold a half smoked blunt in my pocket until after school. I asked them to show me how to sell drugs because I was only getting $18 a month in allowance, and I was always hungry. A lot of the older kids saw potential in me and would tell me to go home and not allow me to sell drugs. I was very thankful for the friends I made there because they looked out for me many times.

Once basketball season came around, I stopped smoking and changed my ways big time. I was inspired by some of the NBA players that had come out of our conference and I wanted to be like them. I started getting my grades up so I would be eligible and I also started behaving on the unit and coming back home on time so I could play basketball for the school. I had to earn basketball with the correct behavior in school and out of school as well as on the unit. Some kids on the unit were jealous of what I was doing so they would try and pick fights with me on purpose, but I never let it get to me. Eventually, I made the basketball team and felt like my life started to have a purpose more and more. I got to go to practice six days a week and came back to the facility late. I started making more friends and even became close with the teachers. Oftentimes teachers would go out of their way to buy me groceries or give me money to get something from the concession stand. It was funny because every game day we were required to wear a shirt and a tie with dress pants and dress shoes so here I am leaving a jail facility and being a kid who wears the same shirts and pants all the time to wearing a shirt and tie. I always loved the away games because every game was in another suburb so I would get to be away longer. I didn't really get along with my teammates because they would always cry about fouls or were not super competitive, so this caused a lot of fights between us. Basketball stopped becoming fun because I could never remember the plays, so I wasn't played very much and this caused me to act out in school and to my other teammates. I stopped wanting to practice and found it more enjoyable to play basketball at the facility then at school on a team. One day I ended up going to school and I was angry with this kid who was laughing at me for wearing an emoji outfit. I was tired of being bullied all the time and I finally snapped. I ended up slapping him. I felt really bad about it because I hated being mean to people, but I was just very frustrated at the time. I eventually got kicked out because the school had a zero tolerance for fighting. I was kicked off the basketball team as well and my freshman season and year came to a complete stop.

I ended up having to attend Lutherbrook School and now my freedom was completely taken away. I no longer had the opportunity to leave the campus, no more good food, no more seeing my friends. I was at an alternative day school stuck with all the other kids from Lutherbrook. I hated everything about this school. We had to stay in one small little room all day long and could not go to different classrooms. Every day we came in we had to be scanned. Each week we had a certain number of points that we had to go by in order to earn a snack. We had to do group sessions every week as well. We went to school every Monday through Thursday then Fridays we were able to go on outings if we had earned all our points and behaved well. I felt like I was a child or a little kid 24/7. Each day I was just handed a sheet of paper and had to work out of the book while the teachers watched us. One day, I got into my first fight with a staff member. I was taken out of the classroom for saying something smart and one of the guys working there grabbed my arm and I swung my arm away from his hand. Then he pushed and threw me up against the corner, having his forearm on my neck. I was so tired of being hit by these staff members and bullied by them that I snapped. I spit in his face for choking me and then it was on. Once I spit in his face, I remember being punched in the face and dropped to the floor. Meanwhile, another staff member had jumped in and held me down while he just kept punching me and kicking me and spit back into my face. I remember just being hit repeatedly and trying to fight back but being held down. I was getting choked and punched at the same time so I couldn't even breathe. Then finally one of the kids I was friends with had come out into the hallway to see what had happened and he pushed them off of me and when I got up, I remember punching him so hard in his face. It then became two kids against two staff, and we were just going at it until everyone from the classroom had come outside and saw what was going on. Finally, I was grabbed and thrown up on the fence and it stopped. After that incident happened, the police never showed up and everyone kept it a secret, but that staff worker had never come back. I really hated every staff member in that facility and wanted to fight all of them. The problem was I was only 15 years old and could not even do 50 pushups without stopping. I saw this happen to many kids but never thought it would happen to me because I wasn't trying to play the tough guy role. I thought about carrying a shank with me or a weapon with me if anything like that ever happened again. What's crazy is that weeks after that incident, a kid from another facility called Alandale was being restrained by staff and ended up dying because they choked him to death. This changed everything on how they would put their hands on us or restrain us.

Staff hitting kids was normal to us. Many times, I remember staff trying to get tough with us. I remember seeing staff punch a kid or enter our rooms to hit us. On my 15th birthday I was headbutted by a staff member. We got into an argument and we were yelling back and forth and he headbutted me right in my noise. I just remember blood was all over my face and my shirt but I was still trying to fight him. Then eventually I was taken down and restrained. Another incident I had called one of the staff workers a "bitch", and he came into my room and choked me until I almost passed out and then I called him a "bitch" again and I remember him pushing me to the ground. A lot of times I would try and fight certain staff just to show them they were not shit. Another incident happened with the same staff that choked and pushed me. I started talking shit to him and I was sitting down, playing a game and out of nowhere he punched me in my side and then I got up and threw the controller at him and he threw me down and kicked me. Then another staff member had to restrain him. Looking back, I really see how pathetic they truly were, grown men hitting 16-17-year-old kids and acting like they are tough. Another incident, I witnessed a kid outside swinging around an extension cord playing not bothering anyone and him getting slammed on his face with his lip all busted up because a staff considered it a weapon. Staff would see how bogus the food we had to eat was as well. We were always given a carton of milk that was usually spoiled. Also, the food we got from the kitchen was always super nasty, so staff would buy food from fast food or restaurants and eat it in front of us to tease us with it. That really bothered us a lot because we would be so hungry and see them eating good food in front of us. But we got our payback on them at times because when we would play basketball staff would play as well and we would foul them super hard to get back at them.

Fights were common but fights vs other units started to happen more often especially once the units were allowed to combine to play games or go on outings together. One incident in particular stands out the most when there was a basketball game and it was my unit vs the Collins Group Home and some of the kids from Collins had gotten into it with some kids on the field. Our unit would play other units maybe like once a week and we had a basketball competition going on between the units. During the game, out of nowhere one of the kids punched another kid and then almost every kid from each unit was fighting. There were at least 15 kids fighting and it was a huge brawl. Some are even hitting staff members. After that incident, a couple of kids were arrested but also there were no more basketball combinations allowed. Fights in the cafeteria were also common because kids from other units would see each other and a fight would just happen. Sometimes kids would take their whole tray and just throw it at another kid or at staff or even at the lunch ladies because the food was nasty. Eventually, everything and everyone was kept separate from each other because of how many fights were occurring.

My behavior was growing better and better and the staff saw how I stopped going on "a run" and how I wasn't involved in any fights or anything. I really changed who I was and who I was becoming. I began getting close with a lot of staff and stopped being defiant. We always had long talks about life and I really started listening and changed. I wanted to become more mature and do better. I knew there was so much more to life than this. My best friend died that summer so that changed me a lot. I understood life really is not a game and it can be taken from you especially doing the stuff I was doing. I never ran away anymore, and I stopped trying to hang out with other kids in my unit all the time. I became very independent and just stuck to basketball and to myself. Eventually, I was switched from the field to Collins, the group home where there was a lot more freedom. Here, I could have a TV and a game system in my room, have a phone, and also be allowed sign outs for a certain amount of time. I was starting to get my freedom back. In fact, I was doing so well that I was allowed back into Addison Trail High School and had made the basketball team again. I started being nicer to people and did not want to be a tough guy or a bad kid anymore. I stopped doing drugs and stopped hanging out with kids who did them as well. I changed my whole life after that first summer. I got myself a free gym membership as well and started working out more and lifting weights and stayed in my own lane. I was even allowed to have a job. I became a completely different kid when my friend passed away.

Greg's Funeral

I was outside playing basketball when I was told I had a phone call. I was surprised because I never got any phone calls, so I was wondering who this was. It was a friend who I used to play basketball with when I went to Lincoln Middle School and he told me Greg Hill passed away. It felt like the world stopped and I hung up the phone. I didn't cry at first because it didn't feel real. How could someone whose house I used to go over and hang out at and see him and his mom after every basketball game, be dead? Somebody who was always smiling with her and laughing? Somebody's house where I stayed the night multiple times and played basketball almost every day inside and outside of school? It was very hard to fathom the reality that one of my best friends passed away. I waited until staff took us to the library that day to get on Facebook and see if this was real. When I got on Facebook all I saw were rest in peace posts to him and then it really hit me. I had a profile picture of us from before and recently had a conversation with him. To think he was gone was very hard to take in. I ended up printing out the picture of us two. Walking back to the group home that night, I was crying to myself because of how hurt I was. I reached out to his mother and sister seeing if they were okay and asked when the funeral was. I saw that there would be a funeral in Chicago that was close to me and got a ride set up to attend this sad moment.

When it was the day of his funeral, we drove a little over an hour and a half to the south side of Chicago to attend the funeral.

When I got out of the car, I saw all my friends who I used to play with at Lincoln and hugged them tightly. I felt upset towards them because none of them ever messaged me or reached out to me to see how I was doing but I let all of that go for this. I sat inside of my pillar. I decided to sit all the way in the back by myself because I didn't want anyone to see me crying. But then his older sister came and sat next to me and I just lost it with her; it was hard to comprehend everything that was going on. I couldn't believe this was actually real and this was happening. Then his mom and other family members walked down the aisle and it was even harder to hold back tears. Once the band began singing and the pastor started preaching, I zoned out to a lot of what was going on because it was just unreal. I remember in my head that day I kept thinking I wish it had been me instead of him. I was just a screwup in a facility, he had a lot of things going for himself and was on his way to doing bigger things than I ever could dream of doing at that age.

Greg Hill was a great basketball player, easily one of the best on our middle school team. When he was in his freshman year of High school he was moved up to varsity as well. He had a lot of friends and everyone liked him. That's why it was hard to see that he was gone. I couldn't believe someone had done this to him or why. I ended up finding out he was killed at a party he went to and that he was not the intended target and this was just heartbreaking. When it came time to pay my respects and walk up to see him in his casket, I chose not to. I was already broken and that would have been even harder for me to see that. Instead, I decided to walk up and pay my respects by speaking highly of him through the microphone.

I met Greg in 5th grade when we played together at Haskell Elementary School. We then reconnected in middle school the first day of 6th grade when the teacher gave us assigned seats right next to each other. From then on, we became good friends, especially when we both played basketball. I was very hurt when I did not make the 6th grade basketball team and that's when he took me under his wing, and we became close. Greg was one of the only people that ever gave me any type of confidence in myself. I always talked down on myself and never felt like I was good at anything but he always made sure I came with him to everything. He always made sure I had a spot with him at the lunch table, always looked out for me especially when it came to basketball. We always talked about one of our idols, Fred VanVleet and how we both wanted to be the next people to make it out of Rockford. I knew I wanted to move to Florida one day and he wanted to play basketball for the University of Duke. When we would talk about these basketball players, we had to learn that it's all about hard work. I was never as talented as the other guys; I was not tall enough or could jump high enough but he always told me and explained to me that it's not about talent it's about hard work. That's when he told me something that stuck with me for the rest of my life: "Hard work beats talent any day." Talent is temporary but hard work will take you places you never thought you could go, he explained. We both just became fascinated with that whole scenario that if we worked hard at everything, we would eventually get all the things we wanted in life. When I spoke into the microphone, I immediately started getting choked up, but I didn't want his mom or people to see me cry so I toughed it out. There were a lot of great memories we shared and will always be in my heart until I die, and I made sure everyone knew just how great of a friend he really was.

After I finished speaking, his mother gave me a big hug. I waited for this horrible day to end. I wished this was a dream and this was not really real. When it became time for the pallbearers to carry his casket outside of the funeral and inside the van and take it to his burial site, I watched as they walked past in complete sadness. That's when his mother said some words that I will never forget: "don't you want to carry your brother?" And I realized, that's exactly what he was, a brother for life. I grabbed one of the ends of the casket and carried him down the steps. It was one of the saddest moments ever, being 15 years old and carrying your best friend's casket. While we carried him down the steps, we later pushed the casket into the van. I was unable to go to his grave site because my ride said they had already waited long enough. Before I left all my other friends that were there made sure to get a picture together with all of us. It was great to see all of us come together like this because this is what he would have wanted. We were all brothers and had been since 6th grade sitting at the lunch table together.

We knew we lost a great friend that day. The city of Rockford, Chicago and the world lost a great young man that day. It's our job to do the right thing so that his legacy will always live through us in a positive way, the way he would have wanted. I realized life is not a joke. Life is not fun and games. Life is very real and it's a beautiful gift to wake up every day and be alive. I decided to change my whole life forever after this. I wanted to be the best man I could be and accomplish all my dreams and goals in life one day.

Sophomore Year

When I came back to Addison Trail High School, I was in the behavior program. I had to show teachers I could show up to class on time and behave well and do my work. I became a very good student and started getting good grades and I practiced once with the varsity team. I was doing a lot better. A lot of the kids I used to hang with had been discharged as well. I didn't have any distractions because I had earned my freedom back. My sophomore year was going well; I was engaged in class and learning better while making more friends. I struggled with algebra at times and was bored with environmental science but who wouldn't be about the study of rocks? Sometimes, I did find myself getting annoyed spending my first four classes down in the basement in the same class with the same kids and the same teacher teaching all four classes. I got into a few arguments with kids and some of my teachers and I had my moments as any 16-year-old sophomore would. I was irritated feeling like this screw up down in the basement being hidden away from all the rest of my friends. Being in a class with a group of kids who just were there to be cool and not learn. I wanted more and I felt like I was better than this. I felt as if I were an outcast down in the basement and that would frustrate me. But I had to prove that I was different with my actions and my behavior by doing the right things consistently and working hard. But once I learned that my teacher was friends with the sophomore basketball coach, I really changed my behavior and learned to listen more and talk less. I stopped getting into arguments with people and did everything I was supposed to do. I did not want to see history repeat itself and be sent back to Lutherbrook School and be unable to play basketball for this school.

In late October, basketball tryouts were coming up. Every day I practiced inside of the Lutherbrook gym to better my skills. A lot of the staff members at Lutherbrook used to play basketball and some even used to coach. I asked a lot of them to help me get better and they showed me lots of drills to do and told me the biggest thing was confidence. I was always scared to play against other people and nervous because I thought I was not good enough. One of my staff members used to take me to the west side of Chicago to a park called Garfield Park and would have me play against all the other bigger kids and adults to get over my fear. I had to get tougher as well because I would always cry about fouls so we would play games without fouls and I would get pushed to the ground, slapped, scratched, everything just to get stronger. When it was time for basketball tryouts to start, I tried out just like everyone else. A lot of kids showed up for the tryouts and I was nervous I would be cut but I remembered everything I worked hard for and used discipline to get over my fear. I didn't get cut the first day, the second day or on the 3rd day. The coach called every player in one by one and I was the very last player called in. He had told me I almost did not make the team because of what had happened last year with me getting kicked off the team. But he was willing to give me a chance and prove my behavior was good both on and off the court. I did just that throughout the entire season. The coach was strict, and I did not show bad attitudes or poor behavior with other teammates. I would write down the plays and study them with some of my teammates just to be better than last year. I wanted to prove to the coach that he would not be let down and to myself after all that hard work I had put in the summer that I was ready.

I played well my sophomore year. I started most of the season and scored a lot more than last year. I was learning all the plays well and playing good offense and defense. In key games against some of our conference rivals, I proved to play well and proved to showcase what I could do. I was making smart plays with the ball and setting good screens and scoring well. At practice, I paid attention well and was really competitive by diving on the floor for loose balls and playing hard. I hated running suicides but every time the coach made us run, I made sure to run hard and beat out my teammates. I wanted it that year and was willing to prove that I did as well. I wanted to work hard every day and beat out everyone. I did have my share of struggles too. I struggled with my dribbling and with getting my shot off quick that year. But I worked on them every day at Lutherbrook and made sure to practice harder than the rest of the kids on my team or who I was going to play against. At lunch time I would even go practice because the teacher gave me the key to one of the gyms. I fell in love with hard work and started to realize that one day all the hard work would pay off if I just believed in myself and stayed consistent. I made sure before every game to get up shots from certain angles and listen to my coach when he talked about the follow through. I had averaged about 10 points a game that season. Even against some of our hardest opponents I scored and played well. My highest scoring game happened that season when I scored 18 points. This was the highest scoring game I had ever had in my life. Even the coach came up to me after the game and told me he was impressed, and greater things were coming if I kept working hard. He also reminded me that around this time last year, I wasn't even on the team so look how much I had changed. It impressed him. I loved that feeling of proving people wrong and impressing people. I wanted to chase that feeling over and over again.

When basketball season ended, I felt myself getting involved at school more and for the first time ever. I grew closer to all of my teachers and started making friends with the other students down in the basement. I even went on field trips which was something I never did. But there was a certain trip that will always stick out to me forever. It was a very unique and life changing trip that had me step out of the box and my comfort zone. The whole year my teachers kept telling me to go on this trip and I said no every time, but something changed in me and I decided to go. I had gone on a field trip to Starved Rock which was out in the woods. I did not like the woods, so this was different for me. It took us about 40 minutes to arrive at the destination which was a state park. When we first got there, we played a game or two and were shown a tour around the building. The cool trip had finally started. I had gotten in a canoe for the first time and as we canoed all over the lake, I remember being so scared. I was scared to get in the canoe and kept saying how I would never do it and here I was smiling and laughing. I had never seen water shine off of the sun like that in my life. When the canoe ride was over, hiking was next. As we all hiked through the woods, I remember seeing how green nature really is. How peaceful the sounds of the woods really are. We ate lunch under a cool waterfall. It was amazing to see nature so beautiful and calm. The smell of the great outdoors and the noises of calm birds chirping and water falling was something I wasn't used to. It was so different not hearing police sirens or busy streets. I had never felt so free and calm before stepping out of my element to try something new was a big thing for me. For the first time, I felt like a little kid running around and hiking in the woods laughing and smiling. It was a feeling I didn't remember or have in a long time.

Once the sophomore school year was over, I finished with A's and B's. I had also improved my behavior enough to where next year all my classes would be upstairs in normal education classes. A lot of teachers and staff were impressed with how much I had grown. I had obtained my first job at Culver's as a crew member and cashier that summer. I was one of the youngest workers at the time, but I worked lots of hours and was very excited to be making money. It was even better being away from Lutherbrook. The only thing on my mind now was when I would be discharged. There was still no foster home in Rockford available for me to go to. My caseworker still never kept in contact with me. In the meantime, I would just work and attend summer basketball camp at Addison Trail.

Later on that summer I came home from work to find out that Lutherbrook was being shut down due to cuts from the state, which would mean I finally would be leaving after two years. The news was shocking to me and a lot of the staff there. Every one of the staff would have to find new jobs and the kids were all going to be placed somewhere else. It was a dream come true because I thought I would be living here for a long time. My caseworker finally got in touch with me after the news and told me I would be switched to a different agency in order to live in this new foster home. I was so happy I would be moving into a foster home in my hometown Rockford, Illinois after almost three years of being gone. I was even more excited to find out I would be getting a chance to play basketball back home again. I missed all of my friends and missed playing basketball against them at the YMCA all the time. I had not seen or heard from any of them in a very long time because I had no phone or way of contacting any of them. A few weeks had gone by and I was one of the last kids in this facility waiting for my turn to go. I met a man who came to visit me named Adam and he would be my new foster parent. Usually, before you move into a new foster home you do an interview with the foster parents and that's what we did. Adam had two other boys living with him during this time and I would have to bunk with one of them, but I did not care, anything to get me out of this facility.

I took a look around and just remembered all the good and bad times of this place and all the different kids I had ever met. There were so many memories that I never would have thought I'd make. I never thought I would come to a place like this before and drink from a water fountain for two years and live in a jail type of facility. It was crazy to see my growth from when I first came here to leaving and how much I changed into a better person. I never thought I would grow into a better person because of this. What was even crazier was, I became very close with a lot of staff and these people became good role models to me when I stopped disobeying them. They helped me find confidence and who I was and what not to be in life. This place changed my life in both negative and positive ways. God blessed me to get through this and was standing by me at the end of the day. I had gone through something not many kids can say they have ever been through. From sleeping through bedbugs, fighting staff, running away and doing bad things, to making a complete 180 change. I used this as motivation in life to work harder. I was ready to achieve my goals and accomplish things and use this as motivation one day to tell kids in the system who are in my shoes currently. Anything is possible with hard work, consistency, faith, and discipline.

Moving into my new foster home-

When I arrived at my new foster home in Rockford, Illinois in June I was staying with a male foster parent named Adam and two other foster kids at the time. This was the same man who visited me while I was at Lutherbrook. His house was very nice and clean in a good and safe neighborhood. I felt very safe there. The only downfall was I would be sharing rooms with another kid my age, but I was just happy to be out of Lutherbrook. It felt so weird not having to live by a scheduled routine every day and how much freedom I had all the time. It was a feeling I was not used to and hadn't felt in a long time. I used my freedom wisely, though. I did not abuse my freedom by hanging out and going to parties like a lot of other kids. All I wanted to do was play basketball at the YMCA. I missed playing basketball with my friends and that's all I thought about. I felt like basketball could be my ticket out if I worked hard enough and that's what my mission was. It was even better because when you are in the foster care system you get a free membership with the YMCA, so I really took advantage of this. I wanted to stay out of trouble and focus on growing more as a person and chasing my basketball dream. I was tired of getting into arguments with people and I wanted everyone to like me and have a lot of friends. Another thing that inspired me a lot was during my 2-year time at Lutherbrook, I had studied a lot of the great athletes like Mike Tyson, Derrick Rose, Stephen Curry, Ray Lewis, and our very own Fred VanVleet. I wanted to be successful like them one day. So instead of sitting around on a unit floor, I would separate myself and I would rent books about these athletes from the library or read online articles about them when I would be sneaky at school. I read all about their work ethic and workouts and made sure to take notes on all the things they did. I even started writing book reports on them because I wanted to remember what I read and get my reading and writing skills better. They all had one thing in common and that was overcoming adversity they faced with hard work. I just became so obsessed with hard work, especially when Greg died, and I just couldn't believe that if I worked hard enough one day, I could accomplish things just like them. All I had to do was work hard and stay consistent and eventually it would pay off. Out of all the athletes I read about, Fred VanVleet inspired me the most because he was from the same city as me. I grew up watching him when he played basketball at Auburn High School and I wanted to play for that school one day just like him.

Another common thing all of these athletes I studied had was they would all wake up early at 4-5 in the morning and workout. I remembered from when Coach Jackson would tell me about this, and I would dribble a basketball that early while living with Linda. They also all had insane work ethics and worked very hard every day. They were all very consistent and it was the consistency and patience that paid off for them. During my time in Lutherbrook, I talked with some of the staff about different ways to be successful in life. But one gentleman that stood out was Tracey Rice who used to coach at Proviso East High School. He would sit down and have talks with me for hours about how hard professional athletes worked. He always brought up a word called discipline. He said if you have a disciplined mind and a disciplined work ethic, the world will be yours one day. I didn't know what discipline meant at the time, so he had to explain it to me, and I learned to fall in love with that word. Tracey would train me in the gym at Lutherbrook and talk to me about how important discipline was on defense. A lot of guys can play offense, but everybody can't play defense, he always said. He always brought up how everything in sports is all mental. As I would play with the other kids in the facility, he would watch me and coach me. If I started crying about fouls, he would tell me we had to leave the gym because basketball is a contact sport not golf and if you can't take contact you don't need to be playing it. I had to learn to get up in my defenders' chest and play physical. I had to play with a killer mindset to where this person was not going to score on me, and I was going to score on him every time. I never got to that level but every day I got closer and closer. I remembered all of these talks we had. Basketball prepares you for the real world so you will become disciplined to doing what is right and working hard and staying consistent to becoming successful in life. I used this as motivation to be successful in life one day. I told my foster parent Adam that I would be going to the YMCA all summer and getting up early to jog there. I did just that the entire summer.

I started getting up at 4:30-5am every day and jogging two miles to the YMCA to practice. I would shoot 400-500 shots a day. Then I would go to the weight room and lift weights. I wanted to get stronger and bigger by the time the season came around. The only problem was I did not have a coach or a trainer helping me so I did not do much. After this, I would jog back and play later on at the park or go back to the gym and run games against the other kids there. I still was not anywhere near where I wanted to be, but I knew it would come in time. But eventually, I started getting help from other people because they saw how hard I was working. That's when I met a trainer who saw me shooting basketball at the park by myself and remembered me from seeing me early every day at the YMCA. He started working me out and introducing me to other players and trainers. Before I knew it, I was working out with two trainers and I had met the assistant coach of the high school basketball team where I would be attending. They taught me the importance of ball handling and had me watch lots of Kyrie Irving's game and handles to get better. We started running hills to work on my endurance and speed. Then when we were inside of the gym, we did lots of cone combinations and began working on my shooting form and arc. I shot the ball too high and it took too long for me to get the ball off, so we worked on this a lot. Eventually, after lots of practicing every day, I was invited to join a travel basketball team that summer because of how much they loved my work ethic. I did not realize that playing on an AAU team was everything because that was how you got noticed by big name college coaches and recruits, the only problem was that I was in foster care and not allowed to leave the state of Illinois without special permission. DCFS would have to do background checks and I would have to get permission every time I left the state, and this was too much. I didn't realize playing travel basketball was so important at the time. I wanted to play for a travel team so bad, but I knew I would be unable to. I just worked out every day that summer without getting on a travel team. As far as being at home I was rarely if ever at the house because I did not trust many foster homes and figured if I was not home, no trouble could be started. All that was asked of me was to let the foster parent know where I was going and to do my daily chores.

Harlem High School Junior Year

When the school year rolled around, and it was the start of my junior year I was attending a new high school called Harlem High School. People usually made fun of Harlem because of how bad they sucked at sports, especially basketball. This school was also known for being a nerdy school full of white people. I knew I was not going to fit in here. I did not know anyone who went to school there at the time, which sucked because I wanted to see all my friends from other schools. It was like I was being teased while I was going to school here, living in Rockford but having to ride the bus 30 minutes when I was 10 minutes from a Rockford school. I just tried to keep a positive attitude and go and make new friends like I had been doing since I was going to school at Addison Trail. As far as working out, I maintained the same routine of getting up early at 4:30 or 5am and jogging two miles to the gym to workout. Then jogging back another two around 7am to get home. I would rush to get ready and have to be at the bus stop by 8:10 am or I would have to walk five miles to school. My foster parent was all about school so if we got in trouble or missed the bus or anything, we would have a two weeks notice threat to be kicked out or get cussed out by him.

Once I started making friends and learning how to fit in with the other students, they followed my social media and saw me getting up early every day and working out. That's when I told people that I played basketball and word got around the school about me and my work ethic and then I started meeting some of the other basketball players there. But I was not close with any of them when I met them. The vibe was off, and I felt a sense of jealousy and competition from most of them. Me and the other basketball players really did not talk that much, and I did not hang out with any of them after school. I was not big into going to football games and hanging out or going to friend's houses and hanging out, I always thought the time I spent hanging out I could be in the gym getting better. Plus, I don't think most of these kids liked me because I was never invited to anything they had going on. I did not even sit at the same lunch table with the other people on my team. I wasn't offended because I was never the type to hang out all the time anyways. But I felt the tension and animosity they had every time I did come around and I knew if I did make the team it would be a very long season. Maybe they felt disrespected when I always told them not to go to parties and hang out, or go out to eat but that's just how I was. I was focused on getting good grades, working the job I had at the time, and being in the gym. Another big reason I was skeptical of people was because my best friend was shot and killed at a party, so I did not trust parties or hanging out with people. This was a lesson I carried with me for the rest of my life.

Once open gym and conditioning workouts after school started, things started getting really competitive. I started seeing a lot of the basketball players from school, last year's team and the kids who planned on trying out at this school as well. There were three new coaches at the varsity level and a lot of transfers to this school and I was one of them. I had already met one of the coaches from working out with him during the summer so at least he knew of me and knew I was a hard worker. This new head coach we had was a very successful coach and I heard from other coaches and people who knew of him that he only wanted players on his team who worked hard. Coach Weathers was the head coach of the Harlem Basketball Program and during the offseason, he had us work hard. Coach Weathers had us run out on the football fields and inside the gym. We also ran stairs and basketball runs during open gym. He usually sat and would watch us play against each other. But this took a turn for me because I got off on the wrong foot early at this school. I played physical, in your chest defense because that's what I was taught and a lot of people were not used to that. I was big on calling people out for being wrong, like ball hogging or taking stupid shots and people did not like that about me either. It always led into a heated argument that almost led into a fist fight. I don't blame them because no teenage kid wants to take accountability in the game of basketball from a teammate, especially not in high school when you think you are the man. It felt like the future teammates of mine were my biggest enemies and I wanted to take it to them every open gym. I did not like any of these kids and I just wanted to kill them on the basketball court. I also wanted to take it to them even more because of how fake they acted outside of basketball during school or outside of school. One player in particular was the school's so-called best player and at open gym he had a wide-open dunk and I came from half court and ran full speed and blocked the ball and he ended up falling on his ankle and twisting it. The coach got mad at me and so did other kids saying I was being too rough. This would end up causing a lot of problems during the season. I started to not even want to play basketball for this school.

During the day at school, I always thought about my other friends at East, Auburn, and Jefferson High School. Being a young African American male in a predominately white school, it's hard at times. I always felt awkward being this poor, half black foster kid going to school with kids who all had parents and lived in nice homes. It was like going to Addison Trail all over again but at least I had a lot more friends there. I felt like I was always alone being here, I never really talked to anyone and just put my headphones in my ears all the time. Going to this school reminded me of being around my dad's side of the family. Me and my sister being the only black people around all white people in our family get togethers. Every time these ignorant people made black people jokes and would talk about black people, the same type of outcast feeling I got from being with my dad's side of the family I got being at this school. I opened up to my foster parent Adam who was black and told him about the stuff they said about the police brutality going on at the time with Travon Martin, Mike Brown, Eric Gardner, and others, but for some reason they always ended up talking down about black people and showed no sympathy for them being killed. I told Adam the things they would say about my mom and her being black would hurt mine and my older sister's feelings. He always told me being black is an amazing thing and I should not be ashamed of it; it's something to be very proud of and a lot of white people want to be like black people nowadays. I told him about how my grandparents casted out my father for marrying a black woman and having kids with a black woman. He was shocked when I told him the first time I had any clue I was black was when my dad beat me and called me a "nigger." It was annoying because people would always come up to me and ask me what my race was. One day at lunch these two girls were sitting at a lunch table just staring at me the entire time then they both came up to me telling me they were arguing about what race I was. I just hated being at this school and was ready to leave.

When basketball season started, I ended up making the basketball team for Harlem. I was very thankful to have made the team but once I did, all hell broke loose at home and it just made basketball so hard to focus on. I had so many problems off the court that caused me lots of trouble in school and out of school. I never had any rides to practice so I usually had to walk five miles to practice and if we did not have school that day, some days I was not given a ride home so I would have to walk five miles home as well. This made me angry and irritated because if a foster parent is an actual foster parent, they are supposed to be a good parent figure in our lives and me and Adam got into it so many times because of this. I did not have a mother and father like all the kids on my team. I did not have people come to my games or support me besides myself. I woke up every day angry and frustrated being inside of this house and going to this school. Me and my foster parent got into many arguments and fights as well. When I confronted him about giving me rides he would say rude and ignorant things like, "I don't have to give you a ride for shit." He would say the only thing he was required to do was give me a bed and food. He was so picky on everything in his house too. If we forgot to put the dishes away, take the trash out, or talk back to him, he would tell our caseworkers and put in a two-week notice to have us removed. Then he would make a group chat with me and the other two foster boys in the house and take pictures of things around the house and send them to us while we were at school starting an argument. This was one of the most immature and stressful people I had ever met in my life. It was always a mental and emotional battle because of the pressure I felt at home to do everything right. I was tired of feeling like this and he reminded me of my father. If something was not perfect or right, he would get mad and complain. It was just like every other foster home and my dad's home: do everything I say, or you will be kicked out or beat. Even if we walked too loud and he was downstairs he would get upset. Adam would get upset about every little thing and it drove all of us crazy. He would watch the cameras in the house and send pictures of us doing things constantly and it was to the point where I did not even want a phone anymore. I couldn't even go to school in peace or play basketball without having to worry about an angry text or message coming from him. I took a lot of emotional abuse as well, when he would get upset, he would say mean things like, "that's why none of your family wants you." Also, at the time I had bad acne on my face, and he would call me names like "pizza face" and just other disrespectful and mean things. He was like a big bully you could not stand up to because if you did you would be put in jail or kicked out of his house. Many times, I wanted to punch him right in his face and he would say things like, "go ahead and do it because that camera doesn't hear me talking. All it sees is you assaulting a foster parent." He was big on having the police called so there was no point in trying anything against him. I seriously thought this man was bipolar or had a mental illness because one minute when you would kiss ass to him and do everything he wanted and he would be good to you, then the minute you messed up he wanted you out of his house. It was so fake to me when he called us his family all the time because I know family does not do this to one another. I was tired of living in foster homes and just wished I could live in a normal household like all of these other kids who went to my school. This foster parent also had a rule that the kitchen was closed at 10pm and I would get home late especially if I walked home and I would be hungry because I was coming from basketball practice and I had not eaten anything since noon at lunch. When I would try to make food or cook, he would bring up how I never listen, and I need to find somewhere else to live. We always had an altercation and I had never been so stressed out in my entire life. Every day when I woke up in that house, I was full of nothing but stress and anger and I hated my life.

On Thanksgiving, we had finally had enough of each other, and we went at it. It started out as a play fight and then while I was eating, he kept grabbing me and squeezing me and that's when I pushed him off of me and got ready to fight him for real. He ended up slamming me on the ground, and while I punched him in his face a few times he started choking me. Once I got up, we both went at it again throwing punches and he hit me and caused me to have a bloody noise and scratches on my arms. I told my basketball coach what happened and sent him pictures and he told me that he had no room in his house for me to live in and that he was sorry. I felt like nobody cared about me and I had no purpose in this world again. That night I ran away and sat outside on a bus stop for hours freezing on a cold November Thanksgiving holiday. Some holiday, right? Thanksgiving is a time where you see family and come together and here I was sitting on a bus stop all alone with a busted nose and scratched up arm hating my life and wishing I was not here. I started to hate my life more and more living with him. I was so tired of always being treated like trash and feeling like all I had was myself. I was tired of going to this school where I always felt alone and like I had nobody. I couldn't even do my homework online for my math class because he refused to let me use his computer and my grades began to suffer. I had cussed at him and he threatened to call the police on me and told me to leave. I had to pack all my stuff in a garbage bag and went outside and waited for hours for my caseworker to come. When she called me, she told me just to apologize because there are no other homes for me to live in.

The other foster kids in this house did not help either. When Adam took another kid in, me and him got into so many fights and arguments because of how disrespectful and rude he was. He always kept me up until 1-2am because he was on the phone with other girls. At the time, I was given a lot of shoes and clothes from staff members in Lutherbrook because of how well I behaved and acted compared to the other kids. However, my clothes began going missing because this foster kid kept stealing them and wearing them to school or wearing them out with friends. Or I would be playing my video game that I bought myself and he would turn it off right in the middle while I was playing or go on my account and delete my stuff. Me and both foster kids ended up getting into fist fights and we were threatened to be arrested. All of this fighting, arguing, and being kept up late took a toll on me. I got so sick of being in this house that some nights I would just walk out of the house and go on long walks in the 30-degree weather and sit on a bus stop or a street corner.

During the beginning of the basketball season while dealing with all the drama and stress at home, I started off getting a lot of minutes. I played a lot because I competed every day in practice and I worked at bettering myself every single day. But I had the same downfall I had been having my entire life and that was playing nervous. I always played nervous and would think too much. I was never able to have fun because I was so scared of messing up and being taken out of the game. I felt like I wanted to play perfectly and I got this from all the abuse from being in foster homes and living with my father. It was so frustrating because I trained and worked so hard to play and there I was acting like this is the first ever game I've played in my life. I worked harder than any other kid on my team and I was always the first one in the gym getting up shots or the last one to leave the gym. On days that we could come in and shoot on the shooting machine, I would be the only one shooting by myself for hours. Some days after practice or a game I would leave from school and go to the YMCA just to practice some more, and every morning I was up at the YMCA, so I just got so frustrated playing basketball. This caused my playtime to decrease over the course of the season to where some games I would never get in the game and this frustrated me, and I let it show on the court. Every day I competed against our starters and I would play physical, hard defense and the coach was not a fan of that. One day I ended up choking one of the kids on our team and got in trouble. I had been thrown out of practice a few times and even had to go to meetings with him. I felt like he did not like me because I competed and played physical and these other kids were soft. I didn't like this coach anyways because of what he said to me that day on Thanksgiving and how he never took the time to talk to me like he did his other players. I hated playing for this coach and I hated playing for this team.

Things at home had only gotten worse. This new foster kid

that moved in with us was big into doing drugs, hanging out with the wrong crowd, and inviting people including girls over while my foster parent was not home and having sex with them. Then breaking things around the house and destroying everything. This really pissed me off because this foster parent Adam always talked about how he was big into not allowing any of us to do drugs or you would be kicked out. Here this kid is breaking every single one of his rules over and over again and he does nothing. I would get so angry with him because he did not do anything about it. This foster kid would wear my clothes while I was not home and steal my things constantly and I was sick of it. We got into numerous fights. This foster kid got into several fights with everyone. Pretty soon this boy was going to be kicked out if he kept up his behavior and he did just that. I was so happy when Adam finally stepped up and was tired of him and ready to kick him out. I could've thrown a party because of how happy I was. But this foster kid was so mad at our foster parent Adam at the time. In fact, he was so angry that he had set all of us up.

The day of my basketball game I was laying on the couch getting ready to walk to school for my game. It had been a normal day like usual but this time it was only me and him alone in the house. I was on my phone watching a motivational video while getting ready for my game, when out of nowhere I looked out the window and saw three masked boys approaching the house. At first, I thought this was a prank because I kept seeing this foster kid going outside and making phone calls and I thought he was inviting people over. But then they stormed in as I was laying on the couch. One of them approached me with a handgun and told me to get up and took my phone. I did not take him seriously at the time and just continued to lay there until he cocked his gun back. Everything happened so fast and, in my head, I knew this was a setup. There was no way in broad daylight that this was really happening. When I got up, he held the gun to the back of my head and made me go inside of a bathroom. I was so angry because all of these boys were like 5 feet tall, tiny, and scrawny and I just wanted to beat the shit out of all of them. I thought about running out of the house because the door was wide open, but he would've shot me in my back if I did that. While I sat inside the bathroom helpless, I heard them just kicking in doors and slamming things and breaking them. They were destroying any and everything inside of this house. I was shocked because the way they moved around the house it seemed like they knew what they were looking for. It also did not make any sense how this foster boy was in the room while I was in the bathroom, usually if you rob somebody you remove all the witnesses. Either these boys were that stupid or this was a set up. That's when I heard the foster boy whispering, telling them what stuff to grab and I knew this was staged. I couldn't believe this sneaky bitch snaked us like that. I wish none of these people had guns because I would've beat the shit out of all of them. I was so angry and mad just sitting there. But there was nothing I could do because I had no gun. I sat inside of the bathroom helplessly and waited for them to leave. When they finally left, I came out to the whole house destroyed. The entire house was shattered, door frames missing, glass broken everywhere, drawers thrown, it was complete chaos. When I went inside of my room everything that I once owned was destroyed or stolen. I had no more clothes or shoes left. All the hard work I put in to get all of these things was just taken from me like it was nothing. Everything happened so fast and I could not comprehend that this was real. I wished so hard that this was a joke. I was so angry as to why this happened to me. I never caused problems with anybody or was a bully. I was so confused and just hurt. When the foster kid came out of the room with a smirk on his face, I knew this was a setup. I grabbed that bitch by his neck and choked him as hard as I could slamming him on the ground. I wanted to kill him right then and there with my bare hands. But something stopped me after choking him. I freaked out when I saw him gasping for air and saw myself as being like my father when he used to beat and choke me, and I stopped. I was surprised he didn't get up and fight back but I was so angry and strong at the moment it wouldn't have been a smart idea. I then went and grabbed the home phone, and I called the police, and called the foster parent, they both knew something was up. When both the police arrived and the foster parent arrived, they separated me and this foster kid for questioning. But my foster parent had given this foster kid a phone and took it away from him because he was behaving poorly. That's when he turned the phone on, and all of the messages popped up because his social media accounts were still logged in. All of the messages of him setting the entire thing up came in. Once the police saw this, they took the phone to use for evidence and he took the foster child to jail that night. From then on, I did not trust a single soul. I did not trust anybody in this world.

Once the robbery was over and the foster kid was finally removed from the house, I returned to practice the next day and explained to my coach and the team what had happened. It was weird because now all of a sudden, this coach and my teammates cared about me, and I felt it was all fake to me. It's funny how something very bad has to happen or you even have to die for people to show love. The coach ended up giving me a ride home that day and he told me he was sorry for all the things I was going through, and I was one of the strongest kids he had ever met. But I really did not care at the time because I was just hurt and angry. I was tired of being in foster care and I wanted to live a normal life like any other kid but that was too much to ask for I guess. Basketball was not even fun anymore, especially playing for this program. I felt like I had zero support and going to that school with little to no friends didn't help either. After the robbery it was hard to focus on basketball. I became a very paranoid 17-year-old boy about everything. Anytime someone came to the door or I was around a friend, I would just think in the back of my mind to be careful because they could snake me at any time. I was very surprised that I stayed on the team. I mainly did it to get away from home. I did not feel safe there anymore; I always felt like someone was after me or watching me.

Once I met with my caseworker and my foster care agency after the robbery, they told me to put down a list of everything that was taken. I had no clothes or shoes or pants, I had little to nothing. This caused me to get made fun of a lot during school because I wore the same clothes over and over again. My foster parent Adam kept telling me not to worry about anything because it would all be replaced with his homeowner's insurance. DCFS also promised me they would give me a certain amount of money back or replace my things as well. Little by little weeks went by, and I still had not seen any money. Every week

I asked my caseworker and the foster care agency what was going on and they just kept saying they were working on it for me. Still to this day, three years later, I have not gotten a penny from DCFS about replacing my things.

For the rest of my junior year, I ended up just having to wear the same clothes and two pairs of shoes all the time because I had no money and my foster parent refused to buy me clothes. Life really sucked and I felt embarrassed all of the time. I really hated going to school and I hated life. I was trying to wrap my head around why bad things like this always seemed to keep happening to me. But no matter how hard I tried, I could not understand why I was always in the unfortunate situations and why things happened the way they did. I started questioning God a lot after that. Why was I beat for all these years? Why was my mother never around? Why did none of my so-called family want me? Why couldn't I have a normal life and a loving family like the rest of these kids? "Why!" was probably my favorite word to say at the time. But then I just had to remember God has a different plan for me. Like the man had told me before, I learned at Aunt Martha's that God works in mysterious ways, but eventually he will come through. Eventually, when I was made fun of by some kids for wearing the same clothes and shoes all the time, I stopped caring and paying attention to it. I just kept my faith strong in God and kept working hard in class and went to the gym like always. Clothes and shoes did not matter to me because you can buy those but you can't buy success or good grades; you have to earn that. That's what I wanted to do was kill people with success because eventually I would overcome it all by working hard. I started going to the YMCA a lot more because I felt safe there and it was my escape from reality. At least here I did not have to worry about what I was going to eat, worry about dealing with this foster parent or hearing his mouth or what would happen to me, I could just play basketball in peace.

Once the end of our basketball season was near, I was getting no playtime anymore. I would only get in the last few minutes of the game or not at all. I was totally embarrassed. A couple of sophomores and even a freshman played more than me. My junior year was just bad in every way you could think of. I felt like I was just a failure every day

I woke up. People would always say I put in all of this hard work just to sit on the bench and never play. I just used it all as motivation to work harder in life because I knew I would overcome this; hard times don't last forever. I was going to make sure all of these people would see me succeed in life one day and they would be sorry. But until then, I had to be a man about things and stop being a baby and feeling sorry for myself. I wanted to transfer to a school where I would be pushed hard, and I would get better every day and I felt like I had a school in mind. I just stayed on the team to work with the assistant coaches on my shooting form and learn new tips and drills, and to be away from my foster home. It was funny because I knew all my teammates and these people wanted me to quit. I heard all of the crap they would talk about and all the stuff other students around school would tell me but I didn't get offended. I just wrote it down as a note to myself and read it every time I felt like giving up. I was going to make sure I went against the odds one day. Too many people in life quit on me but I was not going to quit on myself. I was not going to be a high school dropout over some clothes and shoes. I was not going to be a quitter and I was not going to be a failure in life. I was not going to give anyone the desire to say look I told you he was a quitter.

Every day I kept getting up between 4:30am and 5am, running two miles to the YMCA to work out before school and jogging back two miles to go to school, going to basketball practice, then going back later to the YMCA to work out some more. I always told myself that I have been through too much in life to be basic and too much in life to work a minimum wage fast food job or be someone who was a failure. I used this mindset to keep working harder. Whether it was in the snow, rain, or sun I made sure to be at that gym. In fact, I would even walk in the freezing cold and snow at 4:30am-5am or at night just to get to the gym. I made sure that I wore three coats, a hat, and gloves and I would jog to the gym like this. I would sweat so much that my coat would look like I had peed on myself. The police had stopped me one day because I looked suspicious jogging in the dark with all these coats on and a backpack. I don't blame them because there were a lot of weird things and crime that happened in the city of Rockford. They asked me "Where are you running to?" I told them "To the YMCA to play basketball." They probably thought I was a huge liar, on some type of drug, or I was some delusional kid. The police asked for my bag and searched through it thoroughly. The only thing that was in my bag was a basketball, basketball shoes, a footwork ladder, a tennis ball, and an old granola bar. I know they felt stupid when they saw I was telling the truth. I always had people from school, and even my foster parent asked me how I could wake up that early in this cold of weather just to go play basketball by myself, but it was all determination and God. A word I fell in love with called discipline, doing what you hate to do but doing it like you love it because it will pay off in the long run. Every time I went to sleep, I would listen to a motivational video or just remember everything I went through in life and that would give me the strength to wake up every day and work hard. I was always told that the grind is real, you can't fool it because you will be exposed if you do. I wanted to make sure I worked hard and never cheated myself otherwise I would be exposed and never get better in life.

When the basketball season ended, we were knocked out in the first round by Guilford High School. I felt bad for the two seniors we had on our team because their season was over so quickly. But as far as my own experience, it really was just a horrible year. Everything about my junior year of high school leading up to this point just sucked. It got even worse when we had awards night. I was really hoping to win an award for the hardest worker or just win an award in general because I felt I had earned at least one of them. But when the awards were announced, not one came for me. It was one of the longest nights in my life. Everyone had come with a parent, but I only had myself. The more awards that were handed out, the more my confidence went down. I ended up going home that night with not one single award. When I got home my eyes began to water because of how ashamed I was. I couldn't blame anybody but myself; I was not good enough and did not work hard enough. If I did, I would have won an award as simple as that. The year just kept getting more and more disappointing. It was a very humbling and an eye-opening experience. I'll never forget sitting there and feeling so pathetic, embarrassed, and stupid because I came away empty handed, and I was going to make sure the next year I won an award. This sadness turned into hunger and anger to kill all of these people with success and work harder over the summer. I could not wait to work the hardest I had ever worked over the summer. I was going to make sure I was in the gym at least twice a day. I was ready to get to work.

As the end of the school year rolled around, and this horrible junior year was coming to a close, I was forced to go into counseling with DCFS. They told me that when kids go through traumatizing situations like this, it requires counseling, and you need someone to open up to. Also, my foster parent had me get into this because me and him were not really getting along anyways, so I did it to keep me from getting kicked out of his house right at the end of the school year. I met with my counselor once a week and I actually looked forward to this. I felt like ever since I came into this house, I had nobody to talk to. When I would talk to my foster parent Adam about the stuff I was going through, he would later throw it back in my face when we got into arguments, so I stopped trusting him. I was tired of waking up angry and stressed out every day and feeling like a failure. I wanted to grow into a great man one day who was nice to everyone and had lots of friends. I wanted to just be happy, but I felt like that was always impossible. I did not want to end up like my father one day who was just angry about any little thing and who was a mean person. This gave me the motivation to want to change and I wanted to be like the people in school who everyone was cool with. Once I started counseling, we worked on emotional control and other things that I never really knew much about. It was like I was just blinded from all of these things. I felt like when I was in Lutherbrook I wasted two years of life being stuck in a little unit all the time. I started learning how to cope with things and handle things a lot better. I wanted to keep growing as a person and this helped me a lot.

While I was involved in counseling and learning new things, I stopped being so hard to talk to. While I was in school, I started trying to make friends with people instead of being in my little shell all the time and being quiet. I learned how to have all types of different friends who liked different things instead of only people who liked what I liked and did what I did. I stopped shutting down and started being nicer and opening up. I started getting to know my teachers more and being more involved in school instead of being super quiet or rude. One teacher in particular who I became close with was my Spanish teacher Mrs. Thomas. She was a D1 athlete and had met Dwayne Wade at Marquette University and this inspired me because my dream was to become a D1 athlete as well. I also wanted to go to a big college like her one day instead of going to some community college like Rock Valley. After class, I started coming up to her and asking her about how hard she had to work to get to that Division 1 level of sports. Also, about all the work she had to put in academically as well, because I know universities require a lot of work. Eventually we started talking more about this and she inspired me a lot and opened up my eyes to how much opportunity is out in the world if I work hard to accomplish it. Mrs. Thomas really inspired me to work harder in life and stop complaining or making excuses. I ended up opening up to her and telling her that I was a foster kid. Then explaining some of the hard times I was going through at home and my situations of what it is like being in foster care. I needed more help with my Spanish homework, and she invited me to her class during lunch or just to hang out like the rest of students often did so eventually I came around and started coming to her class. She was always very nice to me and helpful and I really appreciated that. She reminded me of my teachers from back at Addison Trail who actually cared and were nice people.

Once the school year was almost finished and we only had a few weeks left because it was near the end of the month of April, I started telling most of my teachers that I would not be attending school here next year. I was surprised that a lot of my teachers were sad to hear that because I thought they didn't really like me that much. When I told Mrs. Thomas this, she gave me her number and told me if I ever needed any help or even a place to stay, I was welcomed at her home. She was even willing to call my caseworker and have me come live with her in the next two weeks. I thought that was very generous and kind of her to go out of her way for me. A teacher had never done that for me before, that's when I started realizing that I am a good kid and have the potential to be even better. Foster parents in the past always tried to make me seem like I was some horrible kid and a bad person, when it was not the case at all. I was just damaged and needed to learn some things. I didn't have a mother or father around and I had just come out of a jail facility for two years, so I needed some work on myself. The things that my foster parent at home would do made me seem as if I was a terrible person. Especially after I had cleaned out my foster parents' entire garage, just so I could dribble the ball inside and was accused of trying to flood his garage. I took buckets of water with soap and I threw water on the ground inside of the garage. Next, I took a scrub brush and scrubbed the entire floor clean until there was no dirt and it was nothing but shiny. Then I took all the water that was inside of the garage and used a scrunchie to push all the water out of the garage. I was trying to have a better relationship with my foster parent by doing this, but it backfired big time. He ended up telling my caseworker and sending her a picture through his camera of me throwing water down in the garage and making it seem as if I was really flooding it. The part he did not show was me scrubbing his entire floor and using a scrunchie to push all the water out as well. I watered the floors and scrubbed them to get all the dust and dirt out so I could dribble my basketball and work on my dribbling skills, and he sent a video from his camera to my caseworker saying I was trying to flood his garage. I was so pissed off when my foster parent Adam did this and it was the last straw; I was ready to leave his house. Here I was doing something nice for someone and that's what I got. When I would tell some of my teachers the stuff like this that had been going on the entire school year they would be in complete shock and feel sorry for me, they finally understood why I acted the way that I did that school year.

After that incident later that night we both got into an argument and he brought up about when I got robbed and said, "they should've shot your ass" and I ran up to him full speed about to punch him in his fat mouth and he ended up recording that video on me doing this and sent it to my caseworker. After this, they told me I had to find a new foster home to go to and I agreed. I was tired of living with this man and him stressing me out and saying all these mean things to me. After I had a meeting with my caseworker, I was told they found a new placement for me and I would be leaving later that week. I ended up taking my final exam for all my classes early that year because I was moving into a new foster home and this foster parent wanted me out of his house. My foster parent Adam also called the school, and I was given special permission to do this. I was so happy I would be leaving this school and this man's house after months of drama, arguing, fighting, and dealing with other foster kids as well. I was on cloud nine and just ready to move to a new school as well. I was tired of having no friends and not being able to relate to anyone. I was tired of going to this predominantly white school and feeling awkward all the time. I was just ready to have a great senior year at a new school. My last day of school ended up being a week earlier than the normal date that was planned because I was moving. I had to explain to some of my teachers why I was leaving so early and they completely understood. But some of my teachers were nicer and went out of their way to give me a goodbye card. It felt like I had grown a relationship with all my teachers. It was nice to know I made a positive impact as a student on a teacher when most students do the opposite. I was happy I changed my ways around as well. It was a great feeling being called a good student when I was so used to being kicked out of class from my old days in middle school or teachers not liking me. I was proud of myself that despite everything I went through my junior year, considering the physical altercations at home with foster kids and parent, with how basketball did not turn out at all how I wanted it to, being robbed and losing everything, that I did not fail a single class and finished with a couple A's and B's. I saw myself grow over the school year and I was proud of that. I was happy to be leaving this school but kind of sad to say goodbye to some of these great teachers. I had learned a lot my junior year. Whatever adversity you face, you can overcome it especially after going through what I had gone through that year. It doesn't define you and you can still succeed, and I was going to do that in life one day.

Once I finished taking my finals and said goodbye to all of my teachers, I went back to my foster home to pack all my stuff up. I did not have much to pack material wise, but I had my peace, opportunity, and myself to pack and that was enough. When I finished packing, my foster parent ended up taking me to this new foster home. This house was on the west side of Rockford, meaning the worst side of town. I was really skeptical about moving here because I thought this house would be really ghetto and dirty. But when we pulled up the house it was the complete opposite idea of what I had in mind. We pulled up to a very big and beautiful blue house with a nice flower garden planted around it and a clean yard. This house had three floors and was a very quiet house in a bad area of town. As we walked towards the house, an older lady came outside, and I met Mrs. Milly. She was very nice and friendly at first and super welcoming. She offered to help me with my things and was super friendly. It turns out that her and Adam were good friends and had known each other for a while. I did not want to be rude, so I just waited outside with them as they talked for her to show me around her house. After about an hour of standing outside waiting for them to finish talking, we went inside and that's when things changed. We sat inside of her living room and we talked about her rules and expectations of her house. The number one rule was no shoes in the house, and we were not allowed to sit on her couches. I could tell she was a neat freak instantly and very picky. The next rule was cleaning up after ourselves and pushing our chairs in and being mindful. This was easy for me because I always cleaned up after myself well so this was a piece of cake to me. Then she showed me this door that she had and how it locks from the inside and you must have a key to get out. I had never seen a door like this before that locks from the inside as well, this lady had her house very well secured and structured. She had alarms on all her windows, a voice who spoke every time you opened a door, an alarm system where if the door was left open for longer than 10 seconds without putting in the code the alarm would go off, motion sensors that were set every night at a certain time to where if you walked, a very loud alarm would go off, cameras inside of her house and a door that locks from the inside. I felt like I was living with the president of the United States for a second the way this house was secured. At least here I knew I didn't have to worry about getting robbed. Mrs. Milly started explaining how she likes her house very neat and clean and has things set up in a certain order, so she knows if we touch anything. I started getting nervous while she was explaining things to me because I thought I was not going to be able to do anything at all but just sit in my room and that was it.

After Mrs. Milly, also known as "neat freak," finished

explaining the rules to me, she showed me upstairs to my new room. As we walked up the stairs and saw my room, my stomach dropped. How in the world out of this huge house was there this tiny room with no closet or anything? All the room had was a set of bunk beds and a little coat rack. This room was about the size of a jail cell and I was instantly upset and ready to leave this house. Here I am, 17 years old and about to turn 18, a legal adult, sleeping in a bunk bed. I couldn't believe what I was seeing. I had to pinch myself a few times to actually know that this lady and her huge, beautiful house was telling me I would be sleeping in a bunk bed with a room the size of a jail cell. What made things crazier was I would be sharing this room with another foster kid named Randy who was a year older than me. I was just beyond annoyed at this point and I was ready to call my caseworker to come and get me. I didn't want anything to do with this house at first and I knew I was not going to like it. But I just sucked it up and got ready to go to work. At the time I was working at Portillo's because they had an agreement with my foster care agency to let foster kids work for them. This helped me out a lot because I needed a job desperately over the summer so I could have some money until next year's basketball season started. I wanted to travel to a basketball camp over the summer and get more exposure and experience and I couldn't play AAU, so this was my only chance of getting looks outside of Rockford. All I needed to do was save up money and work hard and that's what I was going to do the entire summer on and off the court.

When I went to ask Mrs. Milly for a ride to work, she explained that she would not be giving rides and I had to learn how to take the city bus. I never understood why people signed up to be a foster parent when it has the word parent in it and you're not willing to help the kid out, but I was used to this from living with Adam so it didn't really phase me. It just made me upset how she had a perfectly good running car and was not doing anything at all, but she just did not want to take me to work because she didn't feel like it. I hadn't ridden the city bus since I was a little kid sitting in my mother's lap, but I had to learn how to take it now, I had no choice. I was also going to be given a set of keys to go in and out through the door. She told me if I lost them this was the only set of keys she had, and I would have to sit outside and wait for her to get home or open the door for me to get inside. I was terrible at not losing things, but I had to learn to break that habit quick. I had to learn to break a lot of other habits that I had while living with this neat freak.

Mrs. Milly went and inspected every little thing I did and made sure her house was clean and to her liking. If I left one crumb on the table, she told me about it right when she saw me. If I did not push my chair in all the way she told me about it right when she saw me. Even if I used too much toilet paper, she would write a note on top of the toilet or tell me about it saying "you're only supposed to use two squares each time you wipe, I'm spending too much money on toilet paper." That was the craziest complaint I had ever heard in my life. I've never been told about toilet paper or how many squares I needed to use to wipe my ass when I was almost 18 years old. Even if I left a little water in the sink or did not wash my clothes on washing days I would get in trouble and be told about it. The hardest thing for me out of all of this was pushing in the chair all the way. I would have it pushed in all the way but Mrs. Milly liked it pushed in a certain way and if I didn't do it to her liking it was wrong. I had consequences for my actions if I did not follow her psychopathic ways, and her way of punishing was turning off the WIFI. At first it did not affect me too much because I had phone data, but I wouldn't be able to play my Xbox. She would inspect the house and everything I did to make sure everything was a certain way. But she always complained about something not being correct. It frustrated me a lot, but I had to learn that this is someone else's house and rules and in order to live here I have to abide by them. But the one thing I did not agree with was the way Mrs. Milly fed me. She did not put a lot of food inside of the fridge, so this caused me to be hungry all the time. Her favorite saying was "Once it's gone it's gone" meaning if I came back from the gym, or I ate too much that was it until she got paid again. But when she did put food in the fridge, she never really put good food in the fridge. She bought Hot Pockets, microwavable chicken sandwiches, lunch meat, hot dogs, and once a month she would cook dinner. It was like she fed me cheap food as if I was a dog. This caused me to always be hungry because this would not fill me up. What made it even more annoying was she bought the same food over and over again no matter how many times I asked her for different food. On top of this, I was only allowed to use one plate and one spoon and fork. At 17 years old I made the choice to start buying my own groceries and food. Living with Mrs. Milly taught me to start getting my own things and be more independent.

I started teaching myself how to cook by watching YouTube videos and buying simple foods to begin with. The first thing I learned how to cook was spaghetti, macaroni and cheese, and tacos. But Mrs. Milly didn't want me using her pans and pots, so I had to stop that quickly. I was upset at first but I had to remember this is not my stuff so there was nothing I could do. But I paid attention to what Mrs. Milly ate and I always wondered what the fridge in the basement was for. I would go downstairs to wash my clothes or go use the restroom, and I always noticed a second fridge. Mrs. Milly had cameras all through her house, so I had to be sneaky to open the fridge, and one day I did. I placed a towel over the camera as if I forgot something and had to go back upstairs and I opened up her fridge and was shocked. I saw the fridge in the basement filled with lots of food and stuff she always was eating. It was weird because when I first arrived at her house while she sat down with me and went over her rules, she said the downstairs fridge was off limits because that food was for her brother who would come over to pick it up. But that didn't add up to me because the same food that was in the fridge down in the basement was the same food she was eating. I put the pieces together and knew she was lying. Mrs. Milly kept the food she ate downstairs and the food she put in the fridge for us was the upstairs fridge. I never said anything to her about this, but it made me upset. That is very cruel to do to a kid so I made sure I worked five days a week so I would at least have a meal to eat at work, or if I couldn't get a meal, I would stuff pieces of bread in my pockets from work and eat them when I got home.

I was never home when I lived with Mrs. Milly because I was always at the YMCA trying to get better at basketball and working to get money. The entire summer I was full of determination. My mindset that entire summer was to prove the Harlem basketball coaches, teammates, and entire basketball program wrong. I was so obsessed with proving them wrong that I took a picture of me sitting on the bench and put it as my screensaver on my phone. I wanted to make sure that the days I felt like being lazy I would look at that picture and remember that feeling. To go a step further, I wrote messages to myself on post-it notes and hung them up around my bed with words saying, "You're too slow, you're not strong enough, you can't shoot." I made sure to write every negative messages so that every day when I woke up early in the morning, I would read them and be given motivation to work harder. I also hung up a picture of Fred VanVleet and Kyrie Irving to give me inspiration. These were my two favorite NBA players at the time, and I knew if they could do it, so could I. I wanted to work the hardest that I had ever worked in my life that summer. I would start going to the gym twice a day. After I finished praying in the morning around 7am, I would jog a mile to the gym. Her house was much closer to the YMCA, so it was a lot more convenient for me. Once I got to the gym, I would have to make 400 shots which usually took me two hours. Once I was finished, I would jog back another mile to eat and get a little rest. Once my rest was over, I would go back to the gym to work on my dribble moves and play against people in games so that all the work I was practicing could transition into game style. I was always told playing against people is what gets you better. I cannot do drills all the time and expect to improve.

The entire summer I kept this routine for 5 to 6 days a week and taking only Sundays off for church. I was consistently working on my game and working at my job Portillo's during the time. I was even playing basketball at the outdoor parks against kids who did not have a membership. Every day I played basketball whether it was outside or inside. But when I was outside at an elementary school one day playing, the Guilford High School varsity basketball coach was outside watching people play and I happened to be playing out there that day. He liked what he saw and invited me to their summer camp to workout with them and he told me he could fix my game and make me better. I didn't know what school I was going to yet, so I just said yes and attended. When I attended this camp, I started working on my footwork a lot because my footwork was too slow and, on my jump shot because that was too slow. This Coach played Division I basketball and overseas in Italy, so he knew what he was talking about. I also started learning how to shoot off the dribble and fix my arc from not shooting so high. He would stay after with me and give me lots of tips on what to do to improve my game and I listened and paid attention. He was a big reason why I got better that summer.

After about a week of attending this camp, every day me and another kid would stay after and shoot on the shooting machine. We would shoot about 400-500 shots and it was great because we didn't have to grab each other's rebound. We worked on shooting off the dribble, pull up jump shots and other ways to improve our shooting. One day I made a deal with my friend who I stayed with every day. I told him that I could make ten 3-pointers in a row, all I needed was for him to record me doing it. He agreed to it and we started a competition. The reason I brought this up was because when I was living back in the facility at Lutherbrook, I remembered a gentleman by the name of Ricky Swanigan who was a staff member bet me a Subway sandwich and cookies if I could make ten 3-pointers in a row. He also said only good basketball players can do that, and I wrote it down in my journal one day for things to do. I remembered this conversation a year later and went for it. After a year of practicing, I finally made ten 3-pointers in a row. My friend who I was shooting with was shocked because he had never seen that before and when I posted it on social media, it got 1.6 thousand views in 1 week! People were saying they never saw that before either. That's when I started to see that my hard work was paying off that summer. I finally fixed my jump shot after years of working on it and was getting it off faster and being more consistent.

Afterwards, I got a lot of reactions from it. I started having a lot of people wanting to work out and get in the gym with me, which was really weird because I was used to it being the opposite. So, I started working out with a lot of different people and getting better and better. The only thing was I was too slow on my feet and too slow with going to the rim. This frustrated me and I started lifting weights on my legs a lot more and trying to jump higher. I did a lot of dribbling drills because I was told if you can shoot and finish at the rim you are a good player, and I wanted to be good. After a few weeks went by, I was told about attending summer camp workouts and flying out to other states to get more exposure. Like I mentioned before, I could not play AAU travel ball because I was in DCFS custody and I needed permission to leave and if you stay in a hotel with your team the coaches need background checks, so it was too much. I always hated this because it held me back from having a lot more potential. I just decided to look into a basketball camp over the summer that I was invited to and wait for the right one. I knew if I at least attended one basketball camp I could have a chance at getting noticed and see just how much talent is out here instead of little Rockford.

I was still working out three times a day now and going to work. I felt like I was living on my own as a 17-year-old kid because I never had anyone asking me where I was going or what I was doing today. Mrs. Milly's house was the complete opposite of how Adams' house used to be. She barely ever spoke to me as well and the only time she did was when she would tell me what I was doing wrong around the house. But as far as being hungry, my hunger got worse. I was surviving off 50 cent snacks from the corner store, Subway cookies, and Portillo's for dinner. I barley ate at the house. I did not want to spend too much money on groceries because I wanted to buy other things or save money. So, I kept eating these hot pockets and frozen chicken sandwiches. It was funny riding the city bus because I was always one of the youngest people on it. Riding this bus took so long, every day it was always about a 45-minute ride to work. I didn't mind the ride as much as I hated walking to the bus. I would always try to run to the city bus stop so nobody would mess with me. I lived on the west side of town in one of the worst areas, so it was a little dangerous walking there all the time.

Around my neighborhood or on my block there was always police or a lot of activity at night. Some nights I would be up late and would hear gun shots then a bunch of police sirens right after or all through the night. One day I remember I heard a gunshot a block away from me and when I woke up the next morning someone had been killed. It was the same block that I jogged past every day to get to the gym. I made sure to be in before it was completely dark outside.

Sometimes at night time the police would have both areas blocked because of a shootout or a drug dealer. I hated taking the city bus at night after work and I always tried to stay until closing time so I could get a ride home from someone. If I got off earlier some days, I would wait hours for the person to get off just so I could get a ride home. The reason for this was while I was walking home from the bus stop late at night, I would have people come up to me and harass me to buy drugs off of them. Another time I walked past a kid getting punched in the face by his sister's boyfriend for pulling a gun out to him and after the boy was spitting out blood the man yelled, "next time you pull a gun you better use it!" Then at least twice I had been stopped by a group of men in cars, both times having a gun pointed at me while telling me to empty my pockets but with nothing being in my pockets they would drive off. Another time I was walking home from the city bus stop at night and two men got out of a car with masks and patted me down. That time I did have some change in my pocket, and they took the cash from my pocket and drove off. Stuff like this was normal to me, and that's why I never carried my wallet. I was not as scared of guns or this happening anymore because I was so used to the violence and seeing this type of stuff every day. Drug dealers were all around me and had been around me since I was back at Green Oaks, the only difference was this city was a lot more violent than the suburbs. I just learned to keep walking and mind my business. But it was scary walking to the bus stop every day or around my neighborhood not knowing what would happen to you. There were a few drug dealing houses near where we lived, so at night you would see groups of people standing outside a house trying to buy. There were so many run-down houses on the west side of Rockford and in my neighborhood, it looked like a war zone at times. It was like living on the south side of Chicago, and I see why Mrs. Milly had all this security on her house. Whenever I was outside I went straight to the bus stop or was going to the gym because I knew life is not a joke and I did not want to be involved in any type of activity. That's when Mrs. Milly had a long talk with me about being observant of my surroundings and what I am doing and this was an important talk I would never forget.

Once I entered the month of July and after keeping the same

routine, I was invited to a basketball camp in Tampa, Florida that I wanted to go to. This was the first camp that had a dorm stay and food in the purchase package. This meant I would not have to spend lots of money on a lift or on a bunch of food. It also made it easier to convince my caseworker into letting me attend. I ended up talking to my caseworker about this and saved up my money while also displaying good behavior in Mrs. Milly's house and outside of her house. I showed her enough paperwork to show that this camp was legit. After a few weeks went by and some talking, I was able to go attend the camp. I was so happy because this would be the first time I ever played basketball outside of Illinois. I worked extremely hard leading up to this camp but I was also extremely nervous because I had no idea what to expect or what competition was out there. I began to over think but I had to snap out of doing that and learn to have confidence in myself. I didn't know anyone in this city who was working harder than me, so I needed to use this as motivation.

Leading up to leaving, Mrs. Milly had a long talk with me about how to get through an airport by myself, this was the first time I would be flying alone so I had no idea. I was nervous I would miss my plane or not know where to go. When it was finally time to go, I had taken the Rockford bus to the Chicago O'Hare airport to fly down to Florida. After a 2-hour bus ride to the airport we finally made it, and when I got inside the airport, I was just in shock. There were so many people everywhere and rushing to get where they needed to be and I was lost. I know Mrs. Milly would have been so mad at me because that talk was all for nothing. I ended up asking the front desk lady for help and she showed me how to type my confirmation code into the machine, then where to go to get through security. Once I got through security, I asked some more people for help on how to get to my gate because this airport was so big. I was so embarrassed and laughing to myself because of how lost I was. But eventually I found where I needed to go and sat at my gate getting ready to leave.

The closer it got to getting on the plane the more my stomach dropped, and my heart began to race. I was so scared of planes, and it didn't help because I watched Madagascar 2 the night before and their plane crashed so I was just paranoid. I remember calling one of my friends on the phone and them having to give me tough love to stop being scared. It worked and then it didn't because once I got on the plane, I just got nervous all over again. My seat was in the middle of two very nice ladies and they saw how nervous I was and helped me stay calm. If it wasn't for them, I probably would've had a panic attack and they would've had to take me off the plane. I was just totally paranoid and scared. But after a 2-hour flight, we made it safe and we finally landed in Florida.

I was in complete amazement at how beautiful Florida was. Coming from the west side of Rockford, Illinois to Tampa, Florida was a huge change. I noticed how everyone looked so happy. The beautiful palm trees and nice weather was amazing to go with the clear blue sky with the sun shining down on it all. I noticed how nice all the buildings and scenery were. This was the first place I had ever seen a Lamborghini on the road, along with many other nice fancy cars. It was like being in a totally new world. Even the city buses were super nice and decorated. When I left the airport, I had my Uber take me downtown near the University of Tampa because I arrived too early so I figured I would walk around. I walked around downtown and just saw how beautiful the skyscrapers were. It sucked because I wore jeans and had a sweatshirt on that day which was a big mistake because of how hot it was, and my body was just burning up. But while I walked further downtown, I came across a water sprinkler where little kids were running around laughing together. This was beautiful to see because back home you don't really see too much of that. I saw the beautiful view of all the buildings downtown and I could see how peaceful everyone was. I saw people using scooters all through downtown Tampa laughing and smiling along with all the other people smiling and holding hands. It was like this was heaven on earth compared to Rockford, Illinois. None of these people were worried about a drive by shooting or a gang fight. Everyone just seemed so at peace. I just sat outside for about a little bit with the hot sun beating down on me, breath taken away by how amazing this place was. I wished I could live here and be as happy as these people were one day. As I walked downtown, I saw lots of restaurants and nice condos and everything was just so beautiful. Everyone was eating outside or standing outside laughing and talking and having a good time enjoying themselves. Even though I was sweating like crazy and super-hot it was all worth it to see all of this. I gained a lot of inspiration to make it out of Rockford one day and be one of these happy people. I know people say the grass is not always greener on the other side, but I was willing to take my chances to find out what the grass was like here in Florida. This became my dream city to live in one day and start a new life.

After I finished walking around, it was finally time for me to head to the University of Tampa. I walked over and was amazed at how beautiful this campus was. It overlooked a lake and was right next to the downtown skyscrapers. I headed into the main room where I saw a group of people lined up. This is where I would sign in and be given a pair of keys to the dorm I was staying in. While I waited in line, I noticed how a bunch of players were a lot bigger than me and I started to get nervous again. I thought I was going to get dunked on and be the worst player here. I hated that I always got so nervous all the time, but I got myself together and snapped out of it. I just remembered all of the hard work that I put in to get here. I then shifted my focus to all of the pillows everyone had. For some reason they all had pillows, and that's when I forgot we were supposed to bring our own pillows. All I had was a backpack so there was no way I would be able to fit a pillow inside of it. I just signed in and I walked up to the building where the dorms were. This was where we would be staying for the weekend. This was also where I had met my two roommates for the weekend during this camp. There were three beds in each dorm and then I met the two other roommates of mine, one was from Houston and one was from New York. This was so cool because I had never met anyone from New York or Houston before. Most of the people you meet from Rockford are all from Rockford and you grow up with the same people from kindergarten and see the same people all through the city because of how small it is. It's like being in a cage blinded from how much bigger the world really is. How much more opportunity is really out there in this world if you work hard to get it.

After an hour of staying in the rooms and getting to know my roommates, we went downstairs and walked across to the next building into the dining room. The dining room was unlike anything I had ever seen before. It was absolutely beautiful and had nice marble floors with a lot of space. Here was a huge buffet full of anything you could think of. The buffett even had a whole desert section open and a cereal bar for breakfast. It had almost every drink that you could think of. It was like a mini–Golden Corral inside of a college. After I grabbed a plate full of chicken and pizza I sat down next to both of my roommates, making friends was never hard for me because I was an outgoing person, so we instantly had a big group join us. I started talking to some of the kids and I was amazed how all these players were from all across America. It was very unique to hear all of the different slang and accents. I had never heard anyone from New Orleans, Memphis, or Atlanta talk before and they all had southern accents and slang. A few of us chuckled when we heard them talk because of how different they sounded. A player even flew all the way from Germany to attend this camp.

After we finished eating, the assistant basketball coach told us to walk across the street, that's where the basketball court was and inside to the left there would be a meeting room. This was where we would have all the rules explained to us during our weekend stay at this basketball camp. As we headed over to the basketball court, we were all amazed at how beautiful this campus was. It had a beautiful outdoor court, with an outdoor track field, weight room, volleyball court, and all of this overshadowed by the Tampa skyline. While we made our way past all of this, we headed inside to the basketball gym. Here there were two Spartan statues, one for the outside and one for the inside. While we walked around the gym area, it was amazing seeing all the trophies this school had. Finally, after taking in everything we walked inside of the meeting room. The coaches explained what we would do during our time at this camp, what the mission was, and what the goal of the entire camp was. We were told tonight we would run some drills and get some games in and on Saturday we would be split up into small groups and do drills against our groups to see who the best player of the group was. Later on, Saturday night the groups we were put in and did drills against was our team to play against the other groups that later turned to teams. Finally, on Sunday we would play games early in the morning to see who the best team was, and we would be dismissed later Sunday evening. My stomach dropped like I was on a roller coaster and my hands started getting sweaty immediately once it was time to go to the gym. That feeling of nervousness hit me out of nowhere.

When we got into the gym, we met the University of Tampa men's basketball players. These players were absolutely huge, and some of them were built like John Cena. Once we all sat down on the gym floor, the players spoke to us about the importance of working hard while having fun at the same time. How effort, hard work, and a positive attitude will take you a long way not only in basketball but in life. It was a very motivating and great talk. Once they finished, we lined up and started doing drills like the 3-man weave, layup drills and shooting drills. During these drills, I saw my first ever windmill and off the backboard dunk and this made me discouraged right away. I thought I was the worst player there. I could never do anything like that. I never had the confidence when it came to myself. I always worked very hard, but I was never confident in myself and always got discouraged. A lot of these kids were a lot bigger than me and could dribble way better and I was thinking to myself, "what am I doing here?" I was so pathetic when it came to self-worth, confidence, and believing in myself because I had been abused and treated wrong my entire life. I was passed along as if I was a piece of trash being in foster care and this made me always be angry at myself and life.

After an hour and a half of doing drills, the first night was over and we were told to go back up to the dorms and go to sleep because tomorrow was going to be a long day. During the night, I asked one of my roommates from Houston about how to not be nervous or scared when you play. I was tired of feeling this way and wanted to play freely like everyone else. We had a long talk, and he gave me advice on confidence and how this can be your ticket out to a new future. It was a great talk and it definitely gave me some self-confidence. I had the work ethic and that was the hardest part, now it was time to just start believing in myself. After we both stopped talking and it started getting late, I headed to sleep. But before I passed out that night, I stared out the window and saw how beautiful downtown Tampa was. I remembered how peaceful and how amazing this place is. I did not hear any gun shots, see, or hear any police sirens, see groups of people walking around late at night or drug dealers; it was just a totally different world. I wanted this to be my future one day and I wanted to make it out of Rockford like my idol Fred VanVleet. I was inspired how his stepdad forced him to wake up early in the morning and workout and how he grew up on the west side of Rockford and went to Auburn High School and made it from there. If he came from the same city as me and became very successful, then why couldn't I do the same? I always told myself, "I've been through too much in life to be basic" and I wanted to make a name for myself and chase my dreams. I understood the only way to do this was working very hard and I was willing to put the work in. I had already been getting up at 4-5am and running two miles to the gym every day, working out three times a day and making 400 shots. I was not in the streets, hanging out with friends, trying to party and be cool. I was not having sex, doing drugs, or drinking and I was focused on being the best basketball player I could be while being a decent young man who everyone would like. I was determined to be successful one day and the only thing stopping me was myself. Every motivational video always talked about the importance of discipline, consistency, never being satisfied and being confident and I knew I could accomplish this one day. I wanted to show the world that some foster kid coming from three homeless shelters who lived in a facility for two years, whose mom left him at 7 years old with a dad in prison could do it. I knew that I had been to ten different foster homes and my so-called "family" abandoned me and they thought I'd be a screwup but that only gave me more motivation and added fuel to my fire to prove them wrong.

Once I woke up at 6am to go to the optional shoot around that morning, we were congratulated by the coach as he explained to us "all of you who chose to wake up chose to be disciplined to your work ethic, while other people are sleeping, being lazy you guys are working and this will pay off in the long run if you stay consistent." He told us all to clap it up after and we started this shoot around. I felt like I was back at the YMCA doing this all by myself, the only difference was I had a rebounder. I never knew I was already doing this getting ahead of my opponent and I was given confirmation from him. During the shoot around I worked on my footwork coming into my shot, one dribble pull up jumpers and catch and shoot. Shooting is the biggest art and key to basketball; it takes years to master and the only way to do it is by practicing and getting lots of shots. You have to know your release and how hard you shoot the ball, once you know this you develop muscle memory and shooting becomes easy. After the shoot around lasted for an hour and a half, we finished here and were told to go back to our dorms until 8am and go to the dining hall for the breakfast buffet. I went back to sleep for a little bit because I was so tired from being up late the previous night. But after I finished my little nap, I headed to the dining hall.

The rules of the buffet were: do not eat so much because you will end up playing on a heavy stomach and get belly aches, cramps or possibly throw up. But it was hard for me to resist because of how much great food was inside of here, and I was so used to heating hot pockets and freezer food that I could not help myself. I was tired of eating like a dog at Mrs. Milly's house or surviving off of 50 cent cakes from the corner store, I was hungry. I decided to go all in that morning and have no regrets at the time. I had about eight bowls of various cereals, some breakfast pizza, scrambled eggs, fruit, pancakes, waffles, muffins, some kind of dessert, chocolate milk, orange juice, apple juice and some water. I was eating like I had never ate before, I was in food heaven. No wonder why I was one of the last people to leave the buffet. I'm not sure what that cereal machine was called but if I get rich one day, I'm going to buy that and a slushy machine. After I finished eating, I walked back upstairs to the dorm with a new wobble because of how much food I ate. I had to lay down because I felt like I just entered a food coma. But I could only lay down for a short amount of time because we had to go back to do more basketball drills.

As I wobbled my way downstairs, and across the street into the basketball gym, we were told to sit down. The coaches were placing us into groups for the day. Once we were broken into our groups , we did lots of one-on-one drills, shooting drills, footwork drills, a vertical jump test and a balance test. I never realized how much the little details can improve your game. They taught us the importance of every little detail that will improve your game and your health after basketball. I had a set of my own drills, but I had never done footwork drills with a ladder or did vertical jumps as much as they showed us. There were so many different types of drills that you could do and all I did was stick with the same few all the time, this really opened up my eyes. Then in two of the stations we were explained about the importance of eating healthy and resting our bodies for recovery, and also how to study film and understand the importance of the film room. It was so cool getting to see what these high-level college athletes did. I was totally inspired and amazed the whole time, and I knew this was what I wanted to do one day. I loved competing and getting that killer instinct feeling to take it to someone every time and prove yourself and all your hard work paid off. You cannot cheat the grind, the grind is very real, and it will expose you if you do not work hard.

After doing drills all morning, we were told to go back to our dorms and head to the buffet once again to eat. As we were eating, the coach told us that we would begin running games against other teams after we were done, and this would determine the best team of the camp. Once again, I instantly got nervous, my palms started sweating and I had to use the restroom. I hated this feeling and I wanted to be excited like the rest to play. I just had to pull myself together and remember all the training I had been doing. Once we finished eating, we all headed back up to the dorms to get ready again. I was constantly trying to get over being nervous. I wanted to play perfectly but that's impossible. You just have to play your game, not think so much and have fun. I had another talk with one of my roommates and he told me the same advice I told myself. I used that advice as I got ready and headed to the basketball gym.

During Saturday and Sunday while my team went up against the other teams, I saw so much talent and noticed so many things I needed to improve on. I needed to work on my mental game and get over my fears. But overall, I was happy because I had experience, and nobody could take that from me. This was the first time I had ever traveled outside of Illinois to play basketball and the first time I had ever played against kids from different states. It was just amazing to see how much talent there was during this camp and how athletic people were; you don't see this back-home playing at the YMCA every day. I was also amazed at how much better I could become from this camp and the new drills I learned. I was ready to get back to working even harder and prepare for my senior year. I knew exactly what I needed to work on, and I was ready to get to work as soon as I got back home. I had faith that God was getting me prepared for something bigger He had in store for me.

While waiting for my flight to take off that Sunday night, I was so inspired and thankful I was able to come on this trip. I was inspired to work harder and to chase my dreams even more. I wanted to live peacefully one day like the rest of these people-laughing and smiling. Back home, all you heard about was crime, and more crime and I was tired of this, tired of seeing the same people everywhere I go and living in a city where there is no opportunity. I would love to live in Florida one day, where the opportunity is endless. I would love to never see snow again, wake up to palm trees, in a beautiful city like this. I was so amazed at just how much more there is in this world than just Rockford. My eyes were totally opened to all the opportunity that was out there for me. All it takes is hard work, consistency, and faith in myself and God to achieve the dreams and goals that we want in life. I was willing to use these four important steps to go after everything I wanted to accomplish one day. I'm supposed to lose, and I'm just supposed to be a statistic in foster care, I love that, most people would get discouraged but this gives me even more motivation to beat the odds. That's what I will do one day.

When I got back from Florida, I was actually happy to be back home. I became a different person and I felt so much more motivated, like I had a sense of direction in life. When I was back in the gym going to the YMCA, I used the drills they had given me in Tampa and saw my game improving more and more. I changed the background of my phone screen to the downtown skyline of Tampa because this was where I wanted to live one day. I wanted to remind myself of this every day so I would not get distracted of my goal. The school year was two weeks away and I was about to start my senior year of high school, but I was not sure which high school I would be going to yet. I liked the coach at Guilford, and I liked his basketball program. I had my friends who I've grown up with since I was a little kid at East High School and was offered to stay with them for the school year to play. They were going to be dedicating the season to my friend, Greg Hill, who passed away.They did this because this would have been our senior year playing ball together. I loved that idea, and I missed my friends a lot. But I was not in this for my friends, I was in this for me. As good as all of this sounded and as good as the coach from Guilford was to me, I wanted to follow in the footsteps of my idol. I wanted to be pushed every day on the things I was not good at like sprints, defense, and aggressiveness. I wanted to go somewhere, where I would work hard every single day. I wanted to correct all my flaws and commit to basketball 100% and make a name for myself. I only had one year left to get a college scholarship and give this season my all. I knew what school I wanted to go to; it was the school I wanted to play basketball at since I was 10 years old. I ended up going to Auburn High School and was ready to work the hardest I had ever worked before. I understood the only way to achieve anything in life is to work hard, and that's all Auburn's basketball program was about. They had been down to state a lot while I was a little kid and went again my freshmen year. I wanted to follow in the footsteps of my idol, Fred VanVleet,and be coached by his coach, Coach Scott.

Auburn High School

The first day of school at Auburn, and I loved this school right away. I loved how diverse it was unlike Harlem. It was not a school that was predominately all white, here there was every race. I loved being away from my old foster home at Adams house and not dealing with the drama there. Mrs. Milly's house was a lot quieter and I had my peace while I was going to school at Auburn. I was not stressed out all the time or waking up angry anymore. I loved not having to see my old teammates anymore who I used to argue and fight with but seeing my new future teammates and walking down the hall laughing or planning to play ball after school. I loved how when I walked in the hallway, I didn't have to be very quiet and I would just see all my friends. I was very happy going to Auburn, the happiest I had been in a very long time to go to school. It was great being able to see all my friends again from my childhood, middle school, and the YMCA. It was a great feeling to not feel so alone all the time and dread school. I felt very comfortable here as well. Usually, people always talked down on Auburn because there was a lot of history in the past of bad things. People always said it's a bad high school because it has a lot of gangs, fights, and it's on the west side of Rockford. But while I was going there, I never experienced any trouble or anybody bothering me. It was like I was friends with everyone in the school, even my teachers. My favorite part of coming to school was walking into the gym every day and seeing how the school had Fred VanVleet's high school stats on the wall with all his accomplishments and achievements. I loved seeing that every day and knowing that an NBA player started his journey right in the same gym that I was stepping foot in and the same hallways and classrooms that I was walking in every day. Not only an NBA player but a successful person in life, went to school here. This gave me the motivation every day to chase my dreams and to work hard. I wanted to accomplish my goal of making the honor roll at this school, so every class I had I sat in the front and was very quiet. I wanted to show all my teachers that I was a leader and not a class clown like most of the kids here and I wanted to make the honor roll as well. I knew that education is everything and my plan was to go to college right after high school and I wanted to get a scholarship.

During the first two weeks of school, I continued the same routine that I had over the summer, the routine of getting up early at 5am and jogging to the YMCA and then playing basketball after school. That's when one of my friends told me that I could come workout out at Auburn early in the morning. I just had to come inside the gym through the side door and ask a coach for a basketball. I didn't believe him at first that a coach would just let you practice before the start of school. We were not even in the basketball season yet. So, the next day I watched his Snapchat story and saw he was telling the truth and I was shocked so instantly I changed my routine. I got into the routine of getting up early at 5am and jogging a mile to the YMCA and working out, then around 6:45am walking two miles to go practice in the gym at Auburn, then after school go play more basketball at the YMCA. The very first day I came in the morning I met Coach Scott, the coach that coached Fred VanVleet. He had no idea who I was until I started showing up 4 to 5 times a week and being very consistent with my routine of jogging a mile to the YMCA then leaving from that workout, and then walking two miles to do another workout at Auburn. I was usually the only kid in the gym in the mornings and here I would practice my moves to the rim while putting a cone down in the middle of the floor and attacking the basket. I already would make 400 shots in the morning at the YMCA, so this routine helped me a lot. I was always told if you can dribble, shoot, and drive to the rim you have a complete game and that's what I wanted to have. One day I was practicing by myself at Auburn and Coach Scott came into the gym and watched me practice and do my dribbling moves against the cone. He asked me what my name was and what school I had come from.

After I came back from Tampa, Florida I knew I wanted to go to college in Florida. I did not want to live in Illinois anymore and I wanted to explore new opportunities for a better life. I had no idea how I would get there being a DCFS ward of the state, but I knew with hard work determination anything is possible. I had always heard about foster kids who go to college get more money with Financial Aid and that there are scholarship programs out there for them. Also, when I was going to school at Addison Trail, they had a college board up of all the colleges kids went to and it was all over the state. I wanted to be one of those kids and one of those colleges to be a college in Florida. This was my ultimate goal from now on, moving out of Rockford, Illinois down to Florida. During a student assembly for seniors going to college and for help with financial aid, I always mentioned and looked up schools in Florida. I threw away any opportunity I had at schools in Illinois because I did not want to live here anymore. A lot of teachers and even my school counselor told me that I should stay in Illinois, but I just ignored it. I kept this determination the entire year. I was really hoping to get some sort of scholarship for academics, so I continued what I started at the beginning of the year with sitting in the front of my classes but worked harder and broke habits. I would be on my phone at times during class and now I turned my phone off at the start of class to prevent a distraction. If we had a test coming up, I made sure to study for that test as if my life depended on it. I also became close with all my teachers, almost like a teacher's pet and was very respectful and a quiet student. I stayed after class a lot to look up the different colleges in Florida with my English teacher and try to figure out where to go and what to study. I figured for my first two years I would go to community college because out of state tuition was really expensive and my S.A.T score was not good enough. Then after more meeting and talking I decided I wanted to go to a community college in Tampa, called Hillsborough Community College. This school was in the city I fell in love with, the city of Tampa. A lot of kids at Auburn joked around in class or did not really care about their grades they were just at school to see their friends, but I made sure to put school over my friends in class. It was hard at times trying to be an honor roll student with a class full of people just being in school to be cool. I could only slap myself in the face because had I made the honor roll earlier in school, I would've been in Auburns academic C.A.P.A (Creative and Preforming Arts Program). A lot of my friends would call me two faced because before class I would be talking, laughing, and joking but then as soon as I got in class, I was super quiet. But they understood what I was trying to accomplish and do.

Despite a lot of class clowns in this school, one of the coolest things about coming to Auburn was being able to play basketball almost every day in gym class. It was like going to a basketball prep school. A lot of the people at my school could play basketball and wanted to play, it was not like at Harlem where we had to ride scooters one day and watch a fitness workout channel another day. Even the gym teachers would play basketball with us, so it made the school day even better. During gym class, some days we would all be given a bunch of basketballs and just be able to shot around the entire gym class, or we even have huge games where a class or two classes would all play together. Even better, we would have basketball tournaments where we would play against teams in the gym class. They started asking me if I was trying out and would talk to Coach Scott about me, but he had already seen me practice every morning and no matter what they said I thought that he thought I was not good. I was always nervous every time someone brought up playing on the basketball team because I did not think I was good enough to make it, even as hard as I practiced.

Being a senior in high school and not having to make up any credits gave me the opportunity to leave school early because I only had 4 classes. Meaning, I had to walk home from school every day. I did not realize how dangerous this was walking to school early in the morning and home from school every day on the worst side of town. People in my class would always see me walking as the buses went past and tell me once they saw me "are you crazy? Walking to school?" I was not crazy, my foster parent Mrs. Milly never gave me any rides or helped with anything, so I was used to being a 17-year-old kid who walked everywhere. But almost every day when I walked home from school, I saw a police car or ambulance go past me. I did not really pay much attention to it until I remembered my talk with Mrs. Milly about being observant of my surroundings and that's when I started paying attention to the news more and seeing why. My favorite places to get food after school was Taco Bell and Beef-a-roo because school lunches never filled me up and the fact that both of these restaurants were right next to each other made it easy and helpful. I would sit inside to get Wi-Fi to do schoolwork and I would stay late most nights on days I didn't have to work. Luckily, I had left earlier some nights because both of these places were robbed at gunpoint. The next morning, I would walk past and see Taco Bell with their windows all boarded up. Another incident like this happened when the gas station I passed by every morning to grab a 50-cent cake for breakfast, a man had a shootout with police and was killed there. Another time I was walking to school in the morning and a person offered me a ride to school and I said no, but the next day I saw that person on a mugshot for being arrested. There were low-income apartments next to my high school and there was always a lot of crime going on there. Police were always there at these apartments. There were groups of people standing outside while I walked home from school and a couple of men approached me and patted me down trying to see if I had anything valuable on me. When they saw I had my school I.D. and after not finding anything they told me to "stay in school lil nigga." I didn't have any nice clothes or shoes so there was nothing for them to take, I was broke. I was just thankful God kept protecting me every day I walked to and from school and to and from the YMCA.

Whenever I asked my foster parent Mrs. Milly for rides, she always said no and told me to take the city bus. It frustrated me how she had a perfectly good and running car and would not give me rides knowing we lived on the bad side of town. Some days I would even see her driving to the store while I was walking home or riding the city bus to work after I asked her for rides and she said no. It was like I was risking my life being out here and walking every day. I always felt like I was a dog being in foster care, you have to do everything they say and if you act out, they get rid of you like you're nothing. When I would tell my caseworker about how she never gave me any rides they would say that's not her job and that made me even more frustrated. I hated being treated like trash all the time just because I was a foster kid, and they were getting paid to have me. I hated how I always felt so much pressure being in foster care to be perfect as well, not just in her home but in all homes. But living with Mrs. Milly I felt I had to be a lot more perfect, especially after she would threaten to kick me out of her home for forgetting to push a chair in or using too much toilet paper. It was always a mental battle going to school and not knowing if I would be kicked out of her house for something small. She would tell my caseworker she was tired of repeating herself to me and put in her two weeks' notice one time. It was even more embarrassing walking everywhere and having people record me and post me on their social media as they went past or ask me when they saw me again why I was walking everywhere. On top of that, I always wore the same shoes and did not have many clothes. Going to a school where people have nice shoes and clothes was frustrating as well. I just continued to focus on basketball and school because I knew in the long run if I kept working hard, I would overcome all of this. I started getting myself more involved with God to help bring peace to my life and for me to grow as a person. On Sundays, I would watch church online, and take notes about it in a journal, then I would watch YouTube videos on how to become a better person as well. I just did not want to be stressed out or angry anymore.

After a month of attending Auburn and basketball season was approaching, open gyms and strength and conditioning started. I was surprised because it was only the middle of September. We started way earlier than Harlem High School. Also, this school was very strict, in order to play basketball for this school, it was mandatory to attend strength and conditioning. A lot of kids would try to be sneaky and just go to open gym and not the strength and conditioning, but the coaches let us know about that real quick. They told us that they would be taking attendance on who came and who didn't and they would know. This was unlike Harlem as well because a lot of kids would just go to open gym and not do the conditioning. I had to adjust quickly and get ready. I hated running sprints and I was going to quickly learn to love this, especially playing for Auburn.

After every open gym after school, we had to run suicide sprints in pyramid style. Meaning, we would start by running our way to the highest, then go back down to the lowest. Mind you, we just finished playing basketball, so we were all already tired. What made it even worse was we all had to run it in a certain amount of time and if one person didn't make it, we all had to rerun it again. I would run for my life because I did not want to be the last one to cause everyone to run again. Then, they had us do stairs on the football field. We had to run up each flight upstairs without skipping steps, when I first did this, I got so dizzy from running up and down the flights of stairs I almost fell down them. That scare quickly stopped me from worrying about being tired. Next, we had Indian runs where we each would get in a group and line up and the person in the back of the line had to run as fast as they could to the front of the line, and it would repeat over and over again. Lastly, we had timed mile runs, where you had to get a certain time. This was not hard for me because I had already jogged every day to the YMCA. Three days after we finished running, we went straight into lifting weights. We would do this five times a week, Monday through Friday and it was crazy!

I had never worked so hard before or ran so many sprints in my life. What made it even worse was while I was doing it, the coaches would tease me and say, "don't you wish you stayed at Harlem?" My body would say hell yea, but my mind and heart would say no. I knew I wanted to come here and be pushed every day. Especially when after every workout Coach Scott would say, "if it was easy, everyone would do it." This helped me understand how greatness is achieved. I understood a lot better why very few make it. A lot of kids at my school wanted to go to kickbacks, homecoming, smoke, drink, mess with girls, but I was only focused on being the best. I wanted to be the best so bad that I would've done anything he told me to do. If he told me to stay outside until I caught a rabbit, I would've done it like I loved it without a single complaint. I looked at this coach like he was a God because he had developed an NBA player and so many Division 1 athletes. Eventually, I was in the best shape of my life and after about three weeks of strength and conditioning, I looked forward to doing this while everyone else complained. I would do every single drill the hardest I could because I wanted to be the best. Eventually, the coaches began to notice me beating out a lot of the people in drills and getting good times and I finally had something to be proud of myself for. I would still be paranoid that I was not good enough and go to the YMCA after conditioning and practice as well. I was just such a determined person.

After school everyday strength and conditioning would start. We had to be on time every day or we would be yelled at by one of the coaches. I was usually always on time but one day I walked in late because I was walking to school after I left earlier for the day. Right when I came inside, I was mad because it was Coach Scott, the varsity head coach and not an assistant coach, and he asked me why I was late. I had to explain to him that I had to walk to school because my foster parent doesn't give me rides and he was shocked. I don't think he even knew I was in foster care. Then he asked me if I walked to school in the mornings and I told him that I walk to school in the morning, I walk back home from school after I finish my classes, then I walk to come back to school for strength and conditioning. I was embarrassed saying this in front of the entire gym. At first, I thought he wouldn't want me on his team, I can't even get here on time. But later on, during the week someone told me that Coach Scott said I was the hardest worker right now. I sat back and thought to myself if I was working hard enough, I was already getting up at 5am and going to the YMCA, walking two miles to come to school and working out, working out after school for strength and conditioning, then going back to the gym later to work out. Also, while I was at open gym, I was beating everyone out in the drills. A lot of people thought I had a mental illness, or I was crazy, but I just wanted to achieve greatness like Fred VanVleet one day. I knew I would never be better than him, he's an all-time legend but I wanted to work hard like him. I had never worked so hard before in my life.

There was only a week until tryouts rolled around, and we started doing defensive drills and that's when my lackluster defense was exposed to everyone in the gym. I was too slow on defense when it came to moving my feet, closing out, and shuffling. I knew this would be a problem because Auburn was big on defense first. It got even worse when Coach Scott started yelling,"If you can't play defense you will never play in the game." I really began to wish I stayed at Harlem now, I could not defend. Guys would blow past me off the dribble every time. I hated how slow I was. I was mad at myself that all I did was practice shooting and dribbling when I should have been working on my athletic ability. I had nobody to blame but myself, and sure enough when tryouts came, all we did were defensive drills for almost the entire tryout. I was called out multiple times because of how bad it was. Coach Scott would just let me have it "that's horseshit defense" and I couldn't even blame him. Every kid was faster than me and better than me on defense. Even guys who were taller than me could move their feet faster than me. I had no idea why I was so slow on my feet. To try and get better, I started walking on my toes during the night and day and I would shuffle my feet down in the basement so Mrs. Milly would not hear me at night. I was so afraid I would not make the team, so afraid of all the hard work I had been putting in going to waste.

At the end of each tryout, we had to run something called a "30" where you run down and back 6 times in 30 seconds. Everyone had to beat the time, or we ran it again. This was one of the hardest things I've ever done in my life. We ran 3 "30's" 2 "20's" and 1 "10" for a total of 27 sprints down and back at the end of each tryout. I felt like I was going to die of a heart attack or pass out because of how hard this was. I was just in total shock and gave God lots of praise. I was even able to make time. To help me run faster, I imagined a vicious dog chasing me or the police chasing me from being back in Lutherbrook. It was probably a weird way of getting through time, but I ran full speed and made it. Every time we had to do this my stomach would drop and I got nervous, I kept thinking in my head "what the hell did I get myself into?" We did this for the first two days.

Each morning I was still going to the YMCA and walking to Auburn. I practiced nothing but defense. I did close out drills, slide drills and other drills from the tryout, I was so paranoid I would not make the team. When I would get to school, I saw the same two kids that I had been seeing previously in the mornings. With me being an outgoing person, I asked them to help me do the zig zag defense of slide drills. I was horrible. Thank God they agreed, and we practiced doing it over and over again. I was so nervous that all the hard work I had put in over the summer would fail me and I was going to give it everything I had to make it. As I looked over that morning practicing again and again, I saw coach Scott watching me through the window. I was immediately scared because I was still struggling to defend. I thought for sure after he saw me struggling in a practice that there would be no way I would be able to do it in a tryout. I was kicking myself because of how pathetic I was. That whole day in school I was totally paranoid because this was the third and last day of tryouts. I was nervous all day and I kept asking the other kids from last year who played in this program if they think I'll make the team. They all said yes but I was still scared. When it came time to the third and last day of tryouts, I had gotten slightly better at the defensive drills we were doing and ran as hard as I could at the end while we did our sprinting drills. I gave it everything I had that day; I was tired of losing and tired of failing. My whole life I failed and took losses and I was tired of that. I just asked God to help me win at least one time in my life.

After the third day was over, I was told I would be given one extra day to try out because he was undecided still. The next day I came to school early in the morning and practiced again and when the last day came, I finally improved even better than I did yesterday. When he called me over while everyone was doing an offensive drill, he told me I made the team shortly after tryouts ended. I had never felt so happy before because of how hard I worked to earn this. This is my dream to play at this school and be like my idol Fred VanVleet since I was a little kid watching him. It was one of the happiest days of my life. Finally, I was able to say I accomplished something. That was a great feeling that I wanted to keep achieving not only now but later on in life. I was just so thankful God blessed me after months of working hard. I came from being so intimidated in the very beginning, to using that fear to help me work even harder. It was a great feeling to know I did it. After the tryout was over and I was told that I made the team, I had no ride home. It sucked because my friend who was supposed to wait for me left already. I ended up having to walk two miles home that night and I saw at least three police cars and ambulances fly past me. But I did not care or have any fears in my head, I was just so happy I made the team and filled with an abundance of joy. When I finally made it home safe and thanked God for keeping me safe, I immediately started writing goals for my senior year and the things I wanted to accomplish. This was my last year to get a scholarship somewhere to play college basketball and I was going to give it everything I had. This would not be a repeat of my junior year of never getting in the game and playing nervous. I proved to everyone there and myself that I can do this.

After making the basketball team, we had practiced for two weeks before our first scrimmage to the public. I was learning all the new drills with defense and getting better on attacking as well. The practices at Auburn were much more physical and intense than Harlem's were. I loved the feeling of going to practice every day and competing and working hard. I felt like every day I was getting better and learning something new. I was getting out of my comfort zone while I was here and playing a lot more aggressive as well. Off of the court, I was getting along with all of my teammates and practicing with them at the YMCA after school. In the classroom, I was maintaining an honor roll GPA and being a leader as well. One day, Coach Scott had us get a paper signed by all our teachers explaining how our behavior was in class and all of my teachers wrote good things about me. It was a great feeling being called a great student and a leader in the classroom. It was like I changed into a completely different person from who I used to be. Everything was going well at home too, I made sure to push my chair in and leave no crumbs behind after I was done eating. I did everything Mrs. Milly asked of me and she was proud of me as well. It felt good not having any stress at home or any foster kids bothering me while I was at home. I was actually happy for the first time in a long time. Everything was going well on and off the court.

After school I usually walked to the McDonalds close by or stayed in the library and did homework. These were the quiet places where I would be able to study as well. I did not want to walk all the way home and then back because it was now early November and living in northern Illinois my whole life this is when it starts to get very cold and snowy. I was not a fan of the cold weather so I made sure I would be bundled up. When I would get up in the morning and jog to the YMCA then walk to Auburn, I would wear three hoodies to keep myself warm because of how cold it was. One day we had practice on the weekend, and I could not get a ride, so I walked two miles to school in the freezing wind chill. I made it before everyone else did and I had to sit outside in the cold for 30 minutes. That's when the assistant coach showed up early and let me sit inside of his car because of how freezing he saw me. He ended up telling the coach he offered to pick me up if I ever needed a ride because he usually did this for other kids. I was just so used to getting things done on my own and not relying on other people that I did not even think to ask. Mrs. Milly was still not giving me any rides to go anywhere, but luckily, I managed to get rides home from a few of my teammates or take the city bus. It was nice I did not have to walk home every night or walk to practice anymore in the freezing cold. These teammates cared about me a lot more than my old teammates back at Harlem.

Finally, it was the day of our first scrimmage, I was so happy this day was finally here. I was finally not nervous to play anymore, I was actually confident and ready. All that hard work and competitiveness I put in was going to pay off tonight. I was ready to show all of these coaches and this entire conference that I was a legit basketball player. After we got out of school, we had a little warm up practice before the game. I did every dribbling drill the hardest I had ever done it. During form shooting I worked on my form to make sure it was on point for tonight. I was just so ready and excited; I knew all the hard work I had put in would show tonight. It made it even better knowing my classmates, teachers and people around Rockford were coming tonight. After practice I was told I had to go meet with my caseworker and my foster parent Mrs. Milly before our first scrimmage. I wondered what that was all about but was too excited to worry about anything, so when I walked into the house I was surprised to see a couple of boxes on the floor. That's when I looked down and saw a missed phone call from my old teacher at Addison Trail. He left a long voice message. My case manager and foster parent were waiting for me and my excitement turned to confusion. I was told my foster parent was having surgery on her hand and I could no longer live with her.

At that moment, I was lost for words and had nothing to say. I felt like I just went on the world's tallest roller coaster and went crashing down, my stomach had completely dropped. I felt like someone had just punched me in the face as hard as they could and stabbed me in the heart. I couldn't even talk if I wanted to, I just listened the rest of the time and went upstairs. As I was packing my stuff a wave of sadness just hit me and my eyes began to get watery. I could not believe this was really happening. After all the hard work I had put in over the summer to be better than last year and after flying down to Florida and attending a basketball camp just to get better and play against more competition, I would be leaving. After getting up at 5am every morning before school just to jog to the YMCA and making 400 shots, then walking two miles again to work out before school at Auburn, then going to every single strength and conditioning workout and giving it all I had, it was for nothing. After all the walking I did, risking my safety and even my own life, for what? Most importantly, after all the hard work I had put in it was over just like that, everything I had worked so hard for was gone. That was one of the slowest days I had ever lived because I just felt frozen in those words and shocked. My senior year was over just like that. I was told there were no more foster homes for me to live in and to reach out to my old teacher at Addison Trail High School because he would have more details. I ended up reaching out to the teacher who called me, and he told me that he knew about this for a while. He also told me there was an Addison Trail gym teacher willing to take me in. My teacher told me he would be picking me up the next day and to have all my stuff ready and packed. So, I continued to pack all of my stuff up and that was it. I was still in shock and it was hard for me to comprehend just how fast everything changed. Still ,to this day, I am lost for words and bitter, and for the rest of my life I will have to live with that. I wish foster parents for once could put their foot in our shoes and see how bad it hurts and how much their decisions affect foster kids. We are more than just a paper check; we have feelings and we matter as well. After this happened, I hated being in foster care and I wished I could just live on my own. I was tired of being moved around like I was a piece of trash being passed from one to the next. I could not believe it was really over, all of that hard work just to be told it was over.

The next morning when my teacher from Addison Trail came to pick me up, I was all packed up and ready to go like he said. I finished putting all my things inside of his car. But before we left, we stopped by Auburn to return all my basketball gear and say goodbye to all of my teammates and coaches. Most of my teammates felt sorry for me as well as my coaches. It was just really devastating to end a senior year like that. I made sure to thank all my coaches and teammates for everything and told them this was the best team and program I ever played for. It was really amazing to see how much I grew as a student, person and athlete. If there is one thing in life, I wish I could have a do over every day, it would be playing basketball for Auburn High School and following the footsteps of my idol, Fred VanVleet. I got emotional as I left but I quickly stopped and made sure nobody saw me. Before I walked out the door, I stared at all of Fred VanVleet's memorials and all of Auburn High School's accomplishments. Right then and there I made sure to not give up. Even though I was not going to be able to play basketball for this school I made sure to not give up on my dream. When you fall down in life you have two choices: to sit around and cry and throw yourself a pity party, or you can let this make you stronger and add fuel to your fire to work harder. I understand nothing in life will come to you if you just sit around and wait. You have to work hard for what you want in this world. That's exactly what I was going to do, work hard, have faith in myself and God, and stay consistent. I was going to make sure that all of this would-be motivation for a success story one day and I promised myself I would never stop working hard. The day I stopped working hard will be the day I get buried six feet deep and God calls my name back home.

Mrs. Johnson's House

After saying my bittersweet goodbyes, I got back in the car as we headed towards the city of Chicago. I would be going back to a familiar place where I attended half of my freshmen and sophomore year. I was going back to Addison Trail High School. During my hour and a half ride with my teacher, I just tried to stay positive and think positive. It was very hard to do this realizing that after the hard work, I wouldn't even get to play a single game with Auburn. I already missed being home, regardless if I had to walk everywhere and always ate nasty food. It was still worth it because I was happy. I was happy playing basketball every day and working out. I was happy being an honor roll student and a leader in the classroom. I was a very independent person who just needed food, a bed, and a gym to go to. You never had to worry about me trying to be something I was not or fit in with the wrong crowd because I had already learned my lesson from Lutherbrook and my friend's funeral. I did not want to smoke, drink, have sex with women, gang bang, or anything negative. The only thing I was trying to do was become successful and accomplish all my dreams and goals. I didn't need love or family because I had already been betrayed by my own family and I was done looking for family. I did not trust a family because I did not want to be left again like how they left me to sit in two shelter homes and a facility for two years. I did not even trust my own older sister after she betrayed me too. It made me very bitter how I had a 4-month-old nephew at the time and my older sister never let me see him. Her and

I got into a fall out on her birthday because I found out her baby daddy was beating her while she was pregnant and even after she gave birth. It made me even angrier when I found out he was leaving marks on my little nephew and not helping take care of him at all. Then, after my sister opened up to me and showed me all her bruises, I kicked him out and she let him back in the very next day. My own sister took him back and stuck with him over me and this caused us to get into a big argument. I was so angry that she did this when I found out all the stuff he was doing. Her baby daddy broke into my sister's apartment and beat her then stole her car. I was hurt when I saw all of the bruises on her and she let him right back. She ended up blocking my phone calls and me out of her life while keeping my little nephew away from me. But I learned to just focus on my life and worry about the things I can control; God will handle them one day.

The teacher's name of who I would be living with was Mrs. Johnson. I did not know very much about her. I knew that she was a gym teacher at Addison Trail. I mainly remembered her from when we had a school assembly about cyber bullying, and she was a big part of it. I remember hearing a rumor around school that a student cropped her face from other women sleeping with a student or a nude photo and they chose to make her the victim. I felt very sorry for her when I saw her at the assembly crying because these people tried to ruin her life and her career. They put her and her family through a lot at that time and that was not fair. I remember telling her that I was sorry for her and gave her some words of support and that's the only thing I really remember. We never had any conversations or became close. Another thing I knew about her was that her son played football and was a very good football player. I knew that he played running back and was the best offensive player on the football team for Addison Trail. But a lot of gossip went around the school that he was caught smoking weed and was suspended a few games and that hurt his chances of playing at a very big school. I felt sorry for him as well because you never want to see anyone who works so hard with a bright future ahead of them have it taken away by a mistake. We all make mistakes in this world and nobody is perfect, so I always found it very ignorant of people to throw up the mistakes of others and use it against them.

After a long hour and a half ride full of sadness, anger, and flashbacks we finally made it. At first, I thought we were at the wrong house and I asked my teacher "is this the right house?" and it was. Mrs. Johnson's house was absolutely beautiful. It was a house unlike anything I had ever seen before. Her house reminded me of the houses you used to see on MTV cribs; it was that amazing. When she saw us pull into her driveway, she came outside to greet us. She gave me a big hug while saying welcome home and telling me how happy she was that I was here. I didn't understand why she was happy I was here because I was not anyone special at all. She told me to grab my things and we walked inside, and I was just blown away at how beautiful it was. The inside of her house had a beautiful shiny tile floor to match a shiny chandelier. She was telling me about her house and I was blown away as she explained that her house had three floors, six bathrooms, seven bedrooms, and an indoor bar. Mrs. Johnson had a beautiful fireplace in her living room, right under the TV. The kitchen floors were redone and had marble countertops. While she gave us a mini tour, she opened the fridge, and it was full of food. She had another pantry and fridge full of drinks and food. I asked her if she cooks food for the people here, while she laughed, she said yes almost every night. I was not laughing and very serious and I told her I barely had any food at my last placement and was surviving off of gas station snacks, hot pockets, hot dogs, and school lunches. Mrs. Johnson told me I would never have to worry about going hungry at her house and that those days were over. My mind was just in complete shock because I could not comprehend how quickly everything changed. Coming from the west side of Rockford, all you saw were run down houses everywhere, it was nothing like this.

After the tour was over and my teacher left, I unpacked my things after she showed me which room would be mine. I was in shock the entire time while I was unpacking still at how fast everything changed in one day. I had a weird feeling like all of this was too good to be true. I didn't really know her at all, and I had my guard up and remembered the talk I had with Mrs. Milly about being observant. Once I finished unpacking for a while, she offered to take me to

Portillo's and see if I could get transferred to this location. On our way up to Portillo's she was telling me how she knew the man himself Dave Portillo and I was in shock. Mrs. Johnson told me she knew a lot of other people too and that if I were willing to work hard, she could get me many opportunities with the many people she knew. She also told me that they are trying to get me on the basketball team at Addison Tail and get things set up with the coach. I was told the coach and players already knew I was on my way and I would be able to practice with them shortly. Once we got into Portillo's and I was told I was unable to transfer, I was not upset because I was going to still be able to play basketball. My attitude changed completely after hearing that, even though it would not be playing with Auburn. I was still happy that I had a chance to play my senior year. I was ready to go to practice right away.

Once we got back to the house, I was told Mrs. Johnson needed my help with decorating her Christmas tree. It was still early November and with Christmas right around the corner, Mrs. Johnson's house was completely decked out for the holiday. She had four Christmas trees! I have never seen that before in my life, usually it's just one tree. For a second I thought I was living in the forest with how many Christmas trees there were everywhere. While I was helping decorate the trees, she started telling me about the people who all live in this house. In total there were seven people. She told me it was three of her daughters, her son, me, her, and another lady who lives in the apartment. She was also a teacher but taught at a different school. I was shocked at how there was an apartment inside of this house. I had never heard or seen that before either. She told me that her house is very noisy and there usually are lots of people all the time, from her friends, to her sons and daughter's friends, to people coming over. It was a very open and busy house as she liked to say. She was right because as we were talking, people were making their way in quickly. In the midst of us talking, Mrs. Johnson was telling me how she wanted me to be a part of their family and how I would be loved and safe. The red flags immediately went up in my head once she said this. I hated that word family, and I always felt the feeling of betrayal and hurt when I heard this word. I explained to her a little bit about my background and the foster homes

I had been to. She was in shock by this and told me how all of that was over, but I did not trust anything she was saying. I knew better than to just be gullible and believe every word she was saying. But I heard her out and was respectful about it.

Later on, that night, one of my long friends from freshman year had come over to see me. While we were in the middle of talking, Mrs. Johnson told us that she had been invited with two tickets to go see the Chicago Blackhawks game. She asked us if we wanted to go and I was in shock. The first day I moved in I was already getting to go see a Chicago Blackhawks game at the legendary United Center. My friend and I ended up going that night, and it was just amazing. I let my guard down a lot after that and started seeing that maybe this house would work out just fine. Maybe I just needed to give it a chance. After three days, it was a difficult change for me. I was not used to sitting down all the time and not working out. This area had no basketball gyms but only the school to practice at. I figured Mrs. Johnson wouldn't have a problem with letting me get up shots and work on my game while I was living with her because she was the gym teacher and had a key to all of the gyms in the school. Addison Trail High school had four gyms and I figured since we lived not even a block away from the school that she could open the gym for me and just let me practice and I would walk back when I was finished. She told me that I was not allowed to do this and with three days into living with her it started to annoy me. All I knew was that working out all the time and practicing was my comfort. I knew that because if you don't work hard and practice, you will never improve or get better and I tried to explain this to her. She told me I can get better because I will be practicing with the team shortly but that's not what I meant. I was talking about getting individually better and she didn't understand. This later on would cause us to bump heads and get into arguments. I did not care about the fancy house, the things that she would be able to buy me, the food on the table, I cared about working hard to chase my dreams. All I knew was working hard at basketball everyday and working out 3-4 times a day and now I was told I had to stop all of that. No, I was taught to stand up for what you believe in even if that means losing everything and I believed without hard work I am nothing. in other words, "Hard work beats talent any day."

Addison Trail High School Senior Year

On Monday morning I got ready for my first day back to Addison Trail High School. I felt somewhat happy because I was able to see all my old teachers who I became close with and some old friends. But I felt very weird coming back again. I felt like people all remembered the bad things I did my freshmen and sophomore year while I was living in Lutherbrook going to school here. I had a strong vibe that it was going to be awkward. But I just tried to stay positive and think positive, that's all I could do. Sure enough, as soon as I walked inside, all of my old teachers and some students remembered me. I didn't like that the students remembered me because they always brought up the immature and dumb things I did in class. But it was something I just had to get over and show that I was a different person. When I got into my counselor's office to get my schedule, I was very happy to see my old teacher Mrs. Myers. During my freshman and sophomore year she was the only one I was able to open up to about my problems and she was always nice to me. She always went out of her way to put in a good word for me, buy me things and show lots of support which was something I was never used to. Mrs. Myers even came to visit me at Lutherbrook Academy and brought me lunch to see how I was doing when I got kicked out of Addison Trail towards the end of my freshmen year. She was just one of the greatest people you can ever meet. I was even happier when I found out that all of my grades were able to transfer over from Auburn and I was considered an honor roll student still. Even better, I did not have to have classes in the basement anymore because all of my classes were general ed classes. While we were talking, a few teachers stopped by the office to see me. It was always crazy being at this school because I was better friends with all the teachers than I was students. I have never met such nice, generous, and great teachers before in my life. I couldn't believe they were all happy to see me, I thought most of them did not like me, but I was totally wrong, maybe very few didn't but I never noticed.

Once I finished up in Mrs. Meyer's office, she told me the varsity basketball coach wanted me to meet with him in his office that day. I was excited to talk with him and have a meeting because I wanted to play basketball and get to work. I felt like I had a great chance of getting a scholarship this year; the only thing I needed to do was keep practicing every day. When It was time for me to go see him, I was given a pass to his room. When I met with coach Evans, the varsity head coach of the basketball team, he told me he remembered me from my freshman year in the Addison Trail basketball program and was excited to have me on board. He explained to me that I had to be cleared by the IHSA in order to play because I was on the roster of another school's basketball team, which was Auburn High School. He told me he had no idea how long it would take for me to be cleared to play, but I had a good chance of being cleared because I never played a game with Auburn yet and it was out of my control being a foster kid. I understood everything he said, and I just had to be patient. In the meantime, Coach Evans told me I would be able to practice with them and be on the team bus going to the games with them. Addison Trail had a basketball tournament that was coming up. It was the annual Thanksgiving tournament they had every year. From the sound of everything, I most likely was just going to be a practice player to help the team get better and sit on the bench taking stats. I felt numb about the situation, but I just had to work with what I was given and be the best practice player and stat taker I could be until I was cleared to play.

After this meeting was over, I went down to the basement to

go see one of my favorite teachers, Mr. Andrew. We became very close my sophomore year. It was great to see him again and even better that he and Mrs. Johnson were close friends. I asked him if I could eat my lunch downstairs in the basement like I used to do. We talked for a while then I headed up to the lunchroom to grab lunch and then planned to come back down to his class. While I was in the lunchroom, I saw all of my old friends. They all were happy to see me and welcomed me back. It was nice to see all of them again, but I always felt so left out when it came to hanging out with them because a lot of these students in this school were wealthy and had nice houses and parents and I did not have any parents or nice clothes, shoes or a nice house. During my freshman and sophomore year I didn't have the new phones they had or nice clothes and shoes that they had. I was always the one with beat up and dirty shoes, wearing the same clothes all the time, and asking for their school lunches because I was so hungry when I was living at Lutherbrook. This always made me feel like the odd one out of the group. It was like going to school with all rich kids but being the very few percentages of poor kids in this school. But when I came back during my senior year things changed, especially my appearance and me not begging for their lunches anymore, so it was a plus. But it still felt very awkward and fake because when I left this school none of them ever messaged me or checked on me. I always felt a strong fake vibe being around them even before I left. I learned to just be nice to everybody at school but no matter how hard I tried to make real friends with students at Addison Trail, it was always weird to relate and awkward. But I learned to adjust and I learned how to talk about different things and learn the interests of other people. I had to try a lot harder going to this school because my friends here were so different from my friends back home, but I managed to get through it by being nice and open to any conversation. Being around so many different people for so long helped me learn how to talk to people and make friends with any race, gender, or person. It never mattered what you looked like, had going for yourself, or what your interests were because I learned how to adapt well. A lot of people fail at this skill because they just like to talk to certain people who like what they like or are interested in what they are interested in. But this was never me. Things however did become even more awkward after living with Mrs. Johnson and having students and teachers from school ask me all the time about living with her. I felt like I had all of this weird attention at school and I did not like it. It did help me become close with a lot of other teachers at school though. But ultimately, I felt like I was back to being alone when I went here. I never really hung out with all of my friends I had at this school; it was always small talk or just a quick hallway talk before class and that was it. I wanted to be back at Auburn playing basketball and seeing all my friends back home. I mostly put on a fake happy face and just stayed quiet because inside I was not happy and was very sad. I would just put my headphones in and just go through the school day like usual. They say history repeats itself and it was like being back to my freshmen, sophomore and junior year, going through school most of the day alone and quiet.

After school was over that day, I ended up going to my first practice with Addison Trail. They gave me a practice uniform and a pair of team shoes to wear. I was excited to be back on the court practicing again. During practice we would do some shooting or offense drills with a small group. Then after a while, the starting 5 and other players who were going to get in the game ran against us practice players and we played defense. Once our turn on defense was over, we would run the plays we saw on film that our opponents used, and we would mimic them against the starting 5 and the other players who got in the game and they played defense and tried to stop us. These were probably the most boring practices I've ever had after coming straight from Auburn High School. There was no intensity of competition in this practice at all. Basketball became very boring once I came here. I missed that competitive and aggressive type of style and nature at Auburn. As crazy as this sounds, I missed running "30's" at the end of practice or when someone did something wrong. We rarely ever ran and if we did, they were down and back and it was just boring. I had to learn how to play zone defense from playing full court man and aggressive defense. It was a completely different style of basketball at this school and basketball was just very boring once I came here. After that monotonous first day of practice was over, we went down to the film room and were given a packet on each player's strengths and weaknesses. Then we watched film on the other teams we were getting ready to play against and shortly after were dismissed from practice.

After a few days of doing this same routine, we got ready for the Thanksgiving Day tournament. I was told I did not have to go, but Mrs. Johnson forced me to go because she said this would help me become closer with the team. This caused us to get into arguments because I did not want to go and just sit on a bench taking stats, wishing I could be out on the floor playing. But there was no discussion with her, and I had to go. So, I put on the team travel uniform, which was wearing a shirt and tie, dress pants, and dress shoes and sat on the bus for a ride to school just inside of Chicago. For the entire three-day tournament, I sat on the bench and took stats in my shirt and tie. It was one of the biggest slaps in the face. I felt like I was being teased because of how close I was to playing and wanting to play but having to sit on the bench and wait. It was nobody's fault I had to sit on the bench, and I was not angry at anyone. I just got sad doing this knowing that a little part of my senior year was gone. I would never be able to play in another Thanksgiving tournament again. I wish Mrs. Milly never told me I had to leave because she was having surgery on her hand, it made no sense to me. I was angrier over how that happened. I was taking care of myself while I was living with her anyways and I was 18 years old. It wasn't like she had to spoon feed me and pick me up; it just didn't make any sense to me and it made me angry every time I thought about it. I was just ready to be done with that tournament and go home. I was ready to be cleared to play.

After a week and a half of sitting on the bench and missing six games and a quarter of my senior year, I was finally cleared to play. I was very happy because of how long I waited but even when I was cleared to play, things did not go my way. Coach Evans and I had a talk in his office again after he told me that I was cleared to play. He told me that just because I was cleared does not mean I'm going to be in the starting five or get a lot of minutes yet. This talk frustrated me and essentially pissed me off because every day in practice I worked hard. Every day in practice I competed and did everything the other players on my team did, if not doing it better and harder. Everybody knew I should have been a starter, even Coach Evans and my teammates and people outside of school. There was a reason why every time we mimicked the other team's plays, I was always the main person to focus on stopping. It just really frustrated me when he said this, and I held a grudge towards him after this. I had already known a lot of the plays and studied them, but it was not enough to the coach's satisfaction. It made me impatient as well because I had already missed a quarter of my senior year and pretty soon it would be more than a quarter. As far as getting along with my teammates on the court, I did not do so well with this. I did not like any of the starting five or players that got in the game. It started to become fun when me and the other bench players were always in competition with them and trying to beat them every chance we could get, but we usually lost. This also made me frustrated because it was hard playing with a bunch of players who could not shoot, dribble, pass, and made a lot of dumb decisions with the basketball. I felt like it was always me vs the entire starting five. Although I loved competing, it was not the same anymore. But once we got off the basketball court, I got along with all of my teammates. It was just that competitive nature I had on the court that caused problems, but they knew once we got off of the court it was back to being friends. A few players carried it off the court with them and that was fine. I knew some players did not like me; especially the players that were on my team during practice and were tired of me yelling at them, but I just wanted to win and hated losing. You don't play basketball to lose, you play to win, that's the whole point of basketball. Your feelings should not matter because the only objective is to win basketball games.

Things at home with Mrs. Johnson were not going as good anymore. I got tired of her always telling me what I should and shouldn't do when it came to basketball. It was almost like I had another coach outside of the court. I knew she was just trying to be helpful and I appreciated that, but I already knew what I needed to do to be successful. When I told her I knew what to do to be successful, I was always wrong and she was right. This is where we bumped heads a lot because the main thing I needed her to do was open up the gym and let me practice. I felt and saw how my game was fading and falling off. This was mainly because I never got to practice individually anymore. I never got up 400-500 shots a day like I used to. I never got to work on my dribbling or moves to the rim. The only thing I did have was a weight room at planet fitness to use to get stronger and work on cardio but that never really helped. I never understood why she wouldn't just open up the gym for me and let me practice like I did back home at the YMCA or at Harlem. I was a responsible person and student. We lived right next to the school where it was literally a few steps away. This pissed me off a lot because in order to get better at basketball you have to practice and work hard. Not only practicing with a team but practicing on your game individually, like getting up shots and dribbling. We got into a few big arguments when It came to this, and one day we got into a big enough argument where I walked out of her house and she called my caseworker and put in her two weeks' notice behind my back. Mrs. Johnson always liked to throw up the things she did for me like buying me my favorite food, taking me places, and the nice home she provided me. I appreciated all of this, but I was fine without it. I just wanted to play basketball and go to school and get good grades. It hurt my feelings when my caseworker later told me she did this and then changed her mind and pulled her notice back. It hurt because here she was telling me how she wanted me to be a part of her family and she considered me her own but then did that behind my back and didn't even tell me about it. It made me even angrier when I heard other teachers asking me what was going on with me at her house, because I came to find out she was gossiping to other teachers about our business. I held a grudge after that because it showed me, she was immature, and she tried to embarrass me by giving me a bad reputation. For a grown woman, and a teacher to gossip about an 18-year-old kid and what happens at home is supposed to be private. It says a lot about the type of person that person is. I stopped trusting this woman and I knew all of this kindness was too good to be true.

While I was on the practice team and not playing any games still, I was told I was able to play in the JV games. In other words, I would be playing in a game full of varsity players who don't play in the regular games and play with sophomores and freshmen who they were thinking about moving up. This pissed me off even more playing in these games. It was really just a waste of my time now and like teasing me even more. Here I am beating out the starters in drills and practice and now playing with and against freshmen and sophomores. Then with the same players who I play with on the practice team every day. The same players who never get in the varsity games and who can't dribble, shoot, pass or play defense. In these games it was like everyone was running around like a chicken with their heads cut off. People were turning the ball over like crazy over and over again and it was just a waste of time. I got frustrated and had a poor attitude during one of the JV games for being yelled at and taken out of the game because someone didn't run the play right. At first, I yelled at the players who didn't run it right and was taken out of the game for that. The assistant coach told me in a stern voice that we don't talk to our teammates like that. I knew I was wrong, but I just got to the point where I stopped caring because every practice I worked hard and beat almost everyone out in the drills and I was not playing. I didn't get to practice basketball anymore or workout because Mrs. Johnson wouldn't open up the gym. I was just tired of going to this school and being here. I ended up running my mouth and that's when me and the assistant coach started arguing some more over being respectful to teammates. I was just so frustrated and full of emotion that I didn't stop talking that night when I should have. That's when the assistant coach told me if I keep talking, I'll be sitting on the bench the rest of the game. I sat there and just thought about how there was only 50% left in my senior year as we were already halfway through December heading into the Christmas Tournament. All of the emotion of everything that happened my senior year just hit me, and I was tired of it all. For the first time in my life, I became a quitter and I walked off the bench, went down to the locker room, grabbed my stuff, and I walked home after that. I did not want to live here anymore with Mrs. Johnson. I did not want to play basketball for Addison Trail anymore. Lastly, I did not want to go to school at Addison Trail anymore. I was done with it all.

The next day I was called into Coach Evans office, the varsity head basketball coach. We talked about what had happened that night. Also, he wanted to know what was going on with me in general. I opened up to him about how I felt and explained how I was frustrated. I was just angry about how things happened at Mrs. Milly's house then missing games here, working hard every day at practice and still not playing. I was annoyed with how I already missed 50% of my senior year. Coach Evans told me he understood and got why I was upset. But told me that I can't just come into a new school the way I did and expect to play more than the guys who have been here from the beginning. It all sounded like I was going to just remain on the practice squad and keep being a practice player and this talk just made me more frustrated. It was like I opened up about everything just to be told I would not be able to play still. I was not being a baby about not getting what I wanted because I worked very hard every day in practice to earn my spot. It just got to the point where I did not want to play anymore after this talk because nothing changed. I tried to stay positive and think positive by just working hard in practice and I kept my hopes high that I would be able to play soon. But then another two games went by and I was still not playing, and I was just beyond pissed now. I was tired of basketball and just did not want to play anymore. The last straw for me was during practice in a competing 3v3 drill. I was frustrated because the starters and their team were just scoring on everything. We were getting blown out during this drill. The next time I went out there I played tough defense and blocked the ball but was called for a foul. I told the coach that was not a foul and was being immature and arguing with him and I was told to go stand on the sideline and I wouldn't play anytime soon with that attitude. It was like this coach kept throwing that in my face and it pissed me off the more he did it. The next thing I knew, I took my jersey off and threw it on the floor, and I walked out of practice as the coach yelled, "there goes your senior year!" My senior year was already over by the time I transferred to this garbage basketball school. I went downstairs and grabbed all the stuff I had in my athletic locker. I left all my jerseys, shorts, practice gear, team shoes, and anything else that belonged to this school there. For the second time in my life, I became a quitter. I quit basketball that day and quit on myself because I was tired of being knocked down every time I tried to get back up. I was tired of losing in life, so I figured I might as well stay down then I won't lose anymore.

After I quit the basketball team, the other basketball players did not say a word to me anymore. I did not say a word to Coach Evans when I saw him in the hallways. My mother told me if you don't have anything nice to say, don't say it, so I was just going to keep my mouth shut. There were only a few days anyways until we went on Christmas break. I decided since I was angry at the time, I wanted to do something to make other people happy. I was always feeling sad and upset about the bad hand I was dealt and why the things in life happened to me. I always wondered why it is so hard to be happy. I saw everyone else with a family, loving parents, and everything nice. I always wondered if I would ever really be happy one day. I decided since I was angry and sad that I wanted to make other people happy because that gave me my happiness. It was something about doing something nice to people that gave me a sense of joy. So, I began praying more asking for guidance and reading the bible more asking God to help me grow more as a man and find happiness. I was tired of feeling sad and upset all the time and I wanted to be happy. One of my goals in life was to be a motivational speaker. There are not a lot of people at the age of 18 who have gone through what I have gone through, and this gave me the motivation to be different. I did not want to be like my mom, in and out of jail or my dad in jail for attempted murder. I didn't want to live up to the expectations of being a foster kid and ending up in jail or dead. I had the story to be amazing and it was time I started writing it. A lot of people thought I would fail, and this gave me the motivation to prove them wrong.

One of my lifelong goals was to give back to the people who were in shelter homes, foster care, or low-income families and did not get a lot of things for Christmas. I was able to relate to these people coming from the same struggle. I haven't got any Christmas gifts on Christmas Day for about four years now. I have been in that situation before and know how it feels to not get anything and see the Christmas tree empty on Christmas Day. It was an even better opportunity for me to do this because I had time away from basketball, which was something that I was not used to at all. For all three years in high school, I've played basketball and never had the time to do something like this. I ended up reaching out to the Boys and Girls Club of my hometown of Rockford and started collecting toys for a toy drive. I was going to do my own Christmas Give- away. I gained even more inspiration to do this after seeing Fred VanVleet do his coat give away for the little kids of Rockford. I had to come up with a plan to get people to donate, so I used my social media as a tool for this. I started by posting an experience of what happened to me of not getting any presents and how I wanted to prevent this from happening to other people. My social media post inspired a lot of people and the word of my toy drive spread a lot. I had lots of people share it and tell others about it to help with donation purposes. It helped even more because of all the great teachers from Addison Trail like Mrs. Myers and Mr. Paul who helped me with donations. With their help and the help of many others, I had donations from all over. I had lots of teachers, students, and even people sending me toys and money through the mail. This was the first time I learned that I could be a voice for something. I ended up getting 200 presents donated to me for my give away. This was 100 presents over the original goal. For about a week me and a lot of other helpers ended up getting the presents all wrapped up together and set a date to do this thing. I could not believe I was going to be doing my first ever Christmas giveaway. It was something I always wanted to do and now it became a reality.

Christmas Giveaway

On the day of the Christmas giveaway, Me, Mr. Paul, Mrs. Johnson, and two of Mrs. Johnson's friends were all headed to the Blackhawk Boys and Girls Club of Rockford, Illinois. This was a boys and girls club attached to a project housing authority, meaning these kids lived in the projects. There were so many toys so we ended up taking three cars in total. Mrs. Johnson loaded her car with toys, Mr. Paul loaded his car with toys and so did Mrs. Johnson's friend. It took an hour and a half to get there and on the ride to the boys and girls club I was nervous. I started asking Mr. Paul a bunch of insecure questions and if he thinks this was a good idea. I just wanted everything to go well so I had to just breathe and pray about it. When we finally got to the Blackhawk Boys and Girls Club and were finally in my hometown of Rockford, Illinois. I saw some of my old friends at this event. It was great seeing them, and I even saw my old foster parents as well. I was angry at them for a long time for kicking me out of their house and because of this being sent to a shelter home, but I forgave them and took accountability for my actions. It was like I rekindled a lot of my relationships from the past and I was proud of myself for that because it showed growth as a person on my end. It just goes to show you how relationships with people can change over time into better ones.

Once we got inside, I was taken into an activity room where they had a pool table with a couch and tables all set up for us. It was really amazing and nice of everyone for setting everything up so nice for us. We started unloading the presents and putting them on all the tables they had set up for us while the kids were still playing in the gym. My former foster parents helped and did a cookie part for the kids where the kids would come and sit down at a table full of different colored frosting and decorations to put on their own cookies. I've never seen little kids so creative when it comes to making cookies and I was so impressed I had to go over and make a few of my own. Once the kids were finished making cookies, we assembled an order to where the kids would come in line and grab a present that was wrapped up. We separated the boy presents from the girl presents so the boys and girls would not pick the wrong presents. Once they picked their presents, the boys and girls would come up to me and I would get a picture with them. It was so amazing seeing every kid smile and all of them in complete awe to get presents. At one point I started getting emotional for a second but faked yawning to stop it. I was just so happy to see all of them so excited. For so long I was always angry and upset and it was just a blessing to be a part of this and for everyone who helped. I have never smiled so much in one day before. It was a feeling I will never forget and a memory I will never forget. While I was at Walmart one day, I saw a bike on sale, and I thought this would be amazing to get and give away to one of the kids. I ended up getting the bike, but I did not know who to give it away to. One of the workers who worked at this club picked one of the girls with the best behavior. That made things a lot easier when he did this so none of the little kids got mad at me or thought I was picking favorites and would try and beat me up. When we called her over and I told her the bike was hers and handed it to her, she was in complete shock. This was another memory I will never forget. It was just a very amazing day and time.

After handing out all the presents to the kids and making cookies, I went inside of the basketball gym inside the club and played basketball with some of the kids. I played a few games with some of the kids and the staff there and it was a great time just being able to laugh and smile after being sad and angry for so long. I never wanted the day to end because of how much fun I was having. I wished I could do something like this for every holiday. The feeling of being generous is just a great feeling that hits your heart in a very positive and great way. Some people will do a giveaway or things like this to make their self-image look better or to do this for social media fame. That was never the case for me or my intentions at all. I did this because I had been hurt for so long and I've always wanted to do something like this but never had the time and now that I finally had the time. I came from the same struggle or worse than these kids and understand how it feels and I wanted to change that for them this year. It's very different when someone has been in your shoes before and can give you advice because the advice they will give you is very real. I took the time to get to know some of the kids here because I wanted to leave a positive and inspirational impact on them and not just give away presents and leave. While I was talking to some of the kids, I asked them what their dreams and goals were. I was trying to motivate them and give them good advice by asking these questions in order to chase their dreams. A lot of the boys said professional athletes and some girls said models or actresses. Regardless of what they said, their dream was in life. I made sure to tell them to always work hard and never give up on their goals. I told them once you work hard and stay consistent with your work ethic, you have confidence in yourself and keep that faith through every good and bad thing that happens to you, your dream will become a reality. We all had proof that someone can be successful from this city because of Fred VanVleet. I also told them not to be a follower, a lot of people from this copy everything that everyone else does just to be cool and fit in. If you look down at your fingerprints, there is a reason why nobody in this world has the exact fingerprint as someone else. We were all made to stand out and be different in life. I just wanted all of the kids to hear positivity and motivating words. You don't hear too much positivity in this city or world, it's the same criminal news every day. I just pray and hope these kids get a sense of positivity of what my overall purpose was in doing this giveaway so that way one day they will do their own. It's important to teach our younger generation right so they will change the world. Yes, part of it was about the presents but the overall goal was to inspire, motivate and help emotionally. Rockford, Illinois does not provide the best environment for the average kid looking to grow up in a safe city. Automatically these kids grow up having to go against the odds being from Rockford. Now it's time to let them use that as fuel to the fire to work harder to succeed instead of using it as an excuse to fail in life. I found out a lot about myself during this time and saw the man I can become one day, and I wanted to chase that vision. I saw that God had bigger plans for me, all I had to do was keep working through any mistakes or hard times I will have in my future.

After Christmas Giveaway

Once the Christmas Giveaway was over and Christmas break came to an end, I returned to school hoping to have a great 2019 start. Each month I tried to set new goals for myself as well as at the start of a new year. My goal this year was to find happiness within myself and work hard to find a different route in basketball. I was hoping to get another opportunity to play at another basketball camp somewhere or the last option to try out for a basketball team in college. But things at Mrs. Johnson's house took a turn for the worse and I was ready to move on. I was tired of always sitting inside the house all of the time and not being productive. I felt like I was wasting my life away by just sitting inside all of the time. I eventually got myself a job at the movie theater to get out of the house and to save up some money. I did still have that moving to Florida dream in my mind, but I was not sure how possible it would be now. But when it came to letting me practice playing basketball, me and Mrs. Johnson always bumped heads. I figured since I was not on the basketball team now that she would open a gym up for me and let me shoot around by myself when the other teams were not practicing. But that seldom happened for me and when it did happen, it was during the school day and I only had 30 minutes to shoot and then the next gym class would be coming in. I was frustrated and tired of going to school every day and feeling alone. I knew I had the teachers there for me but it's not the same as having students as your friends. It was like I was being mentally tortured waking up, putting my headphones in and going to school every day barely talking to anyone at all. Then sitting at the house all night or going to work at a movie theater where I stand at a ticket booth and rip tickets, walk up and down every aisle, sweeping up popcorn causing blisters on my hand. Then I would also get cramps in my back from bending up and down all day long. What made this job even worse was I never got paid well and it was not worth it. I was tired of repeating the same pattern all the time and I felt like I was better than this.

Every day I was stressed out from school, frustrated from this crappy paying movie theater job and now dealing with Mrs. Johnson. I was always thankful and appreciative, but I really did not care about living in a nice fancy house and getting food on my plate all the time. As crazy as that sounds, I was just so used to not having it so I didn't care for it; this did not make me happy. Playing basketball, working hard to achieve the dreams and goals that I had, made me happy. From the first day I stepped foot in her house I talked to her so many times about how I wanted to work on my basketball game. I asked her to use her keys to open the gym so many times so I could practice by myself and it was always a no. But the more I heard and started finding out she was talking bad about me to other teachers at the school and telling lies that were not even true, the angrier I became towards her. While I was at work one day, I ended up getting another phone call from my caseworker saying how Mrs. Johnson placed another two week's notice behind my back. Then she did the same thing and decided to pull back on it. I was so confused as to why she was putting her two week's notice in on me. I was not being rude or disrespectful towards her. We got into little arguments, but I didn't know it was enough to where she didn't want me living in her house anymore. It really pissed me off how every relationship I was in I felt like I always had to be perfect. It was always like someone was giving up on me if we got into a little argument or a discussion. But what pissed me off even more was how she lied to my face about her wanting me to be in her family and telling this to me while I was having a two week's notice placed on me. I was sick of the lies and sick of being gossiped about to other teachers and sick of people at school. I was depressed and angry all over again. I just tried to keep that same mentality of moving to Florida one day and getting away from all of this drama and nonsense.

While I was applying for different colleges, I applied to three different schools in Florida: one in Miami, one in Orlando, and one in Tampa. I was so happy when I was accepted into three different Florida colleges and I knew I could move there one day if I kept working hard and believing I could do it. But whenever I would tell Mrs. Johnson about moving to Florida and going to school out there, it was always a negative response. I was told I need to apply to schools here because I have nobody or nothing in Florida. I understood what she was saying and that she was looking out for me but at the same time I needed support in a positive way. It was frustrating how she always tore my dreams down. Even when I would tell her I wanted to do something with my money because I was tired of her always throwing up the things she got for me and did with her money in my face, it was still always negative. I felt like I had no support here anymore and that just frustrated me. Another thing we argued about was how she had two dogs in her house but never potty trained them and let them pee all over the house. I got angry because one time I walked on the floor and stepped completely in a puddle of pee. Another time one of those dogs peed in my room. But when I took the dogs outside and tried to teach them I was the bad guy in the end. I would even be standing outside in the cold with them trying to teach them how to go potty outside. Everything that came out of her mouth was negative and I was sick of it. I was tired of her lies and did not believe anything she had to say anymore or care for what she had to say because it was all negative. She then started telling me about if I was not happy at her house then I could go back to taking the city bus and not having any food on my plate and going hungry back in Rockford. I just started ignoring her and going to work at the movies and working out at the gym as much as I could.

Every day I kept my basketball dream strong and used it as motivation to prove this coach wrong and all the people who doubted me. I had confidence in myself and faith in God that I would overcome this. When I did use the gym, I would get up early in the mornings and jog two miles in the freezing January cold and snow to get to Planet Fitness to lift weights and work on my cardio. My offseason goal was to get stronger, faster, and bigger for the college level. I knew I was nowhere near the body, endurance, or speed of a division one college athlete. I made sure to always stay real with myself and not get a big head or be cocky. There were still a lot of things I needed to work on to get to the next level. But ultimately, I wanted to prove this coach wrong, the only thing that was missing was a basketball court. I was never able to practice in the gym and I got fed up with this. Mrs. Johnson and DCFS worked out a plan for me to stay in her house and I had to get back into counseling. I had not seen my counselor in so long or really had anyone to open up to, so this was nice. I was never ashamed of being in counseling or embarrassed because it helped me grow as a person and I started to see myself changing and using her advice. I thought of opening up to her and explained all the problems and frustrations that I had. I thought that maybe my counselor was able to convince Mrs. Johnson into opening up the gym for me to play basketball. But I was totally wrong. The advice she gave me was just a drop kick in the face. My counselor told me maybe basketball is not the right thing for you to do and I should rethink my plans about moving to Florida. I was very hurt about this because she was the main woman who I trusted, and who I thought would always give me good feedback, not tear me down. I guess it did not sound too realistic to her. I guess what I was trying to do was a miracle in everyone's eyes and nobody believed in me. She then told me that basketball was not for everybody and that there were great schools in Illinois to go to. I just heard her out, I was done with the arguing and fighting with people who did not believe in me. After that meeting with my counselor, I ended up breaking down emotionally that night. Especially after looking at the Rockford news and seeing Auburn in a sold-out home game against East and seeing all my old friends in the game. I would've given anything to have played on senior night and got a picture frame of myself and been playing in a sold-out game. I just remember how many hours I practiced and how bad I wanted to play basketball for my old school. I felt like I had nothing anymore and nobody anymore and I had finally hit rock bottom. I was tired of always feeling like I had nobody and nobody believing in me. It was a very lonely and depressing time.

The next day after my conversation with my counselor the previous night, I just stayed in my lane and continued to work and go to school. I gave up on myself for a few days and was just mad and sad. I was used to being alone and I felt like it was always going to stay this way. I felt like I had no purpose and no goals to achieve anymore. At least there was no point in doing so with a bunch of people who didn't believe in you and no support. Once those few days went by, I got a taste of what being basic is like. I hated being basic, I have been through too much in life to be basic and I wanted to achieve more than this. I started to realize and feel like I was being held back living with Mrs. Johnson and that this was not the right home for me. I was tired of being surrounded with negativity and lies all the time. I hated this boring routine I was in and I was ready to leave this lady's house. I knew there was something greater out there for me and I had the work ethic and determination to achieve it and not just sit around and be basic waiting for something to happen. I knew it was going to be hard, but my whole life has been hard, and God has still carried me through it all this time. I was tired of crying and feeling sorry for myself. I wanted to achieve something. A wise man once told me once you stop making excuses for yourself and hold yourself back, you accomplish more than you thought you could do and step out of your comfort zone. I was ready to do just that and see what other opportunities were for me.

I wanted to do another giveaway because I was always feeling angry and upset again and wanted to make someone else's day. Since the Christmas drive had gone so well it gave me motivation to do another giveaway. I wanted to do something special for women on Valentine's Day. That's when I came up with the idea that I would do a Valentine's Day Giveaway for a women's homeless shelter in Chicago. I chose to do Chicago this time because I already did a giveaway in my hometown Rockford and I wanted to branch off and meet new people, especially since I had already lived in Chicago before. I began planning how I would do this and give away the things I needed to get. That's when I went online and bought 100 boxes of the small chocolates and I would get 100 Valentine's Day cards. I did not need donations for this one because I had a gym, and the items were not expensive. When I brought this idea up to Mrs. Johnson, of course she started being negative right off the bat. I got tired of hearing her mouth, so I was going to walk to the dollar store. She told me she needed to talk to me and told me to wait for her, that she would give me a ride to the dollar store, and I knew this was the day it was time to say goodbye. As we were riding in the car, she was talking about how she had to take her daughter to volleyball practice, and I felt some type of way about this, I'm not sure why but mainly because I felt like I was always asking to practice basketball. I did not keep my mouth shut this time and I confronted her about how she was always helping her daughter with whatever she needed but never me. Especially when I asked to go to the gym that was just a few steps away. I said it was because I was a foster kid and then I opened up to her in the car about how I felt she treats her other son and daughters better than me as well. Mrs. Johnson was pissed and she immediately got defensive and started screaming at me in the car. I could have diffused the situation and not said anything, but I was tired of everything and that's when I started yelling back and explaining my frustration and how I heard her gossiping about me to other teachers. It all spilled out, all the times she lied to my face about being family but put her two week's notice behind my back several times and then removed it. All the times I begged her to open the gym up so I could play basketball and work hard. When I asked her for help with moving to Florida, she made me feel like I was crazy and just talked bad about all my dreams. After a while of yelling back and forth, I told her to pull over and I would walk the rest of the way. I could've handled the situation differently and just been silent, but I was tired of being silent and I wanted to be heard. I was tired of being sad and not happy. God gave me my month for a reason and I'm a human with feelings too.

When she pulled over, I got out of the car and didn't even close the door because of how mad I was. I just went inside the dollar store and purchased 100 Valentine Day cards like I planned to do. I took some space and got myself together. I then walked home two miles in the freezing cold on a January frigid day. I wished I had grabbed my coat that day but all I had was a sweatshirt on because the original plan was for her to wait outside for me but obviously plans had changed. When I made it back, I went inside and walked right upstairs. I did not say a word to Mrs. Johnson. I was tired of her always throwing stuff in my face. I went through all the Christmas gifts she had gotten me and gave them all back to her. Now she didn't have Christmas gifts she had got me to throw in my face anymore. As I placed it in front of her, I told her she can have it all back and that I do not want it. While I placed it on the ground in front of her, she started laughing like I was joking. I went back upstairs, grabbed my phone and called my caseworker. I told my caseworker I was ready to leave this lady's house and did not want to live here anymore. I started packing all my stuff and putting it in a suitcase. While I was packing, I heard her on the phone with someone so I started to go downstairs to listen. While I sat on the stairs, I heard her calling the police on me. She was telling the police I was slamming and breaking stuff while I was sitting on the stairs calm as could be. Now I was really pissed off because this lady was telling more lies and trying to send me to jail. I went over and confronted her about lying to the police and then tried to grab the phone out of her hand. That's when she started yelling to the police on the phone saying, "he is hurting my hand by trying to take the phone away!" Eventually I took it and hung the phone up. I was filled with anger and could not believe she lied to the police now saying I was breaking stuff, when in reality I was packing my stuff up and sitting on the stairs. That's when my counselor called and threatened to have me hospitalized because Mrs. Johnson had lied to her as well and at that point I was just pissed off and angry on a different level. I really did not care to hear anything my counselor had to say either because of what she said to me before and how she was all friends with Mrs. Johnson. I guess if you put two rich white women together, they both become really good liars and shit talkers as well. That's when I yelled at my counselor on the phone "you want to see me break something, watch this!" and I slammed the door over and over again. It was not the best idea, but it was worth it.

Once the police arrived, Mrs. Johnson was so full of shit she ran to the door and screamed, "he's upstairs breaking stuff!" Then the police ran up the stairs and they asked me to stop as he got out his taser gun. Once I saw them coming up the stairs I stopped hitting the door and sat on the bed. I had my hands up and then he put his taser away once he looked in the room and saw nothing was destroyed or broken. They told me to step outside and I explained what happened and what was going on. That's when a different caseworker from Our Children's Homestead showed up. Once my caseworker talked to me in front of the police and Mrs. Johnson, I was told I was going to be taken to a hospital to get checked out and I had to go in an ambulance. I immediately began to panic because I thought I was going to be sent to another hospital like before at Riverside Medical Center in Kankakee, Illinois. All of these negative thoughts started rushing through my head like I was not going to graduate this year, and everything was going to be worse. I freaked out once I saw the ambulance come. But once I got onto the ambulance, they told me they were taking me right down the street and I did not have to be strapped down to a stretcher. I was so happy and relieved once they said this. At least now I would not have to pee laying down again.

Once we got to the hospital, I walked into a room to be checked. My caseworker Gabby met me at the hospital while I sat on the bed waiting for them to take my vitals. I explained everything to her and everything that had happened before this incident. Gabby stopped me from talking and told me she knew Mrs. Johnson was full of shit and her story did not add up. I told her I was nervous and scared of being sent to another hospital and all the other panic thoughts I had. Gabby told me to calm down and that I was not going to be hospitalized. Instead, she gave me some great news, that I would be moving back to Rockford in another foster home and I was so happy. Finally, I did not have to live with this lady anymore and I could go back home to work out and chase my dreams. I could go back to school to see my old friends and not feel alone anymore where I was just friends with the teachers. I was able to go back and see my friends at the gym as well. I was just so happy to be back and so happy I did not have to live with this lady Mrs. Johnson anymore. I was finally free from her and Addison Trail High School. After another 30 minutes went by, we were finally able to leave and head back home. But before we left, Mrs. Johnson pulled up to the hospital to give my stuff to my caseworker. During that time, I did not say a word to her or look at her. But when she saw me, she still had the nerve to ask me to go to lunch with her and keep in touch. I just ignored her and got back into the car. I was ready to get back home and get back to work. As we were headed back home and I was going to my new foster home, I learned a lot about myself and this experience. I learned it's not about the fancy house you live in, how many things you buy for someone, or the people you may know. It's about treating people well, chasing your dreams, and supporting people. I learned that money cannot buy you happiness or love no matter what. I'm sure any other kid would've loved to have that house but sitting around all day was never me. I have been through too much in life to be basic and I wanted to work hard to get to new levels and accomplishments in life.

Back To Rockford

Finally, after a long drive to end this crazy night after having a taser pulled on me and having to ride in an ambulance to the hospital, I was finally back home in Rockford. I was told that my new foster home would be with a lady named Mrs. Tiffany. I had met this lady prior to living with her because I always saw her at the YMCA and Adam and her were good friends. Everything worked out great because she worked at the YMCA, that meant I would always have a ride to their and back from the gym. It was even better that she stayed in a nice subdivision in a neighborhood on the south side of Rockford next to the Cherryvale Mall. At least I wouldn't have to worry about living in a bad area of town like I used to. When I got to her house, I was given a room upstairs. The craziest thing I saw about this room was how many Oreos were on the shelves. There were at least 100 packs of Oreos of all different flavors. I had never seen so many in my life. To top that off, it was a very small and thin room, similar to Mrs. Milly's house but with no bunk bed. At the time there were a total of four people living with her. Me, Mrs. Tiffany, her son Brandon, and her sister. Mrs. Tiffany was like Mrs. Milly, she did not really talk much and always had a mean attitude. I was always nervous to talk to her because of how angry she always looked and sounded; this was probably one of the first women I was afraid of. I was afraid if I said the wrong thing at times, she would knock me out, or at least it looked like she would.

Being in foster care and experiencing as many homes as I have,

I never understood what was the point in being a foster parent if you just treat the kid like garbage? Nobody forced you to sign up and do this, so why do they feel the need to treat us as if we did something horrible to them? This always pissed me off because I knew it was about the money. Half of these foster parents were just in it for a check. I wish they would picture their kids in foster care and then see how that is so disgusting and pathetic. For a grown woman or a grown man to do that to a child and treat them the way they do is pathetic. It's even more pathetic of how the agency will place us foster kids in these types of homes. Then they wonder why a lot of foster kids end up in jail, dead or have some type of mental illness because we are treated like shit because we don't get shown real love and affection. Kids who grow up getting love from one of their parents or family members will never be able to understand a foster kid who didn't get any love from their parents, or family. The love we are shown or at least I was shown my whole life is do everything I say to do, and you won't be kicked out. There is no support, no involvement, no guidance or genuine love. It's all so conditional, and at this point in my life I look back and see that my whole entire life has been based off of conditional love even by my own sister, father, and entire dad's side of the family. I was sick of people at this point in my life. It is even harder when you open up to kids your age and they think you are crazy or don't really want to be your friend because they don't know how to give good advice or support you because of everything you have been through. Being a foster kid is one of the hardest things a child goes through in life because we are taught just to survive. You don't learn and develop like the rest of children do.

After about a week of living with Mrs. Tiffany, I was going back to the YMCA regularly. I would always catch a ride with Mrs. Tiffany on her way to work at the YMCA. I would be there sometimes for more than five hours or stay for almost the entire day. I was just so happy to be back and doing what I loved and that was working hard. It was an even greater feeling being able to play basketball again and see all my friends back at the gym. I was very happy to see a lot of my Auburn teammates again but it kind of sucked because they started asking me how I was doing. It was really fake to me at first because when I moved away not one of them messaged me, but I forgave them and just let it go. It's not good to hold grudges or get mad over little things in life because you have to learn you don't control anyone and so I just began to worry about myself and that's what I did a lot. It was nice to get back into my routine of going to the gym everyday and making 400-500 shots and working on my dribbling and driving to the rim game. I worked the hardest I had ever worked before when I moved in with Mrs. Tiffany spent all that time inside the gym. I was in a zone of just practicing all the time and working out. I loved this feeling of working hard and earning what you wanted. When you see progress and your hard work paying off, it becomes an addictive feeling and that was a feeling I wanted to chase. I never cared about trying to be something I was not, trying to fit in and be cool, talking to girls or getting myself into trouble. I just wanted to be successful in school and play basketball. I was very mature for my age because of everything I had gone through and it made me grow up more. I learned how to be independent and not an attention seeker. I learned the importance of hard work, faith, and consistency at a young age and these were the tools I was focused on. Outside of the basketball court I just wanted to grow my relationship with God, grow into a better man and not have any anger inside of me and be someone who was always nice, generous and respectful to everyone.

Most nights I did not have a ride home with Mrs. Tiffany because she stayed late every night. I usually would just walk to the city bus station and take the city bus home. I understood she was busy and had to make her money, so I was never rude about it. But this always sucked because it was January outside, and living in northern Illinois January is our coldest month of the year. It was below 30 degrees some days and snow and ice covered the ground as well. I ended up having to walk almost two miles to get to the city bus station. Then it took an hour to get to my stop, and once I got off the bus, I had to walk another two miles in the freezing cold home to Mrs. Tiffany's house because the nearest bus stop was at the McDonalds. But this never phased me because I loved the grind and I had to work with what I had and make the best of it. My love for working hard was greater than having to walk home in the snow and cold weather. I just made sure to always wear three coats and a pair of gloves.

Thank God when I did walk home it was in the safe area of Rockford because walking home at night in Rockford was not safe. The worst part about walking home was that I lost my key when I was living with Mrs. Tiffany and I couldn't get it replaced. I always ended up having to knock on the door and wait for her son or her sister to answer the door and they always took at least 15 to 30 minutes, sometimes even longer than this. Mind you, now I am standing outside for another 15 to 20 minutes waiting for them to answer the door. This was the worst part of being outside. It was even worse when some nights none of them would answer and I would have to stand outside for over an hour to wait for Mrs. Tiffany to get home. I would not be able to feel my jaw or ears, my nose was always running and freezing cold. I wish I did not lose my key to get inside otherwise things would have been a lot easier. Another thing that sucked about living with Mrs. Tiffany was that she only cooked on some Sunday's and the food only lasted enough for one plate. The rest of the house would have eaten it all or she would bring it to people at work. She also cooked egg rolls and sold them to people which made me even more hungry because the egg rolls smelled so good, but I was never allowed to have any. The only thing she had was those 100 cases of Oreos. When I asked her why she had all of these Oreos she told me in a very short and quiet response that they were for us kids to snack on. She had this and candy in jars. I was basically surviving off of Oreos and candy or if I got lucky and someone gave me a dollar, a McDonald's McChicken sandwich once I got off the city bus. I felt like I was living with Mrs. Milly again when it came to food. Her and Mrs. Milly were alike because they each had their own food in the fridge, but no one was allowed to eat it. The only difference was Mrs. Tiffany did not have a separate fridge to hide it; she just flat out told you not to eat her stuff with a nasty attitude. I didn't want to get knocked out by this lady, so I made sure I did not touch it. I was so hungry to the point where I was begging people at the gym for spare change to eat something off the dollar menu from McDonald's. I tried applying at all the jobs near me so I could start buying my own food and saving up money but none of them accepted my application or were hiring at the time. No matter how hungry I was though, I still did not wish I were living with Mrs. Johnson because I was happy.

When I was finally enrolled back into school, I was so happy because I would have food to eat again, given that we were given a free breakfast and lunch during the school day. I was also happy because I was getting to learn again and chase making the honor roll a second semester. I always loved school because education is everything and can give you a great job and life one day. Education would also be my way of chasing my dream of moving to Florida one day. I realized that during my senior year, I had now gone to three different high schools. I was not angry about it because I was used to moving a lot, but I was just happy to see all my childhood friends from middle school and from the YMCA again at East. Usually in Rockford, when you grow up on a certain side of town, you grow up with the same kids from middle school, sometimes elementary school and up. I grew up on the East side of Rockford, so I grew up with some of these kids from elementary but most of them from Lincoln middle school. It was crazy to see how much people changed and how different people looked and behaved from back in middle school to now. I used to see my friends in the hallway at East and hang out with them during gym class or at lunch, it was just great to see everyone again. But every day after school when I attended East High School, I had to walk home four miles. This was one of the hardest walks I ever had to do because of how much snow covered the sidewalks and how many busy roads I had to cross with the ground being all icy. I almost hated being a senior in high school because of how early I got out of school and how I never got a ride home. I had to walk home from Auburn and now East and it sucked. Usually, a student would love getting out of school early every day, but it got to the point where I hated it, and this was the worst part of my day.

I had gotten so used to walking so much that it was normal to me. My friends from school, the YMCA, and people around Rockford all thought I was crazy when they would see me walking. I always had kids in school ask me why I wore three coats every day in class and I told them about my walk home and not one of them offered me a ride or even believed me. I was never angry or mad at them because it was their car. It just sucked how they would notice me and honk at me as they kept driving down the street. But walking was the only choice I had, and I didn't mind it at all, it was a coping skill for me and space for me. They say some of the smartest people took walks to get better ideas and this is what I would do. Whenever I walked home, I always pictured myself living in Florida one day and never having to walk in the snow or be freezing again. This gave me the motivation and inspiration to stop complaining and start praying. I had faith that one day I would not have to be doing this anymore. One thing that sucked about walking home every day was how I always had frostbite on my feet from walking through the snow and cold. I was still never able to feel my jaw or ears from walking home because of how long it took. But Every time I would come inside, I could not talk because of how stiff my jaw was. This was the most painful part of the walk; I never thought my jaw would hurt so bad. But when it takes you over an hour to walk home in below zero weather, you can expect that. During this part of January, it was so cold outside to the point where we did not have school for three days because it was negative 22 degrees outside with a windchill of negative 44. It was one of the coldest winters I had ever experienced. But regardless of all of this, I still never wished I was living with Mrs. Johnson. I refused to allow myself to think that I wish I still were living with her because that would mean she won. I would not let her win; I was on a mission to prove her wrong.

After my two weeks of going to East High school, I felt happy again to be seeing all of my friends. The classwork was very easy, and I was getting through it and on track to graduate. But my 2-week time of being a student at East High School would come to a very abrupt end. I was called into my academic counselor's office one day. I did not understand why I was called into his office at the time because I had never met him and was taking all the classes I was required to take. I figured it was information on the graduation ceremony. When I got into his office, he shook my hand and asked me how I was doing and how school was going, just small talk. Then after about five minutes the shocking and horrible news came. The academic counselor told me I was missing a math class and East High School did not offer this math class, so I had to go to an Alternative School called Roosevelt High

School in order to take this math class to graduate. I felt like Mike Tyson just walked into the room and hit me with the hardest uppercut possible. My heart skipped a beat and my stomach dropped as soon as he said this. Now, I would have to be graduating from an alternative high school. A school for kids who did not have enough credits, meaning they failed a lot of classes, or the students that had been kicked out of regular school, or students who went here and were trying to get their G.E.D. Lastly, the school was also for women who got pregnant in high school and had to go there because this school also offered a daycare. I was so angry and confused when he told me this, I did not understand because I had never failed a class in high school in all my four years of going. What made things even worse was I was an honor roll student, and I was passing all of my classes. I was just so pissed off I had to stop myself from talking for a second. I felt like once again I was being knocked down in life.

As I calmed down and then asked him what the reason for this was, the academic counselor explained that the problem was when I went to Auburn High School my academic counselor did not check my transcripts well enough to see that my freshman and sophomore year when I attended Addison Trail High School it was a different school district and a different school system called district 88 not district 205. I took a math class called Pre-Algebra which did not count in district 205. Had my counselor at Auburn checked my credits instead of saying I was all on track and good for my senior year, none of this would have happened. It was an even bigger slap in the face to think all those times I got out of school early I could have been taking that class to graduate. I asked him if there was any other way that I could stay at this high school to graduate with this class and all of my friends and he told me the only way would be to take an online version of beginning Algebra with no teacher or instructor. The academic counselor then proceeded by saying if I failed this, I would have to attend summer school and would graduate late. I knew I sucked at math, so I had to keep it real with myself and know that if I was going to graduate high school on time, I would have to transfer to Roosevelt High School. After we finished that meeting, I walked home after school that day and cried. I felt like Mrs. Johnson won, my dad's side of the family won, and I was a failure having to graduate from an alternative high school. I did everything right academically through high school, I never failed a single class yet I'm being punished over a math class for a mistake that an academic counselor at Auburn made. I would have rather taken that uppercut from Mike Tyson in his prime then graduate from Roosevelt High School. But what was even a bigger slap in the face was I will be graduating high school with more credits than the required amount. I just had a bad night that night. That was one of the worst news I had received, and I felt like life sucked at the time and I just felt in total defeat. I remember asking God that night to just help me think positive and stop crying because I was so depressed. I didn't understand why I was thrown so many obstacles and hit over and over again when I did not bother anyone or start any trouble with anyone. All I was trying to do was the right thing. I already did not ask for much at all and was walking all over Rockford in the freezing cold, surviving off of Oreos, school lunches, and a McDonald's sandwich if I was lucky. I was tired of the bullshit that constantly kept happening to me over and over again in life. I felt like there was no use trying to be successful anymore because I would just keep getting hit over and over again until I finally gave up. I just didn't understand why an 18-year-old kid went through all this and didn't have any support from family or anyone.

I ended up attending the student orientation at Roosevelt High School later that week. As soon as I walked inside this place, I was ready to leave. I hated everything about this school, and I was only inside for thirty seconds. What made it even worse was I could see Mrs. Milly's house from here and all the memories of working hard at Auburn came back. It was just a very depressing time for me. We ended up having a week off of school so Roosevelt could process our papers and set up transportation. After I finished my week of being totally bored at Mrs. Tiffany's house, it was finally time to attend Roosevelt High School. It felt so pathetic waking up at 10:30am every day while walking a mile to get on the bus to go to school. I wanted to wake up at the normal time like all of my other friends. What sucked even more was riding over an hour to get to school, then only going to school for half a day. I was just angry and negative about this whole situation. On my first day at Roosevelt, I met all my teachers and it was explained that this school is a self-paced school, meaning you go at your own speed, so, however much work you complete in a day is up to you. It felt like even more of a waste of time because I was not even learning anymore, I was just working out of a book every day and doing the schoolwork all on my own. It was just embarrassing going to school here. It's mean to say, but I felt like I was in a school for slow people because of how easy it was, and the way things were set up. Even the teachers in school asked me why I was even in this type of a school because of how fast I was flying by with my work. Every day I felt so ashamed of myself, especially seeing all the kids who I remembered from normal school who were kicked out or had to leave. A lot of people made fun of the kids who went to Roosevelt because they knew this school was for "bad/slow" kids. I just had to learn to shut the hell up and focus on my schoolwork. I had to stay positive and stop being so negative. I found a positive quickly when I snapped out of being so negative and saw that I was right next to the YMCA so at least I could walk there every day.

After a week of attending Roosevelt, I started to think more positive and stay positive. I stopped caring what people thought about me and focused on my ultimate goal which was moving to Florida and starting a new life. When I would focus on the positive, I started seeing the good in this school. Like it was a good thing that I was served breakfast and lunch, so I did not have to go hungry all day or eat Oreos to fill my stomach up. I also gained a lot of determination and motivation to fly through this school, finish high school and pass my math class. It was nice with the way this school was set up. Being self-paced, I would just take my schoolbook home, ask all my teachers for all the assignments and complete them all at home. I would sit at the dining room table in Mrs. Tiffany's house for hours just doing work. On Friday, I asked my American Government teacher to give me all my assignments and when I got home, I sat at the dining room table all weekend long and finished 13 assignments. Then, I went to school on Monday and passed both of my final tests and was done with that class. I was knocking out high school quickly and going to have an early summer. Now I only had to take three classes at the time, and I finished two of the classes within a month of being at this school. I became a nerd and an obsessed student with finishing work. The other students and teachers looked at me crazy when I would come back to school after the weekend was over with nothing, but assignments completed. I was just very determined to graduate from this school and work to save up money and move to Florida. That was the only goal I had on my mind: to finish high school early.

While I was still working in the gym every day on my basketball game, I started getting better and better. I was very impressed and proud of myself when I finally made 10 3's in a row again. On top of this, I was flying through school. I was just making the most of my opportunities by working hard because that's what I knew how to do. Then one day I received an email to go to a basketball camp. I always received these types of emails and invites but I never accepted them or looked at them because I did not have the time or money. But that's when I looked back at my experience of going to that Tampa basketball camp, and that's when I figured this would be a great chance for me to get a basketball scholarship. I was not on a basketball team anymore, but I was working out every day and getting better, so this was my chance to prove myself. My motivation for going to the gym everyday was to prove these Addison Trail coaches wrong and show them that I was more than a practice squad player. It was time to get payback. I saw this camp had multiple locations like New York, Houston, Orlando, Atlanta and many other spots. This camp also had a list of all the former NBA and Division I players that attended this skills camp when they were younger. While I continued doing my research on this camp, I saw that it would work out perfectly. For the reason being, that all the camps were on weekends, so I wouldn't have to miss any school. This camp also provided recording footage of how you played at the camp, so I could use this footage to send to coaches and post on social media for my game to be seen by lots of people across the country and not just Rockford. God really sent me a blessing that I had to take advantage of. After how my senior year turned out with always feeling sad and angry, the right opportunity finally presented itself and it was time to take advantage of it and make the most of it. I was nervous how things would work out as far as getting to the camps and playing in them, but there was no time to be nervous.

When I brought this up to DCFS because, of course, I had to get their approval to leave the state. I also had to prove evidence to them that this was a legit camp and get all the paperwork together. I also had to persuade them into letting me go like usual. When I first told my caseworker about it, she immediately denied it saying, "you're in school, how are you going to get to the camp?" and all of these scenarios that would turn me off. DCFS was always so difficult and had held me back a lot in life from traveling and my opportunities with basketball and with not being able to play AAU. I couldn't even go to sleepovers without the entire home having a background check, so this turned a lot of friends off from me because they labeled me as "the police." But God came through and blessed me to find a way. I had some contact with my mom but not a lot at the time, usually every time I talked to her, if I prayed, and how I was doing. Talking to her was like talking to a broken record because it was the same thing and same questions all the time. Our conversations never went anywhere, and it was sad because a lot of kids have good relationships with their mom but I never had this. I ended up reaching out to my mom and we talked, and she told me to find a hotel room, find out how much the camp cost and then get back to her and I did just that. My caseworker also surprisingly came to help. She told me DCFS would pay for the basketball camp and this made me so happy. I was actually going to be able to attend this camp.

After discussing it more with my caseworker, she told me to pick the basketball camp in Atlanta. The reason being was she had a lifelong friend who lived in Atlanta and would be able to pick me up from the airport and bring me to my hotel room. This would help me save a lot of money because a Lyft or an Uber ride was very expensive. I also informed my caseworker that my mom sent me money to pay for my flight and pay for my hotel room, so this was one less issue that we had to check off of the list. The next thing was figuring out how I was going to get to the airport. Mrs. Tiffany did not give me any rides but only to the YMCA, so I had to figure this out. But my caseworker Gabby fixed this issue by setting up a way to buy me a bus ticket that takes me from Rockford, Illinois to the Chicago O'Hare Airport, and back when I returned from Atlanta. Ultimately ,it was the same bus I used for when I went to the basketball camp down in Tampa. The next step was finding out how I was going to eat and get around. I did not want to waste all my money with Uber and Lyft rides, so I made sure to find a hotel close enough to walk to the camp and back. As far as the food situation, my caseworker told me to just let her know when I wanted some food, and she would send me money through PayPal. It was amazing how everything worked out and I was approved to go to this basketball camp. It may not have been in the best fashion but with teamwork we made it happen. I was so lucky to have this great and caring woman Gabby as my caseworker because she actually cared about me and would have long talks with me unlike past caseworkers. I was just so happy because for so long I was feeling depressed, sad and ashamed while I was living with Mrs. Johnson about how my senior year of basketball went. Now I was going to be able to make up for all of this by attending this camp. I was leaving from March 1st through March 3rd and I was going to be in a new state and new city I had never been to before. I had three weeks to prepare for this camp and workout extra hard. But before leaving, I had one very important thing to get ready for, and that was my Valentine's Day giveaway in Chicago.

Valentine's Day Giveaway In Chicago

Even though I had left Mrs. Johnson's house I still wanted to follow through with my Valentine's Day giveaway in Chicago. I had already purchased 100 boxes of chocolates and 100 Valentine Day cards. But I did not find a location yet. But after two days, I found a place in Chicago who would allow me to come inside and hang out with these women. I found a women's shelter called Deborah's Place located on the west side of Chicago. I didn't want to just drop off the boxes and leave, I actually wanted to interact, make new friendships, memories and ultimately make these women feel special for Valentine's Day. I understood they were not in the best financial position or emotional position being in a homeless shelter and think no matter how much money you have or what you have accomplished in life every woman and man deserves to know how beautiful, handsome and special they truly are. A lot of people are sold short in life because they don't understand their self-worth and value, and this causes them to fail or let people mistreat them. But I made sure to hand write a positive and inspiring message in all 100 cards. It took me a few hours to do but it was worth it. But again, I had another obstacle to face in completing this giveaway. Of course, this time that obstacle was once again, finding a ride there and back. My case worker Gabby came through and helped me out once again. She always used to make me laugh by asking me if I thought she was my personal taxi driver. I was 18 and still had no license which was frustrating when you see kids who are 16 years old with one. I took Drivers Ed my junior year when I was attending Harlem. I had my driver's permit and passed the class but none of my foster parents, friends, or family helped me out by letting me use their car to drive in order to get my license. If one of my friends was willing, they didn't have car insurance so this was an automatic ticket that could lead to an arrest and I was not trying to go to jail.

Prior to leaving, I made sure I had all 100 boxes of chocolate and all 100 of my cards ready to go. On Valentine's Day, I wanted to look professional and presentable, so I was a little extra and wore a button up shirt with a vest cover. I was very excited to meet these women and be able to make new friends while inspiring them and lifting them up for the day. When Gabby came to pick me up, she informed me that we had to stop by Mrs. Johnson's house because I had a check at her house from my job at the movie theater and my box of chocolate was on her front porch. I hoped this would be the last time I ever had to see this place again. It frustrated me to get text messages from my friends at Addison Trail telling me that Mrs. Johnson was spreading rumors about me to the students now, but the people who knew me were smart enough to know there are always two sides to every story. Regardless of anything that she was saying, it didn't matter to me anymore because I moved on from that and had to learn to ignore it. I did not want to carry any hate in my heart or anger anymore. I have been angry for too long and want to be happy. My only goal now was to kill her with success because that is the ultimate payback on anyone. I was going to show her that I grew into a great man and was successful regardless. That was not only for her but for all my former foster parents, my dad's side of the family and anyone else who doubted me. Without them, there would've been any motivation or drive to work as hard as I did to become successful and prove them wrong. It was all a part of God's plan for me. I just had to trust it and stay on the right path.

When we finally arrived in Addison after a little over an hour drive, we stopped at Mrs. Johnson's house to pick up my check and to grab my big box of chocolates. Those instant negative memories hit me from the last time of having the police pull a taser out on me and having to leave in an ambulance. At least now my last memory would be grabbing my stuff to head to my giveaway in Chicago. Before we headed to Chicago, I told Gabby to stop at Chase bank so I could deposit my check in the bank. When I opened my check, I was surprised at how much money I had earned from the movie theaters. I guess those blisters on my hand and sore legs and back were worth it after all. Once my check was cashed, I told Gabby to stop by the Dollar Tree Store and little Caesars Pizza, so that everyone was able to get some food for this event. I personally think that there is nothing better to bring people together than some fresh hot pizza and soda. So, I went inside the Dollar Tree and bought seven bottles of soda. Then I went inside of Little Caesars and bought nine boxes of pizza for everyone. Once I got all the food, we packed the sodas in the back, and I held the hot pizzas on my lap. As they burned my leg, we headed to the best city in the world, Chicago. On our way to Chicago, we passed by Lutherbrook Child and Adolescent center and I showed my caseworker where I used to live. She was in shock because of how run down it looked and some of the things I told her during my two years inside of there. I started to get watery eyed and emotional just remembering how far I had come in life. I know one day my story will make sense to me like God has planned. But I couldn't believe people were looking forward to me coming to do a giveaway for them and cheer them up. I had grown so much from then to now and I only wanted to keep growing in life. Seeing this gave me the confirmation from God that I was doing the right thing and gave me the motivation to keep working hard in life because anything is possible. I knew that understanding the importance of and applying hard work, consistency, self-confidence, and faith to my life will take me places I never thought of going one day. I was only getting started in my life.

After another 30 minutes of driving, we finally arrived in Chicago and were at Deborah's Place. When we pulled up to this huge brick building, there was a woman standing outside waiting for us. As we got out of the car, we were greeted by this very nice woman who was one of the managers of the place. As I unloaded the car, she was in complete happiness and shock to see everything I had brought with me. That's when the lady used her walkie talkie to call another worker and told her to grab a cart for all the stuff. We started unloading the pizzas, sodas, and boxes of chocolate onto the cart instead of going back and forth trying to carry all of it. Once we got inside, we were taken through a long hallway with a security scan in. After we passed the security scan, we were taken a little further into a room where lots of tables and chairs were set up very neatly. This was called the rec area, where the ladies did their activities. Gabby and I then started setting everything up by placing the pizza in order from cheese, peperoni, and sausage. Then I got all the sodas lined up and placed a Valentine's Day card on top of every box of chocolate. My caseworker Gabby was going to hand out the pizza and the manager was going to pour the sodas for each lady. It helped out a lot because she grabbed paper plates and cups because I forgot them.

Once the ladies came down, they were all so shocked and happy to see everything all set up. I was surprised that I was not as nervous to meet all of them like I was when I first arrived. I hated being nervous and shy because I was a legal adult now and it was time for me to grow up from that. It made me so happy to see the smiles and happiness on everyone's face during this time. With so much violence and crime going on in this world and in the city of Chicago, and with these ladies being in an unfortunate situation, I wanted to help add happiness and laughter to their day. I could understand how most of them were feeling because I was in this situation before when I was at Aunt Martha's and Nachusa Shelter Home. Also, at a young age, I was inside of a shelter with my mother because we had nowhere to go some nights. One memory in particular that stands out was when my mother told me and my older sister that we were going to a carnival. We were in the car for hours that night and ended up having to sleep in a car because we had nowhere to go. She just told us we were going to a carnival because she did not want to give us the reality of what was really going on. The situation brought me back to when I woke up sleeping on the floor in a shelter while my mom and sister had shared a bed. Doing stuff like this made me feel like it was my job because I felt like these were my people, even though we are not family and we are not related. It's the struggle that brings people together and helps people overcome hard times together. I gained inspiration to give to people when one of my favorite staff members at Lutherbrook named Anthony Battle gave me new Jordan's, pants and shirts. He taught me the importance of giving to people because in the Bible it says to be generous and you will receive blessings back.

We stayed at Deborah's Place for about an hour and a half. We all sat around and enjoyed eating some pizza and talking as I was thanked by every beautiful lady there. After a while, one of the managers made me stand in the middle to introduce myself to everyone because I didn't get a chance to talk to all of the ladies. I started to get nervous, as I was beginning to introduce myself, but I took a deep breath and cut that out quickly. I got up and introduced myself by saying my name and that I was a senior in high school. I told them that I was 18 years old and my goal was to move to Florida one day and go to college and play college basketball. All the ladies clapped loudly and cheered for me. I was in awe because I have never had that type of applause in my life. I couldn't believe people were actually cheering for me outside of a basketball game. It was an amazing feeling I will never forget. It was also crazy how everyone was in shock that I was only 18 at the time. I never thought my age would shock people. I just felt very loved and appreciated during this time. I never really have ever had that feeling in my life, it made me feel awkward. I was always so used to feeling like I was trash being in foster care and being a foster kid. I felt like nobody really cared about me because I was just a check to people being in the system. I felt it even more when my dad's side of the family and my older sister betrayed me. I always felt alone and like I had nobody, because in reality I didn't have anybody or any support. But this showed me that I'm more than a check and that I do have support from people in this world, it may not be a lot, or in a traditional family, but I sure have a start with these women. This Valentine's Day Giveaway showed me that I am a decent young man, and I can be an even greater man one day. My ultimate goal one day is to be a motivational speaker, have a wife and kids, and be a loving father and husband, something that my father never was.

During this event, I noticed how much of a positive impact I can make on people's lives by just being nice and doing kind things like this. Instead of spending money on some new shoes and clothes, people can spend money on something like this and have a bigger impact and make a memory forever. God gave me a sign that I will never forget and a vision of the man I wanted to and can become once again. As we were getting ready to leave, I wanted to get a group picture with these beautiful ladies so I could always remember this moment. I was given lots of great support and motivation from them to keep on working hard in life, never give up and to keep growing as a man. Kind words that meant a lot to me, words that I was not used to hearing. When it was time to leave, I walked with the manager who came outside to greet me. She thanked me for everything, and she told me I always have love and support with them. Also, if I was ever going through a hard time to give them a call and they will help cheer me up. I was just so very grateful for God to lay this on my heart to do. Even more grateful to have met all these fantastic people. This was something in my life that I will never forget and something that can never be taken away from me. As I said goodbye, I gave the lady a hug and thanked her for everything. Once we got inside the car and started driving home, I started thinking to myself that this is who I want to become one day. This is what I would love to do as a more common thing and that is helping people by motivating them in these tough situations. I wanted to inspire people in these situations and circumstances and encourage people that they don't have to play the victim and let these events hold them back from shining for the rest of their life. I want to show people that just because they've had a hard time in life and things may not have been fair, even if they've fallen and failed over and over again, it does not mean that they can't get back up and overcome this to be successful. That just because people grow up in the hood, or in a crime filled city they don't have to be a product of that environment.. On Valentine's Day of 2019 I will forever remember this moment for the rest of my life because of the beautiful, strong, and amazing women at Deborah's Place in Chicago, Illinois.

Getting Ready For Atlanta

When I got back to Mrs. Tiffany's house after an amazing and inspiring day, I wrote a letter to myself about what I was feeling that night before I went to bed. The same gentleman from Lutherbrook, Anthony Battle who taught me the importance of generosity when he used to give us kids nice shoes and clothes, taught me the importance of writing to yourself. Anthony told me that it's not only a coping skill to help control your mind and be aware of how you feel but also, how later on in life you will be able to look back and see how much you have grown. That night I wrote in my notes that one day I wanted to write a book about everything that has happened to me so far in life to help inspire people. Also, I wanted to continue to do more giveaways not just on holidays but at random times too. Lastly, I wanted to be a motivational speaker. I was given a lot of compliments and advice on the things that I've gone through that I thought it would be an amazing story to inspire and tell others one day. After I finished writing in my journal, I started to pack and get ready to leave for my basketball camp in Atlanta. I was so excited because I have always heard great things about this city and how cool it is there. I was even more excited to play basketball and be wearing a jersey again. God blessed me with an opportunity to have my name put out there where I am provided with films of me playing in games, so that people across the country would hopefully see it. I was just so thankful God gave me another chance to do the thing that I love which was play the game of basketball.

There was only a week and a half until I left for my basketball camp in Atlanta. I made sure every day to practice hard. I worked on nothing but form shooting, a quick release, my footwork, and shooting on and off the dribble every time I would do my routine of shooting and making 400 shots. I also made sure to be on my best behavior on and off the court. The last thing I wanted to have happen was being told I could not go over something stupid. But unfortunately, something like this happened to me. The day before leaving for basketball camp, I did my regular routine of making 400 shots and then working on my dribbling moves to the rim. I had a great workout and was feeling very confident in myself. While I was heading out the door, I walked past one of the basketball courts and a little kid shot a basketball from half court and completely airballed it. I just happened to be right below the rim as the ball was coming down. When I went to block the ball from smacking me in the face my ring finger bent all the way back and I felt and heard a crack. Automatically, my ring finger on my left hand began to swell and I could not move it. I grabbed my hand for at least a minute and did not move. I thought I jammed it but it was super hard to move and it did not feel like a jammed finger. After holding my left hand in pain, I walked to the subway inside of the YMCA to put some ice on it. I had never felt so much throbbing pain in my finger before. What was even worse was it just kept swelling up. I walked to the city bus station holding my finger in pain. The entire ride home I kept trying to move it but the pain got worse and worse and the more it hurt. I called my caseworker that night and told her I needed to go to the doctor because the pain in my finger was unreal. She was unable to take me that night, so I had to wait until the morning. But I ended up falling asleep that night with an icepack on my finger, hoping the next day everything would be better. The last thing I wanted was to be told I can't go to camp because of my finger.

When I woke up the next morning my finger was completely swollen, if a finger was able to get pregnant, then my finger was 9 months pregnant. It was so stiff that I could barely move it at all. I had never seen a finger change colors before either, it was all blue and purple. When my caseworker Gabby came to pick me up that morning to take me to the doctor and give me my bus ticket, she took one look at my finger and told me it was broken. She was totally disgusted, and she scared me because I thought I was going to make her throw up for a second. I started to panic right away when she reacted like that. I felt my anxiety go straight up to the point where I was about to have a panic attack. I had never broken anything in my life. She drove me to the doctor and when we got to the doctor, they did x-rays. Once the results came back, the doctor confirmed that my finger was broken. A part of the bone in my left ring finger was chipped off. He told me that I would need 6-weeks off to rest it and not to play basketball in that 6-week time until I went to physical therapy and strengthened my finger back up. I got defensive and told the doctor that I was getting on a flight later today to go to a basketball camp in Atlanta. My caseworker ended up leaving the room to call her supervisor and to tell her what had happened. The doctor ended up taping my finger, giving me pain medication, and a medal splint to keep my finger in place. Once my caseworker Gabby came back inside the room, we talked to her supervisor on the phone along with two other people from the agency. The foster care agency told me that I should not go to the camp for my own benefit and that this was a health hazard. I immediately got defensive again and denied it, there was nothing that was going to stop me from going. They told me fine and that if I broke my finger even more not to be crying about it later. Shortly after I got off the phone with the agency another doctor came in who was a hand doctor and examined my finger. I explained to him that I was leaving for a basketball camp later that day. The hand doctor told me the best thing to do was to wrap two fingers together really tight so it can't bend it or damage it more. So, that's exactly what he did, and I took my medal splint along with my pain killers and we left. It felt really weird having this on my finger but there was nothing that was going to stop me from going, especially after all the hard work I put in. I had been knocked down too many times and this time I was not going to fall, I just stumbled a little. I did not want to waste this great opportunity over a finger.

After we left the doctor's office, my caseworker dropped me off at school and she told me she would be able to pick me up and take me to the bus station that would take me to the airport. While I was in school, I hid my finger inside of my pocket because I did not want to gross anyone out or bring any attention to myself. I just shut up and did a lot of my schoolwork. Once school was over, my case worker was right on time to pick me up and take me to the bus station. While we were in the car she asked me multiple times if I was sure I wanted to go, and I said yes every time. There was nothing that was going to stop me from attending that basketball camp. When we arrived, she handed me my ticket and I said goodbye to her, and I got on the bus going to the airport. My caseworker Gabby then texted me her friend's phone number to call her once I landed so she could come and pick me up. Once I got on the bus I started laughing to myself because of how much I felt like an adult. Here I am riding a bus, getting checked by security and traveling to different cities all by myself. It was just really cool and funny at the same time to think how I used to hate traveling and now I actually enjoy seeing the world. After my hour bus ride to the Chicago O'Hare airport, I grabbed my boarding pass from the computer and headed through the security check out line. I was happy the line was not as long as last time when I flew out to Tampa. When it was my turn to go through security I took my shoes, belt, coat, hat, and backpack off putting it through the scan. I also emptied my pockets removing my phone, wallet and wallet. But as I was going through security I forgot to take the metal splint out of my pocket and the alarm went off. I had all the people staring at me as if I were some terrorist with a bomb in my pocket. The TSA worker told me to get out of line and step to the side and I had to be patted down by an officer. This was embarrassing because he was patting me down thoroughly, meaning touching my butt and groin area. What made it even more embarrassing was it was a man doing this not a woman while a crowd of people were looking at me. When he told me to go inside my pants pocket and take out my medal splint, he asked what it was for in a stern voice and I showed him it was for my finger. The officer then asked me what happened to see if I was lying and I told him what happened and where I was going. At least he gave me a compliment by telling me I was a tough kid for still going to play basketball with a broken finger, especially since I just broke it yesterday. But I will always remember to take everything out of my pockets the next time I go through security.

After that unforgettably weird encounter, I went to find my gate. This time I did not need a lot of help because I knew how to read my ticket now. I know Mrs. Milly would have been proud of me this time unlike the last time after she talked to me for about 40 minutes on how to go through the airport and find my gate and I still couldn't do it by myself. Once I got to my gate, I sat there for an hour and I waited until it was time to board the plane. While I was sitting down I was not as nervous to board the plane as I was when I flew out to Tampa. I ended up watching some cartoons on my phone to keep me from overthinking and to pass time. After about 45 minutes passed by it was time to board the plane. I tried so hard not to overthink and be nervous. I failed and anxiety took over. Once I stepped onto that plane, my anxiety started going up and I had to take some deep breaths to calm down. I tried to use the coping skills of distracting myself by being happy because I had a window seat and I focused on all the beautiful night lights of Chicago from the window. I had never flown before at night, so this helped out a little. Then I checked the weather app before being told to shut my phone off for takeoff and I was happy that the weather in Atlanta was 60 degrees compared to 25-30 degrees on a very cold day in Illinois. As I began to take both of my jackets off I felt the plane moving for takeoff. My heart started racing and my stomach was upset out of nowhere. I felt like I had to take the biggest dump on the toilet in my life. Once the plane got closer to taking off I started praying harder and harder and asking God to keep me safe and forgive me for eating one of Mrs. Tiffany's Jello snacks. I didn't mean to eat it and I wasn't a thief, but I was so hungry that night. I just kept praying and praying and then the plane went from 0 to 100 as if the Drake song just came on. I grabbed the handles on my seat and held on tight and I just kept praying and eventually the plane took off. I remembered what someone once told me, "Faith can move mountains." I kept my faith and relaxed and kept telling myself everything was going to be okay.

After an hour and a half in the air, the plane finally landed. To keep my mind off of being scared I wrote a letter to myself about how I was feeling going into this camp and what I wanted to accomplish. I wrote: score 20 points (because I've never scored that much but I didn't know if I would be able to with a broken finger). Once it was time to start getting off of the plane, I grabbed my backpack and texted my caseworker's friend who was supposed to be picking me up. As I went through the Atlanta airport, I was in complete awe. I was just amazed at how big this airport was. I have always heard how big the Hartsfield-Jackson Atlanta International Airport was but seeing it in person was a whole different level of huge. There were so many restaurants and stores everywhere; it was like being in a huge mall rather than an airport. I had never seen a Buffalo Wild Wings sit down restaurant in any airport ever and that was the coolest thing I saw and I thought Atlanta was an amazing city already. This was the first airport I ever heard hip hop music playing, and I remembered my caseworker telling me that Atlanta is a big hip hop and music industrial city and they have music playing everywhere. It was one of the coolest experiences ever being inside of that airport.

As I gathered my thoughts, I asked for help on how to get outside to find my ride. This airport was so big and had so many areas to get picked up from I had no idea where I was going. My caseworker's friend was getting mad at me because of how long I was taking so I had to hurry up. I couldn't blame her because I spent about 20 minutes taking pictures and walking around. When I finally explained where I was at correctly and stopped confusing her, I got in the car and met her. My first impression was that this lady was very nice. We started talking and she told me all about Atlanta, how much she loved it, and how much opportunity is available for African American people like myself. She was telling me all about the HBCU's (Historically Black Colleges & Universities) here and how great they were. I didn't know I could get enrolled in one of those institutions because I was not fully black. I was half black and when I asked her if it was possible for me to get in one of those because I was half black she started laughing and said "you don't have to be black." I saw the beautiful gold triangles on top of the buildings in Atlanta and the huge Ferris wheel. I knew while I was down here I wanted to check downtown Atlanta out. This lady was a huge help to me because she took me to the store to grab groceries and dropped me off at my hotel. If it was not for her, I would have had to spend a lot of money on a Lyft and an Uber. When I got back inside the car and she saw me with my groceries, which was bread, peanut butter, and jelly she told me I was crazy. "Atlanta has some of the best food in America, haven't you heard of a waffle house?" I understood what she was saying but I told her that I hated spending money going out to eat and buying food from restaurants because of how expensive it was, and I wanted to save the money I was given. I also told her all I'm going to do is finish my plate in 10 minutes then poop it out later so I would rather buy a shirt or shoes and she started laughing. She probably thought I was a comedian but I was being serious.

After we said our goodbyes, I went and checked into my hotel room. While I was at the front desk checking in, I was given a card to swipe in and out and explained the rules of the hotel. I asked him if this hotel served a complimentary breakfast in the morning because I did not want to go to the camp in the morning hungry and the man said yes. That was a plus, at least now I did not have to eat peanut butter and jelly sandwiches the entire time I was here. I headed upstairs to the third floor and when I got to my hotel room I was so happy. It was even better because the Chicago Bulls vs the Atlanta Hawks game was on and they were in 3rd overtime and I finally had cable to watch it. I turned on the game and ate a couple of peanut butter and jelly sandwiches and celebrated the Bulls victory. I thought it was cool how the Chicago Bulls were in Atlanta the same time I was. Speaking of basketball, I went to check my phone because Auburn and East were playing in another sold out playoff game and whichever team lost their season would be over. I saw that Auburn lost that game. I felt sad about it and I reached out to all my old teammates congratulating all of them on a great year. I wish I could've played with those guys, those were some of the best teammates I ever had. The best basketball school I ever attended. But now it was my time to play and go out and see what I could do. Even though I had a broken finger I still was not going to be discouraged or make excuses for myself, I was ready to play basketball and show that all the hard work I put in was going to pay off. I was ready to use all the people who doubted me and everything I had been through as motivation to be successful at this camp.

Atlanta Basketball Camp

I woke up at 8am the next morning and it was time for the first day of camp to start. I did not have to arrive until 10:30 am but I wanted to make sure I was warmed up before I left. I grabbed my basketball, laid down in my king size bed and just did form shooting in the air over and over again. I wanted to make sure my form was on point, despite having a broken finger on my guide hand. Once I finished doing this, I got dressed, packed my bag, and headed downstairs. I smelled breakfast as I entered the lobby. It was amazing to be eating real food instead of Oreos and peanut butter and jelly sandwiches. The hotel breakfast offered pancakes, waffles, yogurt, bagels, cereal, eggs, fruit, biscuits and gravy, and a juice machine. I did not want to pig out because it would give me a stomachache, so I made two plates and went back upstairs and put them in the room fridge for later. At least now I would not have to eat peanut butter and jelly sandwiches the entire time I was in Atlanta. I went back downstairs and made another plate of breakfast. This food tasted so good, I had to stop myself from eating so much.

I walked to the high school where this basketball camp was being held. I used the G.P.S. on my phone to guide me. It was nice that the school was only two miles away, this made for a short walk. It was even better that it was so nice outside and I finally got to feel the feeling of warm Georgia weather. There was no snow on the ground, it was not freezing cold outside, it was just a beautiful 60-degree day in early March. I was hesitant at first walking in an area where I had never been before, but the area was safe and had nothing but nice restaurants and stores all around. When I arrived at the camp, I saw a parking lot full of cars. I also started seeing a lot of kids going inside with their parents with a basketball in their hand. I did not bring my basketball because it was not mandatory, and I did not want mine to get stolen. I did not have the money to replace it so I thought it was better to be safe than sorry. Once I got inside of the gym, there was a piece of paper on top of every jersey with the player's name on it. I found mine and put my jersey on over my undershirt and sat in my line waiting for further instruction.

Once more and more players started coming in, the introduction began. It started off with the man who ran this camp and he explained a little bit about himself and what he does. Then there were 7 or 8 different college basketball coaches and each coach came out and explained who they were and their background to the game of basketball. Every coach there would be watching us and was either the assistant or main head coach to a college in Georgia, from Division I to Division II. I thought this was the perfect opportunity for me to get a college scholarship with college coaches watching and coaching us for two days. I was going to make sure I had a great attitude and worked very hard at everything while trying to be a good teammate. I kept that in mind because the college coaches told us they want to see hard workers, good teammates, smart shots, and good attitudes in players. The coaches also explained the importance of grades in school and having fun on the court. After the introductions, we were broken up into groups and began our basketball drills for the day. We did a lot of basic drills for the first hour and a half like shooting drills, layup drills, 2 on 2 scoring drills and defensive closeout drills. The basic drills that you do in high school. Instead of feeling nervous like usual, I felt very confident because I worked on this all the time while I was at the YMCA. When there was a brief break, I talked to a few of the players and ask wed where they were from and what grade they were in. All of the players at this camp were very friendly and a lot of players were from the south and they all had a different type of accent. I was the only player from the midwest in attendance, everyone else was from different states in the south like Alabama, Florida, Georgia,

Mississippi, South Carolina, or Tennessee. I had never met anyone from these states before besides Florida, so it was a very cool experience.

After an hour and half we were put back into our groups. The man who ran the camp told us they had already picked out teams, and our teams were all the players in each line that we were currently lined up in. It was nice because I had already met all the players who I was playing with from the drills. We were informed about the court assignments for each team and informed that their records would be tracked to determine which team would be the best at the camp. All of the players in my group looked at each other and we were all thinking the same thing: we better win this thing. I really appreciated when he said that because it made the camp even more enjoyable, adding a heightened sense of competition. We were told each team would have a coach that would coach us during each game, and for every ten minutes played, we would all come out of the game for the next five to come in so everyone got a chance to play.

Once the games started, that confidence in myself during the drills went away and I was instantly nervous. I looked around and saw all of these college coaches in front of me and all these other players who were a lot bigger and stronger than me. I thought I was going to embarrass myself in this camp or that someone was either going to break my ankles or dunk on me and none of these coaches would want to talk to me. I hated that I always lacked confidence in myself and thought so negatively all the time. Then again I never really had anybody in life teach me these things going from foster home to foster home and nobody ever came to watch me play so that was probably a big reason why. But I stopped using this as an excuse for myself, I took a deep breath, made sure my broken finger was taped up tight, and I got ready to play. After the first two games, I ended up scoring ten points in each game and was playing well with a broken finger. I was surprised at the good passes, shots, and defense I was playing during those two games. I was impressed with my performance and proved myself wrong. I still had no coach come up to talk to me yet, but I knew if I could score more eventually, they would come. I just kept thinking positive and taking deep breaths trying not to overthink or play nervous. We were 2 and 0 and hadn't lost a game yet. In between games, I ended up watching some of the other players and I always wished I would have done more weightlifting on my legs. I wish I would have practiced jumping as well so I could dunk the ball. I knew if I were able to dunk I would impress a lot more coaches. I needed to get a lot stronger as well because a lot of these players were way stronger than me and could jump high in the air. I stopped letting this kill the confidence in myself and instead used this to inspire me to work harder. I know that anything is possible with hard work. Now, when I got back home, I just needed to hit the weight room, lift more, and focus on improving my vertical jump.

After the first day I was feeling pretty good about myself as I walked back to my hotel room. I was super hungry from playing basketball for hours and I walked past a couple of nice restaurants and fast-food places, but I did not want to waste my money on food. I went back to my hotel room and ate the plates I had saved from the free breakfast that the hotel offered. I wish I did not kill both plates so I could've saved some for dinner, but I was too hungry and not used to eating actual food like this after eating Oreos, Ramon noodles and McChickens for so long. Once I finished eating, I got changed into a nicer outfit to go see downtown Atlanta. I was trying to figure out how to go downtown without paying for an Uber because that would cost me over $20. I ended up going downstairs to the hotel lobby and asking the lady at the front desk how to go downtown. I figured she lives here so she must know. She told me that there was a bus that would come by and take me to the bus station.Then, I had to get on the Metra train with a card. Then once on the Metra train, it would take me to different spots around the city and I had to get off at the stop that says downtown. I stopped listening after she said you get off the bus and take a train. There was no way I was going to be able to make it downtown figuring all of this out for the first time by myself, I was for sure going to get lost. I had a Rockford Public School education, I knew I was not that smart. But I did not want to pay $30 to go downtown and another $30 to come back, so my determination kicked in and I figured I would just ask the other people on the bus who took the bus regularly with help getting downtown. If it were not for that amazing Ferris wheel I saw when I was in the car with my caseworkers friend, I probably would not have gone but I wanted to get on that Ferris wheel.

It was around 7pm at night when I finally decided to head out to catch the next bus that was heading downtown. While I was standing on the bus corner, an old man was standing there as well. I was always an outgoing person and was not shy to talk to people, I figured he lived here so I asked him how to get downtown. He pretty much told me the same thing that the lady at the hotel said, only this time he gave me the bus stop names, and train stop names. I guess this helped out a lot more, but I still had no idea what I was doing or where I was going. I put these stop names in my notes and thought it would help more if I wrote it down so I would not forget. While the old man was explaining how to get downtown, apparently I would have to take two different buses and go through five different train stops to get there using the public transportation system. In my head I thought I should just pay the $30 and stop talking this old man's ear off before he goes deaf from hearing me ask the same question. I checked my bank account and I was very close to being completely broke with no money in my account, I still needed this money to get to the airport and go home. So, I ended up asking him about two more times how to get downtown and to give more detail and the old man said he would just take me downtown and go with me. I think I talked his ear off and annoyed him enough into taking me. I was surprised that he didn't just tell me to "shut the hell up" but instead he said he would show me. Usually back home, people would not even talk to you or they would try and set you up if they agreed to doing this. I made sure I was on alert the entire time, I did not know if he wanted to get rid of my annoying ass or try and sexually touch me, either way if it came down to it, I was going to have to beat an old man up that day if he tried anything.

Once the bus finally came, we both got on the bus and he sat next to me and explained each stop and where we were going. I couldn't believe how nice this old man was to me and how he took the time to show me this. I felt like I learned so much about Atlanta and I had not even been here a full day yet. We rode the bus for about 30 minutes and then we finally got to the bus station. The bus station and the buses were so much nicer than the city buses back home in Rockford. They had nice comfortable cushion seats and clean isles. The ones back home had bugs crawling through the seats at times, so you always had to be cautious of what seat you sat in when going to sit down. This bus station even had huge escalators and signs everywhere with how to get to and from an area. Each bus also had a big sign of what stops it would be taking you to. This made things a lot easier and was a lot more convenient for people traveling. Then the old man started explaining the entire bus station to me, and when we got on and went up the escalators, that's when I saw the train stop. I had never been on a train before or inside of a subway, so this was new and interesting to me. I was shocked that there was no gate preventing you from falling onto the track, someone could push you on and you would be dead in an instant. I was shocked to see how many people were standing so close to the edge. I made sure that I stood all the way back and grabbed something to hang onto every time because I was not trying to die while I was on vacation. When the train finally arrived, we got on and he explained the different areas of Atlanta and the different stops that were ahead. He also explained the map to me on the wall and the different train lines of how to go where. It was like I had my own personal tour guide with me but this one was for free. I started to let my guard down more and see that this man was just being genuinely nice to me. I was not used to this type of stuff, nobody was usually nice to me. While we were riding, the old man pointed out this famous mall called Lenox Square and another area called Buckhead. I guess this was where all the famous people in Atlanta lived. He said, "if a young cat like yourself is trying to pick up an Atlanta girl, stop inside before you leave." At least I knew he was not gay when he said this, so I let my guard down even more.

After an hour and over six stops later, we finally made it to our destination. I was exhausted by this time because of how long it took to get downtown, but at least we finally made it. Once we both got off at the train, I made sure to write down everything he said because he told me he would not be riding back with me. I was nervous because I had to figure out how to get back to my hotel on my own. I showed him my notes for him to check, and he told me everything was good.

I thanked this old man for everything, but he walked off so fast to join his group of friends that I didn't even get his name. When I put my phone in my pocket and got out of the subway, I went up a long flight of stairs. I was wondering where these stairs were taking me to but once I got to the last step I was in shock. I saw the huge and brand-new stadium of the Atlanta Falcons and it was amazing. The Super Bowl was just held there a month before, and the city was still selling cups with the logo on it. Luckily, that night inside the Falcons Stadium they were hosting a huge Monster Truck event. As I walked over towards the stadium to have someone take my picture, one of the workers offered me a free Monster drink because of the event. I was so happy because this helped me get even more energized because I was sleepy. I couldn't help but stare at the incredible stadium, and when I looked across, I saw the Atlanta Hawks Stadium. I thought it was so cool to have both stadiums right next to each other.

As I continued exploring downtown Atlanta, I saw the CNN headquarters and the big Ferris wheel right next to Olympic Park. I always saw pictures of all these things in books or on TV, but to actually be here in person was a surreal feeling. I could not help but laugh remembering being at Lutherbrook and all of us watching Love and Hip-hop Atlanta and asking questions about what the city of Atlanta was like. Now I was here in person, that was something that I will never forget. I ended up paying to get on the Ferris wheel and I almost had a panic attack because of how high up it went and how small that little box was. That machine moved so fast and rocked the box back and forth, so I made sure to sit extra still. I soon regretted getting on it because of how scared I was. I guess heights are just not my thing. But I stopped and pulled myself together and focused on the beautiful view of the city of Atlanta. After the ride I took pictures and explored downtown some more and decided to head back to the subway and go back to my hotel. I was reading my notes the entire time and making sure I knew and understood how to get back to the hotel. I followed all the directions the old man told me to use and he was right after all. I knew exactly which stop was mine and knew where to get off. Eventually, I made it back to the bus station. Now, the only downfall was the buses were done for the night because it was late. But

I couldn't complain, my day was made. I even got luckier when I went to take an Uber back to the hotel because it was only $22 instead of $30. I was a bit bummed that I wasted some money, but I had fun and enjoyed myself. I was really grateful to have met that old man and for him showing me how to get to and from downtown. At least now if I ever decide to come back to Atlanta one day, I know how to get back downtown thanks to him. After my Uber dropped me back off to my hotel room, I ate a peanut butter and jelly sandwich for dinner, took care of my hygiene and went to sleep. I had to get up early again for the last day of camp and I wanted to make sure I gave it everything I had so one of these coaches would talk to me.

On the last day of camp,I followed the same routine as the previous morning, lying on my king-sized bed and repeatedly practicing form-shooting in the air. Then, I went downstairs to the hotel lobby, ate breakfast and left to walk for camp. It felt good walking into the last day of camp knowing my team was undefeated so far. The only thing we needed to do now was win the championship. When I got inside, we got into our groups and lined up waiting for instructions. This time we did not have to do any drills, so we got right into playing our games. During our first two games, we ended up winning them both and my team was still undefeated. It helped having a D1 point guard from Alabama and another D1 guard from Mississippi who could throw the ball down and win games. As far as my performance, I still managed to have 10 points each game. In four games I had a total of 40 points, and this was pathetic because I wanted to score over 10 points. I had never scored over 18 points in a basketball game before and I was looking to break that streak. Regardless if I had a broken finger or not, I came here to show these coaches that I could play and all the hard work I had been putting in the gym was going to pay off. Once the championship game started, we were playing against another undefeated team who had two huge players that were over 6' 4 and they just killed us by rebounding everything. I played very confidently in this game and my team wanted to win so badly. I made almost every shot I took that game and I made some great passes. Unfortunately, we did not have the size to stop both of those players from beating us on the boards and we lost that game. But I managed to score 20 points, and this was the highest I had ever scored before. I accomplished my goal of doing this as I wrote this 20-point goal in my notes while I was on the plane. It was even more impressive that I did it with a broken finger. I knew to not make excuses for myself and it would pay off. At last now I could fly back home having accomplished something I never did before, and made a positive memory that would be with me forever. It was crazy to think that DCFS and the doctor told me I should not go. But I just knew I could not miss this opportunity after having such a disappointing senior year. God had it in his plans for me to go and the hard work paid off.

At the conclusion of the camp, we were given a shirt with a wristband as memorabilia. We took team and individual pictures. I couldn't wait to look back and see how much different I looked from this camp to how I would look in a year from now. I knew I was going to get stronger, bigger and faster during the upcoming offseason. But it was an even greater feeling meeting new people, making new friends, and ultimately playing the game of basketball again and having fun doing it. I made sure to get all my teammates social media so we could stay in touch, just like I did at the Tampa basketball camp. I enjoyed this a lot and I was sad it was over so fast. At least when the YouTube film comes out, I can show people that all the hard work I put in paid off and it was not for nothing. As I was leaving to head back to my hotel room, an assistant basketball coach at a D1 Juco (junior college) in Georgia asked me for my contact info and told me he sees potential in me. I couldn't believe an actual college coach came up to me! I thought I would never be good enough for that level of basketball. He told me we would get in touch soon and I was very happy, but I still wanted to go to school in Florida. But I figured I would ultimately hear him out on what he had to say. I left the camp and I walked back to my hotel room. I had to hurry up and pack all of my things because I had to check out at a certain time. Instead of walking back I ended up running because it started pouring rain. I did not want to waste money on an Uber because I still had to pay to get to the airport, so I had to just deal with getting soaked. I got back to my hotel soaked, and I packed all of my stuff up and checked out. I had to walk again in the pouring rain because I had to stand outside and wait for the bus that would take me to the train station to take the train to the airport. I guess I was going to be soaked for the entire day.

Eventually the bus arrived and I was soaking wet and freezing because the air conditioning was on. I hated being freezing cold, especially when I was tired. I pulled my phone out of my pocket and had to wipe it down because it was wet from being outside in the rain. I looked back at my notes to see how to get to the airport. I remembered the old man telling me if you ride the train all the way to the last stop, it will be the airport. So, I rode the bus all the way to the bus station and I asked the bus driver for help just to get clarification and my notes ended up being right. When I got off the bus at the bus station, I went up the escalators, got on the train, and rode the train all the way to the airport. It was very cool that I got to see the huge and amazing Hartsfield-Jackson Atlanta International Airport from the outside during the daytime just to see how big this airport really was. Once I got off the train and made it to the airport, my flight did not leave until later on at night, so I stayed and hung around the airport for a few hours. I walked through security so I could go and explore this amazing airport some more.

There were four different floors, so to kill time I just got on the tunnel train and rode every floor and walked around amazed at everything it had to offer. I could not believe how many stores and restaurants were inside of this airport. It was almost like being in a huge mall. It was unlike anything I had ever seen before. It was very eye opening to see all the new things that this world had to offer. I always knew there was so much more to this world than the little city of Rockford. It was a blessing that I was able to go to a new state and a new city because as a foster kid, we are not supposed to do things like this. We are just supposed to be a statistic and end up dead or in jail and I refused to live up to this. I wanted to keep traveling and going against the odds. I knew that if I kept working hard I would be able to do this one day. I was just very thankful that God blessed me with this opportunity, and for all the people who taught me the importance of hard work, consistency, self-confidence, and faith. It just goes to show you that if you work hard, no matter the situation and stay positive, you can do it and good things will come. Eventually, I wrote a letter to myself about how much inspiration I gained from seeing more of the world and coming here. I know a lot of people fell asleep on me and stopped believing in me especially when I went to a jail facility but deep down inside I knew I was going to wake them all up one day with my hard work and story. After almost the entire day walking around the airport it was finally time for me to go. I was sad that I had to go back to this foster home because of how much I enjoyed my peace while I was here but that was the reality of things. I was not as nervous when I boarded the plane because I was so tired and so inspired to keep working harder. I took my seat, stared out the window at the beautiful city of Atlanta, and finished my writing to myself. Lastly, I put my headphones on, prayed and asked God to keep me safe on this flight and I went to sleep.

After Atlanta Basketball Camp

After waking up from dozing off on the flight home, it was time to deplane. I almost did not want to get off because of how comfortable I was. I grabbed all of my belongings and began heading off the plane and I instantly felt a freezing cold breeze that hit me. Right then and there I put both my jackets on. I checked the weather app on my phone, and it was only 10 degrees outside. I checked for the windchill and it was -5 degrees and a huge weather change. When I looked down at my ticket for the bus ride home, I only had 10 minutes to get to my stop. If the plane had not got delayed coming home, I would have probably made it a lot faster. I instantly took off running through the Chicago O'Hare Airport and tried to find the Rockford bus that would take me home. I searched through the entire airport for an exit, I ended up taking the elevator downstairs to the bus parking lot. But the only problem was that there were so many different bus stops and different buses coming to pick people up that nobody had any idea what I was talking about. I asked five different workers and bus drivers, and nobody knew anything about this bus that would take you from O'Hare Airport to the Rockford Bus Station. I began to think I was crazy because of the way everyone was staring at me while I was asking about the bus. I did get advice from one person and they told me to go back upstairs and go to the parking lot on the 3rd floor. I took his advice and there was nobody up there and nothing around but this empty parking lot.

By this point, I was freezing cold from standing outside for so long, searching every floor to find where the bus might be. I looked at every area and bus stop trying to find my ride home. I kept asking people and still nobody had any idea about what I was talking about. I was freezing cold and finally when I went to ask a bus driver in the bus shuttle that kept driving around, he gave me some advice by telling me to get on and go over to the international side. So I got on the bus and rode a quick five minutes down to the lower building that was the international gate. I enjoyed the heat after my body was completely frozen from being outside. Once I got off at the international side I asked a lot of the workers and bus drivers here and finally one driver knew what I was talking about. It was like a miracle someone had finally heard about this bus going to Rockford. The bus driver told me that the next bus would be coming at 10:30pm, and it was only 10:25 pm. I was so happy I could have started break dancing in the cold with no jacket on, I was finally going home! I stood outside on the bus stop rocking back and forth humming the song "I'm going home" in the freezing Chicago cold. I waited but still no sign of this bus anywhere. I ended up waiting another 25 minutes and I could no longer feel my face, hands, ears, noise, or feet. I was sure I had frostbite on my feet from the burning sensation. I was done humming and had lost all excitement that I was going home because this bus never showed up. I went inside to the international building and I called my caseworker Gabby, waking her up to tell her what happened. Gabby told me she could not come and get me and to call my foster parent, Tameka. I knew for sure Tameka was not going to pick me up, but I was so freezing cold I did not care and just called her. Tameka said the same thing with a nasty attitude as always. It was now 11:30 pm at night and I was hoping another bus would be coming around soon. Plus, I had school the next morning and you can only miss so many days until Roosevelt kicks you out of their program and I was not trying to have to do another year of high school. I called my caseworker Gabby back and she said there was nothing she could do, and I was going to have to wait at the airport until the next bus came at 6am. I had to face the reality that I was stuck with no ride or nobody to help me.

I had never slept inside of an airport and I did not want to either so I checked the price of an Uber and it was over $200 at the time. I tried to call my mother for help to send me some money, but she was not answering the phone. I thought about calling my older sister, but we had not talked in months and she blocked me. I just had to face the cold fact that I had nobody but myself. It's a deeply lonely and sad feeling when you realize just how alone you are. To help keep me positive I looked around the airport and I saw that other grown people were sleeping. At least I would not be the only one. I just did not understand how they slept so comfortably on these hard chairs. One of the men was even snoring so loud he was that comfortable. Even though I was trying to stay positive I did not want this to be me at all. No matter how positive I tried to be, I could not help feeling completely frustrated and annoyed that I had to sleep in an airport. I was back to being treated like shit and nobody cared for me. I was tired of being a foster kid and going through this stuff. I wished I had loving parents like a lot of kids did who would go out of their way to help their child with anything. I even had a police officer ask me where my parents were after he asked how old I was, and I felt so ashamed. But it was because of incidents like this that made me want to work harder and let people into what it is like to be in my shoes. I just used this as motivation to be a part of my success story one day. I knew that this was going to make me stronger even though I was angry and feeling down at the time. I just believed in myself that one day I would look back in life and tell this story to people. Anything that anyone negative ever did to me I used it as motivation to kill them with success, the best revenge is proving people wrong.

I ended up picking a chair that was furthest away from the door to sleep on because every time the door opened there was a freezing cold breeze. I didn't know how to get comfortable in these metal chairs and I tried every position possible. But no matter how hard I tried, the anger of sleeping inside of an airport would keep me from getting comfortable. I was even more angry because the next morning when I went to school, I was going to be so tired. I had already had to miss a few days due to doctors' appointments and meeting with my caseworker so I could not miss any more days even if I wanted to. This was one of the downfalls of going to an alternative school. I just ended up watching some funny prank videos that night because I was feeling angry and I wanted to laugh. There is nothing better than a laugh to get over things. I followed this up with watching motivational videos about overcoming hardships in life. This just continued to help me gain more and more inspiration and motivation in life. I was always looking for ways to better myself and accomplish more because I had been through too much in life to be basic. I refused to work at some fast-food job for the rest of my life or be a failure and let my dad's side of the family and Mrs. Johnson win. I just had a mentality that regardless of what happens I will refuse to lose and refuse to not work hard.

It was now 3am and I had never seen an airport so quiet and empty before, especially with this being the 3rd busiest airport in the United States. Occasionally, when I would begin to doze off, I would be woken up by police officers talking super loud or somebody being loud inside or walking around. I did not trust anyone, and this kept me from sleeping. One incident in particular that kept me up was when a drunk man came inside and was yelling and screaming about flying to California because he missed his flight home. While he was walking around drunk he kept singing this song about California and it made me never want to go to California ever. I wish I were as big as Mike Tyson to scare him to shut the hell up because of how loud he was. After listening to him for about 15 minutes, the police finally came back around and inside the building. They told him to be quiet and be patient for his next flight in the morning or to leave. I was just so happy this man stopped singing and left. I checked my phone again and only 30 minutes had passed by. It was now 3:30am and I still had a while for this bus to come to take me home. I was so hungry because all I ate was a peanut butter and jelly sandwich and that was like ten hours ago. I was dreading this night and wished it would just be time to leave already. I had no money to buy any food even if I wanted to. I just had to listen to my stomach growl for another three hours until it was time to get on the bus home.

Finally, once it hit 5am I left the upper part of the airport and I got on the shuttle bus to take me down to the international side of the airport. The international side is where I had to wait for the bus that would take me back home to Rockford. I wanted to make sure I would not miss this bus a second time, so I stood there in the freezing cold and I waited. I ended up standing outside for over an hour totally freezing and I got that familiar feeling of being no longer able to feel my feet, ears, jaw, or hands again. Once it finally hit 6am, the bus still did not show up and was nowhere to be found. I was ready to cry now because I had been up all hours of the night and had been freezing cold this entire day walking back and forth and still hadn't eaten anything for hours. This was by far one of the roughest days I had ever had. I ended up leaving because I had lost my patience trying to get on this bus. I ended up walking around to other bus areas asking bus drivers if they knew about this bus. The first thing I asked them was where the stop was. Then I followed this question with asking what time the bus came. I heard the same answer I had been hearing all night long, and they told me they were not sure and had not heard of this bus before. I lost all hope and I finally just decided to snuggle myself up into a ball and sit at this stop and wait until this bus came. I did not even care how cold I was anymore because of how tired I was. I was going to sit here all day until this bus came whether I froze or not because I was trying to see if this bus even existed. My anger and frustration wouldn't allow me to feel the cold anymore.

After sitting here for another 15 minutes snuggled up into an angry ball, the bus finally came. You would have thought I just hit the lottery how fast I got up and cheered. Finally! I made sure to be the first one on the bus, slowly climbing the steps with my frozen, stiff legs. I fumbled to pull my ticket from my pocket, struggling with my numb hands, and finally settled into my seat with relief. I was just so happy to be on this bus, even happier to be feeling heat. This was easily one of the worst nights in my life so far and to think I had school in two hours made it even worse. I was so exhausted, once the bus started up and we began driving, I closed my eyes and I passed out but before I knew it, I was being woken up by the bus driver saying we made it back. That felt like one of the shortest bus rides I had ever been on. But it was an hour and a half bus ride, it just felt so short because of how tired I really was. I had to sit inside of the Rockford Bus Station so I could call my caseworker Gabby to come pick me up. I had to fight myself from falling asleep while waiting and it felt like I was in a boxing match with sleep, fighting to resist the temptation of closing my eyes. After 15 minutes of fighting sleep, my caseworker finally came and got me. I gave her a forceful hug and she yelled, "boy, get off me!" I was just so happy I was finally back. After that quick hug, I told her thank you and didn't speak a word. I was so tired that I passed out again in the short car ride back to my foster house.

Back at my foster house, I knocked on the door and waited for them to answer. Once they answered I instantly went inside, took my bag off, and just laid down face first in the hard medal bed. I set my alarm for one hour because I still had to walk to my bus stop and Ifell into a deep sleep. I had never slept with my shoes still on and feet halfway off the bed with my face first in the pillow with my bag still on my back. I was so exhausted I did not even have the energy to take off my shoes or bag. I always talked about how much I thought sleep was a waste of time because all you do is close your eyes for hours and lay there while you could be doing something productive. But I realized the power of sleep and how real and essential it is for you. After my hour nap, I woke up and didn't even need to get dressed. I still had both of my coats on, shoes on, and everything else I needed for school. As I stepped out the door, the freezing cold instantly hit me, waking me up completely. It was even colder after coming back from 60-degree weather down in Georgia. It was like I played a trick on my body, everything just felt so cold to me. After my dreadfully long walk in the cold to get to my bus stop, I waited and thankfully the bus was right on time. When I got on the bus, I sat in a seat furthest away from everyone and I fell asleep again. It sucked because I only got to sleep for 30-minutes because before I knew it I was right back at school. I only had one class left at the time, and this was Algebra. I had to complete two semesters worth of work in two months, but I was not worried about it because I went to school from 10am to 2pm every day staying later just to complete one class. Some days I stayed after even later to complete more assignments. I was so tired that I didn't even care to do any work that day. I just put my head down in between both of my arms and passed out. I was woken up after a few hours of just sitting like this when my Algebra teacher asked me if I wanted any lunch. I quickly wiped the drool off of the side of my face and went down to eat. I hadn't eaten anything for almost 24 hours and I was starving. That was one of the best Rockford Public School lunches I had ever eaten in my life. Once I finished eating lunch, I went back upstairs and did the same thing over again. I was woken up one more time by my teacher because the school buses were leaving, and it was time for me to go home. I'm sure my teacher was wondering what kind of drugs I was on or how much I had drunk the night before, considering how out of it I seemed. I got on the school bus and went home. I got into a second fight with my body resisting my eyes from closing and trying not to fall asleep because I was afraid of missing my stop. At one point I took both of my fingers and forced my eyelids to stay open.

Finally, it was time to get off the bus and I was headed home. I was so happy to know I could lay down and go to sleep for the rest of the night. I was completely exhausted from this day and just ready to go to sleep. Once I got to the door, I knocked, and I knocked, and I knocked. I was standing outside freezing cold and tired for 25 minutes. I called Mrs. Tiffany's son's phone and he was not answering. Now I was pissed off because I was cold and tired and once again standing outside in the freezing cold, waiting. I felt like I spent the entire day just waiting. I was sick of always standing outside of this house knocking and having to wait for someone to come and answer the damn door. I felt like these people were ignoring me on purpose. I called my foster parent Mrs. Tiffany and she would not answer her phone either. Now I was really pissed off and done. I banged on the door as hard as I could hoping someone would answer, and nobody did. Then I thought maybe if I kicked it someone would hear, so I turned around and kicked the door a few times. This was probably not the smartest idea, but I was so tired I couldn't even think straight. After a few more kicks, the door broke open and I realized I was in some deep shit. I went inside and began to panic because I just broke this lady's door and she was going to kill me. I tried to find a screwdriver inside the house somewhere and fix it, but I could not find one anywhere. I then tried to take the screws and screw them back in with my hand, but they were too tiny. I figured if I just cleaned it up and left no evidence, nobody would notice, so that's what I did. Eventually,

I realized I couldn't keep this secret so I called my caseworker Gabby and told her what happened, but I told her not to tell anyone. Gabby talked some sense into me by saying Mrs. Tiffany had cameras all around her house. I had to face the fact that I was screwed either way, now I was just hoping she would not notice. But in a way I really didn't care anymore. I was tired of this lady treating me like shit and only having Oreos and Ramen noodles for food.I was exhausted from walking in the freezing cold every day and constantly having to stand outside waiting. I was annoyed how this lady always gave me attitude and was rude and barely spoke to me. Finally, I was just done being treated like a dog. I went upstairs and fell asleep.

Once my foster parent Tameka got home, the house turned into World War 3. As soon as she came upstairs, she started screaming and cussing me at me. I couldn't blame her because I just broke her door and I felt bad. I didn't even respond because I was so tired. All I heard was something about a two week's notice and that was it. I went to sleep for the rest of the night but all the while she kept running her mouth about her door. Eventually, she had one of her guy friends come over to fix it. I didn't understand why she was so angry, especially since DCFS was going to fully reimburse her, meaning she wouldn't have to pay anything, and if she did, she'd get her money back right away. I just kept my mouth shut and went to sleep. I woke up the next morning to go to school and I found out what I heard was right. Mrs. Tiffany did put in her 2-week notice and my caseworker had to find a new placement for me. I was already ready to leave this lady's house anyway, so I did not care. After school that day I went to the YMCA like usual and a worker came up to me and asked me about what happened at Mrs. Tiffany's house. Apparently, this lady was telling all the workers about how bad of a kid I was and how I broke her door down. Apparently, I just go around kicking people's door down for no reason because that makes a lot of sense. I just developed this bad habit out of nowhere of kicking people's doors down. It was always so funny to me how foster parents always made foster kids try and look so bad, when really *they* are pathetic because *they* treat foster kids like trash, and they don't know how to take accountability for what *they* do. It's even more pathetic how the foster care agencies license these people and pay them money to take care of us when they can't even do that. They set out garbage food like plastic noodles and hot pockets, don't give us any rides, support, or even talk to us and expect us to be happy. We are pretty much living on our own being in foster care. I was angry that this lady was going around spreading rumors about me to other workers. I was going to confront her, but I did not have a place to stay and the last thing I needed was to go back to a homeless shelter. I just left it alone and let people think how they wanted to about me. Deep down, I knew I wasn't a bad kid or person, and others could see that through my actions both inside and outside the YMCA. Later on that week I talked to my old foster parent Adam who I used to live with when I went to Harlem School and he let me live back in his house. It was on to the next foster home I went to like usual.

Before Indianapolis Basketball Camp

When I arrived at my old foster house, the same house I used to live in when I attended Harlem High School, I rekindled my relationship with my former foster parent Adam. Adam was always a great man and a great foster parent even though we had a lot of issues my junior year. Adam was very different from other foster parents because he never called us his foster kids he called us his "nephews" and told us to call him our "uncle" to make us not feel like foster kids. He always had food in his house for us and his friend Marcus would cook for us as well. When I was living here I did not have to live off of hot pockets, plastic noodles, and 50 cent cakes or Oreos. It was even better because Adam wanted to be involved in our lives. If you allowed him to be involved in your life he would help you and actually be involved giving good advice. He always had a very forgiving and genuine heart and told us as Christian men we have to forgive and move forward because God has something bigger in store for you. I was shocked when he forgave the foster kid who set us up and robbed us. I was even more shocked to find out he was accepting his phone calls and going down to visit him. This inspired me a lot to forgive the people who had hurt me and let go of this rock I was always carrying. We always stayed up late at night and had great conversations about anything. He helped me learn so much about life and taught me lots of things. I told him that I wanted to grow more as a person and did not want to be angry anymore or hold grudges. I wanted to have lots of friends and be someone who was always nice, respectful, and a good friend. He helped me find who Devin Paladino was and helped me grow closer with God. I felt in a way he was a parent figure and a good male role model. When we would have conversations we both were able to relate because Adam grew up in a hard life like me. He grew up in the projects and his dad and mom were never there and were into drugs. He had to live with his grandparents and ended up making the best of his life by going to school and getting a great education. Adam always explained the importance of school and how education is everything in life. With education you can have a great life, great job, and then he would follow up by saying read the Bible and what it says about wisdom and knowledge. This helped motivate me even more and when it came to school, I wanted to have a good career one day, a college degree, and have a great life. I did now want to be working a minimum wage job for the rest of my life because I was better than this. Things just completely changed for the better when I moved back in with him.

When I first moved in with Adam after I had got out of Lutherbrook for two years I was like an uncaged animal he told me. Every word I said had a cuss word in it. I was always hard headed and never wanted to listen. I got into arguments with everybody because I got mad at every little thing that people did. I was just always so angry all the time that nobody wanted to be around me. He told me I had made a complete 180-degree change in coming back to his house this time around. I wanted to keep growing and changing into a better person, I told him, but I needed his help. The first step was growing a relationship with God and having God more involved in my life. I didn't really know how to find God or what God was really about. After some long talks Adam inspired me to join a life group at City First Church and make friends around the church. I would attend church every Sunday and start going to youth groups every Wednesday. It was like history repeated itself when I was back in 8th grade living with Linda, only this time I was a lot more grown and understanding. I started reading the Bible every morning and I started praying more and more. I stopped being on my phone and on social media because I wanted to grow. I felt myself growing more spiritually and as a person during this time because of all the hard work I was putting into myself.

I began making new friends as well. I did not like hanging out with people who did drugs, would drink or try and be in the streets because this was not me or who I was about. I rechecked all my friends and started to separate myself even more because I wanted friends who had standards and values like mine. Adam helped me figure out who I was more as a person and the things I needed to work on more. I noticed I needed to learn more about my emotions and how to control them. I needed to work on patience, remembering things, and listening better. I got myself back into counseling and began working on these things with my counselor. My counselor became very impressed because I started asking her for worksheets and homework on emotional control and other things that would help better myself. My counselor said I was the first ever client to ask for homework and complete an entire book. Adam just inspired me to grow more and more and I became a totally different person. It was like every long conversation we had he was breaking me down and rebuilding me into a better person. I actually figured out who I wanted to be and what I wanted to become. I was tired of being angry, sad, and saying mean things or being rude to people. I wanted everyone to like me, I wanted to grow more as a person, know who I was more and be a great man one day. One day, I want people to talk about how much I have changed into a great person from when they first met me.

Adam also inspired me to rekindle my relationship with my sister again because we were always fighting. He reminded me that we are all that we have, and we need to come together. Adam was always big on family and forgiving because he said it was like a weight you carry and unresolved conflict and that it's not right. It was hard to have any type of relationship with my older sister because she was always stuck and depressed about the past. She was so depressed that she tried to kill herself multiple times and that affected me in negative ways. When I did try to talk to her and have her open up to me, she always shut down and kept everything in her life a secret. Then when I would try to get her to tell me things, she would get angry, block me and not talk to me for weeks, sometimes months. It was like you could not say anything bad or that she did not agree with or it would result in her flipping out and blocking you out of her life. I always hated not being able to have a relationship with my older sister, but it was something I got used to eventually. We were never really involved in each other's lives in any way once we separated and moved to different foster homes. I always felt so bad because I had a baby nephew I wanted to be involved in his life but was never able to. I opened up to Adam about a lot of my past and problems because he was someone who I learned to trust, and he always told me the importance of family and how she was all I had. I learned I had a lot of anger towards her because she always bullied me and lied about things I did when we were younger. I took a lot of beatings for her by our dad and that made me angry as a kid. I had a lot of grudges towards her, but it was time to let that demon inside go. I learned about myself that every time I worked out in the gym or did anything successful, I always thought of the people who did me wrong like my parents, sister, and dad's side of the family and wanted to kill them with success. What Adam was helping me learn and what I was learning more about is that's the wrong motivation to have. You want to do it for yourself because if you don't, you'll always have that grudge with you. The Bible talks about the importance of forgiveness and to have a pure heart. I wanted to forgive them and be at peace with myself, but I always found it so hard to do.

While growing more as a person and on a path to better myself, I began to chase my dream of going to college in Florida. I had already applied to three different colleges and got accepted into all of them. But I knew I wanted to go to school in Tampa. As the school year was coming to an end, I brought this up to Adam more. We started doing research about foster kids in college and the help they could get and that's when we worked on moving to Florida and getting DCFS to help me. I wanted to go to a school called Hillsborough Community College which was a school in Tampa, Florida. This was one of the only community colleges that offered student housing and had a Division 1 JUCObasketball program. Once I got accepted, I began to read the email about the things I needed to complete to enroll in school. So, I began knocking the steps out of the way. The first step was watching the entire student orientation video and I made sure to take notes. Then Adam and I called the school at least twice a day to learn and get all the requirements I needed for school. They told me that I had to apply for financial aid and submit it to the school. Next, I had to send my high school transcripts to this school as well. In the beginning when I talked to DCFS about going to college in Florida, no one showed support or really took me seriously. Adam changed that completely and fought for me to move and make sure they knew I was serious. We both kept calling the foster care agency and bringing it up more and more. It was like they were ignoring us and pushing us aside if we did not harass them constantly. The more we talked about me going to college in Florida, the more they started to come around and help. After my caseworker finally began to help and did some research for us, we ended up finding out that DCFS had a Youth in College Program. This program was like a scholarship, if you were a foster kid in the system and went to college they would give you a certain amount of money each month to help you out financially. Adam was an accountant and was very good with numbers so he ended up calculating this with the student housing rent each month, and the money I would get back from financial aid and we found out this was actually a real possibility.

I wanted to move out of Rockford and down to Florida so bad. I knew if I was going to be successful I needed to leave Rockford because of how little opportunity there was. I was tired of seeing the same people everywhere I went, tired of living in this small city with nothing to do all of the time. I wanted to get out and see the world and move to a place full of opportunity. I gained so much inspiration when I traveled to Tampa and Atlanta. I knew God had bigger plans for me and I had gone through too much in life to be basic. But the only problem was I was a ward of the state of Illinois, meaning I would have to go to court and get a judge's permission to leave the state and attend college down in Florida. I was not sure of how to convince a judge to let me move to Florida, but I stayed positive and made sure to accomplish the things I needed to do in the meantime. For instance, I needed to graduate high school, be on my best behavior, get a job and save money and keep working hard. I ended up doing just that and worked very hard and behaved myself. I landed myself two jobs, one at Olive Garden being a busser and another at Arby's working the cash register and making sandwiches. My life was nothing but working hard. I practiced basketball every morning before school, then attended school. Afterward, I would take the city bus to one of the two jobs I was working. Once I got off of work, if it were not too late, I would go back to the gym to work on my game some more. I was just a delusional 18-year-old kid with nothing but hard work and faith that one day I was going to accomplish this dream of waking up to palm trees, no snow, and more importantly, a new life full of new opportunities.

Every day my routine consisted of getting up at 5:30 am to run two miles to get to the YMCA. While I was at the gym, I would make 400-500 shots to work on my shooting game. Next, I would walk a mile from the YMCA to Roosevelt High School to go to school. Once I got to school I would work on the one and only class I had left which was Algebra and complete a couple of chapters a day to graduate faster. Then I would walk to the city bus station and get on the city bus to go to work. Both of my jobs were down the street from each other, so it made it very convenient for me to take the same bus every day for both jobs. Some nights if I got off of work early on my normal three mile walk home from the bus station, I would stop by the YMCA and play some more games or get another workout in. Every day I began writing in a journal of the things I wanted to accomplish and started setting goals and prioritizing more. Adam always told me to have an organized mind and have backup plans. I took his advice and made sure to write all the things I needed in order. First, I made sure I wrote down the bills I had to pay for each month and budgeted off of that. Then, I made sure to call DCFS once a week about moving to Florida as well as Hillsborough Community College to make sure they had everything they needed. More importantly, I made sure I was working hard on and off the court to become better as a person and a basketball player.

As I attended church every Sunday and got involved in the youth group, I began to realize how negative my thinking was and how much I stressed over everything. It was like I was always in panic mode inside of my head and I had a million thoughts going at once. This was a big reason I would always forget things and lose stuff, my mind was going 1,000 miles per hour. I developed this bad habit from all the abuse I suffered from my father, Lutherbrook and in some foster homes. I was always on alert at the time and stuck inside panic mode. That's when Adam, the pastor, and my youth group taught me the importance of giving things to God and stop worrying all the time. I began praying more and thinking positive thoughts to calm myself down. I started to relax my mind and work on breathing and paying attention to my thoughts and what I would say more. I started stretching and growing my faith that everything would work itself out. It was very hard to do in the beginning but the more I practiced the easier it got. I was constantly looking for new ways to keep growing and break bad habits. I wanted to be more at peace with myself and who I was. I hated always being worried about all of these scenarios of how things would turn out and then being stressed out from this. I just wanted to relax and become calmer.

Once the YouTube video came out from the basketball camp in Atlanta, I posted it on my Instagram and Facebook and got over 2,000 views on it. This was the most views I had ever gotten on anything in my life. I was in total shock to see this many people watching my basketball tape and all the support I was getting with basketball. I realized I could seriously play college basketball one day. Shortly after I posted this, I ended up getting invited to another basketball camp in Indianapolis. It was the same camp from the one I attended in Atlanta. I instantly thought this was another great opportunity to try and get a basketball scholarship. I already had a coach interested in me at a D1 JUCO down in Georgia so I figured if I kept the mindset that I was learning from church and Adam about not stressing out about stuff, staying positive, working hard and praying about it, everything would work out one day and I would get a basketball scholarship. I knew I had the desire, heart and work ethic to back up about how bad I wanted to play college basketball. All I had to do was stay consistent and be patient with myself and my hard work would pay off. I gained confidence in myself and started to truly believe that I could do this. I continued my daily routine of getting up early to work out before school, going to school, going to work, then going back to the gym later on at night again. I never got tired of this because that meant I would be tired of my dream and I was not going to let that happen. I worked hard every day and kept working and praying. I kept my faith strong in God and my confidence in myself. I made sure to work very hard for this camp even though I still had a slightly broken finger, but I kept tape on it. I was never taken to physical therapy to get it properly taken care of and strengthen it back up so I just prayed it would heal correctly. Once it was time to go back to another basketball camp I made sure I was ready and made sure I had enough money saved up. At least this time it would be cheaper because I didn't have to pay for a plane ticket; I would just take a bus.

Indianapolis Basketball Camp

I ended up saving enough money to go to this Indianapolis basketball camp for one day instead of two. I did not want to spend all my money knowing I needed to save for moving to Florida. I talked to my foster parent Adam about helping me get to Chicago by dropping me off at the Greyhound Station, and picking me up when I returned from Indianapolis. He agreed to do both and this helped me out a lot in saving even more money and even being able to go to camp. Adam always loved coming to downtown Chicago so I figured he would say yes. It was late March at the time, and I was leaving Friday night and coming back Sunday night. It was still very cold outside, and I made sure to wear two jackets before we left to head to Chicago. Prior to leaving I was very excited to see the city of Indianapolis and be in a new state where I had never been before. I always knew about this city from Peyton Manning and the Indianapolis Colts. I looked at the downtown area and it looked very nice as well. Once I got out of school on Friday after a long day of doing Algebra work, we headed to the Chicago Greyhound Bus Station in downtown Chicago. It took about two hours to get there because of all the traffic.I hated being stuck in traffic because everything moved so slowly, but I also appreciated it because it helped me develop more patience. When I finally got here it was only 30 minutes until my bus left the station. I had some extra cash on me and went to get some chili cheese fries. These were probably some of the best cheese fries I have ever had in my life. I wanted to take a nap on the bus, and I always enjoyed being full before sleeping, so that was my goal.

It was around 7:30pm at night and I lined up and waited my turn to get on the bus. All I brought with me was my backpack and headphones. Inside of my backpack was an extra day's worth of clothes and my basketball shoes. This made it easier for me to travel because my bag was not so heavy. Before the bus headed out, I got a text message from Adam asking if everything was good and if I knew where I was staying yet. I found a hotel for a very low price on the hotel app, but I did not book the room yet. Instead, I called the hotel earlier that day, and they told me I could just walk in when I arrived. I should have taken Adams' advice about planning ahead on this, because later on that night it would come back to haunt me. I had the aisle to myself, so I laid my head on the window and put my headphones in. I was trying to fall asleep to make the three-hour bus ride go faster. Before I put my phone on do not disturb mode I checked my social media and saw East High School made it down state. I was so happy for them, but at the same time I felt a big slap in the face. I regretted not going to that school to play with all of my friends I grew up with. I had grown up on the East side of Rockford and knew all of those guys since we were little kids going to Lincoln Middle School. I also attended a lot of East High School basketball camps as a little kid. But I let it go because I chose my own fate by deciding to go to Auburn and I did not regret that decision at all. I had been pushed the hardest ever in my life going to Auburn and I saw how much work it really takes to be great. I got off of social media, put my phone back on do not disturb mode and just listened to music the entire bus ride until we got to Indianapolis. I was so happy I ended up falling asleep for some of the 3-hour ride.

Once I woke up I knew we were here by the downtown skyline and seeing the Indianapolis Colts stadium. This was the biggest football stadium I had ever seen before. It was no wonder why they had the NFL combine here every year. It was very cool how the greyhound station was right across the street from Lucas Oil Stadium. Once I got off the bus, I was smacked in the face by the windchill of Indianapolis and quickly woke up. I hated being cold, that's why I always made sure to wear two jackets. Inside the Greyhound Bus Station, it was much nicer and cleaner than the one in Chicago. It was even better that it was less crowded and not full of people like. I found a place to sit and called for a Lyft and after about 15 minutes we headed towards the hotel. I made sure I picked a hotel that was close to the basketball camp so I could just walk there like I did in Georgia. As we were driving to the hotel I saw the beautiful scenery of downtown Indianapolis. This city was a lot prettier than I expected it to be. I got to the hotel and I was ready to go to sleep. I didn't want to be tired for tomorrow's camp, especially since I was only going to be in attendance for one day. I walked up to the front desk and I asked to get a room for the night. This is where the advice of planning ahead that Adam talked about came to haunt me. Instantly my heart dropped when he told me, "I'm sorry son, we are completely booked." I felt so stupid that I did not pay for this hotel ahead of time. I didn't think anything of it because I did the same thing when I was in Georgia. I had little to no money left on me and I was hoping he was joking around when he said this. I asked him to clarify his definition of full because I had just called them four hours prior and they said they were open. The man went into further explanation and I just stopped listening after a while because I was in shock. I just stood there thinking about where I was going to stay now. I felt like this was me sleeping at the airport all over again. I did not realize that it was St. Patrick's Day weekend and this city was going to be packed for this event. I felt like this was sleeping at the airport all over again but even worse. I had no place to sleep this time. I pulled myself together and just tried to stay calm. I called another Lyft to take me to another hotel that was close by but they were completely booked too. I began to panic now, I walked outside and just sat on the sidewalk during this cold Indianapolis night wondering where I was going to stay. I checked my bank account and I was really screwed now because I did not have enough money to pay for a hotel room even if I tried. I had spent too much money on Lyft rides back and forth. After a while of sitting on the sidewalk figuring out what to do, I called another Lyft to drive me back to the Greyhound Station. At least I knew this place was warm and open for 24 hours a day.

Once back at the bus station, I sat inside and tried to figure things out for the night. My phone was dead and the only charger this bus station had was next to the bathroom. I hated having to sit down on this dirty floor and wait for my phone to charge up, but the last thing I needed was my phone getting stolen. Then I would really be out of luck. While I was sitting there I could just smell the disgusting odor from the bathroom. I had to cover my noise with my coats to prevent myself from passing out. I never realized how bad people stink after they finish their business; it was awful. This was definitely the longest time I had ever waited for my phone to charge up before. Finally, I tried reaching out to people for help. I figured maybe all of this would be over if I reached out to someone. So, I called my mom, my caseworker Gabby, and my foster parent Adam asking them for money and they all said no to me. My mom did not have the money at the time. My caseworker Gabby told me her money was too tight. Lastly, my foster parent Adam told me about planning ahead and said now I had to learn my lesson. Now that everyone said no to me, I felt very pissed off and lost. I just sat and stared at the wall feeling stuck and thinking what else I could do. I thought about who else I could have reached out to but I didn't have anyone else to call. I stopped trying to control my thoughts and just turned angry and went into panic mode. Here I am at 18 years old in a new state and a new city. It's freezing cold outside, I don't have any money and haven't eaten anything since the chili cheese fries in Chicago and now I don't know where I'm going to sleep for the next two days. I was just pissed off more at myself that I did not plan ahead. I had nobody to blame but myself.

It was now 11:30 pm and I just decided to sit inside of the greyhound station and wait. I was trying to see if there were any restaurants and fast food places that I could walk inside of, but they were all closed. I did not have a car, so I was out of luck. The food place left was inside of the station and it was closed too. Luckily, I had a little bit of change in my bag and there was a candy machine inside. I walked over to the candy machine and got a handful of Skittles for 25 cents. I didn't care if this was dinner I was just so hungry. I put about six quarters in that machine and just kept eating Skittles because I was so hungry and the only thing to eat was candy. You would have thought it was Halloween the way I was pushing handful after handful of candy into my mouth. I went and sat on one of the benches. I looked around and saw a few other people were asleep and the security guard didn't say anything to them. That's when I got the idea that I would just go to sleep here in the station. Out of nowhere a lady in a wheelchair approached me and asked me what was wrong. I guess my body language was showing something was wrong so I told her what was going on and she said I was best off sleeping here because they won't kick me out as long as I have a ticket. This was confirmation that my idea was not crazy. I had my ticket in my bag so at least I knew I could stay here for the whole night. I ended up putting my headphones on and listened to a speech by Eric Thomas about getting through hard times and not giving up. Just like the time I had to sleep in the airport, whenever I was in an unfortunate situation or feeling and down I would listen to him. Or I would listen to other motivational speeches and read the Bible afterwards. I knew stuff like this was only going to make me stronger and be a part of my success story one day. I had faith that God had bigger plans in store for me as long as I kept putting in hard work and that's what I was going to do.

It was now one in the morning and I was getting sleepy. I still had to be up early in the morning for the camp. The only problem was that I still had nowhere to sleep. I had to face the reality of sleeping inside of this Greyhound Bus Station. I did not trust any of these people inside of here, but I had no choice. It was either sleep here or sleep outside in the freezing cold. It was time to put my big boy pants on and get through this. So, I went and found a bench that was furthest away from everyone. I could not sleep in a chair because that position sleeping straight up was very uncomfortable to me especially with all the bright lights. I picked a bench that would allow me to lay my entire body down. It was very painful at first because the bench was completely made out of metal. Also how my legs were hanging halfway off of the bench. I had to work with what I had and make the best out of this situation. I used my bag as a pillow and both of my coats that I had on as blankets and curled my legs up so my entire body would fit on the bench. Next, I used my hat to cover my eyes so the bright lights would not shine through my eyelids. Before I knew it, I was comfortable in a very unique way. It was now 2:30 in the morning and

I needed to hurry up and go to sleep. I had to be at camp by 8 in the morning which was only 5 and a half hours away. The bus station had gotten really quiet now and that made it easier for me to fall asleep. It sucked having to be in this situation, but I just kept remembering from the speech and stayed motivated and positive from this. I was not going to let this situation crack me, I have been through far worse and life and this would fuel my fire to play harder. I just had to trust God, keep my faith, and stay positive and everything would be okay. I refused to give up like all the other people in my life have. I want to show people later on in life that this will be a part of my success story one day. One day, I will look back on life and say at 18 years old I slept in a Greyhound Station to play basketball in front of college coaches hoping to get a basketball scholarship.

While I was asleep, I felt someone shaking me and saying "sir" and instantly I popped up awake. It was not a dream, it was real. The man who was shaking me was one of the security guards at the station. The security guard was asking to see my bus ticket. I pulled my bus ticket out of my bag to show him. He then went around asking people for a bus ticket. He would begin kicking them out because this bus station was not a place for just anyone off the street to come inside and sleep. Thank God I had mine otherwise I would have been kicked out and had to sleep outside. Once I started to fully wake up from my daze I checked the time on my phone, and it was 5am. This meant I had only been asleep for 2 and a half hours. I was completely exhausted and nervous thinking I was not going to play well.I tried to fall back asleep since I needed the rest for camp and still had at least two more hours of sleep to catch up on. I got back into my comfortable position. and as I laid back down, I could not fall asleep no matter how hard I tried because of how loud everyone was. I was frustrated now because I was still so tired. Also, my stomach was still growling but I was trying to sleep it off so I would not have to think about it. I just stopped trying to fall asleep and stayed awake now. I ended up waiting patiently for the last two hours to pass. But it felt like these were the longest two hours of my life. Maybe if I were not staring at the clock the entire time, the two hours would have passed by a lot quicker, but I just kept waiting and watching. Whenever I would begin to doze off I would hear noise or hear the loud footsteps of people passing by me. So I just decided to wake up once and for all. I was happy there was a McDonald's close by and it was now open. I walked inside and used the little bit of cash I had on me to eat a huge breakfast. Warm food sliding into my stomach and filling it up had never felt so refreshing and good before. I called myself a Lyft, got all my stuff packed inside of my bag and headed to the basketball camp. Even though I only had 2 hours of sleep, I was still going to show these coaches and players what I could do on the court. I was not going to use this as an excuse to not get a basketball scholarship.

On the way to the basketball camp, I automatically began dozing off again. I had to slap myself a few times in the face and the Lyft driver looked at me crazy and thought I was on some drugs. I did not want to fall asleep and I needed to stay awake. There was something about car rides that always made me sleepy. Since I was a little kid riding in the car, especially going on long road trips, I've always ended up sleeping inside of the car. The slaps in the face did not work and I ended up falling asleep in the car as usual. I couldn't be upset with myself because I had only gotten two and a half hours of sleep that night. Once we arrived at the basketball facility, the Lyft driver had to shake me a few times to wake me up. I apologized to him and explained what happened so he wouldn't call the police or ambulance on me. Once I got out of the car, I saw this huge and amazing sports factory. It was absolutely beautiful on the outside and I could tell it was a newer building unlike the buildings I'm used to seeing in Rockford. I still had 20 minutes before the camp started, so I went to Starbucks and sat down. It was still very cold outside, and I needed to change because I did not have any of my basketball gear on. I went to the Starbuck's bathroom and changed into my basketball gear. I was so happy this bathroom had a baby changing table on it so I didn't have to put all my stuff on the dirty floor. I was even happier that the door had a lock on it so nobody could come in while I was changing. I changed into my compression shirt, new basketball shorts and basketball shoes. I also brushed my teeth because I did not want my breath to stink in case a coach came and talked to me. He probably would have smelled my breath and walked away or changed his mind quickly.

After I finished changing, I stuffed all my clothes I wore the night before and my two jackets inside of my bag and I ran to the sports facility next door. I could not believe this was all one gym. This place had an indoor football field and a lounge area before entering the basketball court. There were huge pictures of Jeff Teague up everywhere. I later found out that this was the former NBA player's gym. This indoor sports facility had four basketball courts, it was huge! I had never seen anything so amazing before. Usually you don't see stuff like this back home. I got myself together and began paying attention to the stuff I needed to do. One of the coaches who asked for my name, told me what group I was in. I walked over to that group looking for the jersey that had my name on top of it, just like the set up in Atlanta. Once I saw the piece of paper with my name on it, I sat down in my group and put my jersey on while waiting for further instruction. As the gym became more and more full, the owner of the camp began speaking. The owner of the camp started by telling us the expectations and importance of good grades in school and being a good teammate. After he finished speaking, the college basketball coaches elaborated on what the camp owner had said. The coaches told us they wanted to see hard workers, good teammates, and positive attitudes. I already knew the expectations because I had so many talks with coaches in high school about what college coaches wanted. I made sure to write these down in my notes and study it so I could be a college level player one day.

Soon, they started breaking us up into groups where we started our drills. The same routine as when I was in Atlanta. During the drills it occurred to me because these were the same dribbling, shooting, and defensive drills I did every day at the YMCA. I was dominating and standing out because of how well I was performing during the drills. But every time I would finish my turn during a drill and walk back towards the end of the line, I would be completely drained of energy. But I kept remembering what the speech said about not making excuses and giving up, so I pushed through it. I was not going to allow any opportunity to go past me. If I were able to play on a broken finger, I could easily play on two hours of sleep. After about an hour and a half of doing drills, it was time to start playing games. As I was getting ready, a basketball coach who coached at a D1 JUCO in Chicago came up to me and asked where I was from. He told me he liked what he saw from my game during the drills and asked for my contact information. I was excited because two basketball coaches now had my number—one in Georgia and the other in Chicago. But I still wanted to move to Florida and as far from Illinois as possible. I kept an open mind about possibly playing in Georgia because of how much I liked the assistant coach and when we talked on the phone, he brought up free housing because it would be on a scholarship. He also talked to me about having other things paid for and a little bit about my background. He was shocked when I told him I was in foster care and all the other stuff I had gone through. But ultimately, I still wanted to take my chances of playing down in Florida. Once it was time to start playing games, my team and I gathered up and waited until it was our turn to take the court. I was ready to play in front of these coaches and show them what I could do.

Things didn't go as well as I thought they would go in the first game. I was very frustrated that I was not getting the ball. It was like all the other players on my team were ball hogging and trying to show off for the camera because they paid for the YouTube highlight film and wanted to look good. I had little to no impact at all. The only little impact I had was playing good defense and not allowing my man to score and rebounding the ball. In fact the only time I scored was when I rebounded the ball after one of my teammates shot it. After the first game was over, we ended up winning, which I was happy about because I did not want to be selfish. But I went and talked to a few of my teammates after the first game was over and said we need to start passing the ball more. We also needed to start setting screens for each other more and making a lot more cuts without the ball. There was no movement at all, everyone was stagnant. It was like playing isolation ball at the YMCA or the park. With this type of play, we would be lucky if we won any more games.

Once the second and third games were played, it was the same exact result as the first one. Everything I had discussed before game one was quickly forgotten by everyone or they just didn't care. In all three games, I only had six points each game. I played very pathetic and I was upset with myself. I worked too hard leading up to this camp to produce these types of stats. It was even more frustrating to think I slept in a bus stop and went through all that the night before just to come out and play like this. I had nobody to blame but myself, regardless if my teammates were not passing the ball, that's not an excuse. I always held myself to a high standard and took full accountability for everything I did on and off the court. I hated how I always performed very well when it came to drills but in the real game I always seemed to struggle. This was the biggest downfall of my game and I wanted to fix that. It was a very disappointing day and I was going to use this as motivation to get better. I knew that once I mastered the most challenging part—shooting the ball—the rest of my game would come together easily. I just needed to start working on my athletic ability. If I ever wanted to play at a Division I college I needed to get a lot stronger, faster, and be able to start jumping high. The only way to get this done was to stop being lazy and start lifting weights, running sprints, and working on my vertical. To get a better understanding of what I needed to work on, I asked two of the college coaches after the camp was over. The coaches told me that, based on what they observed at the camp, I needed to work on becoming more athletic. The same thing I had told myself. I knew I was not 6 '5 or had crazy bounce in my legs so I was going to have to work hard to become athletic. Instead of going to the gym and just getting up shots and doing dribble moves, I was going to have to do a lot of work on my body. But I was ready to start working harder because I was tired of being average. I knew in order for me to get to that next level that this is what I was going to have to do. I had to ask myself how bad I really wanted it, not by answering in my head but proving it with my actions when I worked out.

When the camp was over, I walked over to the Starbucks to change again. I had an extra days' worth of clothes and wanted to get out of these sweaty clothes. Then, I sat inside of Starbucks and I waited for my Lyft to pick me up. I had to figure out where I was going to sleep for the night, so I just decided to go back to the bus station and I found an empty bench. I was prepared to have another long night and then leave the next morning. In the meantime, I saw that the ticket booth was open. I didn't know what this meant but I figured I would ask them about my ticket and see if I could have my day changed for leaving today instead of early tomorrow and it was possible to change my ticket for a small fee. I was so happy and thankful that I did not have to spend another long night here again. I was just completely thrilled to know I was leaving this place and never had to come back again, no offense to the beautiful city of Indianapolis. God really came through and answered my prayer and I couldn't thank him enough. The devil will always try and throw obstacles at you because God has big plans for you and the devil doesn't want you to prevail. It's your job to not fall into the temptation of giving up but letting experiences like this make you stronger and grow. They told me that the next bus going to Chicago was not leaving for another two hours, so I sat around and waited. I kept dozing off but set a timer on my phone so I would know when to get up. Time flew by unlike the morning when I was just staring at the clock. I was the first in life to get on that bus. I had never been so ready to leave a place in my life. I was so hungry because the last time I had eaten was around 7am and it was now 5:30pm. I made sure to grab a handful of Skittles for the bus ride home. At least then my stomach wouldn't growl as much. I contacted Adam about what was going on. He was in Chicago already with his friends, so this worked out perfectly. While I was sitting on the bus I prayed and gave thanks to God again. I was just very thankful he kept me safe through all of this. Before the bus took off, I made sure to ask the bus driver around what time we were going to be back in Chicago so I could set a timer on my phone and go to sleep. I set an alarm on my phone and fell asleep during the 3-hour ride home. What a life-altering experience this was.

After Indianapolis Basketball Camp

Once my timer went off I was so happy to find out that I was back in Chicago. As I got off the bus and sat inside another bus station I called Adam to let him know I was back, ordered some cheese fries and waited. Once I killed my cheese fries, Adam arrived and I got in the car and thanked him. He asked me if I learned my lesson about planning ahead and all I could do was laugh because he was right. A hard lesson learned for the rest of my life. After a two-hour ride back home to Rockford, we finally made it. I was so happy to be sleeping on a bed and not a hard metal bench. God taught me not to take the little things for granted with this experience. Before I went to bed, I prayed again giving thanks to God and I slept like a newborn baby that night, hoping I would have enough rest for school in the morning.

Once the month of April started, I continued my routine of getting up in the morning at 5:30am-6am and jogging two miles to work out before school, then school and Algebra, and walking to the city bus station to head to one of my two jobs. After work, I would take the city bus home and go back to the gym. I loved this routine because my days always flew by and I felt like I was always accomplishing a lot. I just needed to work harder in my Algebra class if I planned on graduating high school on time and moving to Florida. I still had one whole semester's worth of work and only one month left to finish. I was never very good at Algebra, so this was a challenge for me, but I was lucky to have a great teacher, Mr. Brooks, who helped me out a lot. It was up to me to stay disciplined on my work during class because it was a self-paced school. Meaning, if I just sat on my phone the whole day and got no work done then that was my fault. I started turning my phone off to stay focused more because I needed to get through this and finish. As far as going to college in Florida, me and Adam continued planning ahead and figuring things out. We needed to figure out exactly how much money I needed to save. He was telling me how bad it would be if in the middle of school I could not afford to pay rent. Then that would lead to me having nowhere to live and not being able to show up for my classes and leading me to fail out my first semester. But we were both very confident I would get this DCFS scholarship by graduating on time.

While I was continuing this routine of working hard, I also started to work on myself heavily. I continued going to my youth groups once a week and going to church every Sunday at City First Church. Each time I came here, I couldn't help but remember living with my former foster parent, Linda, and how terrified I was on my first day—crying alone in a corner. It was amazing to see my growth from then to now. That's what my goal was in life: to keep growing more as a young man and strengthen my relationship with God. I wanted to be a great man one day. I wanted to be someone who everyone would say, "Devin is a nice, funny, great person and a great friend." We all have to die one day but I wanted to leave a legacy of being someone who impacted people in a positive way and was a great man. I never wanted to be labeled as a mean, rude, or disrespectful person because then nobody would want to be around me. In the beginning it was always hard because of how shut down I was and how I did not trust anyone. I was always angry and rude to people a lot of the time and that's not who I wanted to be. I was starting to get rid of that defensive and angry side I had. I was learning how to control it more and think before I do things. But one thing that I had to work on was respecting my mother and father as it says in the Bible.

It was very hard for me to follow the Bible about respecting my mother and father, especially after all the things they did to me. How can I respect a man who beat the crap out of me for years and damaged me? Also, how can I respect a woman who abandoned me and fed me so many lies and stories for years? They both damaged me, and I ended up having so many problems because of them. I was always angry at God because he dealt me two shitty parents, but I learned that these are my earthly parents. My ultimate parent is God and I had to work with what I was given and know it could always be worse. This gave me the strength to overcome. I had to learn to let the grudge inside of me go so I could grow more. I talked to my foster parent Adam about this and he gave me some great advice to get in touch with my mom. Instead of always having short conversations with her and her just asking me if I needed money and if I was okay, I started opening up to her. I tried to get a better understanding by talking to her more and getting to know who she was because I really did not know much about her other than she was a liar. I already knew I did not want anything to do with my dad anymore, even when he got out of prison. I lost all respect for him and I can't allow someone like that to be in my life or be around my children one day. Especially after everything I witnessed as a child. I just decided to write letters to him that I was never going to send but I wanted to forgive him and move on for my own sake and peace. As far as my older sister and my relationship with her, I tried to mend our relationship again. I ended up inviting her to my life group at church and inviting her to come on Sundays as well and after some conversation she agreed to come. But this would be the day that she crossed the line with me.

I let her know that every first Wednesday of the month a guest speaker would come and speak at City First Church. It was not going to be a life group service, it would be an actual church service. After some convincing, my older sister agreed to come to service. She told me that she would be picking me up from my house and to wait outside for her. So I got ready and I waited outside for her to come. Once she came I got in the car and saw my little nephew was in the back seat, so I was very happy to see him. We had a good talk in the car on our way to service and everything. seemed good. But things suddenly changed once we got into the parking lot of the church. She dropped me at the front door, and I was confused because I thought she was coming with me. But she ended up telling me to go ahead and go inside before I was late and find us a spot while she went and found a parking spot to park the car. So I went inside the church and sat down and saved a seat for her and waited, and waited. A little over an hour went by and she never came inside the service. I was so confused as to what was going on. Once service was over, I called her and asked where she was because she was my ride home. She told me she was coming to get me and to wait out front for her to. After fifteen minutes had passed by and she never showed up, I was getting pissed off and annoyed because I felt like she was playing games with me. I called her and she said she was parked in the parking lot and to walk to her. I searched all around the parking lot and could not find her. She gave me no hints, no clues, or nothing. She just said, "I'm in the parking lot." The parking lot at church was completely full because it was a packed service.

After ten minutes of walking around trying to find my sister's car I finally found it. Her car was not hard to miss because the entire front of it was ripped off. Once I got inside, I immediately started asking her what was wrong and why she did not come into the service. She disregarded everything I said and simply turned the music up to its maximum volume. Next, she went from 0 to 100 and sped down the road as she drove me home. I began to panic and felt myself having an anxiety attack. My dad used to do this every time he got mad, just drive full speed and I used to get so scared he would kill us all. I remembered my stepmom used to scream and cry begging for my father to stop. I had flashbacks of this and I couldn't believe she was doing this with her 7-month-old son in the back seat. I turned the volume down and asked her what was going on and what's wrong. Then, she started screaming and crying and at this point I thought we were going to crash. My older sister has had a history of acting out while driving. One time, she got mad and tried to jump out of a moving car and I promised myself after this that I would never ride with her in a car again. I told her to pull over and let me out of the car. When we finally got off of the busy intersection and into a street close to where I lived, she stopped the car and I got out. I called her a psychopath and told her don't ever give me a ride again and before I could close the door, she went from tore away and ran over my foot while the passenger door was open. My foot was shooting in pain. I was just lucky I had boots on that day and my ankle didn't roll otherwise she would have broken a toe or possibly my ankle. I could not believe this incident happened, especially with my 7-month-old nephew in the back seat of her car. She could have killed both of us or even worse her own damn son. I was just so thankful his car seat was strapped all the way in because he could have flung out of it the way she was driving.

She slammed on the brakes because the passenger door was still wide open and the door closed from the impact. Once the door shut she took off driving down the road. I was just enraged with anger, I couldn't believe my own sister just ran over my foot with her car and turned into a complete psycho on the road for no reason, almost killing us. I was so tired of giving her chance after chance and her screwing me over. She had been doing this ever since we were little kids. I walked home that night and I told Adam what happened. I wanted to get back at her by calling the police on her and have her arrested for doing stupid stuff like that. I was scared for my little nephew more than anything. But Adam took it the complete wrong way. He got upset with me and went on about how you don't have family arrested—that it's messed up. If that was the case then how come anytime I ever did something wrong he threatened to have the police called on me but then claimed we were family? He then mentioned my 9-month-old nephew and how he would be taken away and sent to a foster home and it would be my fault if he grew up messed up or abused. I couldn't believe Adam was saying all of that stuff. I stopped talking to him and went to my room for the rest of the night. I was just pissed off and tired of the fake shit in my life. I was tired of being lied to and betrayed by people. I didn't want anything to do with my older sister again.

After that incident, I became very bitter and angry. I was tired of having all these crappy people in my life and being treated like garbage all the time. I didn't understand how hard it was just to be happy. I felt like I would never be happy unless I was alone. It pissed me off even more to hear how Adam told me I was in the wrong for wanting to have my sister arrested or having her get some serious mental help because of what she just did. I don't think he understood that she could have killed all of us in the car that day. I bet that if it was me doing that to him he would've had me arrested that night. I was just tired of being wronged by people in life and ready to walk away. I wanted to move away from everyone and just start a new life. I hated how Adam always threw up the importance of family and how important they were and how I would never be a good or successful man in life until I worked on my relationship with them. Overtime, that pissed me off more and more and started to make me feel horrible about myself as a person. He had no idea all the things that I had gone through with my dad's side of the family and my older sister. It was like things were going back to how they first were when I was going to school at Harlem and first moved in with him. I understood he was trying to help but he had a very rude way of giving advice. It's like I'm supposed to keep letting people walk all over me and forgive them as if nothing happened. I don't think he understands everyone is different and might not do it his way. I can forgive people from a distance and not be involved in their lives. No matter how much he talked about forgiving family, I couldn't repair my relationship with my dad's side of the family, who were racist, abandoned me in shelter homes, a facility, and a hospital, and never once took me in or offered any help. Especially since I also had aunts and uncles and none of them wanted me. I did not want anything to do with those people again. I just wanted to pray about it and ask God to take away the anger and hatred I had towards them. I did not want to carry that bag of rocks on my back anymore.

I always had questions for God when I prayed as to why I had the father and mother that I had. Why did I have the older sister that I had? I don't think my friends and people understand how lucky they are to have a mother or a father who loves them unconditionally and supports them through whatever. I see why it is so important to raise a child the correct way while they are young, so they don't have these problems as they get older. I felt like my whole life I never felt real and unconditional love. I knew I hadn't because my entire life I was abused physically and mentally by my father, my dad's side of the family, in foster homes and in Lutherbrook. I hated hugs, I hated anything to do with love and I would shut down. My mother and father, the people who were supposed to love me and care for me never did and abused me mentally and physically. I was so scared by this and hurt for years. Once I entered foster care I stopped caring about love. I felt like I was always a cold soul. I was nice to people but never wanted to be attached to them because I felt like they would betray me. Especially after I was robbed at gunpoint by a foster kid who I used to be friends with. I tried to explain to my foster parent Adam about all of this but he didn't understand and said I was making excuses and needed to grow up. He was right in a way because I did need to grow from this and use it as motivation. But in another way it hurt because sometimes I felt I had nobody to talk to and had to keep this bottled up. I was just so tired of all the stress, anger and hard times that kept coming in my life. People always told me God gives his hardest battles to his toughest soldiers, but I didn't ask to be a tough soldier. I didn't ask for any of this in life. Some days I got really depressed and just felt like I had nobody and no purpose. I was tired of living this hard life.

Sometimes I got so tired of living this life that I would try to commit suicide. I would walk to Walmart, buy a small bottle of NyQuil and soda, pour the NyQuil into my soda, mix it together and drink it, hoping I wouldn't wake up or the days would go faster. I used to do this all the time while I was at Lutherbrook. Whenever I walked home from the bus station I would stop by the Dollar Tree and steal a bottle of NyQuil and drink it so the days would go faster. At first, I did not think it was suicide I thought it was just getting through the days faster, but the first time I realized I was trying to kill myself was on my 15th birthday. Staff at Lutherbrook kept noticing how I went to bed early all the time. At first, they thought it was just from me being tired but eventually they realized it was not normal. On my 15th birthday I went to sleep early, and they knew this was not normal because nobody goes to sleep as early as I was going, especially at 15 years old. A staff member went into my room while I was asleep and saw the empty bottle of NyQuil. I must've been clumsy that day because I usually hid it in the trash, but they found it. Lutherbrook ended up calling the ambulance and I woke up to the paramedics shaking me. They took my vitals and did other checks on me and told me if I had drunk a normal sized bottle of NyQuil I would have overdosed. I felt pathetic doing this, but I was tired of living this shitty life and tired of always being stressed out and angry. I was tired of going through this bullshit and hurt. I was just a very bitter and quiet person at times, numb to life. I felt like I had no support, part of it was my fault because I did not allow friends to know what was going on, but I just shut down. I reached my limit with being treated like shit in foster homes, always going hungry and having to walk so far in the cold. I was tired of not having a family and tired of feeling like I had nobody in my life. I was tired of feeling alone, at least if I was dead I knew I would no longer be alone or have to live this life that I had.

It was now early May, and I only had about 3 weeks left to graduate high school on time. I decided to use all the bullshit and stress going on around me as motivation to succeed. I read my bible, prayed, continued my routine of working hard, and stayed focused on what mattered. I had to accept that I change or control people, but I can change who comes in my life and who I allow to be involved in my life. I can also change who I want to become as a man. I made the decision to stop letting others distract me and prevent me from pushing forward.There is no room in this life for a quitter and I know God has bigger plans for me. The devil was just trying to throw me off my path, but it made me stronger. In the classroom, I continued to turn my phone off and focus. Algebra was still hard for me, but I was not going to back down. I managed to work hard enough to where I completed two semesters worth of work in four months and now I only had three chapters left until I would be able to graduate on time. I was very determined and ready to achieve this. The main coping skill I used to help me was going to the YMCA. The YMCA was like my home and my escape from everything. There was something about dribbling and shooting a ball for hours that helped me gain confidence in myself and feel some type of achievement. But it helped me to not be inside of my foster homes. I was always trying to stay away from my foster homes as much as possible to avoid any drama or conflict. I figured if I were not home, no drama or problems would be able to start. So, I always tried to do this at every foster home I was at. Even when I went to work, I stayed quiet to avoid any conflict. I just wanted to graduate high school and move to Florida to start a new life.

When I did have to be in my foster home, I tried to stay in my room and kept quiet. I did not want to risk losing anything or start any drama. But Adam always wanted to pick a fight by saying smartass things or he would throw the stuff I did wrong up in my face constantly like it was a joke or a game. I tried to tell him many times that when he would do stuff like this, it frustrated me and hurt my feelings. I was not trying to play a tough guy role anymore where I took everything in and didn't care. I felt I had a voice and needed to address it the right way. It was like he would bully me in a way and tear me down when he did this. I know those were not his intentions but when someone tells you they don't like something, and you keep doing it, then it's a problem. The more he kept throwing the things I did wrong and what I opened up to him about in my face, the more it made me angry. He was always trying to antagonize people and trying to get a rise out of them. It was not new to me because he had been doing this since I first lived with him back when I was 16, calling me pizza face because of my acne and saying how nobody in my family loved me and how when I got robbed they should have shot me. I never understood if he was bipolar or what, but it was exhausting living with him at times. One minute everything would be fine, and he would be telling you he loved you. It was always hard living in foster homes, not just in his house but in all of them. You never knew when a foster parent would put their two week's notice in and want you removed. I felt like I always had to be perfect throughout my entire life because while I was living with my father he would beat the shit out of me if I did not do exactly as he said and messed up. Then living in foster homes, if I messed up, they wanted me gone. As time went on Adam kept antagonizing me by throwing stuff in my face and I finally got sick of his mouth and I snapped on him after trying so hard not to.

I had to do chores around the house in order to live there. I had been doing chores my entire life, so this was nothing new. In fact, I liked doing chores because I knew it would help me be responsible and clean as an adult later on in life. But sometimes I would forget to do my chores, and this would piss him off. This was the first foster home I was in where if I forgot to do my chores, he would take pictures and send them to my phone and then threaten to kick me out. It was very annoying when he did this because I would be in the middle of school or check my phone while I was at the gym and see a picture of a chore and I forgot to do it with a rude message attached to it and a threat to put in his two week's notice. I felt like he was always trying to pick a fight with someone. Part of it was my fault because sometimes I forgot but the second I slipped up it was like none of that mattered. It was something I had to get used to, it was just a lot of pressure to never forget constantly and it caused a lot of stress on me to be perfect. But Just like Mrs. Milly, Adam was very big on chores. Adam's next big chore was to clean his yard. All of us had to go outside and help otherwise we would get in trouble. While we were cleaning the yard up, we started trimming leaves, mowing the yard, raking the branches and trash up in the yard, and picking up dog poop. When it came to doing yard work outside with Adam and the other foster kids, I hated it because I always ended up doing most of the work.

We had been doing yard work for almost four days now and we all were getting tired of it. I had scratches all over my arms and back from crawling under the branches. I also had a few blisters on my hand from raking for so long. I guess I should've taken the advice I was given about wearing gloves while using a rake. On the 4th day outside, it was me, another foster kid, and Adam in the yard. But while we were out here Adam kept making smart comments to me while we were having conversations. I was already annoyed because he had been doing this for so long and I was busting my ass helping him and doing most of the work. Then, he made one last smart comment and I was finally done. When he threw the incident up about what happened with me and my sister in my face I was just enraged. I threw the rake down and walked away before things escalated. I was fed up and tired of his smart and rude comments. I just went inside and sat in my room to cool down.

While I was trying to cool down inside, he kept sending me text messages telling me to pack my stuff up and that he was putting in his two week's notice if I didn't come back outside and help. I was so sick and tired of that. I let my anger get the best of me and I went back outside and started arguing with him. For a while we were just talking a bunch of crap to each other embarrassing ourselves. But once he told me to "shut the fuck up" twice and raked branches and leaves onto my feet and pants, I went all in. I got into his face and just cussed him out calling him a bunch of rude things and we both threatened to fight each other. It was like all the coping skills I had learned from counseling were just thrown out of the window at this point. That's when I walked past him to go inside the house one final time and I shoulder bumped him. This is a 280 pound grown man compared to my 160 pounds. I shoulder bumped him so lightly that he didn't even move. I was really just waiting for him to put his hands on me so I would have a reason to knock his fat ass out. Whenever it came to Adam he was all about the police in these moments and if one of us was going to get arrested, I was going to make sure it would have been him for touching me fist.

Adam headed inside and the other foster kid told me I shouldn't have done that because I can get arrested for that. I didn't think that a shoulder bump would result in jail time, especially on a grown man. When I finally walked back inside, I decided to pack my bag up and go to the YMCA. At least I could get away from this house and get a peace of mind dribbling and shooting a basketball. As I was packing my gym bag, I heard a walkie talkie going off and it sounded like a police officer was inside. Sure enough I was right, and two police officers walked into my room. I was confused at how in the world they got here so fast when this incident just happened. I told the officers I was going to the gym and to move and they told me to stay in the room because they had a few questions about what happened outside. So, I had to sit down and explain everything. I told the officers that Adam and I got into a heated argument, he raked some branches and leaves onto my body and we got into each other's face and threatened to hit each other. None of us ended up hitting one another and I walked away, and I went to leave and go to the gym to clear my head.

After explaining my story, the police officer told me to put my hands behind my back and told me that I was being arrested for domestic violence. Apparently that little shoulder bump was enough to get me arrested. Now, I was really pissed off because if I had known this I would've punched him in his fat ass face as hard as I could, at least then it would be worth getting arrested for. My anger was getting the best of me and I started becoming loud with the police officers and I refused to put my hands behind my back because I didn't do anything. I really did not like police anyways from all the previous encounters I had with them while I was younger and with white cops killing unarmed black people. The officer kept saying sir put your hands behind your back and if I didn't cooperate they would use force and I would be charged for resisting arrest. I started to escalate things and told the officer to go ahead and use force then. That's when he called the other officer inside for backup to help. I started getting disrespectful with the officer and calling him a bitch a few times and other mean names because he had to call another police officer for help. I ended up putting my arms behind my back so I wouldn't get a second charge and next thing I knew I was walking out in handcuffs to a police car.

I was just so angry. I was so pissed off how a shoulder bump is considered an act of violence. I was tired of living in these foster homes and being treated like shit all the time. I was tired of always having to be perfect and the minute I made a mistake everything was over. I felt like I was betrayed again and that this was a horrible cycle that kept on happening in my life. When I did finally calm down the officer asked me who this man was, and I told him he was my foster parent. He told me he felt bad for me because a lot of foster kids go through this kind of thing, but I did not care what he had to say. If he really cared he would have taken these handcuffs off and let me go. The officer did tell me not to worry because it was around 4pm on a Sunday and I would see a judge the very next day and possibly get out. He told me I had a very high chance of getting out the next day over something small like this. I had an even higher chance because I was not on probation or had any adult arrest records before. I was just so angry I couldn't believe this man betrayed me like this. After all the long talks and trust I gave him, for him to do this to me I felt like I got stabbed in the back. I was completely filled with nothing but hate and anger. I felt like I was such a fool for trusting this man. After 15 minutes in the back of a cop car handcuffed, we finally pulled off. I was now going to be an inmate at the Winnebago County Jail at just 18 years old.

Winnebago County Jail

After a very long 15-minute ride in the back of a cop car facing the reality that I was going to be in adult jail for the first time in my life, we made it downtown to the police station. The police officer pulled in through the back part of the jail. I was happy I was finally able to get out of this car because of how squished I was. The officer walked behind me and took me inside with handcuffs on. Once I got inside, he took my handcuffs off and left, and I had to sit on a bench and wait for what was next. The entire time I waited I didn't say a single word. I was too angry and sad about what just happened to me. I felt nothing but betrayal. I was also in shock the entire time trying to figure out how crazy everything was. Everything had changed so quickly. One minute I was a free man the next I'm in handcuffs being placed in jail. It was just crazy to me how things can change that fast. While I sat and waited angrily on the bench for 15 minutes, the processing officer came inside and got me. He took me to another room to get processed. At least this room had a TV on and a place where you could make a phone call. The only problem was I had no one to call, I had nobody but myself. I was back to feeling alone again. Since I had nobody to call, I ended up just sitting in this chair for 20 minutes watching this game of baseball waiting to be called up. This was where I was going to get fingerprinted and my mugshot taken. Once the officer called my name, I walked over to him and he grabbed a few of my fingers and scanned them through this finger printing machine. Then I had to have my mugshot taken. I was so embarrassed and angry during this time I still could not talk or say anything. I felt so ashamed of myself to know my picture would be posted for everyone to see. This made it all the more embarrassing. I wasn't even a bad kid or a street kid. I went to Church, played basketball, went to work, and went to school. I never bothered anyone and always tried my best to be nice to people. Going through this I felt very low about myself. I felt like a complete failure, it was one of the most upsetting times in my life.

After another 20 minutes of waiting, another officer called my name. This officer came to me and had a bin in his hand. He told me I had to change out of my clothes and put them in this bin. He handed me another bin with a set of clothes in it. I had to go into a room with a curtain and take all my clothes off to change into this 1-piece jumpsuit. This felt very uncomfortable and weird. I couldn't believe I wasn't even allowed to wear my own socks anymore. I had to put on these weird smiley face ankle socks. I was just pissed off and annoyed to think I was going through all of this over a shoulder bump. Once I got done changing into this dirty jumpsuit, I gave all my clothes away to them in a bin. Then I took the bin I was given and carried it with me and walked down to my unit. There were so many security doors we had to go through just to get to my unit. You would've thought they had El Chapo or some other crazy criminals locked up inside of here. It felt like it was one of the longest walks I had taken in my life.

I finally got down to my unit. This was the unit where I would be sleeping and staying. Once I got here and the door closed behind me, I really had to face the hard fact I was in jail now. Everywhere I looked there was nothing but cells all around the walls. I was already ready to leave this place. Other than the cells everywhere, they had three pentagon shaped tables welded to the ground. As I walked further along, I saw two small televisions on the wall with a bunch of plastic chairs all around. There were four phones on the walls and there was a little room where you could walk around in a circle or back and forth. There were probably about twenty other men here and I was clearly the youngest and the most ashamed of myself. After I finished walking around and seeing what this unit was like, I went into my cell where there was a bunk bed and a toilet. I found it crazy how this was supposed to be for two people considering how small it was. I could not imagine being locked up inside of here for a long time. I hadn't even been here 24 hours and I was ready to leave. I just sat inside of my cell while everyone else was watching the televised basketball game. I got on the top of the bunkbed and just laid down and stared at the ceiling and got lost inside my thoughts.

I was still in complete shock by how fast everything happened. I couldn't believe that all of this was real, it felt like I was in a bad dream. I felt so betrayed and stabbed in the back. I really trusted Adam and thought we had a great relationship. I opened up to him more than anyone else and I was so mad at myself for this. I hated that I trusted him, and I did not want to trust anyone ever again. I felt like everybody was a liar, especially these foster parents. I hated foster homes and I never wanted to stay in another one after this. I would have rather been homeless then lay my head down in a foster parents house knowing they are getting paid to have me. I felt like everyone who I trusted was going to screw me over in a way. My mom, dad, sister, aunts, uncles, grandparents, friends, and foster parents all did it. I was amazed at how many people had screwed me over in life, to think these people are supposed to be the ones who do good by your side. It was almost unreal to me how people in this world managed to have loving families. All I had was nothing but shitty person after shitty person in my life. I was so mad and confused as to why God placed such shitty people in my life and the more I thought about it, the angrier I got. I wished I would've punched that man straight in his fatass face if I had known I would be going to jail for shoulder bumping him. Since I was 16 Adam and I had an on and off relationship and I was just so mad at myself that I let him back in. I just prayed to God and asked him to forgive me for being stupid and making this mistake. Here I am trying to grow more as a man and become successful and look at where I am. There were so many different ways I could've handled this situation and I chose to handle it the wrong way. I had nobody to blame but myself. I felt like my pathetic father and was ashamed of myself. I knew I was better than this and could do better. I was going to use this as a lesson to never come back here in life.

Eventually I stopped overthinking and got out of my head

when my cellmate walked in the room. We started talking right away, he was a nice person. He was in his late 30's and had been arrested for stealing something from the grocery store. When he asked me what I was arrested for and I explained it to him, he started laughing right away. He had never heard of anyone being arrested for something as dumb as that before. I agreed with him, the next thing I was going to be arrested for was for pinching someone or looking at someone the wrong way. After a while of talking, we both went out to the common area and met some of the other people out there. Everyone was watching the NBA playoffs, especially since the Toronto Raptors were playing and Fred VanVleet was in the game. Watching him on TV while I was in jail gave me hope that everything was going to be okay. If someone from the same city I was from and went to the same high school I went to could overcome all adversity and be successful, then I was going to do the same thing one day. During the game I started talking to the other inmates, I never had any trouble making friends or talking to people because I had been around all different types of people my entire life. One of the inmates asked how old I was and what I was in here for while we were talking about the basketball game. As I explained the scenario for a second time, he started bursting out laughing and called like ten other guys to come listen to my situation. Everyone else started hovering around me, as I recalled the day's events and they all started laughing. I guess nobody had ever heard of someone getting arrested for bumping somebody with your shoulder. I felt like I was a comedian because I had already made my cellmate, the man next to me and now almost the entire unit laugh. I was laughing on the outside but crying on the inside, I was so mad. Then they asked if it was an old lady or something. I told them no it was almost a 300 pound fat, grown man. When I explained that I was in foster care, they all understood it more. They all knew foster parents would do mean stuff like that to foster kids, in fact some of the inmates used to be foster kids. Then they started telling me the stuff foster parents would do to them and it was just a vicious cycle of abuse and mistreatment. I wanted to be someone who would change this all one day. Eventually the guard came over and asked what was going on because of all the noise we were making. When I told him, he told me that I would be gone by tomorrow and not to worry about being held here. The guard was actually really nice and apologized for me being in foster care and knew about the abuse inside of the system from what he had and seen on the news from other foster kids. I actually started laughing to myself after hearing so many people's reaction to how much of a piece of shit Adam was. It was funny to me how he portrayed himself as a nice and helpful man, but he was really a backstabbing piece of shit. Over time, I stopped being so angry and mad at myself after everyone's reaction and advice. I just knew that my day to succeed would come and all I had to do was keep my faith in God and work hard.

Soon, it was time to eat dinner. Our trays came down in a cart, the same cart they used while I was at Riverside Medical Center. The officer turned off the TV and we all had to get in a line to receive our trays and they passed them out one by one. When I received my tray, I was disgusted. The food was so nasty, it looked like dog food. But at least it was better than eating Ramen Noodles, Oreos or Hot Pockets, it was actual food. But the food looked very weird, it was like a liquid pile of crap. What made it even worse was all the liquid spread into the other things on my tray and I lost my appetite. I just had to shut up and eat it because this was all I was going to be able to eat until the morning. But I couldn't help myself from thinking where is Gordon Ramsay when you need him? I watched so many shows with him, he would've flipped out if he had seen this. After eating, we were told to go back into our cells. This was the first time since I stepped foot inside of jail that I started to get a slight panic attack. I hated having doors locked on me and being stuck inside places with no way out because it always reminded me of the time my father beat the shit out of me and locked me in my room for an entire day. I had to pee on myself because I couldn't get up from the beating he gave me. But being inside of this very little hot room with another man made me nervous. I heard all about the gay stuff that happened in jail and I was not trying to get it in the butt. I made sure I didn't take a shower or have any soap because I heard the rule about dropping the soap. As the door locked I was now trapped inside. But what helped me calm down was when my cell mate started talking to me about how his girl was supposed to bail him out and he was going to have sex with her right when he got out. That calmed me down a lot because at least I knew he wasn't going to try any gay stuff on me.

While I was locked inside of my cell and laying on top of the bunk bed, I was trying to fall asleep so the night would fly by faster. But it was only 7pm and it felt like the longest day of my life. I had never been ready to leave from somewhere in my life. I was ready to see what God had planned for me once I got out of here. I was told that in the morning if we wanted to eat, we had to get up early. I did not want to miss breakfast because then I would go hungry for the rest of the day. As I laid down I began to stop thinking so much and relax. I prayed and asked God to help me use this experience to motivate me to be successful. One of my favorite stories in the Bible was how God delivered Moses and the Israelites out of Egypt after 400 years of slavery. After reading that I knew I had a God on my side who works miracles. The devil was just throwing this obstacle in my path to try and distract me from what God has planned for me. I also thought about all the athletes I was inspired by and how they got out of the hard times they were in and became successful. I just refused to lose my faith in God regardless if I was in a huge mansion or in a jail cell. I knew that I had been through way worse and people out there were in way worse situations than I was. It's easier to get discouraged when you go through hard times because that's what people and the devil want to have happen. But I made sure I was not going to let this happen. Before I went to sleep I prayed and thanked God for putting me in this situation because it was going to help me grow more as a man. You will never be able to grow in life if you never go through challenging times and I was thankful for this experience. I also prayed for God to keep me safe through the night and to wake me up tomorrow as I do every night. My faith in God and my motivation to succeed in life got stronger tonight. I knew one day that this was going to be a part of my success story, all I had to do was keep working hard and believe in myself.

When I woke up, it was breakfast time. I hurried up and jumped from the top of my bunk because I was hungry. I'm not sure why I woke up so excited after what I had for dinner the night before, but I was. We had to get in a single file line as the guard passed out trays just as he did at dinner time. I grabbed my tray disappointed and disgusted and sat down. The food looked even worse than dinner. It looked as if there was white dog crap all over my plate. When I asked what it was they told me it was supposed to be biscuits and gravy, but this was way worse. The only good thing from breakfast was the jelly packet and the dry piece of bread that was supposed to be toast.I knew jail food wouldn't be great, and I'm not expecting a gourmet meal, but this was unlike anything I'd ever encountered. Like I said, I always grew up poor and eating poor my entire life, so I just sucked the jelly packet down by itself and I ate that dry piece of bread and called it breakfast. It wasn't my first time eating a nasty breakfast and I was just happy I was given food to eat. It could always be a lot worse in life, I didn't want to make God angry, so I tried to stay grateful. I was even happier that later on that day, I would be leaving. That was just one of the many other positive things that came to mind.

Once I finished eating, I had to wait my turn to use the phone. I had to speak with a public defender through the machine so he could help me get out of here. Once I got on the phone with the public defender, he asked me questions about what happened that led up to my arrest and I explained it to him. This was the first person I told the story to and did not laugh so I was happy about that. I was informed that I would be having court later on that day and to expect to get a recognizance bond. I had no idea what that meant so I got nervous right when I got off the phone. I thought that meant I was going to be kept inside of jail longer and I immediately got upset and began to panic. But I ended up asking another inmate what a recognizance bond meant and he told me that's where you don't have to pay to get out of jail. I felt like I was bipolar for a second because I went from angry to happy in the matter of a minute. Now I just had to wait around for a few hours until my court time came up. I ended up watching a fishing show on TV with another inmate who had been here for a few months, so he had the privilege to watch the TV. I had never seen anyone so entertained by a fishing show in my life, it was funny and cool to see how different we all were from each other. After waiting for about two hours, it was finally time to leave to go upstairs to court. We all had to get in a single file line again, as they cuffed us up. This time it was not handcuffs, we had to be shackled from our hands down to our feet and have this belly chain on. You would've thought I committed murder the way I was shackled up. As we started walking my feet were starting to hurt so bad because every time someone walked too fast, the chain would yank at my skin. It was like these other inmates were used to this or had done this and knew the correct form to walk. I felt so embarrassed having these chains all around me. All of this for a stupid shoulder bump. In my head, I was thinking that I should've called the police on him during Thanksgiving last year when he slammed me on the ground, choked me and smacked me and left me with bruises on my arm and face. But I forgave him and moved on from that incident. I feel like people always take my kindness and forgiveness for granted because I feel like I do it so often. I was just frustrated that I was even in this position to begin with. But I just kept my faith strong and stayed positive. I knew God was going to get me through this as he had done time and time again.

Once we got upstairs, we all simultaneously sat down inside of a specific room. I was given a piece of paper which was the statement from Adam stating what happened from his point of view. It made me even angrier to see the words "shoulder bump." I wish it would've said a lot of other things instead of a shoulder bump. But at the same time I was glad that was all it said because I was ready to get out of here. After they broke us up into specific waiting rooms, we waited to be called into court one by one. This was like torture sitting in a room full of dirty and sweaty men waiting for our fates in front of a judge. I really learned to appreciate women after this because they really are a gift from God. It also inspired me to never be like these men, listening to the conversations they had inside of here because they made all men seem like filthy pigs. I knew I never wanted to talk like that or end up like that in my life. As the other inmates started going in one by one I was happy to hear that some of the others who did worse stuff than me got recognizance bonds. This helped boost my confidence and faith that I would be given oneness well. After a while of waiting I was finally called into the courtroom. Before I went inside they shackled me up once again and my ankles started hurting right away. As they opened the door, I walked into court with my shackles on. I looked in the crowd area and saw my cousin sitting on the bench watching. I was in complete shock that he knew I was here and that he was even in attendance. We were not really that close and didn't talk much. But I quickly turned around and faced the judge as he started talking to me. I pretty much zoned everything he said out and was just listening for what was going to happen. He was using such fancy language that I didn't really understand either, but I knew that I needed to advance my vocabulary. I zoned out thinking about how I was going through all of this over a shoulder bump. All of this court bullshit was pathetic and a joke. I really got to understand and see why so many foster kids end up dead or in jail. Considering everything I've been through so far, it's hard to believe there are kids who have experienced much worse. I also got to understand why so many people protest the United States justice system. Once I refocused, the judge informed me that I would be returning to my foster home and granted me a recognizance bond. I made sure to give my thanks to God for this. I was so happy and thankful to hear I would be leaving jail. I was so sick of being inside and sitting around all day wasting my life and opportunities. I felt like I was back at Mrs. Johnson's house where I used to just sit around all the time. I had too much faith, hard work, and belief in myself to not succeed one day, and sitting around made me feel like I was just wasting time on the path to get there. I had a purpose driven life regardless of my living situation. God had something bigger planned for me and that's why he helped me get out of here.

After court was over, the guards escorted us all back down to our units. We were told we had to wait here until we were going to get discharged. They never gave us a time the guards just told us it would be sometime during the night. I was just happy I was leaving that night, so I had no room to complain at all. I sat around and watched some of the NBA playoffs on TV with the rest of the inmates. I was surprised at how peaceful this jail was because I always heard that there would be lots of fighting and violence. Nobody ever bothered me the entire time I was in here. We stopped watching TV once the dinner cart came down. We all had to get in a single file line and wait for our tray to be handed out as usual. I was so happy to see it was good food this time.

We got spaghetti, salad, bread with butter, and a piece of cake. I had never eaten so fast before; I was so hungry. I was even asking other people if they were going to finish their food and I got lucky and had extras. I called it a going away and never coming back meal. Once we finished eating we all had to go to our cells for the night and wait. Me and my cellmate were both being discharged so we had to wait until we were called. This felt like it took forever because we were constantly waiting for the guards to call our names. I just sat on top of my bunk bed and got lost in my thoughts asking myself what would be after this? What was next for me in my life? I felt like my chances of moving to Florida were ruined. I felt like I was a huge failure now and was going to be living in Rockford for the rest of my life. Seeing the same people from middle school everywhere I go doing the same stuff all the time. I felt like I blew my chances to be successful. A negative wave of emotions began to hit me all at once. I was trying to remain positive, but it was hard for me not to think realistic. But I had to remember I had a God on my side who works miracles, the devil was just trying to get inside of my head.

Soon out of nowhere our cell door unlocked and the guard told me, and my cellmate, it was time for us to leave. Right then and there I knew that was the power of God. The guard told us to pack all of our stuff up inside of our bin. So, I grabbed my mattress, blanket, and cup and put it inside of the bin like I was told to do. Afterwards all the people who were getting discharged that night had to line up. I felt like I was in kindergarten again the way we had to get in a single file line every time. The heavy metal doors finally opened, and it was time to leave. I was so happy we didn't have to walk out in shackles this time and have my ankles yanked at again. We went through about five different doors and we finally made it to the discharge area. Fresh air never smelled so good before. In the discharge area, we had to return our bins that we were given when we first entered our units. I took my bin and slid it through a door, and then they gave me my bin with my stuff that I had before I changed into my jail uniform. I was so happy to be wearing my clothes again and not some one-piece jumpsuit. I was even happier to be wearing underwear again, wearing underwear had never felt so good before. I got dressed behind a curtain and made sure that I had all my belongings. As I was getting ready to walk out of the door, I was given a court slip of when my next court date was. I signed a copy of the paper stating that I received it and before I left I was told by the officer to be on my best behavior. As I walked out the door I was almost in tears of joy. I had never been so happy to be outside before, it's very eye opening how we take so much for granted on a regular basis. I was beginning to put my headphones in and walk three miles home, but before I left the parking lot I heard a car horn. It was my cousin, the same cousin that showed up at my court date and he was parked outside waiting for me. He told me I was not going back to Adam's house and I was coming home to live with him.

Before High School Graduation

Once I heard this, I was in shock. We were not really that close. Especially since when we were younger and all he used to do was bully me and my other cousin. We had gotten into a lot of arguments and fights in the past as well. I couldn't stand him after the time he threw a juice box at my face full speed and cut me with it. As we got older and occasionally ran into each other, he remained very controlling, always insisting on things going his way, or he'd get upset. But we did get a little close my junior year when I attended Harlem and he would come to some of my basketball games. We both tried to have a relationship, but it was hard being around him when he would get upset about every little thing you did. He reminded me of my dad in a way. For instance, if we were watching a football game and the Chicago Bears were playing and I rooted against them he would get extremely mad. Or the few times we were in the weight room and I didn't spot him correctly or if we played basketball in the gym and I didn't pass him the ball enough he would say mean things and get mad. My cousin always got upset over little things and I hated being around people like this. He was also very mean to my older sister calling her disrespectful names. I was not looking forward to living with him at all. I especially didn't want to live with him because he had two small boys: a 1 year old and a newborn. Don't get me wrong, I love kids, but I don't like to hear them scream and cry 24/7 and deal with the throw up, boogers, and biting. There was something about little kids biting me that always kept me on the lookout around them. But I had nowhere else to go and had to learn how to deal with it. As we were driving to his house we began to talk about his rules and expectations. My cousin also started telling me about how he and his wife do things at their house. I was not defiant or rude because I'm going to someone else's house and I just had to make adjustments as I had been doing my whole life. This adjustment was just a lot bigger than a lot of the foster homes I had been in previously. Once he finished talking about his rules and expectations he brought up how my older sister was saying bad things about me while I was in jail. I was very angry how Adam gossiped to her and spread lies on my name and she had nothing to do with what happened. But at this point I was so used to being screwed over by both of them that I did not care what either of them had to say about me. Especially after my older sister almost killed me and her son that day coming home from church and running over my foot. I definitely did not care about what this fat piece of shit Adam had to say either after he betrayed me and threw me in jail for a shoulder bump. All the times he told me he loved me and said we were family and turned his back on me like that. Both of them were nonexistent in my life and I learned to start cutting people off who were not helping me or benefiting me in my life.

After a car ride full of rules and gossip with my older sister, the drama got worse. The second I turned my phone on, I saw nothing but messages blowing up come across my screen. It was all from Facebook. I'm never really on Facebook unless I make a post after a long time, so this was weird for me. That's when I was ready to throw away my phone and delete all my social media. Rockford Mugshots posted my mugshot from jail on their Facebook page and everyone saw it. I was really pissed off at how Rockford Mugshot's has a Facebook page, that was so childish and attention seeking to me. Usually a mugshot goes on a jail website, not a social media account. That just goes to show you how small the city of Rockford really is. If you are from Rockford or live in Rockford you don't even have to watch the news because the news is all on Facebook. In fact Facebook in Rockford gives you more information than the news does. That's how sad it is. But I was shocked once I began to read the comments. I had a lot of people post on my page saying free me and how they had my back. I was in shock because these were people I didn't even talk to or haven't talked to in years. Then once I went onto the Rockford Mugshot page I read all of the comments underneath and these people were all sticking up for me. They were even posting pictures of the Christmas and Valentine's Day giveaways in Rockford and Chicago. I was in complete shock and had the wrong impression. I thought all of these comments were going to be of people laughing and making fun of me. I never expected or realized how many people were really sporting me out here. Here I was always thinking I'm all alone and always depressed inside of these foster homes and I was completely wrong. There were even people I had never talked to before or in years sticking up for me like we just talked yesterday. God showed me that my voice and the impact I had on others were far greater than I ever imagined. It was a sign of motivation to become something in life. This was one of the first moments in my life that I actually felt positive and real support from people. I saw another post that said I beat a female up because I had been arrested for domestic violence. I made sure to clear the air on what really happened. I did not need a rumor going around that I was some type of woman abuser. So, I decided to post about what really happened and take a picture of the written statement that Adam said about me. I also told the truth about how I was actually arrested for shoulder bumping someone. Not just anyone, someone that claimed we were family, said they loved me like a son, and was a grown ass 300 pound man. Once I posted this, my social media really blew up and that woman abuser rumor went away quickly. I was not trying to bash my foster parent Adam but if a foster parent has the audacity to try and ruin my reputation and life, then I'm just as brave to stick up for my reputation and my life and ruin theirs. I was not going to be another statistic of a foster kid who ended up dead or in jail, no matter how hard these foster parents or DCFS foster care agencies wanted me to fail. This is my life and if they think I was going to just lay down and let them control it they had another thing coming. I refuse to fail and lose in life. I've been through too much to be basic and I know God gave his hardest battle to me because I am a fighting soldier. Once I made a post on my Facebook, I turned my phone off and was ready to go to sleep. I had enough for today. My cousin showed me where I would be sleeping, which was in his basement. He had everything all nice and set up a bed and told me we would be grabbing the rest of my stuff from Adam's house tomorrow. I made sure to thank him for everything before I went to sleep and got ready to go to school the next day.

The next day I got up to go to school. I turned my phone on and saw my Facebook had blown up again. I went to check it and saw I had 664 reactions and over 200 shares, this is the most reactions I had ever gotten before, and I was in complete shock. All of the reactions and shares I got was nothing but support, not one single negative comment. God gave me an even bigger sign and showed me that I have an inspirational story. People really do listen to me and I can inspire many people one day. As I was getting ready to walk out the door and walk to school my cousin's wife stopped me and told me she would be taking me. I was just expecting to walk like I did every morning and explained to her that's all I did in these foster homes no matter the weather and she was shocked. Her and my cousin told me if I ever needed any rides and they were not busy to let them know, I wouldn't have to walk all over Rockford anymore. My mindset of living here changed after that because I saw how it wouldn't be that bad. Maybe this would be a great home for me if I just gave it a chance. Once she dropped me off at school, that's when the embarrassment started. As soon as I walked inside the door I had a whole bunch of students ask me if I was okay because they had seen my mugshot. I appreciated them checking on me, but I didn't like all of the attention. Once I walked into my Algebra class, my teacher pulled me to the side to ask if I was okay because he had seen it too. I was just completely embarrassed that everyone had seen my mugshot. But I just pulled myself together during the school day and focused on what needed to be done and that was graduating high school. I only had two weeks left to finish three chapters in order to graduate on time and I was very determined to get through this and get out of Illinois to move to Florida. I was not going to let this minor setback stop me from being successful.

Once I finished school that day I got on the Rockford city bus to head to one of the two jobs that I still had. Today I was working at

Olive Garden, after the 45-minute bus ride, the embarrassment went even further. As soon as I entered work and headed to the back to hang my sweatshirt up, some of the servers, bussers and a manager asked me if I was okay because they had seen my mugshot as well. Now I was really wondering where else my mugshot was posted because there was no way this many people had seen it. Either that or that's just the cost of living in a small city where everyone hears about everyone. But all of the workers were very nice about it, they told me they felt sorry for me and they were sorry I was in foster care. As much as I was embarrassed I was happy at the same time because finally a light was shining on kids in foster care. So many times I would tell people I was in foster care and they had no idea what that meant or was. You never hear anybody really advertise or talk about foster kids, so I felt this was an educating and opening time. I just never liked all of this attention all at once. Even a couple who came in to work to eat that night, while I was cleaning off their table said they saw my mugshot and heard what happened, and they were sorry for me. After a long night of work, I finally got some peace on the city bus. It was nice just to put my headphones in and relax without anyone bothering me. Many times when I rode the city bus I always daydreamed about the things I wanted to accomplish and the story I would write for my life. I knew one day this 18-year-old kid riding the Rockford city bus would be something in life, I had the work ethic, dedication, and faith in myself and God to back it up. I got off the bus and walked to the YMCA and went to play some basketball to clear my head more. I always had my backpack with me packed with my basketball stuff, so I would be able to play basketball before and after work. As soon as I got inside the gym the embarrassment started again. I was close with all of the staff here and I would have great talks with some of them. I just didn't want them to see me in a mugshot and give them the wrong impression that I was some dangerous youth because I wasn't. These were people that I wanted to make proud one day. But they understood completely and a lot of them told me if I ever needed any help I could reach out to them or call them. Once I got up to the basketball gym, I saw a lot of my friends and people who I usually saw at the YMCA, and they asked me what happened and if I was straight. I made sure to tell all of them thank you and that I was okay, but I just wanted to shoot the basketball by myself that day. I was very thankful to have all the support but I didn't want people to feel sorry for me, I wanted a change to happen in the foster care system and I wanted to be successful and run with this incident. I did not want the incident to just be another story, I wanted it to be a moving and touching reason to help others.

After a very long day filled with lots of emotion and attention, I left the gym and I walked the four miles to my cousin's house. I didn't mind walking because it was a coping skill for me ever since I was younger and helped give me space. My cousin and his wife offered to pick me up, but I told them no because I wanted to cope with things and to make it easier on them. My cousin just told me to use the key he gave me to get inside because by the time I got back they would all be asleep because he gets up at 4am to go to work. Once inside, I went downstairs quietly and went to sleep to get ready for the next day. I was just hoping that all of the attention I had would go away tomorrow. In the morning I started my routine of going to the gym. I really wanted to go early this time so I wouldn't have to worry about anyone bothering me. I got up and walked to the YMCA and worked out. I made 400 shots before going to school that morning. Once I finished shooting, it was time for me to head to school and I started walking over to Roosevelt High School. In the middle of my walk I got a call from DCFS. Before I was arrested I was supposed to be going down to Springfield, Illinois along with other foster kids in DCFS to speak and share our stories about being in foster care. I thought they were calling me to ask how I was doing at first, but I was wrong. DCFS called me to tell me that my speech had gotten canceled because I ended up going to jail. I hung up because I didn't care for what they had to say to me. I was pissed off about this because I had a speech all planned out and it made me very upset because I was really looking forward to going. But I stopped being angry and looked and turned that anger into hunger to use it as fuel to the fire to keep working hard. I was not going to let these people break me, I was going to make my own opportunities in life one day.

Going to jail really changed my outlook on life. Once you have your freedom taken away it's very eye opening to see how quickly things can change for the worse. It shows you how real life is, and our time here is limited. I just used it as another wake up call to work harder and leave a legacy behind me. I knew I had been through a lot in life at 18 years old then a lot of adults and I had a reason to get up every day and work hard. I learned at a very young age that nothing will ever come true in life if you sit around and wait for things to happen, feel sorry for yourself and don't work hard. I learned to believe that if you want to make something happen you have to work hard every day and believe that you can do it and that's what I was going to do. I didn't need anyone to ever tell me to work hard because that's all I knew my entire life. I was going to make sure I used my work ethic to bring me success one day. I had to be patient until I would get my next opportunity. I made sure to continue my routine of getting up early and reading the Bible in the morning and praying. I wanted to grow my relationship more with God and keep growing into a better man. My urge to show people that just because you grow up rough doesn't give you the excuse to be mean or rude to people and act crazy. I wanted to have a wife and children as well one day and be a great uncle to my nephew, so this gave me the motivation even more to grow as a person. While I prayed and worked on my relationship with God I also wanted to get rid of any anger I had. I did not want to be a mean or an angry person, I hated being angry. One of my biggest fears in life was ending up like my father and becoming abusive or toxic. I was going to make sure I never ended up like this regardless if I had to do counseling, cut off friends, or leave a relationship. I just did not want to be angry. I also started writing in a journal everyday about how I was feeling and what I was going through. This was a healthy coping skill for me in my growth process. Then I would start my workout. I never wanted to use an excuse as to why I was not going to the gym and working out because that would show I didn't want to be successful enough. Once I got to the gym I would make 400 shots and lift weights on my legs. Then I would walk a mile to Roosevelt High school and work on my one and only class I had left which was algebra. Once I finished school I would get on the city bus to head to work at one of my two jobs or unless my cousin or his wife told me they would take me to work. Then once I got off work I would go back to the gym for one last workout which usually was me working on my ball handling.

This was my routine with a little tweaks here and there. ROutine made me feel safe and in control. I knew God had bigger plans for me in the long run and this was just a stepping stone. My friend's grandma always told me to pay my dues, so I just had to be patient and pay them for the time being. The aftermath of me quitting one of my jobs and continuing my routine for the next two weeks paid off. After spending hours a day in one single math class and working very hard while staying consistent I was able to graduate a week before the deadline. I made sure to thank Mr. Brooks for all the help he had given me, he was easily one of the best teachers I had ever had. Without him I wouldn't have been able to graduate. It was unreal to think that I was done with high school and on to the next chapter of my life. But before I left his class to go grab my cap and gown, Mr. Brooks told me that I was one of the hardest and dedicated students he had ever had. He told me if I kept working as hard as I did in math in life that I would go very far. I used these words he gave me as motivation and inspiration to keep working harder in life. It was up to me if I really wanted to be successful or not.

Once I left Mr. Brooks' class and headed downstairs to grab my cap and gown, they made an announcement over the intercom as they did with every student that finished and would be graduating. I told them not to do this because I didn't want all of the attention, but it felt nice to hear it was my name this time. All I could do was give praisc to God and be thankful and proud. What a journey it had been through my four years of high school. I summed everything all up- from my freshman year living in a jail facility and getting kicked out of normal high school to being sent to an alternative school and thinking it was over and I would not amount to anything in life, to God blessing me with an amazing work ethic and working very hard to get back into normal high school. Finally towards the end of my sophomore year I was blessed with a second chance to go back to a normal high school. The next step was moving back to the city of Rockford and living in a new foster home, my first foster home in two years and going to a new high school at Harlem to start my junior year, and all of the adversity

I faced while living inside Adam's house and being set up by one of the foster kids with a gun held to my head. I lost everything that year and had to wear the same few clothes over again and be made fun of. Playing on the Harlem basketball team and eventually never playing in the games and sitting on the bench most of the year. Next, my senior year I went to four different high schools and moved to five different foster homes and never played a single regulation basketball game after working so hard during the summer. Being told I had to graduate from an alternative high school after never failing a single class was another setback. Having to sleep inside of an airport, and a bus station because no one would come and get me was a haunting memory. Surviving on school lunches and barely having any food to eat in these foster homes was another obstacle. Then being placed in jail I just thought everything was over. There were so many moments in my senior year I was ready to give up but God made a way every single time. It was crazy to look at this cap and gown in my hand and to think of all the adversity I had to face just to get this. But I was proud of myself because God gave me these challenges for a reason and I came into my freshmen year being a boy, but I was graduating being a man and a soldier. I was even prouder to see all the growth I made as a person, as a faithful follower and as a student. I was just so thankful that God blessed me and got me through all of this. I knew this was only the beginning of what was left for me to accomplish later in life.

High School Graduation

Once the day of my high school graduation came, none of it felt real. To me it just felt like just any other day. The reason being was I didn't have anybody come to my graduation. Also, I was not graduating with any of my friends either, so I felt very alone. Usually it's a very big and exciting day and the whole family comes together but I didn't have any of that. I decided to go to the YMCA before my graduation that day just to take my mind off of things. Deep down it hurt inside to know that nobody was coming but I didn't want to show it. I ended up walking four miles to the gym and making 400 shots. Then I went to the weight room and lifted weights. Whenever I was feeling down I tried to do things like work out or be productive to use my sadness as motivation to be successful. The days of me sitting around and crying were over because there is no room in this world for self-pity, life goes on. But it was hard for me not to think about my parents and family not attending one of my biggest days and accomplishments in life. These are the days that you look back in life and have good memories about but none of that was going to be here. I just had to be proud of myself. Once I finished my workout, I walked four miles back to my cousin's house. But walking back was not as easy this time for me. I almost wanted to skip going to my own graduation to avoid the sadness and hurt. Halfway, I turned all the way around and sat outside the YMCA and started thinking to myself. I began questioning myself if I really wanted to attend my high school graduation ceremony. I was thinking that I should just ask them to hand me my high school diploma instead of walking the stage and not having anyone afterwards. Right then and there I heard somebody on the phone walking past me saying "I'm going to be successful with or without yawl, this is for me." That was God right then and there! After I heard that I knew I needed to go. I was not going to let the sadness or hurt of my mother, father, older sister, or dad's side of the family hurt me anymore. I was tired of holding myself back in life and this was something I needed to do. I went through all the foster homes, shelter homes, and a facility by myself. I struggled and went through hard times by myself. The least I could do is walk across a stage by myself and give myself the respect and credit of knowing I did it. This was my moment and what I rightfully earned.

Once I heard those words from a random phone conversation, I got back up and jogged to my cousin's house because it was almost time to go. As soon as I got inside I heard my cousin's wife telling me to hurry up because I was going to be late for my own graduation. I went downstairs and I got ready to go. I wore my shirt and tie along with my dress shoes and dress pants. Then when I looked down there was just a wave of sad emotions that hit me. My last day of school, I was asked how many tickets I wanted for my graduation. I told the school receptionist that I wanted eight tickets which was the max amount of tickets you were able to get. I knew I didn't need eight tickets, but I wanted to use this as motivation for my future self-one day. Each ticket had a meaning on the back of it for me, so on the first two tickets I wrote "mom" and the other one said "dad." This was motivation for me that one day when I become a parent that I show up at my kid's graduation. This would be my inspiration to be a better father to my children one day. On the 3rd ticket I wrote a list of my uncle's names who weren't showing up. This motivation was for my nephew when he grew up to make sure I was there for him even though he is not my son. I wanted to be a great uncle to him one day because I'm the only uncle he has. The 4th ticket I wrote my older sister's name who was not showing up. I wanted to inspire and teach my children one day to have each other's back and not grow up how me and my sister did and be mean and hateful towards each other. Siblings have to grow up loving and taking care of each other. The 5th and 6th tickets had my grandparents name on it to remind me of how they used to tell me I would end up dead or just like my father in jail when I was suspended at R.E.S.A and had to stay at their house. The 7th and 8th tickets had 2 important friends who made excuses at the very last minute of not showing up. This gave me the motivation to keep my word and be a great friend to people. It was very hard for me to write the names on the back of the tickets of people who were not showing up, but I managed to get through it.

Once I finished getting ready, my cousin's wife told me to hurry up and get in the car because we were running late. The graduation was being held at Rock Valley College, which was a 25-minute drive, so it was pretty far from where we lived. It didn't help either knowing I had to be there at 4pm and it was already 3:50pm. But I managed to arrive just a few minutes late thanks to her driving skills. Once we made it to the ceremony, I hurried up and went downstairs hoping I did not miss anything. I saw the teachers lining the students up in order, while all the students had their graduation outfits on. I had to hurry up and change into my cap and gown and I put the long dress-like gown over my shirt and tie. Then I fixed the string over my cap that said "Class of 2019." Then one of the teachers told me I was lucky I got here at the time I did because in five minutes we would be walking out on stage. I was lucky I was even able to walk on stage because I did not show up at the graduation rehearsal and they told us if we did not show up we would not be able to walk the stage. I was very fortunate to have made it this day. Once the teacher lined me up in the correct order and after another 5 minutes of waiting, we began walking upstairs to head to our ceremony. Once upstairs, there was nothing but people all in the crowd cheering for us with the music playing. It pissed me off to look around and see a gymnasium full of people and to know that I didn't have a single person. When I did focus back on the graduation and not the crowd I looked around to see what chair I was supposed to sit in. I had no idea where I was going or how to walk up on the stage because I didn't attend the graduation practice. I was just hoping that the chair that was mine was all the way in the back so I could watch other students go before me. The last thing I wanted to do was embarrass myself even more. But there were teachers standing at each row as we walked in one by one and I found my seat in the second to last row. Thank God for this, now I really didn't have to walk up first, and my nervousness went away.

Once all of the students were seated, the principal and a few teachers had motivational and encouraging speeches for all of us congratulating us on graduating high school and accomplishing a very important goal. Once the principal and a few of the teachers were done speaking, a few students began to speak to us as well. The students talked to us about personal hardships they had to go through to graduate and all the times they felt like giving up but didn't. Some of the students even began crying in the middle of their speech and some students sitting next to me started to cry too. I thought to myself, if I went up there and told them all the things I had to go through from the start of my freshmen year to now, the entire gymnasium would've flooded with tears. But I just took my seat and stayed quiet while everyone spoke. I knew I was going to tell my story one day, but it was not going to be today. Another thing I thought was how everybody kept saying how proud we should be and how big of an achievement it is to graduate from high school. I felt like this was nothing to be super proud over and that this really was not a huge accomplishment. A high school diploma to me was the bare minimum of basic. That's what you're supposed to do. I have been through too much in life to be basic, what I wanted was a college degree from the University of Florida or another big university down in Florida. I understood the importance of school at a very young age, and I knew a high school diploma wouldn't get me anything but another fast-food job. But with a college degree, I knew I could have the potential to have a career one day. I would be able to have a salary and benefits. Plus, I wanted to accomplish more than my pathetic mother, father, or sister has ever done before. My mother had never even gone to college. My father went to college, then dropped out to go to the Marines, then got kicked out of the Marines for abusing my mother and ended up becoming a manager at Golden Corral. My older sister went to college, then she left, then went back, then left again and she ended up getting pregnant and now has a baby and is struggling. I had grown up in the struggle my entire life and the struggle was real even during my high school graduation. But I had faith in God, faith in myself and the hard work ethic to not struggle anymore one day. I wanted to have a life where I didn't have to struggle with bills or get evicted for not being able to pay the rent. I wanted to have a good life one day. I had to grow up poor because of my parents' mistakes but this was my chance and opportunity to be better than they ever were. I was going to make sure I proved the foster care statistics, my older sister, my dad's side of the family and anyone who ever doubted me in life one day wrong by becoming successful.

When it was finally time to walk up to the stage and get my diploma, it felt unreal. I could not believe this was my last day of high school already. Time seemed like it flew by, mainly because I was unable to play basketball for a school team this year. I knew for the rest of my life I would wish I were able to redo my senior year of high school because of how things went but I had to let that go. It was time for the next chapter in life, a chapter that was going to be full of a lot more ups than downs. As the lines went one by one the slower time went. My heart started to raise, and my fingers began to sweat. I had no idea why I was so nervous when it was only me here. Finally, it was my turn to get lined up and head towards the stage. I made sure to follow the order I was told so I wouldn't screw anything up. The closer I got to the stage the more surreal this moment felt. Once my foot hit the stairs to walk onto the stage the longer the moment felt. I could not believe that in a few seconds they were going to call my name, hand me my diploma and I was done with high school. I became more and more nervous, but I didn't want to show it on my face. Thank God for the gown over my white shirt because you would easily see my sweat through my white dress shirt. Finally there was only one more person in front of me and now it was my turn. These were some of the longest seconds I had ever felt before. To think that I would not see half or any of these people ever again. I would never get a chance to play high school basketball again. I possibly would never be living in this city again, it was an unreal moment for me. All of the moments in high school I grew and overcame for this one moment right here. Then they called my name and the moment was finally over. I walked up and shook a few teachers' hands before having my diploma handed to me.

It felt very amazing to hear every teacher say congratulations, that was a word I wanted to hear over and over again in life one day. As I walked down from the stage I made sure to walk extra slow so I wouldn't fall or trip and embarrass myself. Once I got to my seat I just stared at my diploma picturing it being a college degree one day. After the other students walked up to the stage and received their diplomas, the principal gave one final speech about cherishing this moment and how we will go onto do bigger things in life. We had the choice to throw our caps in their air or keep them on and I chose to just keep mine. I wanted to keep it as a souvenir and did not want to risk losing it. Soon the music blared on and the rest of the students walked out in line. We were immediately told that our real diplomas are downstairs. The entire time I thought my diploma was inside of my booklet they gave me, but it wasn't. So, I had to hurry up and head downstairs while fighting through a huge crowd of people to get my diploma. I owed $50 in fines to the Rockford Public School System for lost books over the years from other foster homes. I was told I wouldn't be able to graduate unless I paid that fine, so I made sure to pay it on the last day of school. Once I walked up to the lady who was in control of giving out diplomas, I told her my name and she checked the list then handed it to me right away. Now, I had the real diploma and it looked beautiful. I had never seen such fancy paper before. As I stared at my diploma, I got a text from my cousin telling me to hurry up because they were outside waiting for me.

As soon as I walked outside that's when all of the emotions of sadness and anger hit me. Everywhere I looked I saw all of these students with their family and friends smiling, laughing, and hugging while taking pictures and I had nobody but myself. It was beautiful to see all the ladies getting handed flowers and balloons and the guys getting congratulated. I loved to see people happy and not upset but being in this moment and seeing all of this was a big reason why I didn't want to come to my graduation ceremony in the first place. This was the hardest day I had ever faced without having my parents there. It was crazy to think that I still wanted both of them to come after everything they had done to me but that was the forgiving and generous heart that I had. I wanted to cry, feeling so alone with no one but myself, standing there with nobody by my side, but I couldn't—I was numb. I had to make sure that I stayed strong and used this anger and sadness to be successful one day. I knew God was my eternal Father and as long as I did good things in life that was all that mattered. But I made sure to remember this feeling of not having anyone, I was going to write in my journal later about how I was feeling so I would always remember it. As much as I was hurt and angry by this I was so thankful God put me in this moment because I gained so much motivation. I was going to make sure that I would get through college one day, get a degree and accomplish a lot more in life then both of my pathetic parents ever would. I was going to kill anyone who got in my way with success and beat everybody out one day because I wanted to be successful more than anything else in this world. I knew deep down inside that nobody had the work ethic, heart or desire to want it as bad as I wanted it. I didn't care about being cool, trying to impress women, having friends, the only thing that mattered to me was being successful. I walked away from my high school graduation a different person. I became a lot hungrier than I had ever been before.

Once I got inside the car, my cousin asked what restaurant I wanted to go to as my graduation treat. I told him I didn't want to go anywhere at first, but he told me I had to pick somewhere. I mostly just wanted to be left alone because of how sad and angry I was feeling. I just wanted to lay in my bed at my cousin's house and fall asleep so this day would be over with. I had talked to my cousin earlier and told him how I didn't really want to go to my high school graduation, and he gave me some good advice which encouraged me to go. I ended up just saying that I wanted to go to a pizza buffet because pizza is one of my favorite foods. At least I would have leftovers and go to sleep on a full stomach if I ate at a buffet. I couldn't go to Golden Corral because a lot of my dad's friends worked there and every time I stepped inside of there, a lot of the staff recognized me, so it made things very awkward. As my cousin began driving to the pizza buffet, I started opening up to him about how I felt. I told him I felt very sad and alone during my graduation and how hard it was not having anyone there for me. Once I said this the conversation took a bad turn. My cousin told me he didn't really know what to say to me and he got offended because he thought I was calling him and his wife out by saying they were not there for me when they were. But that was not what I meant at all. I tried explaining what I meant by feeling alone to him, but he was upset. I felt alone not having my parents and other family members, but he wasn't hearing it. I guess he felt like he was not being appreciated and this ticked him off. Once we got to the pizza buffet he didn't really say much to me and was rushing everyone the entire time because he was ready to leave. It really pissed me off because once again he was mad over something little. I couldn't even try to enjoy myself because here he was throwing a fit about something small. I just ate my food, acted nice and friendly to them and went downstairs once we got back to his house. I didn't want to offend him or cause a problem and risk getting kicked out of this house and not having anywhere to go.

Before Virginia Basketball Camp

After my high school graduation, I stopped wanting to be at my cousin's house. I just worked at Arby's and stayed at the YMCA as much as I could. I asked my manager if I could work every day and on days I was not working I was at the gym. I figured if I were not at the house or around him then no problems would be able to happen. I did not want to be around someone who got mad over every little thing. My cousin reminded me so much of my dad and this was a big reason why I didn't want to live with him and why we were not close in the first place. But no matter how hard I tried to stay out of the house, my cousin found a way to get upset with me and once again got mad over little things. For example, my cousin loved to play video games, that's all he did when he was not working, and I never played video games because I never had a game system. I saw that he owned two controllers so one day I finally asked if I could play with him and he told me no because this is his only time off he has to enjoy himself. I couldn't get mad at that because that was his game system and this was his house. I didn't want to watch someone play a video game because that was boring, so I went and grabbed my comic book and started reading it on the couch next to him. Suddenly, he accused me of having an attitude because I wanted to read one of my new books instead of watching him play. Another incident was during a pouring rain storm, my cousin wanted to be funny and play basketball outside on the outdoor hoop he had in the front of his garage. He told me he was tired of playing his video game and handed me the controller and said I could play. But five minutes later, he came inside the house soaking wet and stood right in the middle of the TV trying to be funny and get me to look at him. If I did that to him it would have been World War 3! All I said was "watch out, I'm going to die" because I was in the middle of a game. Then he turned the TV and the game system off and told me not to talk to him in his house like that. By now I was getting sick of being around this grown man who acted like a sensitive little baby all the time. But the incident that really did it for me was when I was walking to the YMCA. I was on the phone with my DCFS caseworker talking about my upcoming court date, getting on the youth in college scholarship program and my plan of moving to Florida. In the middle of my phone call my cousin called me and I was unable to answer because I was already on the phone with my caseworker talking about important stuff. So, I texted my cousin while I was on the phone with my caseworker telling him that I would call him back. Right after I sent this text to him he called me ten more times and was just blowing up my phone like crazy. I was worried that something went wrong or happened at the house, so I told my caseworker I was going to call her back tomorrow. When I finally answered my cousin's phone call I asked him why he was calling me so much and what the issue was. He cut me off in the middle of talking to tell me to "shut the fuck up and answer the phone when I call you the first time, now are you coming home for dinner?" Right after he said that, I moved the phone away from my ear and brought it down to my eye level to look and see if I had the right phone in my hand because I couldn't believe he was talking to me like that. I didn't want to believe that in the middle of an important phone call with my caseworker that a grown ass man called me 15 times just to ask me if I was coming home for dinner. I hung up instantly and I blocked his number. Soon, he started calling me off of fake numbers and his wife started messaging me telling me I was wrong for hanging up on someone who is taking care of me. I didn't even respond, I was just ready to leave his house. I refused to be treated like shit by foster parents. I was tired of rolling over on my back and taking it over and over again. I had been treated like shit and beaten since I was five years old. These foster parents and my own cousin had another thing coming if they thought I was just going to kiss ass and be seen and not heard.

Eventually my cousin did apologize for what he said to me over the phone. But when we sat down and talked he was telling me how he was frustrated how DCFS was not paying him for me being here and how money was tight. I understood what he was saying because he was the only one working in that house with two kids who weren't even a year old yet. His wife couldn't work because she had to stay home and take care of them. He said he had called the DCFS licensing agency to get paid and was doing all the stuff they required him to do but they weren't working with him or they were taking too long. I knew he had gotten into it with someone at my foster care agency because my caseworker texted me saying he was very disrespectful with one of their licensing workers. But I started to realize he didn't just take me in to be nice, he took me in to get paid as well. This hurt my feelings. I thought he was really doing it to help me. Also, his frustration with the agency not paying him led him to taking it out on me and getting mad at any little thing I did as if it was my fault. I was just so tired of being in homes where people looked at me like a paycheck. It was like I didn't matter as a person anymore. My feelings, how I felt, or what I was going through didn't matter either. The only person who I was ever able to sit down and open up with was my old foster parent Adam and I couldn't even do that because he would later throw it back in my face as a joke or when he got upset with me. I started to wake up angry every day again after this and did not want to be around anyone.

One day as I was heading to work and my cousin's wife took me in her car and had a talk with me. She told me how she had a long talk with my cousin, and he started crying and saying that I don't like him and that I didn't want to live here. I was confused as to why he was crying because he was the one who was causing all of this if anything I should've been crying. That's when she opened up about how he was being rude with me and treating me wrong. It was nice to have someone to talk to after all of this built up frustration. I told her that I was just upset with how he got mad at every little thing and how was taking his anger out on me because he was not getting paid from the agency. His wife was really understanding, and she apologized. She told me that she made my cousin get into counseling because he had done abusive things towards her and she almost didn't want to be with him at one point either. She opened up to me about how during her pregnancy my cousin would get mad and drive full speed then stop so her stomach would hit the dashboard. Then another time he had grabbed her arm and that's when she finally threatened to leave him and got him into counseling. She felt that he and I wouldn't be able to live together for much longer because our personalities clashed. She was afraid that eventually, we'd have a big argument, and I would end up leaving. She would be right about that later on. But my cousin's wife also brought up how money was tight, and they were doing this to help me. I was really thankful they did this, but I almost wish they didn't help me out because I felt like I was making their money tighter and they were more stressed out with me living in their house. Eventually, my cousin and I started to bond when we watched the NBA playoffs together, or I would watch him play video games. Sometimes he was a lot nicer than other times, it's just you never knew how he was going to react. My cousin was a nice person, it's just he had anger problems. But I couldn't blame him, both of his parents divorced when he was young, and his mom stopped being involved in his life once he moved in with his dad. It was like she left him just as my mom left so we could relate in a way. He always talked about how hard it was having to choose sides all the time and how it built up anger inside of him. But at the same time you can't use this excuse to treat people wrong. If that was the case I should have every excuse to treat people wrong because look at how hard and messed up my life was. When we did talk, it was nice to connect over some things. Eventually, he started helping me practice my driving skills so I could get my license, and we also began playing basketball outside in his driveway. We had a very on and off relationship at times. I usually would just stay quiet around him and agree with everything he said not to cause any problems. When he did get upset I would just hear him out and agree with him because I didn't want to risk losing this placement and having nowhere to go. I also continued going to the YMCA and stayed in the basement often.

Once June arrived, I got an invite to another basketball skills camp in Charlottesville, Virginia. This was the same camp I went to in Atlanta and Indianapolis, and this time I was even happier because this was the All-American Basketball Skills Camp. This meant that some of the top basketball players in the country were going to be in attendance. It got even better because the same weekend, the basketball camp was holding their All-American camp in Charlottesville, Virginia, alongside another prestigious camp for the top players in the country called the "Top 100 Basketball Camp." This was the perfect opportunity to get a basketball scholarship because all of the top prep schools and college basketball schools were going to be sending their coaches and recruiters. If I had any shot of getting a basketball scholarship, this would be the chance to get one. The only problem was I would have to use all the money I had saved up from work just to pay for a flight and a four-day stay in a hotel. I started to use my resources and see what help I would be able to get from people. The first person I thought I'd reach out to was my caseworker because they had previously paid for one of the basketball camps in Atlanta. I got declined by my caseworker and DCFS the second time I went to Indianapolis because it was on such short notice, so I made sure this one was good timing. The only problem was the agency's office was closed so I had to wait until the morning. Then the next person I was going to reach out to was my mother because she was always asking me if I needed money and we both were starting to talk more. So later that night while I was talking to my mom and asking her for money my cousin and his wife heard me. That's when they started asking me about it and they wanted to help me. I was in shock because me and my cousin's relationship was still kind of shaky. At first I was not going to accept their money because I didn't want them to throw it back up in my face later. But then I thought about how my mom had just told me she didn't have the money to give me at the time, so this was really my only option. I sat down with my cousin and his wife and explained how important this camp was, sharing that I had already attended two of them and that it was crucial for me to go if I had any chance of earning a basketball scholarship. Shockingly they were all for it and decided to help me. I was in shock that they agreed to even help me at all. I told them that DCFS would reimburse them for the money they spent and they just had to email DCFS the receipts. So, they really weren't spending any money at all. But to play things safe they told me to wait until the morning when they talked to DCFS about going and we would figure things out. I didn't want to lie to them and have them pay for something they wouldn't get their money back for, only to have my cousin and his wife get upset with me because the information I gave them was false.

The next day me, my cousin, his wife, and my caseworker all talked on the phone about me going to this basketball camp in Virginia. The phone call went great because DCFS was going to pay for my roundtrip flight, and my cousin was going to pay for the basketball camp and DCFS was going to reimburse him once he sent them the receipt. The only thing I had to do was pay my cousin back for the hotel and pay for my own food and Lyft rides. I was in shock at how everything worked out in my favor.I truly got to witness how powerful prayer and supportive people can be. I thought this was going to be another missed opportunity but that was not the case anymore. But the only thing standing in my way of going was court. Since I had been arrested just a few weeks ago I was not allowed to leave the state of Illinois and had to attend all my court dates or I would be arrested again. I waited for my next court date later that week, and once I learned the outcome, the plan between my cousin, DCFS, and me would go through, allowing me to attend the All-American basketball camp. I was nervous because I didn't know what the judge would say. But I prayed about it and talked to God asking him to help me with this opportunity. I knew I had the work ethic, hunger, and commitment, all I needed was a chance to play and showcase it in front of people. My chance had already been taken from me due to how things turned out my senior year. I just had to trust God no matter how many reasons I gave him of why I should be able to go. The hardest and scariest thing about faith to me was the part of not knowing if your prayers would be answered. I remember I told the pastor this one day and he told me God doesn't want you to see your future because then you may not work as hard for it or you'll get discouraged. He said the part of not knowing what's going to happen is how God knows who his followers really are. If you are a true follower you have to trust in God even when you're going through the hardest and darkest times and you think you can't do it or it's not going to happen. That is the true power of the almighty God. I just remembered what that pastor had told me and kept this in my head before my court date.

Once my court date did finally arrive, my cousin's wife took me to the courthouse in downtown Rockford, Illinois. I had to meet with one of the public defenders I was given and talk about what was going on with me and he updated me on what was going on in this case as well. He informed me that the victim, Adam, did not want to press charges and wanted everything to be dropped; all he wanted me to do was get into counseling. I was happy about this because now I didn't have to worry about going back to jail or being put on probation. I told him that I was trying to go to a basketball camp in Virginia and showed him paperwork as proof to show the judge and ask if I would be able to go. After our private 10-minute conversation it was now time for the moment of truth in front of the judge. But as soon as I saw the judge and realized this was a woman, I thought it was going to be an automatic no. Based on what I had seen on TV, especially with all the women judges like Judge Judy, I had lost any hope of going and was mentally prepared for a "no." Once I took my seat I started to change my thinking and stay positive hoping that this lady would be a lot nicer. Maybe I was just overthinking things and needed to give her a chance. But after I saw a handful of people go before me and witness how strict she was with them and how she had sent someone to jail and they started crying in the courtroom, I thought for sure I was going to be the next person crying. After another 20 minutes of waiting, my name was finally called. As soon as I got up my heart started racing and my adrenaline kicked in. My hands and armpits were filled with sweat and I was just hoping I didn't have to lift my arms up. I tried not to make eye contact with her because of how nervous I was and kept looking down at the floor. But eventually I had to when she told me to introduce myself and began asking me yes or no questions. I just had to calm myself down and breathe. Once I finished answering her questions the public defender did most of the talking. I was happy about this because I was beginning to stutter and

I was not the best convincer. He was a lawyer so I was sure he would be able to convince someone a lot better than I would. Once he introduced the topic of me up leaving the state of Illinois to attend the basketball camp in Virginia, my stomach dropped again, and I felt the sweat from my armpits just roll down my arms. She gave me one long look and asked me if I knew who Fred VanVleet was and of course I said yes. I had no idea why she asked me that question, maybe she was really trying to see if I played basketball or knew about basketball. But after she asked me that question and I gave her my response, she paused and stared at me a few more seconds and then told me I could go. I was in complete shock! But I was even more shocked by how amazing God was, the power of prayer and faith is something very real.

After court was over, I called my caseworker and let her know what happened. She told me that I would hear from her later on that week about the plane tickets they were getting me. Once my cousin got back from work he went ahead and paid for my hotel room. I was so happy I was able to go and ready to make the most of this amazing opportunity that I had in front of me. With the basketball camp now only being three weeks away, I wanted to make sure I was ready. I trained the hardest that I had ever trained before. Every morning I jogged four miles to get to the YMCA. I wanted to make sure that my conditioning was in good shape. Kyrie Irving once said being in shape is not being able to run up and down the floor for long periods of time, it's being able to play offense and defense for a long period of time and have an impact on the game. I had problems with getting tired too fast, so I started eating healthy as well to help with my conditioning. Next, I continued shooting and making 500 shots a day. But instead of just catching and shooting while standing in one spot, I started working on shooting off the dribble in different ways. One way was by putting a chair in the middle of the floor and running full speed and coming off the chair like it was a screen and shooting. I knew I was not the biggest or strongest, so I had to work on shooting off the screen. I followed working on my shooting by dribbling and making a move full speed into a pull up jump shot. Then when it came to dribbling I put a plastic bag over my basketball and started doing what Kyrie Irving used to do to get my handles better and tighter. Next, I did a tennis ball drill where I would dribble a basketball down the court while dribbling behind the back, between the legs, or making a crossover and while I was doing this throwing a tennis ball in the air and catching it before it hit the floor. Then I would get cones out and pretend that the cones were defenders while making moves and working at attacking the rim. Then I would play games against other kids in the gym to work on what I had been practicing in game situations. But the only problem was I still was not able to dunk, I was not strong enough, and wasn't fast enough. The hard truth I had to face was that I wasn't athletic enough to get a basketball scholarship. Part of it came from my genes but the other part of it was because I did not work hard enough. Instead of shooting jump shots and dribbling all of the time, I should have been in the weight room lifting weights 4 times a week, running hills and sprints, and I should have been practicing trying to dunk. I watched YouTube videos on what separates players from a Division I school to a Division 3 school and they all said the biggest key was their athletic abilities. This really pissed me off because my game was all there. I just didn't push myself hard enough when it came to the athletic side of things. I had nobody to blame but myself, I didn't want to be a Division 1 basketball player bad enough. If I really wanted it I would have worked on these things every day. This would later on come back to bite me once the camp started.

Soon it was time to leave for camp. I was very happy because during these three weeks nothing negative was going on in my life. I had no more drama and no more arguments with my cousin or at work. Things were going very well, and I was actually happy for the first time in a while. The night before I was leaving my cousin gave me $100 and told me to have some fun while I was there. This meant a lot to me because nobody has ever just handed me $100 out of nowhere. Him and his wife also bought me some snacks just in case I was hungry in between games. I felt like my relationship with them had gotten way better because I understood my cousin's behaviors more, and how to be more mindful of what I did and said. Once I finished talking with my cousin, I went downstairs, and I made sure to pack all of my stuff up during the night. I had to wake up at 4am because my flight was leaving at 7am and it took an hour and a half to drive from Rockford to Chicago, O'Hare Airport. One of my friends was coming to pick me up and take me to the airport because my cousin had to work early in the morning that day. After I finished packing, I set five alarms on my phone and made sure that the volume was all the way up so I'd be sure to hear it when it went off. I also slept on the couch that night so I wouldn't fall into a deep sleep and could leave the house more quietly. The last thing I needed was to oversleep and miss my flight or start an argument for being too loud.

After five hours of sleep, my alarm went off and I jumped up off the couch to turn it off. I didn't want to wake anyone up in the house, especially my cousin's two sons. I hurried up and got dressed right away and I made sure to brush my teeth so my breath wouldn't stink. Nobody wants to be around someone whose breath stinks in the morning. Once I finished my hygiene, I planned on eating breakfast, but my friend was already outside waiting for me. Instead of trying to stuff my face all at once I just decided I was going to wait and eat once I got to the airport. I just made sure I had everything that I needed one last time before we left. The last thing I needed was to forget something. Finally, I got in the car and we headed straight to the airport. I tried not to fall asleep because I wanted to sleep on the plane but that didn't work out. I was so exhausted from working out so hard these last few weeks. I woke up to my friend shaking me because we had made it to the airport already. I only had my backpack with me, so I just grabbed that and got out of the car quickly because we were right in the middle of traffic. As soon as I got inside of the airport, I went to the machine and typed in my code to get my boarding pass. The airport was packed already and the line to get through security was huge. I was not trying to wait any longer than I had to, so I hurried up and got in line with my boarding pass in my hand. While I waited in line, I couldn't help but look back at and remember when I walked around all night trying to find the bus home back to Rockford and ended up having to sleep inside of here. Or when I was going through security and the alarm went off because I forgot my medal splint in my pocket for my broken finger resulting in me having to be patted down. I was just happy and thankful that this time around I was healthy and didn't have any broken bones. Playing with a broken finger in the past camps in Atlanta and Indianapolis was very annoying. I just wish someone would've taken me to physical therapy instead of self-healing it because now my left ring finger is slightly crooked. Soon it was time to go through security. I made sure to take everything out of my pockets so I wouldn't embarrass myself this time. Thankfully, I made it through nice and smooth this time around.

After making it through security, I was on a trek to find some breakfast. It sucked because a lot of the cheaper shops were not open yet because of how early it was, so I ended up just going to McDonald's to get some food thinking they were going to be cheap. I was completely wrong about that, the McDonald's inside of this airport didn't even have a dollar menu. I hated how they made airport food so expensive, it was such a rip off. The same bagel, egg, and cheese sandwich that would've cost me $1 cost me $4. I just had to shut the hell up and pay for it because my stomach was growling super loud. I was happy that the hot sauce and water cup were free though. Once I finished eating, I walked over to my gate and sat and watched cartoons on my phone until it was time to go. I did this to stop myself from falling asleep because I wanted to make sure I got on the plane. I still had an hour left before takeoff. I hated the waiting part about traveling. I wish somebody had invented a teleporter where you could just walk inside of it and you would be at your destination in a second. I was just happy my flight was not very long because I would hate it. I couldn't imagine flying over ten hours somewhere while being awake, I would need to get a shot that would put me to sleep. But I did enjoy waiting at the same time because it helped me become more patient and grow in that area. It seems like everyone nowadays is so much ruder because they lack the skills of being patient. It's something that you see every day on the road, at restaurants and fast-food places, grocery stores and many other places. That's not who I wanted to be because impatient people are always angry, and I wanted to have patience and be happy.

After an hour of waiting, it was finally time to board the plane. I was so happy because I was about to pass out and go to sleep. I was not as nervous anymore because I had flown so much within the last year that I was used to it now. But all that nervousness came back once I stepped on this plane. This was the smallest plane I had ever been on or seen before, it was more like a private jet. There were only eight rows and each row only had two seats. I had never seen such a crammed and tiny plane before. This plane was so small when I started walking to go to my seat I had to duck because my head was able to touch the ceiling. All the confidence I had just went right out the window, I lost all hopes of having a smooth plane ride and falling asleep because of how nervous I was. I always heard that small planes are easily damaged and more likely to crash especially after Aaliyah died. But I just breathed and prayed extra hard for God to keep me safe on this plane. I always felt better when I prayed because I knew I was giving my problems to God. I felt a good sense of relief as well when I got a row all to myself. At least now I wouldn't have to be squished and I would have plenty of legroom. Once the plane captain spoke to us and told us we were getting ready for takeoff, I put my headphones on and just tried to fall asleep. But right before taking off one the headphones earpiece blew out. I was super annoyed because I had just bought those no even a week ago. This was going to be a long and boring plane ride. I tried plugging my ear with one of my fingers and listening to music in the other and that did not work either. I just had to deal with it and focus on what really mattered and that was getting to my destination safely.

Virginia Basketball Camp

After an hour and a half of riding in the smallest airplane I've ever been in before and not having any music to listen too, the plane finally landed. I was so happy that I made it her safe, I made sure to pray and thank God immediately after. However when I was looking out the plane window Virginia looked very country. I did not see any city skyline or anything urban, the only thing I saw were mountains and green fields everywhere. I had a bad feeling that this meant I was in the country, and sure enough I was. I hated everything about the country because it seemed super boring with the accents, and the farmlands. I loved living in big cities where there was always something fun and new to do. I wish this basketball camp would have been in Florida or another fun state like the girls all American Camp was. As I was beginning to make my way off the plane, I saw that people were not walking through the tunnel as usual once you get off and walk into the airport. It turns out that we actually had to walk down the stairs of this tiny plane. I felt like I was in the movies or on a sports team the way they walk off their private planes. It was a very unique and cool experience. As I made my way into the actual Charlottesville, Virginia Airport I was shocked to see how small it was. This was definitely the smallest airport I had ever been in and now it made sense as to why the plane was so small. There was only one floor to this airport, and it had five different gates, one restaurant and only one shop. I really appreciated living in a big city once I saw this. But I do admit, it was very nice in a way because it was not so crowded and busy.

Once I made my way out of the airport I sat on one of the benches and waited for my Lyft to come pick me up and take me to my hotel. As I was waiting I was wondering if I would see any basketball players who were attending the camps. I knew that all of the players were going to be in this small city for the weekend and sure enough I saw one. I looked up and saw this huge, muscular dude and it looked like one of the guys I followed on Instagram named Kyree Walker. I looked up his Instagram and watched his story and sure enough it was him. He was one of the players in the Top 100 Camp and one of the best high school basketball players in the nation. Right when I saw him and realized we were both in the same grade, I knew I had a lot more work that I needed to do if I ever wanted to play at the Division 1 level. Soon, my Lyft arrived and as soon as I got inside the car the Lyft driver welcomed me and was very friendly and nice. I always loved people in the south because of their southern hospitality, it was very real compared to Illinois rude hospitality. I had never really heard anything about the state of Virginia before, so I told the Lyft driver the city that I was staying in and asked what fun things they had to offer during my four-day stay here. He told me that Charlottesville, Virginia was a college town. This was where the University of Virginia was, and I thought that was amazing. This was the school that had just won the NCAA March Madness Tournament for men's basketball. He also told me that the three former presidents of the United States were from here and their names were Thomas Jefferson, Jamie Madison, and Jamie Monroe. This city was so historic that a lot of the buildings and roads were made out of brick. After hearing this I changed my mindset on this country town and had a lot more respect for it knowing that this was such a historic area. But this Lyft driver did tell me something very disturbing that there was a protest regarding a Robert E. Lee statue that was in Charlottesville, Virginia. A crowd did a peaceful protest to remove the statue because Robert E. Lee was a Confederate General and back during the Civil War, he was for slavery so many people including myself felt that it should be taken down because we want to get rid of racism in the United States. But a person who was a part of the White Supremacist group decided to drive his car into the crowd and killed a woman. He was shocked that I had never heard about it because it was all over the news. I never had cable, so I wasn't able to pay much attention to the news unless I saw it on social media. Hearing that made me sick to my stomach. It's so disgusting to hear that racism still goes on in our country even after all of the great people like Dr. Martin Luther King fought to stop it. I will never be able to understand why people judge other people over race when we are all of the same race and that is the human race.

Once we made it to my hotel, I thanked this very nice man for informing me about this city more and for being very kind. It's not every day you come across a Lyft driver who is actually friendly and open to have a conversation with you. I checked in at the front desk and grabbed my key and went to my room. It sucked because this hotel was not offering any free breakfast, but I figured I would just go to Walmart and get a couple of groceries while I was here. When I checked in, I grabbed a couple of brochures to see what things there were to do around here. I also grabbed them because I liked to collect the brochures from all the places I have been to. This was a cheaper hobby of mine than buying a hat from every place I traveled to. Once I walked inside my room, I was so happy. I had a king-sized bed again just like I had in Atlanta and I was ready to go to sleep. I had been up since 4am and I wanted to make sure I was well rested before the first day of camp tomorrow. But I had two problem, one of them was I was very hungry, and the other one was that it was only 1pm. If I went to sleep now my sleep schedule would be all screwed up and I would be awake at 2 to 3 in the morning and I'd miss the Toronto Raptors game. I couldn't miss it knowing Fred VanVleet was playing in the NBA finals and had a chance to be the first ever person from Rockford, Illinois to win an NBA championship. So, I got on my phone and watched some YouTube videos and did some searches on google of what fun things there were to do in Charlottesville, Virginia. In the video I saw that this place had a famous and a very historic outdoor mall that everyone one went to. The mall had plenty of places to eat and a movie theater so I figured I would just spend the day walking around there, get something to eat and watch a movie to kill time. I only had so much money with me, so I made a budget and made sure to only pay for Lyft rides to the basketball camps and back and to the airport for my final day of being here. I wanted to do what I did in Atlanta and take the public transportation system to save money. This town was not anywhere near as big as Atlanta was, so I had a feeling it would be a lot easier to take the bus around here. Now I just had to figure out if anyone would be able to teach me or show me where the stops and routes were.

After I finished unpacking my bag and I grabbed the stuff I needed before I left my hotel room, I headed downstairs again to the hotel lobby. I was hoping to see if someone at the front desk would be able to help me with figuring out the public bus stop routes and stops so I could get around Charlottesville without having to pay for a Lyft. When I got to the lobby I walked up to the front desk and saw that the hotel worker was not helping anyone, so I went and asked her for help. This lady was very nice to me and extremely helpful, if it wasn't for her I would've never been able to get on the bus. She showed me the website of the bus transportation system that had all the routes and stops on it and what times they would be arriving. Then she showed me where the bus, which was right across the street from the hotel I was staying at. I was happy to learn that I would not have to take a train anywhere or ride the bus over 30 minutes to get downtown to this outdoor mall. It was going to be a very fast and smooth ride. After the lady at the front desk showed me where the bus stop was I thanked her and went and stood outside waiting for the bus to come. I was happy I didn't have to wait another 45 minutes for the next bus to come, instead I got lucky and only had to wait 10 minutes for the next bus. Once the bus showed up, I got on and took a picture of all the routes that this bus makes just in case the website would not load on my phone because of the bad connection around this area. The last thing I needed was to get lost here. It was nice to see how there weren't very many routes that the bus traveled to, so I knew it would be very easy for me to get around. After a 15-minute bus ride we made it downtown. This downtown had a totally different style compared to a downtown in Chicago. There were no huge skylines or skyscrapers anywhere. There wasn't really even a bus station downtown either, it was just a bunch of buses lined up underneath a stairwell with a few benches. It was a very different setting compared to what I was used to. As I made my way off the bus and walked up the steps there was nothing but brick floors and brick buildings just like the Lyft driver told me. As soon as I got all the way up the stairs and turned my head left, I saw nothing, but a long brick road filled with lots of brick buildings. This was one of the coolest and most historic malls I had ever seen before.

While I was walking around and exploring this amazing outdoor mall here in Charlottesville, Virginia I not only noticed how historic and unique this mall was, but how peaceful and happy everyone was. Seeing this really changed my mind on living in a small town or living in the country. It was crazy to me how packed this outdoor mall really was and how everyone had their big groups of friends and families together just enjoying it all. This showed me that you don't have to live in a big city or a rich area to be happy, you can find happiness wherever you live but, it's ultimately up to you. Another thing that amazed me was that every building with a small shop inside was bustling with business. Whereas back home in Rockford, Illinois the same type of buildings they had here would be run down, torn down, sitting vacant, or drug houses. I wish Rockford would use all of its buildings and turn them into small shops just like this place did, instead of just having them be empty and run down and not bringing the city any money or new business. Seeing this just proved how rough and poor the city of Rockford is. But it motivated me even more to make it out of there and see how much more opportunity in this world there really is. I used to always be so angry and upset that I was from there, but every time I traveled to a new city I was proud to be from there because when you grow up in a rough and poor city it gives you the heart, toughness and hunger to want to be successful in life even more. While I continued walking I started to look for a place to eat. This mall had a ton of restaurants to choose from, but I was not trying to spend a lot of money and was hoping for something more basic and cheaper. That's when I came across this pizza place and this made my day. Pizza is my most favorite food in the whole word, and what made this pizza my favorite pizza in Virginia without even trying it was the cheap prices I saw displayed in the window. I walked right inside once

I saw that it fit my budget, and I was just amazed at the huge slices and selections that this little shop had. This place had a taco pizza, meatloaf pizza, hamburger pizza and many other choices. Me being me I knew I was only going to get a cheese pizza, but it was still very cool to see all of the options. I was glad I was eating alone because I had stopped eating beef and pork to be healthier, and all I ate was cheese pizza. People started to dislike me when it came to ordering or eating pizza together. At least now I didn't have to hear anyone complain or pick off anything on the pizza and I could just eat it. After I finished waiting in line I went ahead and ordered myself two huge slices of cheese pizza, a water cup and a side of hot peppers to put on top of my pizza. I had never devoured pizza so fast in my life, especially not these big slices. I was still a little hungry after I finished eating both slices, so I went ahead and ordered myself another two more slices as if I were in a buffet. I loved getting so full to the point where your stomach felt bloated because then I would go to sleep faster, and I wouldn't be hungry for the rest of the night.

Once I finished stuffing my face with four huge slices of pizza, I walked back outside and walked around the mall searching for something else to do while feeling like I had just gained 400lbs. That's when I came across this very odd, shaped building that was a movie theater. I couldn't believe that this movie theater had two floors inside of it, I had never seen a theater like that in my life. I checked my phone to see what movies they had playing because if I was going to spend money I wanted to at least watch a good movie. I saw that they had "The Secret Life of Pets 2" playing and just decided to see that. A lot of my friends made fun of me because I always watched little kid shows but I hated watching horror movies and cop movies because that's all my dad forced me to watch when I was a little kid and that traumatized me. I really understood why they had an age limit for movies because some of the movies my dad had me watch as a little 7 or 8 year old kid scared me so bad to the point where I was afraid to get up and use the bathroom at night or go downstairs to the basement. He always thought it was funny to scare me all the time by forcing me to watch these movies, and that is a big reason why I really only watch cartoons, romances, and superhero movies now. I get so sick of hearing and seeing violence as well and that's why I don't care for those types of movies either. Its already bad enough we have all of these killings and horrible crimes in our society every day, we don't need to make it worse by turning them into movies as entertainment. Once I bought my ticket, I walked upstairs into a cozy, dark, and cool movie theater, enjoying the refreshing air conditioning. I felt even better once I sat down and saw how the seats reclined all the way back to where I could lay down for this hour and a half film. Once I nestled in and reclined my chair, out of nowhere the movie was over. I was so mad at myself that I had fallen asleep and wasted my money. I only got to watch 15 minutes of the previews and didn't even get to watch any of the movie. But I couldn't blame myself because of how tired I was, at least I got myself a little nap in and the NBA finals game was about to start. As I was leaving the theater and getting ready to go back on the bus to head to my hotel, I saw this huge crowd gathered inside this restaurant with a bunch of security. I started to panic because I thought there was a fight or a shooting that happened, but people were just saying there was a famous basketball player inside. I felt a sense of relief after hearing that because I was not trying to have anything happen to me while I had a basketball camp to go to the next day. But I was curious to see what famous basketball player they were talking about. That's when I looked through one of the windows and heard people say that it was Dwayne Wade. I was in complete shock, I couldn't believe one of the all-time great players from Chicago and in the NBA was here in this little college town. Then I remembered that his son plays basketball and was attending the Top 100 basketball camp at the University of Virginia. I wish I would've been able to get his autograph but there were too many people and I didn't want to miss the NBA finals game.

Once I got off the bus after a short 15-minute ride, I got back inside of my hotel and headed upstairs to get ready to watch the NBA finals between the Toronto Raptors, and the Golden State Warriors. It was crazy that two of my favorite NBA players, Fred VanVleet and Stephen Curry were playing against each other. But it was unreal how Fred VanVleet from Rockford, Illinois was playing in the NBA finals. This was probably the only time in my life I wished I were in Rockford because they had a watch party downtown where everyone would come and watch the games on a big screen. I was mad they decided to start that right when I left. But lucky me, my big screen was a tiny and outdated iPhone 7 because the hotel had no TV. So, I just decided to watch the game on my tiny phone screen. I was just thankful I had WIFI so I could even watch the games. This game was so big and a must watch for me because it was game 6 and all the Raptors had to do was win one game and they would be NBA Champions for the first time in franchise history. But as soon as the game started, I couldn't get any service while laying on this king-sized bed, so I had to lay on the floor right next to the WIFI box just to get a clear quality vision and connection. Man, my arms were all sore from holding this little tiny phone screen up for 2 hours and laying on this carpet. It was even worse when I had to plug my phone into the charger because I recently lost my charger and I had to borrow my cousins and it was only a foot long. But all of this was worth it, and I refuse to complain because it could always be worse. I was just thankful and happy to have had the chance to watch history possibly be made. This was one of the greatest finals games ever played because of how back and forth it was. But in the 4th quarter it became even greater because that's when Fred VanVleet made some of the biggest shots for the raptors and basically won them the game. He had a total of 22 points and 12 of his 22 points were in the 4th quarter alone, that's how much he took over and stepped up. It was just simply amazing to witness this. But during the final minutes, the Raptors were up by 1 point with 9.6 seconds left in the game. I was nervous because the Warriors had some great 3-point shooters on their team like Stephen Curry. As the warriors inbounded the ball and time was trickling down, Stephen Curry had a wide-open 3 point shot and missed it. The Raptors rebounded the ball and the Warriors fouled them trying to stop the clock and hoping they would miss their free throws, but they didn't. They made both free throws and as time expired the Toronto Raptors won their first ever NBA Championship. More importantly, someone who came from the same city I was from, who attended the same high school I went to had just became an NBA Champion. After the game was over, Fred got interviewed and towards the very end of the interview he yelled "Rockford, it's for you!" and that was just amazing. I remembered every single day I walked to Auburn High School in the morning before I shot a basketball, I would stare at his memorial on the gym wall and be inspired by him. Fred VanVleet gave the entire city hope, showing us that we don't have to fall into the streets, get caught up in drugs, be involved in shootings, or associate with the violent crimes that plague Rockford. He was like the Batman symbol in a city full of darkness. He gave kids like me hope and inspiration that we can be successful one day if we work hard in life and chase our dreams. He always had a motto that said, "bet on yourself" and I never was able to understand it at first, but I understood it more and more. I knew I didn't have a mother, father, family and really nobody else but myself but that was all I needed. I started telling myself this saying to stop making excuses and feel sorry for myself. I knew I would never be better than Fred VanVleet but if he could come from the same city as me and be successful, then why can't I? We all have a hero that we look up to in life, and Fred was that hero to me. After seeing this I was left with nothing but motivation and inspiration. I knew I could achieve anything I wanted in life one day, but it was up to me to work hard and go get it. The night I saw someone from Rockford, Illinois win the NBA Championship was the night I really understood that with hard work all things are possible.

The next morning I woke up refreshed because it was time for the first day of basketball camp to start. I forgot to go to Walmart and get groceries for breakfast, so I just ate a bunch of fruit snacks and granola bars. I felt very nervous because these were some of the top players around the country that I was going to be playing against. But I just prayed and remembered all the hard work I had put in to get to this point. I needed to have that self-confidence if I was going to play well. I decided to write to myself in my notes like I usually did before camps and big events. I told myself that my biggest goal was to have 20 points in one of these games to show people that I could play against tough competition. Instead of just being labeled as a shooter I wanted to show people that I could play defense, communicate, score at the rim and make good passes. After I finished writing to myself I checked the time and I had to leave. I got all my basketball gear and other stuff that I needed packed inside of my bag and I headed downstairs to the hotel lobby, waiting for my Lyft driver to come and pick me up. On the ride there, I put my headphones on and stayed quiet to focus and get my mind ready for camp. The basketball camp was being held at a high school in Virginia and it was huge. I wish we could've played at the University of Virginia but either way I was just thankful and happy to be here. My Lyft driver drove around to the back where the other cars were, and the parking lot was packed. Out of all the basketball camps I had gone to, it was never this packed before. I got out of the car grabbing all of my things and headed inside the basketball camp. I still felt nervous, but I was just focusing on all the hard work I put in to get here. I didn't fly all the way out here and convince a judge into letting me come just to be scary, I had something to prove. As I made my way up the stairs to get inside the gym, I saw a line of jerseys with a piece of paper on top of each jersey. It was the same set up as in Atlanta and Indianapolis. After finding my name, I sat down, put on my basketball shoes and jersey, and waited for further instructions.

There weren't as many player's inside yet but after another 10 minutes, they all started flooding in both boys and girls. A lot of these players all had EYBL shoes, shirts, and bags and all I had was a half-torn backpack and a pair of slightly ripped basketball shoes. I knew these players were going to be good right when I saw their gear because the EYBL is one of the biggest AAU circuits for the top basketball teams and players in the country and most of those players go Division 1. As more and more players arrived, the coaches began speaking to us. The first person who spoke was the man who ran this camp, the same person I had seen from the two previous camps. Once he finished talking a former NBA player and ESPN recruit spoke to us. I felt like I was the only one in the gym amazed that an old NBA player was talking to us, but I guess that's from playing at the YMCA all the time. Most of these players played for an NBA players EYBL team or had been coached by one of them so they were used to it. He gave us a lecture on what college coaches want to see in a player on and off the court, and also explained the importance of grades, hard work and having fun with a positive attitude. Then all of the other college basketball coaches who were in attendance introduced themselves and gave us a lecture as well. I really took in the information they gave us and was going to make sure I wrote it in my notes once the first day of camp was over.

Once the coaches finished speaking to us, we started our basketball drills. I felt so much more prepared because I didn't have a broken finger or any aches or pains in my body. I was ready to start playing, I felt like these basketball drills would help warm me up even more and take away the little nervousness I felt. We were broken up into groups and sent to three different coaches. With each coach, we did a different drill. I did very well in the drills and hardly made any mistakes or missed any shots because these were mostly the same exact drills I practice every day for hours. It was all basic to me, like running off a flare or tight screen and making sure your footwork and your shooting arm was in your pocket as soon as you caught it, then doing stationary ball handling drills while dribbling two basketballs, catching a tennis ball or going full court. Then a defensive close out drill where you had to close out on your defender once they caught the ball and communicate and shift properly on defense. A lot of players just wanted to play in the games and never wanted to perfect their craft during these drills. They were drills that would make you better and give you the skill to perform well in the game. But I did have to learn that no matter how good you do in the drills it doesn't have as big of an impact as how you play in a basketball game. This is where I ultimately struggled—overthinking, playing nervously, and realizing the athletic abilities I hadn't worked on. During this camp, I was really exposed to how unathletic I was.

Once the time limit ran out on the clock, the horn went off and we were told to sit back down in our group while they were going to tell us what we would be doing next. So, we all lined back up and then we were told that every person in our line was going to be our team for the camp. I was happy because I had some good players on my team who did really well during the basketball drills, so I felt confident that my team was going to do well too. The coaches then told us that we would be starting basketball games now and six teams would be playing at once because we had three different gyms to use and just like the other two previous camps I attended, they were keeping track of each team's record and the best team would win the camp. To keep things better organized they posted a schedule on the wall of all the teams that would be playing and the record of each team after every game. It turned out that my team was actually going to be playing first on court number one. In a way I wish we didn't because I wanted to watch and see what type of competition I was really going to be playing against, but I just had to be confident. After the coaches finished talking, each team went to the correct basketball court they were assigned. I was really hoping I would perform well, so I made sure to tie my shoes up extra tight and stretch a little more just so I would be ready. We were assigned a coach to coach us during the camp and once he came out he gave us a little speech about having fun and playing hard. Then he picked out his starting 5 from what he saw in the drills and I was happy to be in the starting five. But for some reason I kept having this nervous feeling and I was trying to get it out of me. I was just intimidated with all of these college coaches watching us play and I was scared I was going to mess up and embarrass myself. To take my mind off of it I told everyone to match up with who their man was that they would be guarding. Then the opening tip off started and the game was on. Right after the first game was finished I was shocked because I had never played with or against such athletic players before in my life. I saw one of the players on the other team do a windmill dunk, and a reverse 2-handed dunk on a few fast breaks and that was the first time I had ever seen that in person. All of these layers here were so explosive, strong, fast, and could jump out of the gym. I really saw what separates a Division 1 athlete to a Division 3 athlete here. After the first game was over a bunch of coaches went to talk to the player who did a couple of those crazy dunks and one of the players on my team. I didn't know that one of the players on my team was a 6'5 ranked freshman in the ESPN top 100. It was a totally different ball game and competition from back home at the YMCA. Once the first game was over my team played one more game making it a total of two games the first day and I had 10 points in each game. I was very frustrated with myself because with all the hard work I had put in I should be scoring 16 or 20 with ease but my athletic ability was just horrible. I would be lucky if any coach even came up and spoke to me. My footwork was way too slow on defense and I was just too slow in general. I could not dunk or be explosive off the dribble. I wasn't even strong enough to get past a lot of my defenders. Every player in this gym was so much bigger, stronger and faster than I was. I was starting to feel like I flew out here for nothing. I was not good enough and didn't belong here because of how mediocre I was. I was just very disappointed in myself and had nobody to blame but me for not working harder on my athletic abilities.

After the first day of camp was over, I called a Lyft and headed back to my hotel after a rough first day. I just stared out the window the entire car ride and once I got back to my hotel I began to wonder what God had planned for me. I was starting to think that I was just wasting my time with basketball. I was done with high school basketball and had no offers anywhere, the best possible choice I had was trying out for a basketball team and hoping I would make it somewhere. It was so frustrating to think that every day I woke up at 6am and walked 4 miles to get to the basketball gym just to make 400-500 shots a day. Then I would come back later on at night and practice some more. I dedicated my entire life and worked so much harder than anyone I had ever known at the game of basketball. Every single coach I had ever come across always told me I was the hardest worker they had. I had even changed the way I ate just so I could perform better. I was just pissed off to think of all the hard work I had been putting in since I left Lutherbrook just to still be average with no offers or scholarships anywhere. But I had to stop thinking so negatively and realize if I was ever going to play at a high-level basketball school I had to work on my athletic ability. It was so much harder for me to be athletic because my dad was only 5 '7 and my mom was 5 foot but somehow I was 6 foot almost 6' 1. But my height was no excuse because there were players at this camp smaller than me and NBA players that were smaller than me who could dunk and were crazy athletic. I knew deep inside that guys were always going to be naturally more athletic than me and if I was going to be successful I was going to have to work a lot harder than them. This is where I remembered what my best friend Greg always told me before he passed away. Greg and I always had long talks about NBA players and how hard they worked. Then we would go to the YMCA for hours, sometimes even the entire day and do a bunch of drills because he always explained to me that hard work beats talent any day. Even though I was a terrible basketball player back in middle school he always forced me to play and get better instead of sitting around. I just had to go back to those memories and use that talk over this off season to get my athletic ability better. My game was already there, and I had got the hardest thing down which was learning how to shoot the ball. Now all I needed was to add more muscle, speed, and bounce. Scoring and the game of basketball would be so much easier for me once I got this down. I began looking back and seeing how I had made it this far to a camp in Virginia when I'm not even supposed to be here, so what was the point in stopping now? Especially after watching Fred VanVleet do the impossible and win an NBA championship. I just had to believe in myself and keep working harder and harder. Eventually my hard work would pay off. I just had to be patient. I just needed to use this basketball camp as a lesson from what separates a division 1 player to a Division 3 player and make that choice of what division I wanted to be.

When day two of camp rolled around, it was even more competitive than yesterday was. A lot more college scouts came over from the Top 100 Camp to our All-American Camp because of all the skilled and talented players that were here. On the second day the top ranked 8th grader in Canada and a projected NBA player in just 8th grade was in attendance. He was 6'4 and played like a grown man. I have never seen an 8th grader dunk on someone or have his basketball game so advanced. It was almost hard to believe he was even in 8th grade the way he would bully people in the paint and dunk on people at the rim. No wonder why he had over 7 Division 1 offers already. Our team and his team quickly became the center of attention because we had an ESPN top 100 ranked freshman who was 6 '5 and they had the top 8th grader in Canada who was also ranked in the ESPN top 100 and everyone wanted to watch those two go head to head. As soon as our game started up every single scout and coach came over to our court to watch us play. We were the only two teams that were undefeated and this was a battle for first place. I knew if I was going to make a name for myself and impress the scouts and coaches with my game now was the time to step up and do it. But unfortunately I did not perform well enough and we lost that game. That was our only loss of the basketball camp so far. Now my team's record was 3 wins and 1 loss, making the team that we lost to the only undefeated and first place team. As for me as a player, I had another mediocre day scoring 10 points in both games. I now had a pathetic total of 40 points in 4 games. This was nowhere near as good as some of the other players in this camp. But I didn't let it discourage me. I used this as a lesson for how much I needed to improve as a basketball player.

After the rest of the games and teams finished playing, they decided to hold a dunk contest. This dunk contest was just amazing to watch and see. I couldn't believe how high some of these basketball players were able to jump. There were players shorter than me who were able to do windmills and between the leg dunks. One player even threw it off the backboard, caught it in the air and did a windmill dunk. I started thinking to myself and began wondering what they were eating or what type of workouts they were doing to be able to jump so damn high. Seeing this really made me take a good long look at myself and inspired me to work harder and take my game to new levels. If I'm seeing people shorter than me do these crazy dunks then I sure as hell know I can dunk a basketball. I couldn't believe what I saw. As soon as the dunk contest was over and day two of the basketball camp was finished, I went over to ask some of the players for advice. I figured since a lot of these players are better than me I could use some of their advice and tips to help me and my game as a player. The first person I asked was the player who had won the dunk contest, and I asked him how he jumps so damn high. He started laughing and then gave me a few leg workouts to do and said it really comes from just practicing trying to dunk a basketball over and over and then the leg workouts make your legs stronger to help with your vertical. The main point he made was you have to actually practice jumping, you can't just lift weights on your legs and expect to dunk and that's the part where I messed up at. If I had put anywhere near as much work into my legs as I did on my shooting, making 400-500 shots a day I would be jumping out of the gym.

Once I finished talking with him I went and asked another player who was on my team and ranked in the ESPN top 100 about how to get better at basketball and what drills I could do. I had told him all the workouts and training I did by getting up and going to the gym 2-3 times a day and showed him some of my basketball videos. He told me to just keep doing what I was doing because that was a great work ethic, but I needed to start lifting weights and working on my athletic ability. He told me a guard who is a strong finisher at the rim, can shoot and knock down open jump shots and can throw it down at the rim is an instant Division 1 player. I had the hardest part down which was being able to shoot the ball consistently and knock down open shots and shoot with a defender in my face. I could make 11 3 pointers in a row without missing and most people my age couldn't even do that. But I ultimately knew if I was going to play Division 1 basketball I had to get my athletic ability up. As soon as I got back home in Rockford, I was going to head straight into the weight room. Once I got back to my hotel room later that night I watched some YouTube videos on how to lift weights properly for each muscle and I made myself a weight room workout plan. I was going to start lifting weights 4 times a week on my arms, and 2 times a week on my legs. Then I watched some videos on how to get my footwork faster and my speed up. The videos showed me that I needed a footwork ladder and a parachute, so I went and bought myself a parachute, and a footwork ladder to start running sprints and to get my footwork faster. I was done with making excuses for myself and being basic, I wanted to take my game to the next level. I had been through too much in life to be basic. I knew if I worked hard enough and stayed consistent with my work ethic eventually the hard work would pay off. I just had to stick with it and be patient. But the first and most important step was having the hunger and desire to want to be better and I had that, now it was just time to put it together and work hard.

Once the third and final day of camp started, we found out that our team would be playing one game. That one and final game would be for the second-place ranking in the camp. It was very disappointing we couldn't be the first-place team especially after coming second in the Atlanta basketball camp as well. I was hoping we would be the best team in this camp, but second place was not bad for how much talent and skill there was. Once I arrived at the camp, we had to wait for all the other teams to finish playing so we could finally play. It sucked that this was the final game of the camp and the last time I would be playing with these players. I made sure to get their social media accounts and to stay in touch just like I did at every camp I had been to. You never knew what connection you would be able to have and it was cool to have friends all over the United States and not just in Illinois. I was really hoping we would be able to get a workout in sometime because I knew some of these guys were going to be Division 1 players for sure. After an hour of waiting it was finally our turn to play. This was the last game we were going to play, so I needed to make this game count. I was hoping I would be able to score 20 points or over, at least then I would have accomplished one of my goals of being here. I was picked to be in the starting five again and I was ready to show out this time.

Although my team had won the game and we came in second place, I ended up playing another mediocre and pathetic game once again. I had only finished with 7 points which was the worst game I had played so far. I was so frustrated and upset with myself because I knew I could score way more than this. I ended up having a total of 47 points in 5 games and didn't accomplish my in-game goal of scoring 20 points or over. I was upset with myself, but I just had to use this as a learning experience going forward. Once the game was over and the final day of camp was done, I said goodbye to my coach and asked him about what things I could do to improve my basketball game. He said the same thing as everyone else which was working on my athletic ability. But then he asked me what grade I was in and I told him I was a senior with no offers. This coach told me the best way to go was to play basketball at a prep school. I had a prep school reach out to me in Florida and try to recruit me, but I was not interested in going to a prep school. I told him that my main goal was to play at a Division 1 basketball JUCO down in Florida. This coach then made a comment to me that I'll never forget. He said "son, Florida, Texas, and Kansas are the most skilled Division 1 JUCOs in the nation, if you don't have an offer from them yet your best bet is to look at other options or play for a lower division." I was not upset that he was being honest with me because I knew I was nowhere near the division one level, but that comment was just what I needed to add fuel to my fire. I knew I had the hunger to play Division 1 because the old me would've gotten discouraged and started wondering if I should play basketball anymore or just give up. But I knew that this was what I wanted to do in life one day. No dream was ever going to come true if every time someone said something negative about it I gave up and quit. That is supposed to be a part of your dream, that's what makes you work hard and want it more. At the end of the day, if a dream were easy everyone would do it, but every person doesn't have the heart, work ethic, and hunger for it. All the great athletes and accomplished people in this world at some point faced adversity and a challenge in their lifetime. I was not going to let some coach who barely knew me decide my future and just throw my basketball dream down the drain because he said this to me. I was not going to start crying like a little bitch and feel sorry for myself and give up. My whole life all people did was give up on me and I knew for damn sure I was not going to give up on myself. I was going to prove him wrong just like I have done with everyone my entire life. The only thing I knew how to do was work hard every day and out work my opponent. I was willing to give it everything I had and die for this because a man once told me if you're not willing to die for what you want then you don't love it or want it bad enough. That's the killer mindset I was installing more and more inside of my head. At the end of the day the opportunities in life were endless for me, it was up to me to work hard to get them or sit around and make excuses not to. I left that basketball camp with a completely different mindset on not just basketball but in life.

Once I finished talking to that coach, I called my Lyft and left for the last and final time. I headed back to my hotel room because I needed to pack all of my things up before the checkout time. I always hated how early hotels made you check out because if your flight was at night, you still had a lot of time to wait around and this was my case. I went on Google and searched for things to do and checked how much money I had left to spend. Thankfully, I had just enough money left in my account to do something fun to kill time, so I decided to go to an arcade. I was like a big little kid when it came to arcades because of how much fun they were. If I was ever feeling sad, upset, or just wanted to go out and have fun my first option would be an arcade not anything else. A lot of people my age thought I was weird because I would rather go to an arcade and I always said no to parties, kickbacks, and other suspect events. But the truth was I didn't care to be cool, drink, smoke, or try and fit in, I just wanted to be myself and surround myself with the correct environment. Once I got all of my stuff packed up, I handed my card to the front desk and checked out of the hotel for the final time. I called myself a Lyft ride to the nearest arcade I found on Google. I wanted to make sure it was close to the airport so I wouldn't spend too much money on Lyft rides back and forth. After a 10-minute Lyft ride I arrived at this humongous and beautiful arcade. This was way better than the run-down Chuck E. Cheese and Nickel World back home in Rockford. As soon as I got inside I saw they had a special deal going on for the weekend where you could play unlimited games for one hour. I instantly bought myself this card because all I had was an hour until I went to the airport. Just when I thought the arcade deal was great they had a special on pizzas as well, so I got myself my own personal pizza and played a bunch of arcade games. I started out with playing a bunch of basketball games because I always wanted to break the highest score that was set previously. Then I liked other games where you could win a bunch of tickets and cash them out at the arcade store once you finished.

But 15 minutes into playing at this arcade, I saw a group of little kids looking under the machines and begging their parents to get them more tokens. I was all by myself and I only had 45 minutes left on the card. I was still feeling pretty down about how I played during this basketball camp, but I wanted to make someone else's day. So, I walked up to the group of little kids who were begging their parents for more tokens and I handed them my card explaining it was unlimited for another 45 minutes and that they all would be able to play. The parents said no at first but I told them I was leaving to go to the airport after this anyways and I wanted to do this. I loved going out of my way to help and do nice things for people. This world we live in today is so negative and full of crime, hate and violence so why not be generous like the Bible tells us to do? Also, being a good man was more important to me than an unlimited arcade card, shoes, being cool, nice clothes, or anything like that. We only have so much time on this earth and that's why it's important to leave a legacy behind. I want my legacy to be remembered as a great person to people. I did not want to be a mean, disrespectful or angry person like I used to be or like my father. Once I gave the kids my card, I sat in the chairs and waited for my Lyft ride to come pick me up and take me to the airport. That's when I saw more little kids joined the kids I gave the card to and eventually there were at least 8 kids playing and having fun together and that's what it's all about. Even though I did not play as well as I wanted to at the basketball camp, it was nice to know my last day in Virginia I put a smile on a bunch of little kids faces and watched them all come together as one to have fun.

Once my Lyft driver showed up, I got in and as we headed to the Charlottesville airport. I stayed quiet the entire car ride and just looked out the window wondering what was next for me in my life. I started to get nervous and worried because I realized that this would be my last basketball camp that I would ever be in again as a high school player. It was just crazy to me how fast time flew by from my freshmen year to now. It was always challenging for me to keep my faith in God in times of uncertainty like this. I began wondering if I would ever get my athletic ability up to be a division one basketball player one day. If I ever would go to college outside of Rockford or be stuck in these foster homes through college as well. I was just scared for what was next for me in my life. My mind started getting filled with all of these negative and worried thoughts about me and my future because I didn't know what was next for me. But I remembered reading about all the successful people in life and how uncertain and hard times didn't throw them off their path or discourage them into giving up. I had to learn to let these times push me to work harder and believe in myself more. A lot of times at church, the pastor and my life groups always talked about how God has big plans for people but our faith will be tested by the devil during times like this. The devil will always try to blind you of your future and greatness by throwing obstacles in your path but if you remain faithful and continue to work hard you will succeed. Thankfully, I already had the hunger, work ethic and desire to be successful now it was all about keeping my faith and believing in myself.

Once I got to the Charlottesville airport, I went to the kiosk machine to print out my boarding pass. I was shocked at how empty this airport still was. Even when I had to sleep at the Chicago O'Hare airport it was more packed there than it was inside of here, and this was broad daylight. Once I printed out my boarding pass, I went through this very small security area and did all the security procedures to get through. I always thought the most annoying part was having to take your shoes off and your belt off. A lot of times I tied my shoes up really tight and had a lot of hand-me-down jeans that my friends gave me, so it was always a hassle of trying to find a place where it wasn't crowded to bend down and tie your shoes and then not look awkward by pulling my shirt up and trying to get my belt to fit back on around these huge saggy jeans. I was just thankful this airport was very small and slow. As I waited at my gate to board the plane, the flight got delayed two different times so it felt like I was sitting in here all day. I started getting hungry so I went down to the one and only tiny food shop this airport had and got myself a banana muffin and chips. I tried to keep a cheap budget because I still wanted to have money left for when I got back home to Rockford. I was happy this place had Wi-Fi to, so during the delay I was able to watch a few movies. Then I got another text message alert telling me the flight got delayed for a third time. I was now three hours behind schedule from when I was supposed to be home. I started to get worried I would have to sleep in the airport again because of how behind schedule I was. My cousin still had to get up early and go to work the next morning and that was my ride. I had to text him and let him know that I was still in Virginia due to my flight being delayed. Luckily, the time back home was central and not eastern meaning it was an hour behind the time it was now so it was not as late. Also the flight was just over an hour so I would be back quickly.

Finally after another 30 minutes of waiting it was finally time to board the plane. I was so happy to go back home and get out of this small country town and state. I did not like the country, I was a city boy and I'm pretty sure I always will be until I turn 80 years old and have hearing aids. I loved the feeling of having something new with lots of stuff to do every day, the traffic, skyline and all the attention it brought. Maybe that was the ADHD inside of me or the desire for all the many opportunities that this life had to offer. But what I was really happy and excited about was getting back to work and working on my basketball game. I felt like my hunger had been turned up a lot more after that comment the basketball coach at the camp gave me about playing Division 3. Also, just seeing people smaller than me do windmill dunks and seeing how explosive and great these players were at basketball gave me the motivation to strive to be a way better player. Playing basketball at the YMCA you don't see these great players everyday so, regardless of how I played I was really grateful I felt what it was like to play against Division 1 athletes. It showed me that I had a lot more work to do and gave me humbleness. As I boarded the plane and sat down in my seat, I took my phone out and began taking notes on how I was feeling in this particular moment. I wanted to remember how I was feeling so I could look back and read it later on in life and see if I proved myself wrong and changed my mindset or if I failed. I was really doing this to challenge myself to keep working harder and harder to be better and succeed in life. I also wanted to challenge my mindset and grow my thinking into more mature and positive thinking. I just wanted to be the best man I could be and be great in life. I was always told goals are nothing without action plans to achieve them so I broke achieving the goals down into steps. The first goal was getting stronger in the weight room. My action plan for that was lifting weights on my arms 4 times a week and on my legs 2 times a week.In addition to this, buying protein powder and eating healthier to see better physical results. The second goal was to start running sprints and doing footwork drills. I had already bought myself a parachute, a footwork ladder, and some cones for my action plan in getting started with this. My third and final goal was to start working on my jumping and vertical abilities so that way I could dunk and become more explosive. My action plan for this was practicing dunking every day and working on jumping straight up and recording my progress to keep track if I was jumping higher or not. I was so excited and ready to get back home and get to work. Now I was just praying for a safe flight home.

Leaving My Cousins House

After an hour and 20-minute flight, I gave thanks to God for making it back home safely. As soon as I turned my phone back on I checked the time and saw it was now 9:30 pm and I had a bunch of text messages from my cousin saying he was at the airport waiting for me and to hurry up because he had to work in the morning. I didn't want to be rude or make him angry so I hurried up and grabbed all of my belongings and I made my way off the plane. The only problem was that I had to go number 2 really bad and I was not going to be able to hold in for another long hour and a half car ride back home to Rockford. I wasn't sure what I had ate but it upset my stomach bigtime. I always tried to avoid public bathrooms because of how nasty and disgusting they are but I just had to deal with it this time. Once I found the bathroom and put toilet paper all over the toilet seat and got ready to handle my business, but my cousin kept calling me back to back to back. I finally had the chance to answer the phone, and when I did he kept telling me he was downstairs waiting for me in the pickup area. I didn't tell him I was using the bathroom because I didn't want to make him upset, so I lied and said I just landed and was making my way off the plane. Once I finished using the bathroom, I hurried up and rushed my way out of the airport and downstairs to the tunnel area. This is where almost at the cars, shuttles, and different type of busses would come and pick you up at. This also meant that there was a crap ton of traffic all in this small three lane area that did not allow any parking. So, all you could do was hurry up and drop people off or hurry up and rush to get inside of the car, and in my case I was trying to hurry up and rush into the car. My cousin started to get pissed off because every time he didn't see me he would have to go all the way around in the circle again because there was no parking allowed. I didn't blame him because he went around this circle about 4 times now as if he was riding a Ferris wheel. I called him and told him I was in the third lane and had my hands waving in the air so he wouldn't be able to miss me this time around. Finally he pulled off to the side just in time for me to run out and get inside of the car. As soon as I got inside of the car, he instantly asked me what took me so long and I told him that the flight had been delayed 3 hours and it was super busy inside. I still did not want to tell him I took so long because I was handling business inside of the bathroom and didn't want to make him even more upset. I just made sure to thank him over and over again and opened up to him about what happened last time while I was living with Mrs. Tiffany and had to sleep inside of an airport because nobody would pick me up. He just gave me a small talk about being mindful of people's time and to let him know ahead of time what was going on. My cousin was right because I still struggled with planning ahead and communicating at times. But either way I was just thankful to be back home and get to work in the gym.

Once I got up to go to the gym the next morning, I continued my routine of reading the Bible and praying before I did anything. I needed that confidence in myself and God that I could do this new routine I was going to start doing. I also did this because I wanted to grow into a better person more and more. My life group had told me reading God's word every day will keep you on a straighter path in life and that's the path I wanted. All I wanted my life to be around was basketball, God, work and becoming a better person. I didn't really care to have friends because I did not trust hanging out with people outside of the gym, unless they were a part of my church life group. I knew I needed to break this bad habit of not trusting people and starting to get closer with friends but I always felt a lot of friends were fake to me and they all come and go. I did not want to be distracted in life, I just wanted to focus on achieving and accomplishing all my goals. I was always nice to everyone and cool with everyone, making friends was not hard for me it was just having a best friend and someone who I trusted to hang out with outside of the gym that I had a problem with. After I walked 4 miles and got to the YMCA, I met up with a couple of my weightlifting friends. They were much older than me but I went to school with their younger brother at Harlem and saw they were a wrestling and weightlifting family.

I didn't really know much about any weightlifting workouts or how to get started, so I asked them for help with new workouts for my biceps, triceps, back, chest, and legs. I also watched a few YouTube videos and asked them to show me the proper technique of how to do the exercise correctly so I wouldn't hurt myself and actually see results from doing it. After about an hour of them showing me all types of different workouts and how to correctly lift, they started explaining to me the importance of building my body up. I learned that when you lift weights you have to be patient, you're not going to turn into a Lebron James overnight and this is what discourages people a lot and makes them quit. You also have to build your reps up, don't just start lifting the heaviest amount of weight because then you will end up hurting yourself, you have to start out small and slowly increase over time the amount of weight and sets. My old basketball teammate and his brothers showed me pictures of then and now and that was a year or two of constant weightlifting. I had a hard time being patient because I wanted everything to happen now, so lifting weights was therapeutic for me because it taught me patience, was a great stress reliever and helped me build confidence in myself by sticking with it and seeing results over time. After an hour of these brothers showing me and teaching me how to lift weights, they started telling me about supplements to take that will help me with seeing results faster. At first I thought they were trying to get me hooked on steroids and I was about to stop talking to them after this. But then they told me all of this was legal and started explaining the importance of protein shakes, creatine, BCAA's and eating more protein packed food. I had no idea you had to do all of this just to see results, I thought it was just coming into the weight room and lifting weights but it was way more than that. I couldn't believe how many different types of protein shakes and different kinds of supplements there were too. It was crazy to me. But eventually we came to an agreement on which one I should take and that was a mass gainer protein because I wanted to have my body puff out and see quicker results. I was also going to have to start eating a lot more baked chicken, fish, rice, beans, fruits and veggies if I wanted to see results as well. I was going to really have to commit myself to this, there was no more time for half-assing stuff if I wanted to be a division one athlete. It was really time to put my money where my mouth was and know that it was up to me to make it happen. No more just coming into the gym and making 400-500 shots because that wasn't good enough and I saw that at the camp in Virginia. I had to come up with a completely different workout routine.

After I finished spending a few hours at the YMCA and learning all about lifting weights, supplements and eating protein filled foods, I walked 4 miles back to my cousin's house. I was hoping to get my cousin motivated to lift weights with me because when I was younger he used to pick me up and take me to the weight room with him to lift weights and learn. He also used to be a wrestler and knew all about weightlifting so I figured we could become closer and benefit from this. But once I got back to the house and started telling him all about how we should work out together and the protein shakes and food I was going to start getting, it all went south. He told me he couldn't work out with me because he had to work to provide for his family even more after spending almost $500 on me and my basketball camp. Then he followed that up with a smart remark by saying that instead of spending money on lifting weights how about I pay him back with the money I owe them. I was totally confused as to what he was talking about. I got defensive and told him that I didn't owe him $500, all I owed him was money for the hotel and things started getting escalated. Apparently, DCFS screwed my cousin over and told him that they were not going to reimburse him for the basketball camp that I went to. My cousin told me he didn't have money to spend like that, being the only person with income trying to feed 4 people now, not including himself. It was like everything was my fault now and I was the one to blame for all of this. Me and him started getting into an argument about how I've been living here for free and he hasn't gotten paid from DCFS since I've moved in with him and now for this basketball camp and that I owed him. After some more back and forth I just walked away from this conversation before things started to get more escalated than they needed to be. I knew me and my cousin both had tempers and the last thing I needed was a fallout and nowhere else to live. I just couldn't believe how he was taking his anger out on me for DCFS not paying him. I was not in control of money. If I was, I would've paid him instantly. I was barely making any money working at Arby's because I was given so little hours. It was like he wanted me to give him every single paycheck and I wasn't going to do that because I still needed to move to Florida.

As I started walking away and going downstairs to get ready for work my cousin followed me and went on and on about the situation and I just ignored him because at this point one of us was one word away from throwing punches. His wife was supposed to take me to work but I just walked out of the house after I grabbed all my stuff and was going to take the city bus. Apparently I owed him gas money for all the times they took me to work as well. But even when I walked outside my cousin kept following me and then he made one final smart-ass comment and I was done. He told me "walk away from everything just like your piece of shit mom and dad did." I don't know why that made me so angry because I don't even like my own damn parents but I guess there is still a respect or care for them deep down inside. I was also sick of my cousin saying rude and disrespectful smartass comments to me and me just taking it over and over again and not saying anything. I turned around and just went off on him. Now we were outside in broad daylight with a few neighbors outside and cars driving past us making ourselves look like fools in front of them. We both said some mean and really mean and hurtful things to each other. I hated saying mean stuff or being mean to people but during this time I did not care. I was tired of being treated like shit in all of these foster homes and being backstabbed. Now I felt like my own cousin was backstabbing me over money and it wasn't even my fault. Eventually my cousin's wife came outside and stopped us from arguing. She told me to get in the car and that she was going to be taking me to work. My cousin kept telling her no and saying mean things like how I'm 18 years old and want to argue with a grown up like I'm grown so my broke bitch ass needs to get my own car and license. He was right because there were 16-year-old kids that already had their own car and license and I still didn't have any. I couldn't blame myself though because no foster parents would take me to the DMV to help me out or teach me how to drive. The only driving I did was last year at Harlem High School during my drivers ed class and that was only about 30 minutes each time. Pretty soon I was going to be 19 with no car or license still and I was sick of walking around everywhere and taking the city bus. I was even sicker of spending all this money on Lyft and Uber rides. It would cost me almost $20 in a Lyft or Uber ride just to get from my cousin's house to the YMCA. Thank God my legs worked because I would be broker than what I was now. But to piss my cousin off more I turned his insult into a joke and said I don't need one when you'll take me to work and spend your gas money on me. My old foster parent Adam always told me the best way to get someone pissed off is to turn their insult into a joke and make them look stupid because it didn't hurt them and now you are insulting them.

After my cousin's wife finally screamed at both of us and told us to stop acting like a bunch of bitches, she slammed the car door and revved the engine up as she began driving me to work. I didn't blame her for getting mad at both of us because we were making ourselves look so childish and acting like bitches. After she took a few deep breaths my cousin's wife finally began talking to me. At first I didn't want to hear anything she had to say because she was on my cousin's side but the first words she said was that she wasn't taking anyone's side because we were both wrong. She explained to me in a very calm and respectful tone that my cousin was not upset with me, he was upset with DCFS and how tight their money is. His wife started telling me that they both were hurt to see me in jail and that they went out of their way to help me even though they didn't have the funds to take me in. They both thought they would receive some sort of payment from DCFS for having me but they didn't. They told me that I eat a lot in the house and it costs money to be there and cause bills which I understood completely. I also understood why they were upset over the basketball camp after DCFS told them they would be reimbursed for it. But as much as they were going out of their way to help me and being generous, I felt that they still were looking at me as some sort of paycheck for having me. I understand that money is tight nowadays and people are barely making ends meet in today's world, but it hurt my feelings for someone who I have known since birth took me in not only to be generous but to receive some sort of payment from the state. I wonder what would've happened if there were no payments attached to me. Would they still have done the same thing? Probably not and that's what disgusted me. Once again, I felt a sense of betrayal and double-crossed. I basically just zoned her voice out and was just ready to get out of the car. All I wanted to do now was just make enough money to pay my cousin back so he would shut the hell up. As much as I wanted to move to Florida and go to college, it was going to be hard to pay my cousin $500 back and have enough money saved up to pay for my flight to Florida and first month's rent in student housing which was $800. There was no way I was going to be able to do all of this in a month and a half while making $9.25 an hour. I started to lose hope in myself and my dream. I guess it was time to just apply to Rock Valley College and face the hard fact that I'm probably going to be stuck in Rockford for a long time and have to live in these foster homes and continue to deal with this bullshit all through college as well.

After I got off of work that day, I ended up taking the city bus to avoid any more conflict or being accused of owing them more money. I also wanted to defuse the situation and not have things escalate anymore. As I was riding the bus home that night I started wondering if the problem was me. Why is it that every home I've been to it seems like I have a problem with everybody? Maybe I'm just a bad person and need to take a good long look at myself and figure out if I'm causing the problems. When I walked 4 miles from the bus station and back to my cousin's house that night I didn't see any of them because they were already asleep. I sent a text message to my youth group leader at City First Church and asked him if we could get together the next day and talk about things. I knew I was eventually going to have to speak to my cousin about what just transpired between both of us, and I wanted to get advice from a man of the church and just open up to him about how I was feeling and what was wrong with me. I learned the importance of seeking wise counsel and advice very early after I left Lutherbrook and saw how advice can work out but it all depends on who is giving it to you. After I reached out to my youth group leader, he agreed to come and pick me up tomorrow. In the morning, I still didn't see my cousin because he got up to go to work early so at least a problem wouldn't go off just yet. When my youth group leader showed up that afternoon I went with him and we both ended up going to a small restaurant where we could talk about things. I told him that I felt like I was the problem in all of these foster homes and that I was a bad person. I had been kicked out of so many homes within the last year and it was crazy to me. I was having problems with my cousin now and my older sister and maybe I was just a horrible person. He stopped me and told me I was not a bad person at all, I just dealt with a lot in my past and in these foster homes that wasn't my fault. But I didn't want to keep using the past as an excuse for my behavior nowadays.

I wanted to grow as a person and overcome the many obstacles and challenges that I had faced throughout my life. I knew that I had problems with being patient, controlling my words when I got upset and keeping my attitude in check at times. I really realized while talking to him that I need to work on these issues if I want to become a better person and have people want to be around me. I didn't want to grow up like my father and be abusive and angry to people, I wanted to be very nice, respectful, loving, caring and a great man and friend. I just hated how hard it was for me to do this. I almost began breaking down because of how frustrated I was and how bad I wanted to become a better person. My youth group leader told me to just be patient with myself and keep doing what I was doing. He told me I was doing a lot better than a lot of people because I wasn't drinking, smoking, having sex, I was going to college and I had just graduated high school. The only things I did were go to the YMCA, go to church, and work. He told me that my problem was that I overthink too much and needed to learn how to get my mentality fixed and that I was a paranoid person. He was right about that because I was always paranoid that I was not good enough, I wasn't working hard enough and overthinking all the time and this caused me to be stressed out a lot. I never knew the feeling of what it was like to just relax and be happy, maybe sit on the couch and just watch tv all day for once. Change would come in time and I just needed to keep doing what I was doing and stay patient with myself, but I did need to get my anger fixed because I did not want to keep escalating situations or be mean to people. My biggest fear was ending up like my dad one day and becoming abusive and not having a wife and children and I wanted that one day and I wanted to have a loving relationship. I wanted to have friends and I wanted to be a great man and have people like me and talk good about me.

Later that day, I saw my cousin once he got off of work and we had a sit-down conversation and I apologized to him. I told him that I was sorry that DCFS had screwed him over and I apologized for the mean stuff I said to him. I opened up to him about the robbery I suffered and how DCFS promised to replace my stuff and even had me write down all the things that I was missing. They took pictures of the boxes as evidence and proof of my missing things but didn't replace a damn thing. My cousin was very understanding and he accepted my apology and apologized to me as well by telling me he was not mad at me. It was just that their money was tight and they made a sacrifice that they didn't have trying to help me out. I completely understood everything he was saying and I told him I would help him out and give him some money and do a lot more chores around the house to help out with things. I did the dishes, took out the trash, and even cleaned up dog poop to help more. I started organizing the living room after the two little kids would get done playing so they wouldn't have to do it. That was the least I could do knowing he had gone out of his way to help me when he didn't even have the money to do so. I stopped asking my cousin to give me rides to places and started taking the city bus more to help them save gas money. I tried to do a lot more instead of just going to the gym, work and hiding in the basement all the time. I would come upstairs and watch my cousin play video games or try and watch a tv show he and his wife were watching to bond with them more. I had to learn to take the initiative when it came to making relationships with people and trying to get closer with them. He even started letting me play his video game more, but both of our personalities and tempers would come to us having a complete fallout. It all started with something as stupid as a video game once again.

My cousin had told me about a new video game that was free on the PlayStation network called NBA2K20 and that he was going to download it so we both would be able to play it. I was not really into playing video games because I felt the time I sat around playing video games was time I could be using to get better in the gym or work on myself. I especially was not into video games while living at my cousin's house and using his game system because of how strict he was with all of his games. I didn't want to start any problems or be accused of messing anything up. But I looked at this as a time to bond and felt like this would be a good opportunity to do that. So, later on during the week after I watched my cousin play this new game, he handed me his controller and told me I could play and make my own basketball player in the "my career" area of this game. I guess making your own basketball player was the best thing about this game and the reason why so many people played it. So, I did just what my cousin told me to do and I made myself my own basketball player and made sure to not touch his basketball player that he made. My cousin had his own fictional basketball guy and I now had my own fictional basketball guy. I didn't realize just how fun this game really was and I decided to stay up all night and play it as if I was really living my own career as an up and coming NBA star. It was like I was in my own fantasy world and I was escaping from reality and that's what made it so fun.

But the next day when my cousin came down to get on and play with his character the problems over video games started once again. I was in the kitchen washing dishes and watching some Jimmy Neutron on my small little iPhone 7. I usually always had my phone on do not disturb mode when I was watching a movie or a tv show because I hated whenever I was in the middle of watching something and I would get all of these alerts or something that would distract me. All I wanted to do was watch my cartoons in peace whenever I actually would get the time to sit down and actually watch them. I had both of my earbuds in because my cousin and his wife were in the other room and I didn't want to disturb them or be rude by playing my stuff out loud. But a few minutes into me watching my cartoon show and washing the dishes out of nowhere I felt someone yank one of my earbuds out of my ear. I turned around so fast that my phone fell into the dish water and was soaking wet now. When I turned around it was my cousin and he was pissed off. As he yanked out my earbud he yelled, "Can you not fucking hear me?" My adrenaline went from 0 to 100 because he scared me and he just spoke to me in a very disrespectful way. I did not want to cause any type of argument or problem so I calmly answered him and told him that my phone was on do not disturb mode and I was watching cartoons while I was washing the dishes. I was trying to defuse the situation and not escalate things any more than they already were. But I was pissed off once he told me his reason for doing what he did was. His reason for approaching me was apparently I messed up his NBA2k20 "my career" and he now had to start an entire new career. All of the defusing the situation tactics that I had learned and tried to do just got thrown right out of the window. It was so silly to me that he was that angry over a damn video game. I instantly started to get defensive and began to raise my tone a little because I was upset that he accused me of doing something I didn't do and just yanked my earbud out. That's when he told me to "shut the fuck up" because I was raising my voice to him. Once he spoke to me like that I just turned around and stayed quiet and continued to wash the dishes. I was so angry that he just did all of this after everything was going so well between us and I just ignored him completely as he was talking to me. My only response to him was by me saying that I would never play another video game on his game system ever again because of stupid problems like this. After I said that I walked right downstairs and stayed down there for the rest of the night. I did not want to talk to him or see him for the rest of the night. My cousin reminded me so much of my dad the way he just flew off of the handle over something as small as a video game after all the progress we made. I was really tired of living here now and tired of being accused that I owed him money and doing all of this stuff to help them out just to be talked to like I was a dog. I looked at the messages he sent me through text and they were even worse. I was just tired of being treated like shit all of the time and I was ready to leave this house and just live on my own.

Later on that night after I heard everyone go upstairs to bed while I was downstairs in the basement, I went into the kitchen and ate a bagel with cream cheese. I didn't eat dinner because I stayed downstairs avoiding further conflict, so I was really hungry. After I finished eating my bagel, I made sure there were no crumbs on the table or anywhere and that my chair was pushed all the way in. For a second I thought I was living with Mrs. Milly, but it was just the old habits she installed in me and they stuck. Now I always made sure my chair was pushed in all the way and always checked for any little bit of crumbs I could have possibly left. The last thing I needed was to hear my cousin's mouth about leaving a mess or complaining about something knowing he was already mad at me. After I finished eating my bagel, I went back downstairs and got ready to go to sleep because it was late. I still had to be up early in the morning to work out and then go to work the next day. Regardless of what was going on in this house, I was going to make sure I dedicated myself to my basketball grind. The next morning when I woke up, I was surprised to hear all the loud noises and everyone got up so early. It was only 7am, but I guess my cousin had off from work today and everyone was up early for some odd reason. Usually around this time the house was super quiet so this was very strange. But I went right over to the desk area and read my Bible and prayed. Then after I finished spending time with God I grabbed my gym bag and got dressed to go on my 4-mile walk to the YMCA and get my morning workout in. As I was headed up the stairs, I heard my cousin's voice in the kitchen. I started thinking to myself wondering if I should open the basement door now where he could see me and I could see him, or should I just wait till he left the room and go after that? But I had to think logically, we don't live in a huge mansion so either way I'm going to have to see him. So in my head I just thought screw it and decided to open up the basement door. My plan was to just walk right past him and leave out of the front door to go straight to the gym but that plan I had failed. He instantly got my attention and called my name as I tried to zoom past him. I was mad at myself because I couldn't pretend like I wasn't able to hear my cousin because I forgot to put my headphones inside of my ears. Apparently I did not tie up the bag of bagels to his liking and this is what he was complaining about. My cousin said in a very rude and stern tone, "instead of tying the bagels up with the bag, use the twister that comes with it, that's what it's for." Then he started complaining about where I put the cream cheese in the fridge and told me he wants his stuff in a certain order. It was 7 in the morning and it was too damn early to be hearing someone complain over something this little. I really didn't even want to answer or talk to him the way he spoke to me last night, so I just kept saying "ok, ok, ok" and that's when he told me to "shut the fuck up" again. Now I was really done holding my tongue and both of our tempers let loose. I told him "you shut the fuck up" and we both started going at it and yelling. Then the yelling turned into him throwing things and before I knew it my cousin flipped over the entire table and was screaming at the top of his lungs. His wife rushed into the kitchen to grab their little son because he almost crushed his foot by flipping the table over. Now his son was screaming, crying, as well as his. He was yelling and I was just standing there patiently waiting for him to put his hands on me. I was only looking at one thing and that was the knife that was right next to me. Today was the day that I was going to use a knife on someone in self-defense. He kept threatening to slam me on my face and me being me I kept egging him on telling him to do it. I was done backing down from people and letting people walk all over me. I was standing up for myself waiting to see if he was really going to be a man of his word and do it. His wife came back in the kitchen and tried to calm my cousin down but he just kept yelling for me to get out of his house. His wife started begging me to walk away, so I went downstairs and grabbed my bag and then as I was leaving out the front door, my cousin told me he wanted his house key. So I went in my bag and dropped it on the floor as I walked outside and the next thing I knew he slammed and locked the door behind me. I felt like breaking down and crying for some odd reason but I was used to going from home to home. It just hurt how my own family turned on me once again. I made a promise that this would be the last time I ever associated myself with any of my dad's side of the family. This was the last time I would be betrayed by any of them ever again.

I walked to the local McDonalds that was close by and I called my caseworker to let her know what just happened. My caseworker was not very happy about what happened and she began telling me how there were no more foster homes in Rockford for me. We almost got into a little argument because she said I had been to so many homes within the last few months that they were running out of options of where to place me. The way my caseworker was talking it sounded like I was going to be moving to Chicago again. I started getting defiant and I told her that I was not leaving Rockford, I was going to stay here until I moved to Florida. She just kept saying there weren't any homes for her to place me in and told me she would be calling me back later to let me know where I was going. In the meantime I just walked 4 miles to the bike path near downtown Rockford where the YMCA was. But during my entire time of walking my cousin kept texting me off of random phone numbers harassing me and calling me over and over again. This was like the biggest crybaby I had ever met in my entire life. I really felt sorry for his wife and his kids because they were going to have to deal with that person and I wasn't anymore. I just turned my phone off so it wouldn't even bother me anymore. Once I got to the bike path near the YMCA and downtown Rockford I just sat down far away from everyone so I could be at peace and not be bothered at the time. But me overthinking and stressing out was bothering me more than anything. I just started thinking to myself why is my life so damn hard? I don't ask for anything but just a bed and food. Everything else I do independently yet it's so damn hard just to live somewhere. Now I have no idea where I am going to be living later today or where I'm going to be in the future. It just frustrated me as to why it was so damn hard just to live somewhere. I wanted to be a normal kid just like the rest of my friends. I saw so many people walking with their families along this bike path laughing and smiling having a great time. I even saw a huge group of ducks walking in an organized single file line all peacefully floating on the water together. I read the Bible every day, I prayed every day, I did not cause problems or trouble with anybody. All I did was go to school, work, church, and play basketball yet my life is so hard. I didn't ask for 2 pathetic parents, a fake family, to grow up in foster care, or any of the bad things that happened to me. To think that I was only 18 years old and all of this stuff was happening to me, I couldn't imagine what was next for me once I became a full-grown adult. I really began to hate my life again, I knew things could always be a lot worse but I felt like I was almost there. I was so tired of all the drama, stress, and bad things that kept happening to me over and over again. Maybe my life would be better if I just gave up and stopped trying. It felt like everyone had already done that to me so I began feeling like I should do the same, I was tired.

Eventually, I stopped throwing myself a pity party and stopped feeling sorry for myself. I knew nothing would ever change in life if I just sat around and complained all the time. I had to be the change I wanted to see in the world one day and that's what I was going to do. I have been through too much in life to be basic and I refuse to just give up. I decided to pick up the phone and started reaching out to people asking if I could live with them. I was determined to find somewhere in Rockford to live and not have to move to an entirely different city. The first person I reached out to was my older sister because she had been trying to get in contact with me for a long time. Once I called her, I told her what had happened between me and our cousin and she wasn't surprised one bit because of how rude he was to her and everyone. At least me and her were finally able to agree on something after all. But what I needed from her was a place to stay. I told her I didn't have any place to live at the moment and for some crazy reason I asked to live with her. I knew she had her own apartment and had plenty of space so I figured I would just give it a shot regardless of our past history. But she quickly turned that idea down and told me no I couldn't stay with her. I couldn't even get mad because my older sister had screwed me over so many times throughout my life and it was her place. It just sucked how siblings usually always have each other's back and she didn't have mine at all. I was about to get off the phone with her because that was all I needed to know, but then she brought up how I could go back and live with Adam. My stomach dropped as soon as she said his name, I felt like I was going to throw up. I was surprised how she even knew him but I guess she and him are good friends now. I quickly rejected that offer and told her that I would rather be homeless then go back and live with that man. This was the same man who called the police on me and put me in jail for a damn shoulder bump. My older sister didn't show me any sympathy and she told me to go ahead and be homeless then because that's the only option left in Rockford right now. I told her I was going to call her back because my caseworker was calling me and when I picked up the phone she told me that they found a placement for me near Aurora, Illinois. I told her I was not going and that I had found another placement in Rockford that I was going to be going to and then hung up on her. I was sick of these caseworkers and foster care agencies placing me where they wanted me to go and having to go by what they said all the time. I was not the same 14-year-old kid who was going to allow that to happen anymore. This was my life and I was going to take charge of it. I called my older sister back and I just decided to take her advice and go back live with Adam for the third time. At least I would have food, a bed, and still be able to go to the gym and work. I also knew he was a very forgiving man and didn't hold grudges. I also knew he cared about me a lot, it was just we always had an on and off relationship. This was my only choice, it was either here or go live in another random foster home so I was going to have to make this work.

Before Taking My Nephew In

Once I called my older sister back telling her I was going to take her advice and move back in with Adam, she told me she was going to call him and let him know. So I sat on the bench like I had been doing the entire day and I waited for her to call me back. I put my phone on my lap and just waited to hear a response and instead I got a random text message of a code. It was Adam texting me the code to get in through his garage. I didn't know what to say back, I hated when things were awkward and I felt like this was a very awkward situation. I knew there was going to be an elephant in the room as soon as I saw him. Or maybe I was just overthinking things and stuck in my head. When my older sister called me back she said that he was happy to take me back and he wasn't angry at me. She told me to walk to his house and talk it out with him. As many times as me and Adam had gotten into it and had an on and off relationship, he was unlike any person I had ever met before. This man had such a forgiving heart not only for me but for everyone. Even when this foster kid who was once living in his house planned the robbery and had set us up, he still went to visit him in jail and accepted all his jail calls. Any foster kid who had ever wronged him or he had gotten into it with, he still forgave them and would help them out as if nothing ever happened. I remember he had always told me that he never wanted to see any foster kids out on the streets or in jail. He always considered any kid that used to live with him his own kid and family. In fact he wouldn't even call us foster kids he would call us his nephews or nieces.

I was just shocked because I had never seen anyone with a forgiving heart that fast. No matter what happened between us I knew one thing that was for sure, and that was he was there for me more than my own family. I couldn't believe my own cousin threw me out of his house to be on the street and this was someone I had known since birth and a stranger would never let that happen.

OnceI got off the phone with my sister, I walked 2 miles to Adam's house that night. Once there, I typed in the code to the garage to get inside. When I got inside everything was completely dark and nobody was home. This made things even more awkward because I was walking into his house without speaking to him first but this was how he was. His home was always open to anyone who needed it, even back when I was living with Mrs. Milly and barely had any food to eat, Adam would give me the code to his garage when he wasn't home and tell me to eat some food that he had. I guess things were only going to be awkward if I made them awkward. Once I walked into my old room I started to unpack the clothes I had left in my bag and put them in the drawers. I didn't have any of my stuff because it was all still at my cousin's house, that is if he didn't throw my stuff out on the street like he said he was. I couldn't even worry because of how I was full of exhaustion. It felt like today was one of the longest days I had ever lived. I was just very thankful I had a safe place to sleep and lay my head. I was just going to talk to Adam in the morning when I saw him. When I woke up the next morning, sure enough I saw him first thing sitting at the kitchen table. This would be the first time we had talked since we both got into a heated argument outside and I went to jail. I decided to take the elephant out of the room right away by sitting down and telling him "thank you so much for taking me back for the 3rd time." I didn't want things to be weird between us or our relationship to be screwed up anymore. He gave me a very short response and followed that up by telling me that my caseworker was trying to get a hold of me because they didn't know where I was at. This was the last person I wanted to talk to right when I woke up first thing in the morning but I called my caseworker and spoke with her and she was angry to hear that I was back at Adam's house again. I told her that I wanted to live here and had to convince her that everything would be okay. She then asked to speak to Adam and Adam told her it was fine that I was living here. Once she and Adam finished talking, my caseworker talked to me in a very stern tone informing me that if another incident pops up, it's my ass. I was going to make sure nothing happened because I was focused on my ultimate goal of moving to Florida and going to college there. This placement would only be temporary, I had no proof of it I just had faith that things would work out especially since I was back at Adam's house. All I needed was to keep working hard like I had been doing and stay focused on the things that mattered.

After a week of being back in Adam's house, our relationship had gotten way better and things stopped being so awkward. We both started talking more and we finally had a sit-down talk about what transpired between the two of us that day I went to jail. I feel like a lot of problems in this world can be resolved if people actually have a sit-down conversation and put their egos aside. Adam told me he was teaching me a lesson by sending me to jail because I wanted to call the police on my older sister for the incident that happened after church and wanted her in jail. He told me family doesn't do that to family, instead they look out and help each other. I was just confused because he always told me I was his family but yet he sent me to jail and always threatened to put in his two week's notice when I made him upset. But I just listened and heard him out because I didn't want to be defiant or risk another argument and possibly be kicked out of this home. I was upset though after he told me how he was teaching me a lesson of sending me to jail. Once he finished talking I got up and went and walked inside of my room and just started thinking to myself. I didn't send him to jail when he put his hands on me during Thanksgiving last year but I should've taught him a lesson right? I really realized just how hard it is to be in foster care. Half of these foster parents don't even give a rats ass about you, they don't do anything for you, they are not involved in any way with your life for support, all they want is that check that comes in once a month for having you. But they want you to kiss their ass and never mess up in order for you to live in these homes. What's crazy is how my entire life I had been living this way. Even with my own father I lived almost the exact same way, the only difference was I wasn't getting beat in these foster homes. If this man told me to do something and I didn't do it right he beat the shit out of me. I was beat for everything and anything I messed up on. It always felt so frustrated and exhausted living a life like this. I was always stressed out, depressed, and angry almost every day I woke up. I wish people would really understand that nobody is perfect in this world, especially not an 18-year-old who has been physically and emotionally abused almost his entire life. I always felt such an emotional toll from this. I was just thankful God made me an outgoing person and that I wasn't afraid to open up to people because if I wasn't I probably would've committed suicide from holding all my depressions and anger in all the time. But it did hurt when I would open up to people, especially Adam because a lot of times he would throw it back at me if we got into an argument or he would do it jokingly. if we got into an argument. I just felt like I would never be a happy person or a great man in life because of how angry and sad I was all the time. I felt like I just needed one person who would unconditionally be good to me, actually be involved in my life through the ups and downs, and really just help me grow in life. All I am is just a student in this world learning new things every day. The only problem was I was a student who was further behind than others because of the lack of support and guidance in my life.

As my court date was right around the corner, I had a lot of concerns as to what my future would hold. I didn't know if I was going to be placed on probation or if I was going to be charged. Either way I was just nervous this was going to prevent me from moving to Florida. But I sat down and had another long talk with Adam about what was going to happen during this court process. I was worried and I opened up to him and I told him about what my goal was and the things I still wanted to accomplish with school and shockingly enough he agreed to help me move to Florida again. He also told me he was not going to press charges and did not want anything on my record. I never had anything on my adult background so I was sure I was going to get off anyway. Later on that week me, my caseworker, and Adam both went down to the courthouse in downtown Rockford. Adam had written a letter to the judge saying that he did not want to press charges or want to continue any further with this case. The only thing he wanted to get me involved in was a court ordered anger management class or some sort of therapy. He was telling me how Florida is a stand your ground state and he didn't want me to end up like Travon Martin because of some altercation. But I was already in therapy with the foster care agency Our Children's Homestead and met with a therapist once a week. So, my caseworker got a written signature from my therapist of all the sessions I had been in to prove I was in counseling once a week. I always loved going to counseling and therapy because someone would actually listen to me and give me good and helpful advice to grow as a person. That was all I wanted to do and later on in life when I had the funds I was looking to get into an anger management class. I didn't have bad anger problems or a bad temper. I just wanted to make sure I never ended up like my father and I wanted to be nice to people. I was tired of being stressed out, frustrated, depressed and angry about things and I wanted to learn how to get rid of that or control it way better. I knew one day I wanted to have my own family with my own wife and kids and I wanted to be a great husband and a great father not some piece of shit abusive person like my father was.

While we were waiting outside in the lobby area the public defender came and spoke to me and my caseworker. He spoke to Adam privately as well. We all got the understanding that the case was going to be dropped today and all I needed to do was stay in counseling and prove that I was already enrolled. After we all finished talking, we waited about 15 more minutes until it was time to go inside. When the judge called my name, it was the same lady from last time who allowed me to go to the basketball camp in Virginia. As I walked up to the stand and stood with my public defender, he explained what the plan was. He also handed the judge a few papers showing her that I was already in counseling and then she had found out I was in foster care. I was so shocked because once she heard that this judge told me that she was sorry for all the things I have been going through in the state's system and that she knows how tough it is being a foster kid. I was blown away by her saying that because I always thought judges were mean but she proved me wrong. However the judge did tell me before she was going to completely dismiss this case, she wanted me to get enrolled at Rosecrans and show her my enrollment papers. Rosecrans was another type of therapy and this meant that I would be attending two different types of therapy once a week. I didn't mind it at all because this just meant I was going to better myself more and more. After we were dismissed from court, my caseworker took me over to Rosecrans to get enrolled and show the judge these papers so this case would be dismissed for good. As me and my caseworker were talking she had told me that before DCFS could even think of letting me move to Florida I had to do my counseling and have this case with my foster parent Adam closed. So this was now my biggest goal, I wanted to be able to show this judge that I was serious about counseling so she would drop this. But as soon as I thought after this case was over I would be allowed to move to Florida, my caseworker stopped me and told me not to get ahead of myself because I would have to see an entirely new judge. It turns out that this judge was a DCFS judge and I would have to convince him and the state of Illinois to allow me to leave the state. I started to get a huge headache after my caseworker told me this because she told me they rarely if ever allowed foster kids to just leave the state and if they did they were completely cut off of all state aid. This meant no Youth in College Scholarship money or any type of financial help while I was in college. There was no way I was going to be able to work full time and go to school just to pay rent, my phone bill, and for groceries. It was hard enough working a job in high school and that was just part time, college is a lot more work and way harder. My biggest fear was ending up homeless again and I did not want this to happen to me if I moved down to Florida. I just had to pray, continue to work hard, and trust that everything was going to work out.

After another week had gone by, it was now mid-July. It was time for me to go back to court and show the judge that I had gotten myself enrolled in Rosecrans so this case would be dropped for good. So, me, my foster parent and my caseworker headed back to the courthouse in downtown Rockford to report back to the judge on my final hopefully final court date. While we all sat out in the lobby waiting to be called inside the courtroom, I met with the public defender to make sure that I had everything that I needed so I wouldn't have to come back again. He told me everything looked great and there should be no issues, this made me a little happy knowing I would be done with one judge. Once we went inside the courtroom, I turned my phone off like usual and we all sat down waiting for our names to be called by the judge. This felt like it was the longest court session I had ever been in because of how much anticipation I had of being done. I just needed to hear it from this judge's mouth one final time. When she finally called my name, I walked up to the stand hoping this would be my last time being here after 4 different times and I stood next to my public defender as he showed her the paperwork I had of me getting enrolled in counseling at Rosecrans. She took a good long look at it and told me okay. Finally this case was closed and nothing would go on my adult record. I was so thankful to not be placed on probation or any type of action that would stop me from being able to move to Florida or affect my record. Before I left the stand this judge told me something I would never forget, she said “there will always be a judge in the state of Illinois rooting for you and that judge is me.” I was totally blown away that she had just told me this, it was crazy to think of how much my mindset had changed from first meeting her to now leaving her. This was a judge that I would never forget and always be thankful for meeting. Now there was only one more judge that I needed to cheer for me and be on my side, and that was the state of Illinois. I had no idea how I was going to convince him into letting me leave the state of Illinois, especially after I had just been arrested. Even if I was allowed to leave there was still going to be a very big problem. Not only was I going to have to convince this judge into letting me leave the state, but also convince him to not close my case so I would still be able to receive services and aid while I was in Florida. My foster parent Adam kept telling me to just apply at the local community college here called Rock Valley and just go to school here for a semester. I really started considering his advice and decided to take it by applying to this school as well. He always told me the importance of planning ahead and having a plan A, B, and C. I should know this better than anyone after I didn’t take his advice when I was in Indianapolis and had to sleep inside of a bus station because I didn’t plan ahead or have a backup plan. I also really did not want to be out of college completely and just end up sitting around all day doing nothing and feeling like a bum. I wanted to get started with my college career right after I got out of high school to get things moving quicker so that why one day I would get a college degree and make a good living for myself. But I really wanted to start a new life and have lots of opportunities for myself down in Florida. I knew being stuck in Rockford would not open doors for me or give me the opportunities that I needed in life. I just prayed and I prayed and I prayed hoping that after everything I had been through in life God would come through for me and give me a new life.

After another week of waiting it was now late July and my court date was finally here. This was the moment of truth to find out what my future would be. I felt so nervous and sick to my stomach not knowing what was going to happen with my life. I did not want to live in Rockford anymore seeing the same people I had known since elementary and doing the same things all the time. I wanted to wake up to palm trees one day, never see snow again, meet all kinds of new people from all over the world, and have a life full of opportunities. Once my caseworker came to pick me up to head to court, Adam decided he wanted to show up with me for support and to know what the plan was going to be. While we were waiting inside of the courtroom lobby to be called, Adam saw that I was nervous and I began to open up to him about how I was feeling. Once again he told me like always that everything was going to be fine and to pray about it. But he also added how he knew that I was going to succeed at whatever I decided to do in life because of my work ethic and determination, regardless if that was in Rockford or down in Florida. I was happy that he told me he was all for me moving to Florida and me being a foster kid that actually wanted to do something with my life. Adam told me so many stories of all the foster kids he had taken in before me who weren't doing anything with their lives or are in jail to this day. He told me I was one of the reasons he still did foster care because it showed him that there are good foster kids in the system who are willing to listen and want more out of life. That's exactly what I wanted to do with my life, I wanted to beat this statistic and prove everyone who ever doubted me wrong.

After 15 minutes of waiting in the lobby, we were finally called into the courtroom. I felt like I was about to go on the world's tallest roller coaster and just drop straight down. I was so nervous and scared if I was going to be able to move or not. I knew I was going to cry if this judge said no because that would mean I would have to continue living in these foster homes and stay in the city of Rockford. I have never wanted something so bad as I wanted this opportunity. I knew if I could have the chance to just move and go to school in a completely new state, city, and environment I could have way bigger chances at succeeding in life, becoming successful and actually feeling safe and happy. The city of Rockford is a very violent and dangerous city, every day there is a shooting, robbery, rape or some other sort of crime. There is a reason why it's so hard to make it out of this city and why it's always on the top 10 worst cities to live in. As I made my way into the courtroom I sat next to my caseworker and Adam as the judge started reading and going over the report. While he was speaking my heart started racing, my stomach kept dropping, my hands were all sweaty, I was just a nervous wreck. This judge started asking me questions about what school I wanted to go to in Florida and I told him a school called Hillsborough Community College, which is in the city of Tampa. Then once I got my 2-year degree from there I wanted to attend the University of Florida or the University of South Florida. He asked me why this school in particular and I told him that I wanted to play basketball for this school and they had a Division 1 JUCO men's basketball team that I wanted to play for. I also showed him paperwork that I had already been accepted into the school and completed my freshmen orientation packet along with my financial aid and high school transcripts. I made sure that I had everything that I needed to show this judge that I was serious about moving and I wanted this. Once I finished talking, the state's attorney of Illinois started bashing it saying it was too much of a risk and a huge leap. They also brought up how if I had left the state all my benefits would be completely cut off and stopped. When it came time for my caseworker to speak she told the judge great things about me but she did agree with the states attorney of Illinois for me to stay. At this point I thought I knew it was over, I had my caseworker, and the state's attorney against me. It was now two against one and I just felt a wave of sadness shoot up through my body because I knew it was over. After everyone finished talking the judge started talking and agreed that it was a big jump and a huge leap but he shocked the entire courtroom. This judge brought up how many foster kids he has seen and out of all of them I was one of the rarest he had heard of me trying to better my life and do something with it. That's when he did something that was never done before. He said "if there is a foster kid wanting to go and find new opportunities outside of Illinois then why stop him? Let's give him a chance and if Florida doesn't work out then we will leave his case open so he can always come back and still be in state care." This meant that even when I left to go to school in Florida my case would still be open, and I would have a caseworker in Illinois while I was in Florida. I would be allowed to get on the Youth in College Program and get financial benefits and help being a foster kid in college. My caseworker and Adam were both in complete shock because this rarely if ever happens. I was speechless, I could not believe what had just happened. If I could have gone up there and given him a big hug I would've but there was a huge security guard and a few police officers inside and I was not trying to go to jail again. Before he dismissed the court I told him thank you so much for this chance. I could not believe this was actually going to come true. Inside of that courtroom I began to feel God had something bigger in store for me.

After the shocking news, I was just full of complete joy and happiness. I couldn't believe I was actually getting to move and start a new life. My entire life I had been wanting to make it out of Rockford and now that dream was finally coming true. After all the hard times and the adversity I faced over and over again in my life and in just the past few months I finally got one of the biggest blessings of my entire life. All the tears I cried, all the times I kept getting knocked down over and over again, getting robbed and losing everything I had, going from foster home to foster home, all the times I felt like I was never going to amount to anything or be anything and now God came through and blessed me with the chance to be something. I used to always be so angry and upset as to why all of this stuff was happening to me but it was all worth it and going to be a part of my journey in life. God always gives his strongest battles to his strongest soldiers and I felt like a soldier more and more. When me, my caseworker, and Adam got together and met outside we began talking about what was going to be the next step. When was I going to be leaving Illinois now? That was something we had to figure out both financially and logically. My caseworker told me to contact her once me and Adam started figuring out this move to Florida and how this was going to work out. There was no way I was going to be able to go to school in August because I didn't have enough money saved up to pay off the first month's rent. I still had to pay for groceries and my phone bill monthly as well. But I had a plan and thought that it may work best for me.

Once I got back to the house that night, I was thinking about contacting an old friend of mine who I grew up and used to live with when I attended R.E.S.A Middle School who had moved down to Florida. This was the same person whose mom had slammed my head up against the wall and had me arrested for pushing her to get off of me as I ran away in a blizzard January day back in 8th grade. But these were also the same people who protected me and my older sister from my abusive father and helped us learn what he was doing wasn't right and we needed to stick up for ourselves. They cared for us like we were their own family and went out of their way so much just to help us and all we were was just neighbors who used to play with each other as little kids. After a few years had gone by I ended up rekindling my relationship with them, and while I was at the Tampa basketball camp last summer they offered to come pick me up and stay with them at their house. I visited him, his grandma, his mom, his sister and we all became close again. While I was down there they kept telling me if I ever wanted to move to Florida or come to school down there for college I could stay with them until I got things figured out. They were a big motivation and inspiration for me when they told and showed me how much opportunity and things there were to do there instead of Rockford. I figured maybe I could move in with them in August so I could get my in-state residency faster for the next school year so tuition would be cheaper and do nothing but work and save up money for school. I needed to save up money for my first month's rent to move in for student housing. Then in January I would go off to college at Hillsborough Community College in Tampa and start the second semester there. I thought this was a very logical and smart plan and to be sure I talked to Adam about it and he agreed with me. So, I contacted my friend, his grandma, and his mom and asked if I could stay with them just until January so I could get my money together and speed up my in-state tuition for school. Shockingly enough he, his mom, and his grandma all agreed to my plan and were all for me moving to Florida with them. I had them talk to my foster parent Adam just so we all could get an understanding of this plan and agree together and everyone did. After we all agreed the next thing I knew we were talking about what date in August would work best for them for me to move in their house and they told me August 22nd. It all felt so unreal, I couldn't believe all of this was actually happening and I was actually going to be moving to Florida.

The next day me and Adam talked to my caseworker about my plan for moving to Florida and moving in with my friend who I used to live with. As usual I had to run my plans by DCFS and wait for them to get approved and she had to do background checks on my friend and his family that I was going to be living with. But through all of this I wasn't worried at all because I had already got approved by a judge to move to Florida so there wasn't much stopping me. I was just waiting for a phone call from my caseworker later on during the week telling me everything was all set to go. But I ended up getting another phone call later that week that was completely unexpected and random. That phone call would be from my older sister. It was very shocking that she called me because we were not close at all, we would go months sometimes close to a year without talking. So I knew something was up right away when I saw her calling me. As soon as I said "hello" she answered me crying, and I was very concerned. Even though me and my sister were not close at all, I still had respect and cared about her. At first I thought her baby daddy was hitting her again but then I thought to myself that it wouldn't make much sense for her to call me for that when she never did in the first place. Once my sister calmed down and stopped crying she told me that she went to court and DCFS took her son, my nephew away and placed him in a foster home. I was in complete shock and I could not believe what I had just heard. I asked her why DCFS did that and she said it was because once her baby daddy got out of jail for hitting her she lifted the restraining order she had and brought him back around the baby and her. The evil side of me wanted to laugh and say, "see I told you so" and throw up how stupid she was for taking him back and not listening to me. I also wanted to laugh at how the tables had turned after years of her treating me like shit and me just asking her for help. How she said no and now all of a sudden wanted my help. But I didn't do that because that would be very wrong and cruel. I can't call myself a Christian man and expect God to help me if I am mean and unforgiving to people. I asked her what I could do and she asked if me and Adam would be willing to take him in for the time being. I didn't really know my nephew that well because my sister always kept him from me every time she got upset at me. It hurt my feelings a lot how she wouldn't ever let me see him or be around him so I felt this was the best opportunity for me to bond with him and step up to be a good uncle. After all, I am the only uncle that he has. I told her I was going to talk to Adam about what was going on once he got off of work. So, as soon as Adam got off of work I told him about what was going on and he said he was all for taking him in and having me learn how to take care of a baby even though I had no idea how. We called my sister's caseworker and got things worked out to where he would be staying with us in 3 days. Once again life had hit me with another complete turnaround, now we all would be taking care of a 10-month-old baby.

Taking Care Of My Nephew

While we were all getting prepared for my 10-month-old nephew, my older sister ended up coming over to drop off a lot of his stuff. She brought his crib, diaper bag, baby bottles, toys and a bunch of other stuff he needed. I couldn't believe a little baby needed all of this stuff, he had more stuff than I had and I was 18 years old. It felt so strange having all of his things because it was as if the house had completely transformed into a baby's space. After we finished moving all my nephew's stuff inside, Adam, his friend Marcus who lived with him, my sister, and I all sat down to discuss what was going on. We also talked about what the future was going to look like and if this was going to be a short- term or a long-term thing. But none of us had any idea of when she would get custody of him again. All we knew was her son was going to be moving in with us in 2 days and we were going to take care of him until further notice. I was truly grateful that God placed it on my heart, and that Adam's heart was willing to step in. It was a blessing that everything worked out, allowing us to take care of him. My nephew did not deserve to grow up how we did in foster care. I did not want him to grow up getting abused or mistreated in any type of way. The cycle of abuse and neglect needed to end, and it all started with me and my older sister. My sister needed to move on and use this as a lesson to find someone new in life and know her worth. I was hoping that this moment would bring us closer again to where we would have a good relationship and talk more. It was embarrassing to have a sibling who you never talked to and didn't get along with. But taking care of my nephew was going to be new for me. I never really had been around a lot of babies but I was not going to use this as an excuse, I wanted to use this time that I had to bond with my nephew until I left for Florida.

A day later, my 10-month-old nephew came, and it was just love at first sight. He was so adorable with his little blanket and bald baby head. I instantly went to hold him and didn't want to let go. It was crazy to think that this was the next generation in front of me and we were related, literally blood relatives. One day my children would play with him and they were going to be cousins. It was so funny to me but crazy at the same time. I have never been so attached to a baby before in my life. Every time I was around him I just wanted to hold and play with him. While he was sitting on my lap and my sister's caseworker was talking to Adam, I started getting him to laugh and smile. That was so heartwarming for me to be able to get him smiling already. He was such a good baby, he rarely if ever cried or threw a fit, he was always calm so this wasn't an issue at all. But then I forgot there was going to be an issue and that was the poop and throw up. I had never changed a diaper in my life before and I was not looking forward to doing it. The only way I was going to change a diaper was with a doctor's mask and gloves, I was so afraid of getting poop on me. I also have never been thrown up on and did not plan on it either. I had no safety precautions of not getting thrown up on in mind but to just keep my distance after he finished eating. I also didn't know how to give a baby a bath or how many scoops of formula he needed. The more I thought about things the more I began to realize that I needed to educate myself more on taking care of babies. This was going to be a unique but amazing learning experience for me. Luckily, Adam and his friend Marcus both had kids of their own in the past and knew how to take care of babies, otherwise I would've been screwed. Before my sister left she showed me how to give my nephew a bath. The first thing we did was check the temperature, it couldn't be steaming hot how I liked it, it had to be mild to barely hot. Thank God she was there for the temperature because I would've had that water hot as heck. Once my sister got my nephew ready to get in the bathtub, I grabbed his baby chair and a cup to put the water in. As soon as we started putting water and soap on him the smile instantly went off of his face and he started screaming at the top of his lungs. I hated loud noises because they gave me bad anxiety. So I quickly left the room to go and grab my headphones so I could play music while he cried to make it not so loud and annoying. My sister started hysterically laughing and I was trying to figure out what was so funny so I took my headphones off. She told me you can't do that, you have to be alert and listen to how a baby cries. This just sucked, I guess now I had to just listen to him cry and try to get him to stop. I had no idea how to get a baby to stop crying either and whenever I didn't know how to do something I always went to YouTube. YouTube has the answers to everything and it's free, so I watched a couple of videos on how to get babies to stop crying and tried to do this for my nephew. Sadly, none of them worked at all and he just kept screaming. After the bath and the scream fest was over, we went to change his diaper and put on clothes. My sister started showing me how to put his shirt, pants, and socks on and this was just a complete nightmare. I never realized how rough of a person I was and my roughness started to make him cry all over again. My sister always thought everything I did was so funny and now I had a baby crying, her laughing, and I was just so confused on what was happening. We weren't even an hour into doing parent and uncle duties and I was already tired. Thank God I didn't have any kids and I was going to use this lesson to not have any kids anytime soon.

Finally, after we bathed him and got him changed into his clothes, it was now time for something easier and that was play time. I thought playing with babies was so much fun because you could easily amaze them and get them to smile at anything you did—all it took was a high-pitched, cheerful voice. I started by giving him my phone and playing this baby game with him and he liked that a lot. Next, I went and grabbed his toy car and pushed him around the living room a bunch of times. Then I put him in his new baby chair that Adam got him the day before at Walmart, and he watched this baby learning video that had a bunch of singing. I have not seen a baby that was so happy and entertained before from all of this, I loved it. My nephew helped me learn that I don't suck with entertaining babies after all. I just sucked when it came to changing diapers and being around any throw up. But I was going to learn how to get better at that. I just needed some time to get used to doing it, that was all. Once it was time to feed him, I was shown how many scoops of formula to put into one of his baby bottles and then how to shake it up for him. I just couldn't believe that this nasty smelling white powdered formula was food for him. After I finished getting it ready and went to bring his bottle to him, he instantly started crying once he saw it. The minute I gave it to him he sucked that thing down and held it up with his own hands; I had no idea he could do that. It was like he turned into a grown baby for a second. My nephew did not play when it was time for his food. After he finished sucking down his formula, I saw how to burp him gently by patting him on his back. It was important for him to burp because he might start throwing up, getting gassy or becoming cranky and we didn't want that. After my sister left, I turned cartoons on because it started to get late. I loved watching cartoons so I sat with him and we watched it together. Regardless of how long this day was, I enjoyed all of it and wouldn't trade it for the world. I learned so much about babies and how to be gentler and take care of them. But I also learned a lot about myself and that was how much love I have in my heart. Even though the situation was a negative for my sister, we all made it a positive by coming together for my nephew. I was very thankful to know I would be able to bond with him before I moved to Florida. This would be a memory that I would never forget.

It took a few days for me to get used to taking care of a 10-month-old baby, but I learned to love it more and more. That's the beautiful thing about being a human, we learn to adapt and adjust over time to our situations. I began by adjusting my gym schedule again, I started by getting up early in the morning around 6am like I used to do while I was in school and jogging 2 miles to get to the YMCA. I wanted to start working out before everyone woke up, also so I would have more time to spend with my nephew. But the thing I also loved about having my nephew around was Adam and his friend Marcus. They made taking care of him easier because of how much they loved my nephew, they treated him as if he was their own blood family. Adam and Marcus helped out so much and went out of their way time and time again to help me and my nephew and I was just so thankful and grateful for them. It started to get even better because Adam started inviting his little grandchildren over to the house to play with my nephew and pretty soon there were little kids running and playing all over. I loved to see all the little kids playing together and laughing while using their own imaginations to play together. It was funny to think I was once one of those kids who didn't need to sit on social media or have to worry about money, I just played and had fun. I even started joining in with them and chasing them during tag or wrestling with some of the little kids. It started to become a lot of fun being around little kids again.

Later on that day, we took a trip to downtown Chicago because one of Adam's grandkids wanted to see the big Ferris wheel. So, me, Adam, Marcus, my nephew and his other grandkid all squeezed inside the car for the ride downtown. I always loved this about Adam because he actually did stuff with us foster kids and his grandkids. He always took us to downtown Chicago, to the movies, to the car show they had every year, and other places if he wasn't busy with work or was in the mood to do it. Most of the time he paid for it out of his own pocket and would also pay for our food too, he was way better than a lot of other foster parents that I had ever lived with. After a long and crammed 2-hour drive to downtown Chicago, we finally made it. As soon as I got out of the car I stretched my entire body out, this was the downfall of having really long legs. Next, we unbuckled both my little nephew and Adam's grandson as Marcus got the diaper bag and stroller ready. It was so crazy because I never thought I would ever be pushing a stroller around on uncle duties while being downtown. Once we all got on the elevator and headed to Navy Pier to see the Ferris wheel, we were all blown away by how packed the city was tonight. Every sidewalk was filled with people, the roads were packed with cars and took forever to cross, something had to have been going on in Chicago tonight. As we kept walking and I was trying to push this stroller through all of this huge crowd, we noticed a huge set up with a bunch of loud noises. That's when we realized that Lollapalooza was going on, one of the biggest outdoor concerts in America. We just had to pick this day to come downtown out of all days. But we didn't mind it because of how cool all of this was to see. Once we got to a less crowded area downtown, Adam took his drone out that he had brought so he could fly it high in the air and record incredible videos of the city. Before we went downtown, I always would spend time watching him learn how to fly this cool drone. I eventually wanted to save up and get my own because of how cool it was that this little airplane could fly for miles and get up super high in the air while recording videos. As it began getting darker, we started heading to Navy Pier and stood in line waiting to get on the Ferris wheel. I had never seen what it was like to ride it at nighttime so this was going to be a new experience for me. After about 15 minutes of waiting, it was our turn to finally get on and ride. As we loaded onto this small box, we slowly started making our way up and the view was just beautiful. The whole entire city and skyscrapers were all lit up and glowing, this was way better than riding during the daytime. Everyone's face began to just light up in amazement, even my nephew started staring at everything and this was a moment I will never forget. After the ride was over, we started making our way back to the car because of how late it was getting. But this was one of the best days I'd had in a long time. It was filled with laughter and smiles. For the first time in ages, I almost felt like I had a family because of how much fun we had.

Once we got into the car and headed home after a long day of being in Chicago, I posted pictures of me and my nephew downtown. I decided to fire shots at DCFS explaining how they tried to take my nephew away and put a 10-month-old baby in foster care. I never liked DCFS so I felt it was appropriate at the time. Also, in my post I talked about all the stuff I was learning to do with taking care of a baby. I posted it on my social media and got a lot of positive reaction from my sister. My sister did not like the post and she was heated. I was shocked how she even got my social media account because she told me she didn't have any. That meant someone was stalking my page or one of her little friends was stalking me trying to see what I was doing. She sent me a very rude and demanding text telling me not to post her baby on social media and all of her business. Then she followed this up by saying I wasn't even the one who took him in, Adam was and because of him he was living there. She also said a few more mean and hurtful things, but I was used to it because that's how my older sister was. Not just her, but almost everyone in my entire 18 years of life—every time you do something someone doesn't like, they turn on you and talk about you like you're nothing. But when it came to my older sister she was worse, if you would do or say one wrong thing to her, she would cut you off and block you until she felt like she wanted to come back around. It was crazy because she treated her baby daddy, who was abusing her, better than her own brother, who was trying to help her. But it was funny because this time she couldn't block me or ignore me because we had her baby at the house, and she needed to keep in contact with me. But it was really pathetic of her to say all that rude stuff when I didn't say anything wrong or send shots at her through my social media. I never told her she was a bad mother or mentioned her name, she was just acting like a child as always. Now we were back to square one in our relationship, back to her getting upset about little things and her overreacting. It was things like this that made my relationship with her so frustrating and annoying. It was like this childish repetitive cycle that kept going on over and over again and that is why our relationship was never going to grow or get anywhere. We had been doing the same childish shit for years now and I was sick of her bullying me and treating me like a dog. The only reason why I tried to have her involved in my life was because of my nephew. It just sucked this time around because she would keep me from seeing her son now every time we argued. It's sad to say but our bad relationship is the reason why he will probably grow up without his uncle being involved in his life. Not only because I'm moving to Florida but because of the relationship we have.

When my sister came over to the house the next day to see her son, she had the nerve to smile in my face as if she didn't just say the things that she said to me through text last night. Seeing that really pissed me off because she thought it was a big joke. So to show her I was serious, I stopped speaking to her completely. If she was in the same room that I was in I would leave the room. if she tried talking to me, I acted as if I didn't understand or speak English. She really crossed the line this time with me and I was tired of her treating me this way. Of course, she ended up telling Adam because they were close and he would lecture me about how she was all I had and we needed to stop it. But I wasn't falling for that this time, I was done being a sucker and having people walk all over me and forgiving them right away. I ended up ignoring her and acting the way I did towards her for about a week. Until one day she came into the room I was in while I was watching TV and told me that I was acting childish. She also explained how I wasn't going to be seeing her for a very long time once I moved to Florida and to just let it go. In a way she was right but I still didn't even get an apology, so it wasn't sincere enough. But eventually I had to get over it so I stopped holding this anger I had because it wasn't healthy. The Bible says to forgive and when I hold grudges all it does is holds me down and feels like I'm carrying a bag of rocks. The best thing I could do is forgive, let it go and make the choice if I wanted her involved in my life once I moved. Once I began learning my self-worth more and more I stopped letting people walk all over me and decided who I wanted in and out of my life, I became more independent and started working on growing as a man more. You can't grow if you have negative people in your life and around you, so I had a choice to make.

It was now the middle of August and it was almost time for me to leave and move to Florida in a couple of weeks.. At first the days felt so long but once my nephew came the days felt shorter and shorter. The closer it got for me to leave the harder the days became. The bond I had grown with my foster parent Adam, my nephew and his friend Marcus was the best and closest we had ever become. Also, going to the gym every day and seeing all my friends while lifting weights and playing basketball was great. It seemed like all of my relationships in life were well, besides the one I had with my sister. It didn't really hit me yet that I probably wouldn't be seeing a lot these people for a very long time, maybe never again. I felt my emotions changing and it was very weird. I was actually beginning to miss my hometown of Rockford, Illinois and felt scared about leaving. But that didn't make any sense to me because my entire life I had been wanting to make it out of Rockford. That is the majority of everyone's goal who is from there. Maybe I was just not getting enough sleep, or I ate something that had me feeling weird. But I was pretty sure this feeling was very real. I was nervous about moving to Florida. I didn't know anyone besides my friend's family and I was going to be starting all over. I was going to be completely on my own. I started second guessing and asking myself what if I'm making the wrong choice? What if I don't make any friends and I'm even more alone than what I feel being here at times when I know lots of people? I decided to open up to Adam about how I was feeling and he told me that was normal because I was making a big change. People are always nervous when they move somewhere new. He started telling me how I was going to meet people from all over the world, people of all different cultures and even some famous people. He thought it was amazing that not only me as a person but a foster kid had gone through everything that I had been through and was trying to do something with my life. Adam's favorite line for me when I began to think too much was "shut your ass up" that was a jokingly code word for stop overthinking everything. But I did change the subject and tell him that I felt like if I did this move that I would be a bad uncle to just leave my nephew here like this. I was going to miss out on a lot of his life. But he just continued to tell me to stop overthinking and everything was going to be fine.

A few more days passed, and soon there was only one day left before I had to leave. I got up at 6am like usual to read the Bible, pray and spend time with God. Then I jogged 2 miles to the gym. I realized that today was the last day I would be doing this. I couldn't get up tomorrow to do it because my flight was leaving early in the morning, so this was my last time going to the YMCA in Rockford. I texted a couple of my friends to see if they wanted to get one last workout in with me before I moved tomorrow and none of them answered. I knew all of them were asleep at the time. All of my friends always used to call me crazy because of how early I woke up to go to the gym and how I jogged regardless of what the weather was like outside. They also thought I was crazy because of how many times a day I went to the gym. I didn't think I was crazy, I just thought I was a very paranoid and dedicated person. I was never the type of person to sit down for hours and watch tv, play video games or anything like that. I was always scared that there was someone out there working harder than me and that caused me to always be paranoid that someone was going to take my spot in life. I knew that if I had any shot at becoming successful that it was going to have to be up to me to work hard every day and that was something that needed to be done. I never made any excuses for myself to not work hard or miss a day not only in the gym but in life. Once I put my hoodie and backpack on, I made sure my nephew was still asleep and I quietly left the house to make sure I didn't wake anyone else up. After I finished my 2-mile jog, I went straight to the weight room and lifted weights on my arms. Once I finished that, I went up to the gym and made 500 shots. After three and a half hours, I had finally finished my first workout of the day. On my way back, in the middle of my jog, my caseworker called me to make sure that I had my plane ticket and to call her once I landed tomorrow. She also checked to see if I had my stuff packed and all my important and necessary documents that I needed like my birth certificate and social security card. Then my friend and his grandma called me asking if I was excited and checked in with me again on what time I was flying in. I made sure to thank them over and over again for helping me until I went off to college. I was very grateful to have generous and great people like them in my life. It still was unreal to me that this was actually happening. Once I got back to the house, I saw my nephew was awake and I took him out of his baby chair and held him for a long time. I wanted to spend as much time with him as I could before I left.

My friends messaged me saying they were at the gym now. I wanted to make sure I spent time with them and played a few more basketball games together before I left. So, I put my hoodie and backpack back on as I got ready to go jog another 2 miles to the gym to play ball. I decided I was just going to pack later when I got back from the gym, I didn't feel like doing it at the time. I was starting to feel sad again and I didn't want those emotions to come back up. After I finished my jog, I was back at the gym. I checked in and headed up to the basketball courts where I saw all of my friends. It was so funny how empty and quiet the gym always was in the morning compared to how it was in the evening. I hurried up and put my basketball shoes on and stretched before I got to play next on the court. I spent two hours playing basketball with all of my friends one last time and it was one of the best times I've ever had. Nobody was crying over fouls, arguing about the score, or coming close to fist fighting, we all just had fun.

Once I checked the time I saw it was getting late and I still had to pack and wanted to spend more time with my nephew before he was put to bed. I told all of them I had to go and this was one of the hardest moments, saying goodbye to all of them. It made it even harder because I had no idea when the next time I would be back was. But I knew deep down inside I wasn't coming back for a long time. I started feeling a strong wave of sad emotions hitting me and I had to stop. The last thing I wanted to do was start getting emotional in front of all of them. I just told them I would be back over Christmas break to stop myself from overthinking and getting sad. As I dapped everyone up and said goodbye, it felt really good when they all told me how proud they were of me and how far I had come. They all told me to keep working hard and to just keep doing what I have been doing because it was going to pay off in the long run and that I was going places in life. After hearing all their goodbyes, it got harder for me to hold back my tears. I hated how they all waited till the last minute to say all of this stuff knowing I was already sad. But I was thankful for all of them and I was going to make sure I would make them proud one day. As I headed out of the gym I made sure to say goodbye to some of the staff at the YMCA. I was friends with a lot of the YMCA workers because they would see me up there 2 to 3 times a day so they all pretty much knew me. The YMCA was one of the greatest things that happened to me, even though it was just a gym it was my escape from being in my foster homes and staying out of trouble. I felt like in a way that was my home and I was sad to be saying goodbye to it.

Once I got home that night, it was almost time for my nephew to go to bed so I held him until he went to sleep and played a few more games with him. I almost wish I could take him with me and hire someone to clean up the poop and throw up, but I didn't have money like that. I just stayed positive and knew that I would be able to facetime him and come back sometime to see him. I pushed him around the house in his toy car some more and I let him play his little kid game on my phone that he liked. I have never been so attached to a baby before, being around him made me think of my kids one day. I knew I was going to be a way better father than my dad ever was to me. Being around my nephew made me see the potential I have to be a great man one day. I saw all the love and generosity I had not only for him but for people. After about an hour, it was time for my nephew to go to sleep. We usually just put on his baby music videos and stayed in the room with him until he fell asleep or was distracted all the way. He hated it when you just went into the room and left him there by himself, so I watched a few of these baby shows with him. By the time I watched the same video for the 5th time, I had memorized almost every song and I was answering the questions before they even asked because I knew every scene that was coming up. I didn't mind though because I was spending time with my nephew, but when I looked down I realized my nephew was fast asleep and I was just sitting there watching the show on my own. I guess a baby show had me entertained after all.

I quietly left the room and closed the door. I still had to get my stuff packed and wanted to spend time with Adam and Marcus since I didn't know when I would be seeing them again. I went out to the kitchen and saw them both talking at the table and I joined in. I thanked them both for everything they had done for me over the years and that I was sorry for all the hard times I ever caused. That's when they both told me how proud they were of me and how far I had come as a person. Adam told me when I first moved into his house, I was like an uncaged animal with the way I acted. He said I was very disrespectful and defiant, every word I spoke had a cuss word in it, I never listened to anybody and got upset about everything. They just kept going on about how bad of a person I used to be. It made me cringe and laugh listening to all of the bad stuff I used to do. I couldn't blame myself though because I had been in a jail facility for two years with nothing but a lot of bad kids everywhere. Every day there was a fight with another kid or a staff member and each day was structured with a bunch of rules. Once I got out of there all that rude and disrespect I saw from those kids rubbed off on me a little bit. But it was no wonder why me and Adam got into so many arguments and why I really didn't get along with anyone inside of his house. They both followed all of this up with saying how proud they were of me. Adam and Marcus told me how much of a 180 change I made as a person and that is one of the most important things in life. If you never grow or change as a person you will never see how much opportunity is out in the world for you, you'll always stay the same and be miserable. Instead of having a fixed mindset I learned through a lot of counseling and conversations to have an open mindset about a lot of things in life. This is what I wanted to keep doing—growing and maturing into a better man. I couldn't have done it without all the help from this foster home. Even though we had ups and downs through it all, we still stuck around and worked all of our problems out. God had placed these people in my life for a reason, and there was a reason why they both didn't give up on me like a lot of people in my life did.

Before I finished talking with Adam and Marcus that night to go and pack, I wanted to get advice on how to keep growing as a person. My biggest fear in life was becoming like my father and being abusive and mean towards people. I wanted to have a wife and kids one day and I wanted people to talk positively about me. I didn't want to end up being alone in life and some rude person who didn't have any friends. That's why I always pushed myself to do therapy, stayed in church, surrounded myself with the right groups and friends, and kept working on myself all the time. I was very paranoid about my image and how I treated people, I did not like being resentful or having anger because that pushed people away. When I told him this, he immediately commented on how it was amazing what I had just shared. Then he followed this up by telling me I used to only care about fitting in, expensive name brand shoes and clothes, and trying to be cool. It was weird because a year and a half later I didn't care about any of those things anymore, I just cared about who I was going to be. I realized wearing fancy clothes and shoes won't leave an impact on people as much as helping, being nice and respecting people. Adam told me to keep doing exactly what I was doing, and that I was the only foster kid he ever had that was not drinking, smoking, having sex, in jail, or trying to gang bang. I was actually doing something in my life because I wanted to work hard and change. But the biggest thing he told me that I needed to change was my anger. Learning to think before I speak and not speak or do things out of anger. If I didn't learn to fix and control my anger in healthier ways than my anger was going to hold me back the most in life and ruin a lot of opportunities. This is what I was most determined to fix about myself because it was the only thing stopping me from being a great man and having a great life.

Soon, it was now midnight. I had to be up early in the morning and at the airport by 8am because my flight was leaving at 10am. I still did not finish packing so I went back to my room to finish. I borrowed one of Adam's big suitcases and a duffle bag he had to pack full of clothes to make sure I had enough when I moved. The only problem was most of my clothes were long sleeve and mostly jeans because of how Illinois weather was. In Illinois there are four seasons and it was going to be a huge weather change moving to Florida which was the hottest state year-round. I didn't stress too much about it because I would just use some of the money I made from work to buy some new clothes every now and then. As I was packing all of my clothes up I started bringing some of the very few memories I still had with me. I packed up my pictures that I had printed out from both the Rockford Boys and Girls Club, Christmas Giveaway and the Valentine's Day Giveaway I did in Chicago. I liked to keep these pictures up on my desk to give me motivation to keep becoming a better man in life and helping people. I also grabbed a few cards that people had written to me and my graduation tickets as motivation for me. After I finished packing all of my clothes, certain memories, and important things that I needed, I put all my bags in the truck so I wouldn't have to do it in the morning. I also put my clothes out a day ahead because I hated trying to figure out what I wanted to wear in the morning. It was less time consuming and convenient as well. I knew I wasn't going to be able to use my phone on the plane so I looked for a few of my toys that I had over the years to keep me entertained. Yes, I was a legal adult and I still played with a fidget spinner, silly putty, a slinky and a Rubix Cube every now and then. But what was crazy about each of these toys was that they were given to me by a staff member or other kids in Aunt Martha's and Nachusa Shelter Home. It was like each toy I found was like a memory of how far I had come in life. After I finished everything, I double-checked to make sure I hadn't forgotten anything and that I was all set to go the next day. Before I went to sleep I took a long look at the room and just thought to myself, I could not believe this was actually happening.

One Last Goodbye

Once my alarm went off at 6:30am and I woke after four hours of sleep, I hurried up and got ready. Then I went to wake my nephew up and get him ready. I changed his diaper and put a fresh one on, got him all dressed and made his bottle for the morning. I was so happy that he was not a fussy baby because that would've made mornings hard but with him they were easy. While my nephew was drinking his bottle, I went and made sure that I had everything I needed. The last thing I needed to do was forget something and have to come all the way back. Once my nephew finished his bottle and the time got closer for us to leave, I went and buckled him up in the car and sat inside with him while I waited for Marcus. Sadly, I still didn't have a license or a car yet, but these were both of my goals for the upcoming future when I moved. Since no foster parents wanted to help me out with getting a license, I was going to get myself enrolled into a driving class where they would teach me the proper way of how to drive. I was tired of asking people for help, it would be easier if I just paid the driver's class cost. Once Marcus finished getting ready and got in the car, he had given me a letter that my sister wrote to me and told me not to read it until I got on the plane. I really didn't care to read it because it was the same cycle between us but I didn't want to be rude, so I just put it in my pocket and waited to read it. He asked me to go back in the house to make sure that I had everything that I needed because I was always forgetting something. Sure enough he was right, I forgot to grab a few of my toys that I was going to play with once I got on the plane. I hurried up and grabbed them and got back in the car as we got ready to head to the airport.

After about 10 minutes, I felt my emotions starting to change drastically. My eyes began to water and I felt myself getting sadder and sadder. I couldn't figure out why I was so emotional, this is what I have wanted and been talking about since I was a little kid. I was finally making it out and going onto bigger and better things filled with opportunities. I thought maybe it was just the song I was listening to, so I turned my music off. That's when we passed Auburn High School and the tears just started flowing from my eyes little by little. I tried to cover up my face with my hand so nobody would see me cry. I knew these were mostly tears of joy then tears of sadness. It was just hard for me because I remembered being a 17-year-old kid who had just got out of jail-like Lutherbrook, and nobody believed in me, not even myself. I thought I was never going to amount to anything in this world and I was going to be a failure and everyone was going to be right about me failing and not doing anything with my life. I was so afraid of living up to a statistic and people being right about me becoming a failure that it drove me crazy. Once I got out of that facility I promised myself that I was going to work hard and prove people wrong. I had no idea what the hell I was doing or what God had planned for me, I just listened and remembered what all the people taught me about working hard and what Greg Hill had told me before he passed away and that was,"Hard work beats talent any day." I was inspired by him and my idol Fred VanVleet and I just became obsessed with working hard. No matter what the weather was outside or what I was going through in life I made sure I got in the gym and I worked hard outside of the gym. I always used to get mad and question God as to why I was going through everything I went through in life. I never asked to have two shitty parents and grow up getting abused by my father, in some of these foster homes and inside of Lutherbrook by some staff. I used to hate my life so much because I was always getting bullied and made fun of. When I was living in these foster homes they barely fed me, never gave me rides anywhere, a lot of them didn't care about me, they were just in it for the money, and I even got robbed and lost all of my stuff. I was tired of sitting on the bench then not even being able to play my senior year. I hated not being able to have a family or have someone that was there for me and genuinely cared about me. I hated my life so much that I tried to kill myself on my 15th birthday and thought about what it would be like if I wasn't alive. Never in a million years did I ever think that I would be in the position I was in no matter how hard I tried to believe I could and keep my faith in God.

Once I arrived at the airport, I was still crying and covering up my face trying not to let anyone see me. I quickly got out of the car and went to the back where the trunk was to wipe away my tears. I didn't want anyone to see me cry or embarrass myself anymore. I took a few deep breaths and grabbed my suitcases and all the other stuff I brought with me to take down to Florida. I made sure I had everything before closing the trunk and then went to the front of the car to make sure I had everything. Finally it was time for the hardest part and that was saying goodbye to my nephew. I took one long look at him and my eyes instantly started watering again. I didn't care anymore of trying to hide myself from crying, I was going to miss my nephew a lot. I hated how he moved in with us right when I was about to move to Florida, this is what made it so hard. I felt like I was being a selfish and horrible uncle just leaving him here knowing I was going to miss out on a lot of his life. His 1st birthday was only a week away and it sucked that I wouldn't be there to celebrate it with him. But I stopped thinking so negatively and thought back to all the people who I was inspired by. Every person who ever became successful in life had to make sacrifices to get to the position they were in, no matter how big or small. I had sacrificed a lot in life but this by far was the most hurtful one. As I picked my nephew up out of his car seat, I hugged him so tight and gave him one big, huge kiss. I had never loved a baby so much in my life as much as I have loved him. It was so hard to let go, I just wanted to sneak him in my suitcase and give him a new life in Florida too. I'd find someone to change his diapers and clean up the throw up. But unfortunately, it was time to let go of him and say goodbye.

Once I walked inside the airport, I was surprised at how small it was. The Rockford Airport was almost the same size as the Charlottesville airport in Virginia. I was happy because it was going to be a lot easier to get around the airport than it would be at Chicago

O'Hare. I walked up to the check in desk and printed my ticket out on the kiosk machine, then I went to get my suitcases weighed in and checked. I went through security very fast and easily and walked up stairs to find my gate. There were not very many gates around this airport at all so finding it was very simple and easy. While I was sitting down I couldn't help but go back and reminisce in my mind about the past. I started smiling to myself remembering how nervous and scared I was flying to this Tampa basketball camp all by myself. This was the first time I had ever traveled anywhere alone, and the first time I had been on a plane. But it was unreal how that one basketball camp would inspire me and open up my eyes to how much more opportunity and better life can be outside of Rockford. I never thought that I would turn that dream of moving to Florida into a reality one day, especially since I used to always hate traveling and going on vacations because of how scared I was. I used to always want to just stay in Rockford all the time. It was crazy to me how much my mindset had grown and how much I changed as a person. I guess hard work really does pay off in time. I don't know how I managed to stay patient through the entire process that I went through after being knocked down over and over again. Nobody believed in my dream and everyone thought I was crazy, but the entire time I didn't need anyone but myself and God. There was an old saying that I read once that said, "the first step into chasing any dream is believing you can do it, once you believe you're halfway there."

After waiting at my gate for a while, it was finally time to board the plane. I got in line and waited until it was my turn to show the airline worker my ticket so she could scan it and I could get on the plane. When I got to my seat I was happy that I had the window seat. I always loved looking out the airplane window to see the amazing view. Plus, I liked to use the window seat as a wall to lay my head on to help me fall asleep faster. While I was sitting, I just stared out the window thinking about what a journey I had been on in life. From being physically and verbally abused almost every day by my father for anything until I was 13 years old to being in 7th grade and going to school one day, and in the middle of a test being called out of class by a principal. Then being taken into a room where there was a bunch of police and my older sister was sitting there crying as she told me that our dad had stabbed our former stepmom and we weren't going home anymore. Once we left school we were taken to the Rockford Police Station downtown and were taken to my aunt and uncle's house. This was a bad idea because it resulted in me and my sister getting kicked out of there and causing no one else on my dad's side of the family to want to take me and my older sister in. This resulted in us getting split up and being sent to different homes. This caused me to start acting out and getting arrested three different times at the age of 14. I was tired of getting bullied, made fun of all the time, and treated badly by these foster homes and kids in school. After I kept going from home to home, DCFS finally ran out of options of where to put me and sent me to a homeless shelter in Aurora, Illinois while I was still only in 8th grade. There, I got bullied by a few of the older kids and lost all my freedom that I normally would have. Then I was taken into another foster home. When I got to this foster home I acted out again and got kicked out again. Once I was kicked out of that foster home DCFS didn't have any homes to put me in again and I was sent to another homeless shelter but this time it was in Dixon, Illinois. While I was in the Nachusa Shelter Home I kept acting out and didn't want to listen to the staff because I was angry. I couldn't be normal like the rest of my friends and had to follow a structured schedule every day. I also was mad that I lost a lot of my freedom again and this caused me to act up and get arrested twice while I was there, one was for throwing a chair at a window and the other one was for running away from the shelter. Once the police officer slammed me face first onto his car, he threatened to get his dog out on me if I tried to run away. That was the first time I ever had to ride in the back of a K-9-unit police car. I thought my life was horrible and I couldn't control myself. Just when I thought things couldn't get any worse I was sent to a hospital and had to ride on a stretcher for three hours all the way to Kankakee, Illinois.

Once I got inside of this hospital, my freedom was taken away even further to where I couldn't wear my clothes, shoes, or have any of my stuff anymore and I was only allowed to make one phone call a day. I had to sit in groups all day and follow everything on the schedule otherwise they would give me shots, make me stay in my room all day until I behaved. Then once I got out of this hospital, DCFS decided that I was no longer fit for foster homes and I was sent to a jail-like residential facility in Addison, Illinois to correct my behavior while I was still only 14 years old and in 8th grade. Once I had got to this facility, I was so angry and bitter with my life and I felt like I was never going to amount to anything and be a failure just like my father and end up in jail. I was angry at my family for not wanting to take me in and angry at all the people who gave up on me. I stopped caring about my life and started getting involved in the wrong crowd. This caused me to start doing drugs, stealing from cars, fighting staff, other kids, and running away every night. I acted up so much that I was later placed on probation at 14 years old and ended up getting kicked out of high school my freshman year for fighting. That's when I became so depressed and hated my life so much that I started drinking Nyquil all the time and tried to kill myself because I was so tired of being bullied, not having anyone, and feeling like I was never going to be anything in life. I reached my lowest point and I was all alone. I was not close to God and had no one helping me anymore. That's when one day I found out that my best friend passed away and I had to attend his funeral and carry his casket. On that day I really saw how life was not a joke anymore and it can be over in a second. This put a lot of fear inside of me and inspired me to turn my entire life completely around. I made a total 180-degree change in my behavior both in and out of school. I stopped being hard headed and trying to fight staff and instead began listening to them and following the directions they gave. I would actually listen to the advice they began giving me. I also stopped hanging with the other kids in my unit and following their stupid behaviors like running away, stealing, doing drugs, and fighting. Instead I became a leader and wanted more out of my life so I saw how much easier life was when you listened and lived it the right way, which was listening and being nice to people. That's when my behavior was so good at the alternative school and on the unit that they let me back into normal high school and allowed me to play on the basketball team again for my sophomore year. Then I was changed to a different unit and placed in the group home because of my good behavior and gained more and more of my freedom back and started becoming more responsible. I got myself my first job, improved my grades in school, became a better teammate and player on my basketball team and started becoming very independent and responsible while behaving well. After spending two years at this facility, I came home from school one day and was told that Lutherbrook was being closed down. I had no idea that this would be one of my biggest blessings to my future. During my entire two years at Lutherbrook, DCFS told me there were no foster homes open for me in Rockford, but this place was closing out of nowhere a foster home opened back up for me in Rockford, Illinois. I was so happy I was going to be back home to see all of my friends again and get my freedom back. I was even happier I was going to be playing high school basketball for a team back home. I felt like God had blessed me with a second chance after changing my behavior.

When I moved into my new foster home, I dedicated all of my time to work, school and being in the gym. I started getting up at 5am every morning to go and workout before school and made a whole basketball workout routine because I wanted to be like some of my idols. But once my junior year started at this new high school and in this new foster home it was the complete opposite of what I wanted. I had to go through all the fighting and arguing with my foster parent and other foster kids in that home. I ended up getting set up by one of the foster kids and robbed at gunpoint, resulting in me losing almost everything. Basketball didn't work out for me at all and I ended up sitting on the bench almost the entire year and never getting in the game anymore. I was back to feeling angry and depressed all the time that I drank Nyquil some days. I even began walking five miles to school and home after basketball practice or school because I would be so angry at how school was going and my life at home. I was upset with how my life was going again but this time around I didn't give up or quit. Instead I ended up leaving that school and foster home and went to a new foster home and a new high school. I dedicated my entire life to being in the gym and working hard the entire summer to be better at basketball than I was last year. Once the beginning of the school year started, I made the team and things were going well at school. I was an honor roll student and all my teachers considered me a leader and a great student. I began growing more a student and a person, maturing into a better version of myself. Things at my foster home were well besides barely being fed, not having any support, and never being taken anywhere. Instead I learned to become more independent and started learning how to take the city bus and worked a job while I was in school.

When the basketball season finally came around my senior year after putting in all of this hard work and working the hardest I had ever worked in my life, life knocked me down again. The day before our first scrimmage game to the public I had to leave that home because my foster parent was getting surgery on her hand. This caused me to be angry and bitter again, and once I was sent to this new foster home, things didn't go well. I was angry I was not able to work out any more like I was able to do at the YMCA and I was even angrier when I got on this basketball team and was told I was only going to be a part of the practice squad. This caused me to quit the basketball team and be angry all the time. But I still had the desire to grow more as a person and help people. I tried to just walk away from basketball for a while because of my inability to practice. But I ended up leaving that foster home and I was sent back to Rockford where I would live in yet another foster home again. I was back to having no support and barley getting fed, instead I was surviving off of just eating Oreos and Ramen Noodles. Then I was told I would not be graduating from normal high school anymore and instead I had to graduate from an alternative high school all because a high school counselor made a mistake with one of my math classes. Once again life knocked me down and I was feeling sad and depressed all the time but instead of throwing myself a pity party I kept working hard and found another way to help people.

I wanted to continue to keep growing as a person and helping people. Shortly after this I was blessed with an opportunity to play at a camp in Atlanta and convinced my caseworker into letting me go despite having broken my finger. But shortly after the camp was over I had another crazy experience where I had to sleep inside of the Chicago O'Hare Airport because nobody would come and get me. Shortly after I was kicked out of that foster home and was sent to another one of my former foster homes. But I continued to work hard in school, stay in the gym, and work on changing myself into a better person and becoming closer with God. I was blessed with another opportunity to attend a basketball camp in Indianapolis but had another crazy sleeping experience. Instead of sleeping inside of an airport this time I had to sleep inside of a bus station. Once I got back from my basketball camp I started getting myself more involved in church. I got myself into a youth group and started going to church every Sunday. I began chasing my dream of moving to Florida one day and going to college there. Everything was going well but then I was sent to jail for a shoulder bump. Once I got to jail I thought everything I had worked so hard for was all over and that I was a failure. I thought my dream of moving was done and I was going to be stuck in Rockford for the rest of my life.

Once I got out of jail, I went to live with my cousin. I continued to work by staying in the gym all the time and working on myself and my relationship with God despite all the arguments me and my cousin had gotten into. God blessed me with another chance at basketball and I flew out to a camp in Virginia to play against some of the best basketball players in the country. Things were going well but they suddenly took a drastic turn again and I was kicked out of my cousin's house and I went back to live with my old foster parent for the 3rd time. I worked hard and things started going well between us again and in my life. Somehow, I managed to have 2 different judges work in my favor with one dropping my case and the other granting me an opportunity to leave the state of Illinois and move to Florida to go to college while still getting financial benefits from the foster care system. Now after all of this I am sitting here on a plane, getting ready to take off for the next chapter of my life to go to college in Florida.

What an amazing journey it has been throughout my 18 years of living. Life has knocked me down over and over again to the point where I wanted to give up and even try and commit suicide. Life has caused me so much pain and heart break with being abused physically and verbally almost my entire life and losing my best friend, my "family" and so much of my childhood and opportunities. Life has caused me to question God over and over again as to why all of this was happening to me. There were so many times I wanted to just give up and live up to the statistics of foster care, stop trying to chase my dreams and settle, and stop working hard. But there was a reason I went through everything that I had gone through. Hard times don't break people, instead they make people. On the other side of pain and sadness is happiness and success. Now I am more confident, faithful, successful, and happier than ever before. Life has shown me that with hard work, faith in God, confidence in yourself, and consistency to keep working every day one day your dreams will come true in life. Once you learn to turn all the pain, anger, and sadness you experience and feel into fuel to your fire to be successful, nothing will hold you back but yourself. God gives his strongest battles to his strongest soldiers for a reason. All of us go through something in life and we all get knocked down, some people get knocked down more than others. But we all have a story to tell, let your story be a success story because you didn't give up. I don't know what my future holds for me, I don't know what will happen next, but I do know that if I am going to be successful in life it is up to me. So, I will continue to work hard, keep my faith strong, stay consistent, and believe in myself through it all because I know God has a plan for me. My name is Devin Paladino and one day my success story will be told.

www.ingramcontent.com/pod-product-compliance
Lightning Source LLC
Chambersburg PA
CBHW040725120726
48010CB00001B/15

* 9 7 9 8 3 3 0 2 4 9 2 8 2 *